"In celebration of its centennial anniversary in 2018, the authors have researched and written a history not only of Mortar Board, but also a history of the evolution and complexities of four centuries of American higher education as the context for Mortar Board's development through the twentieth and twenty-first centuries. Additionally, the authors have referenced many of the corresponding national and world events that were occurring over the decades and that often shaped or influenced the activities and growth of Mortar Board. Originally established as an honor society to recognize college senior women for their scholarship, leadership, and commitment to service, Mortar Board continues into its next century now recognizing both college senior women and men who continue to reflect these ideals. The authors have captured the challenges that Mortar Board has withstood across the decades, with the earliest challenge being that of a women's organization in a man's world of higher education."

—Mabel G. Freeman, The Ohio State University (retired)
and Mortar Board National College Senior Honor
Society (past National President)

"Virginia Gordon and Jane Hamblin provide a captivating history of Mortar Board and identify innovative programs established by chapters that are now woven in the fabric of higher education—career programs for women, freshman orientation programs, and leadership programs. Mortar Board members modeled collaboration and, during World War II, contributed to the war effort, including serving as airplane spotters. Mortar Board's strong historical foundation challenges chapters and members to make a difference on their campuses and in their communities—to act on compelling issues that, as a group, they are uniquely well suited to address. One will learn much about students and the commitment of alumni in this rich story of a highly acclaimed honor society."

—Marylu K. McEwen, Associate Professor Emerita,
University of Maryland, College Park

"A wise person commented, 'One can drive safely only by periodically checking the rearview mirror.' Through this comprehensive history of Mortar Board, we can 'check the rearview mirror' to review its evolution over the past 100 years. We are reminded Mortar Board began at a time when women did not have the right to vote and fewer than 4% of women in the United States had completed a bachelor's degree. With utmost clarity we see the impact of historical events shaping Mortar Board—the Great Depression, WWII, the student protests of the 1960s, the Civil Rights Movement, and Title IX. Familiar names of chapter and national leaders remind us of the visionaries who were determined 'The Torch' would always be held high."

—Betty M. Nelson, Dean of Students Emerita, Purdue University

"*Mortar Board: A Century of Scholars, Chosen for Leadership, United to Serve* is far more than a skillfully written history of Mortar Board. Embedded in the richly detailed stories of Mortar Board's founding and expansion are the histories—and herstories—of U.S. higher education, women's rights, civil rights, and first-person accounts of the impact of Title IX. Through the use of period-sensitive language over the century, the reader gains insight as 'girls' become 'women,' 'Miss' transitions to 'Ms.,' and 'alumnae' expands to include 'alumni.' The painstaking research and original sources result in a scholarly product suitable for classrooms and coffee tables alike."

—Marlesa A. Roney, Professor of Practice, Higher
Education Administration, University of Kansas

"This book is different from many organization histories in that it is well founded in the history of our country. The authors tie the history of Mortar Board to the events that were shaping the United States and the world. This is a story of women in academia, World War II, women's rights, civil rights, professional development, Title IX, and how these events helped guide the formation of a national collegiate honorary dedicated to promoting equal opportunities among all people and emphasizing the advancement of the status of women."

—Mary Sadowski, Professor, Purdue University

"This remarkable history not only chronicles the founding, expansion, and operation of Mortar Board, but it also provides an insightful look at how various societal and educational changes had an impact on higher education and the development of honor societies. From the time women were first enrolled in colleges and universities to the passage and implementation of Title IX to the challenges of today, this book does an excellent job of explaining how Mortar Board adapted and continued to grow as a thriving organization that celebrates and supports collegiate scholarship, leadership, and service."

—Tara S. Singer, Executive Director, Omicron Delta Kappa

"There is nothing like a good story, and *Mortar Board* offers storytelling at its best, taking the reader from the organization's beginning through its evolution to the present time. Mortar Board's unwavering commitment to scholarship, leadership, and service has never changed during its one hundred years. Remarkable women, later joined by men, have steadily guided this honor society, always seeking ways to ensure its survival through inevitable challenges. Values, membership, and funding are constant issues, and they are addressed in this very interesting book. Mortar Board is now one hundred years old. With continued careful stewardship, it will be good for another one hundred!"

—Jane K. Smith, Assistant Vice President, Academic Services Emerita, San Diego State University; Trustee, Mortar Board Foundation; and Jane K. Smith Cap and Gown Chapter Adviser

"In 1918, five college women who wanted a national honor society recognizing women's achievements in scholarship, leadership, and service created Mortar Board. At that time, World War I and a flu epidemic were wracking the nation, men dominated society, and women could not vote. One hundred years later, the founders' vision remains alive in Mortar Board, the premier national college senior honor society. Mortar Board members come together as 'family,' sharing their commitments to leadership, service, and lifelong learning. While Title IX brought controversy and male membership in 1975, advancement for women remains a core purpose."

—Martha Lewis Starling, The Pennsylvania State University (retired); Mortar Board National College Senior Honor Society (past National President); and President, Mortar Board National Foundation

"An outstanding read for Mortar Boards of all ages. In addition to being a narrative on the first one hundred years of Mortar Board—covering the overall organization, the collegiate chapters, the alumni chapters, and the Foundation—readers will find wonderful information on the history of higher education in the United States."

—David Lynn Whitman, National President, Mortar Board National College Senior Honor Society and Professor Emeritus, University of Wyoming

Mortar Board

A Century of Scholars, Chosen for Leadership,
United to Serve

Virginia N. Gordon
Jane A. Hamblin
with Susan R. Komives

Edited by Jane A. Hamblin

Printed in the United States of America.

Cataloging-in-Publication data available from the Library of Congress.

ISBN: 978-1-55753-793-5

On the cover: This June 1920 photograph shows the impressive public ceremony for new members held by Mortar Board at The Ohio State University. A procession of candidates wearing white, accompanied by outgoing members in robes, led to Mirror Lake, a legendary campus location, where the initiation was held. A breakfast followed. The Ohio State chapter still conducts an elaborate procession and "linking" of new members observed by family and friends. An indoor location for the initiation now controls for weather uncertainties since classes now end early in May.

All photographs in this book are copyright Mortar Board, Inc. or The Ohio State University Archives unless otherwise noted.

Additional material about Mortar Board, Inc. history can be found at docs.lib.purdue.edu/mortarboard.

This publication is intended to provide accurate and authoritative information based on reliable, original sources.

Contents

Author **Virginia N. Gordon**, PhD, was assistant dean emerita and associate professor at The Ohio State University. A critical force behind the nation's growth in academic advising, Dr. Gordon wrote fifty books, monographs, book chapters, and journal articles on career counseling, advising administration, advising undecided college students, and advisor training. She was past president of the National Academic Advising Association and the founder and first director of the National Clearinghouse on Academic Advising. She was elected to Mortar Board in 1948 at The Ohio State University. Dr. Gordon passed away on November 21, 2017.

Author-editor **Jane A. Hamblin**, JD, CAE, COA, is the executive director of Mortar Board, Inc., and the Mortar Board National Foundation and editor in chief of the *Mortar Board Forum*. She has played senior student affairs roles at Purdue University and the University of Maryland–Baltimore County and has been an instructor at Trinity Washington University (Washington, D.C.) and Purdue. Before coming to Mortar Board in 2009, Ms. Hamblin had been a senior leader at three D.C.-based higher education associations. She was elected to Mortar Board in 1973 at Purdue University.

Contributor **Susan R. Komives**, EdD, internationally known scholar and observer of leadership development, is professor emerita at the University of Maryland at College Park. Executive editor of the inaugural *New Directions in Student Leadership* series, she has authored or edited a dozen books on leadership and student affairs. Dr. Komives is past president of the Council for the Advancement of Standards in Higher Education and the American College Personnel Association and served two colleges as vice president. She was elected to Mortar Board in 1967 by the Torchbearer chapter at Florida State University.

Acknowledgments

Mortar Board gratefully acknowledges:

—the Historical Publication Steering Committee members who have worked on vision, research, writing, interviewing, transcription, photo finding, marketing, arrangements, and fact checking:

Diane Miller Selby (The Ohio State University, 1961)
Martha Nichols Tykodi (Ohio State, 1951)
Mary Lou Nichols Fairall (Ohio State, 1956)
Joan Slattery Wall (Ohio State, 1988)
Sheila Castellarin (Ohio State, 1956)
Alicia Notestone Shoults (Ohio State, 2005)
Becky Zell Fullmer (Ohio State, 1999)
Jane McMaster (Miami University, 1968)
Denise L. Rode (Northern Illinois University, 1971)
Sharon Martin (Central Michigan University, 1988)

and staff members:

Tracey Fox
Bridget Williams Golden (Purdue University, 1997)
Francie Kaufman (Wittenberg University, 2017)
Audrey White (Ohio State, 2014)

—the staff of The Ohio State University Archives

—Susan Komives (Florida State University, 1967) for adding her knowledge of leadership development, higher education, and love of Mortar Board to this publication

and especially:

Virginia Niswonger Gordon (Ohio State, 1948)

Identifying and Referring to Members and Referring to Chapters and Institutions

It is Mortar Board's custom to identify members, when their names appear in writing on first reference, by a parenthetical with their institution and the year of their initiation into Mortar Board: for example, Esther Lloyd-Jones (Northwestern University, 1922). This custom is continued in this publication. It is also Mortar Board's custom, in its other publications, to identify postgraduate initiates by the year of their chapter's installation. However, for this publication, we believe that it provides much richer historical information to supply the year the member was initiated into a local society that predated Mortar Board.

It was customary in the minutes of early meetings to refer to the delegate by the name of the school (e.g., Ohio State for Secretary, Swarthmore for Treasurer, and Syracuse for Historian). We retain this convention.

Though scores of national leaders (eleven of twenty-eight national presidents) held or hold doctorates or other terminal degrees, we eliminate most honorifics for ease of reading and on the theory that all members are equal. However, we refer to subjects with terms like Dean, Dr., or Prof. as a sign of respect for these Mortar Board and higher education icons.

What to call members of Mortar Board is a long-standing debate. "Members of Mortar Board" is always correct. In this work, we interchange this with "Mortar Boards," a usage common throughout the country. "Mortar Boarders" is not preferred, although many chapter members refer to themselves with this shorthand.

Before 1975, all Mortar Board members were women, so we refer to them with the Latin feminine "alumna/alumnae" to make distinctions between members who had graduated and collegiate members. After men joined our Society, Mortar Board has come to use the catch-all plural "alumni" for those who are no longer collegiate members. The words "college" and "university" are used interchangeably throughout the work in reference to an institution of higher education.

On second and subsequent references to an institution, we use an identifiable but shortened version of its name—for instance, University of Hawaii at Manoa becomes Hawaii beyond the first reference.

When appropriate, and depending on the time period, we have used "Miss" or "Ms." (a title that gained momentum in the early 1970s' women's movement) along with a woman's last name. In captions, we have often simply used a first name on second reference.

In spite of Mortar Board's belief in the advancement of women and equal treatment of women and men, we have let stand the word "girls" without further explanation or apology to provide context for society's expectations for college women through much of the last century.

—JAH

Dedication

Advisors

Every collegiate chapter must have at least one advisor, and as we in the National Office tell chapter leaders all the time, a team of advisors works best for the "most successful chapters." The National Council has great expectations that chapters will reflect Mortar Board's purpose well and do good things year after year to provide high-impact practices that add to the quality of student life. But the nature of a mostly one-year senior collegiate experience requires that there be "institutional memory" to ensure that the chapter keeps performing well. The advisor provides this essential historical ingredient to pour into the mixing bowl when officers make the transition at the end of the school year.

There's another ingredient: being there to challenge, honor, and support your members. I ran across this well-reasoned advising philosophy written by one of our newly minted certified organization advisors:

> It's not my job to be their pal, even though I enjoy "my" chapter members. I believe that cocurricular learning through Mortar Board is icing on the cake of these high achievers. If I help them plan and learn and then reflect, I feel great. But I can't do that remotely. I have to be there to support them as they are learning. Otherwise, I don't get my reward.[1]

"So," the advisor continued, "even though it's not in my job description to advise Mortar Board, I believe that it suits who I am as an educator. I make it work within the context of my family, my position, and my classes. It is energizing, challenging, and often hysterically funny. I'd miss a lot if I weren't there."

We dedicate this book to Mortar Board chapter advisors who believe in "being there."

—JAH

Note

1. M. A. Roney, "Why Advising Matters," keynote, Leadership Excellence and Advisor Development Certification Program, San Diego, October 8, 2016.

Editor's Note

Mortar Board Historian Emerita

Virginia N. Gordon, Ph.D.

(1937–2017)[1]

For all of her professional achievements in higher education, Virginia Gordon—Ginger—really saw herself as an amateur historian. She completed an extensive family history, a history of the Ohio State University Retirees Association, and the one-hundred-year history of the Ohio State chapter of Mortar Board, to name a few.

After many years on the national steering committee that developed the idea for some type of centennial publication, Ginger, in 2014, formally volunteered to write our one-hundred-year history. For a year-and-a-half, she worked in the National Office, at the Archives of Ohio State, and in her home office handling some 8,000 separate documents—minutes, letters and cards, telegrams, and transcripts—and reviewing at least 400 issues of our magazine, newsletters, and conference handbooks. Following the lead of historians of Mortar Board who came before her, she carried the right tone that makes for this one-of-a-kind publication.

After the overall history was written, in 2016 it was time for the histories of each of our chapters. Ginger was willing to let me bring archive boxes, a couple at a time, to the sofa by her desk in her comfortable home in Columbus. More often than not, by the next day she would e-mail with the message, "I'm ready for more." I would bring even more boxes to the sofa, and darned if she didn't e-mail me within a day or so, writing, "I'm ready for more." Avidly and steadily, in a way that would match the methodology and drive of any professional historian, Ginger researched the founding histories of nearly 230 chapters. The stories she uncovered are a vital part of this book.

When it came to chapters five and six, it was Ginger who set the direction. Late in October 2017, at what turned out to be our last strategy dinner, she formulated a plan for completing the document that would highlight the one hundred Torchbearers of Mortar Board for our centennial.

Dr. Virginia Gordon did more behind the scenes in our Society than any member in all of our one hundred years. She always put the *more* in Mortar Board, and I would give anything for an e-mail from her right now that says, "I'm ready for more."

—JAH

Note

1. Early in 2018, the National Council awarded the title of Historian Emerita posthumously to Dr. Gordon.

Introduction

One hundred years ago women students from five institutions of higher learning in the United States had the vision to form a national organization to honor outstanding college senior women. Although honor societies had traditionally existed for men on college campuses, there was no comparable national honor society for senior women. The seniors, who represented four established local women's honor societies, met to form a national organization in February 1918. Their vision resulted in the founding of the Mortar Board National College Senior Honor Society. Today the number of chapters has expanded to 232 colleges and universities, and the total number of members initiated into Mortar Board has surpassed a quarter of a million.

The general purpose of Mortar Board as envisioned by its founders has not changed over a hundred years. The preamble to the original constitution read:

> We, the undersigned, recognizing the advantages of a national union of Senior Honorary Societies for women, do hereby bind ourselves together to form a national fraternity whose purpose shall be to provide for the cooperation between these societies, to promote college loyalty, to advance the spirit of service and fellowship among university women, to maintain a high standard

of scholarship and to recognize and encourage leadership, and to stimulate and develop a finer type of college women.[1]

Although some of the words composing this purpose have been changed or rearranged over the years (i.e., the reference to college women), the original reason for forming the Society has remained constant. Ninety-four years later at the 2012 national conference, the Society's purpose still contained the same points:

> [Our purpose shall be to] ... emphasize the advancement of the status of women, to support the ideals of the university, to advance a spirit of scholarship, to recognize and encourage leadership, to provide service, and to establish the opportunity for a meaningful exchange of ideas as individuals and as a group.[2]

The Setting

Mortar Board was founded in an era of great societal and world unrest. When the college women representing the five local societies met to form the new national honor society, the United States had been involved in World War I for almost a year. These young women were born at the very end of the nineteenth century as part of what Strauss and Howe call (quoting Ernest Hemingway) the Lost Generation.[3] This generation was reaching maturity during and just after World War I, when the country was in a period of great instability. The war had a profound effect on youths' changing attitudes and values. As one young man declared after the World War I armistice, "We have in our unregenerate youth . . . been forced to become realists."[4] The United States was a country of many immigrants—over nine million members of the Lost Generation were born abroad, more than any other generation up to that time. Over one fifth of all children worked in sweatshops. Many young people died in the great influenza epidemic of 1918.

At a time when many Americans were illiterate, an interesting paradox is that college attendance was increasing (the total college enrollment in 1916 was over 330,000 students).[5] There was an enormous expansion of state universities and state colleges of agriculture and mechanical arts. As detailed in the history of higher education in chapter 1, the "democratization of a college education" was unfolding, and the college curriculum was expanding.[6] Higher education increasingly was recognized as a way to improve one's social status and earning power.

By the end of the nineteenth century, the number of women attending college greatly increased. This was due partly to the rise of women's colleges and the admission of women to regular colleges. Women obtained 19 percent of all undergraduate college degrees at the beginning of the twentieth century.[7] Many other events had a strong influence on the status of women during this period, the most important being the passage of the Nineteenth Amendment to the U.S. Constitution in 1920 that gave women the right to vote. In addition to women's suffrage, this era also was known for prohibition, organized crime, jazz,

and the flapper, who set a fashion statement with her short bobbed hair, use of makeup, and knee-revealing dresses. One story relayed in the Mortar Board archives describes "one rebellious member with a bob who didn't want the dean of women to know about her haircut. So she saved her shorn hair to wear as an early version of hair extensions, known as a 'fall,' when required to meet with the dean."[8] Those in the generation before the Lost Generation who lived a conservative Victorian lifestyle found the antics of these new youths disgraceful.

So this was the world in which the Mortar Board founders lived. Traveling through Mortar Board's hundred-year history, one is struck by how the changing societal, economic, and cultural milieu reflects the values and interests of each generation of Mortar Board members. Chapter activities and service projects reveal the interests and values of its members at different times during the span of a hundred years. The Great Depression and World War II affected college students in profound ways, and the minutes of local chapter meetings recorded how their members were involved. The advancement of the status of women and women's role in the workplace are illustrated in many Mortar Board chapter activities and programs. During the 1970s national Mortar Board expanded into new types of institutions, and the profile of its members became more diverse. Title IX had a dramatic effect on the organization, as it made the transition from a traditional women's organization to coed membership. Delegates to the 2003 national conference adopted Reading Is Leading as the national project so that all chapters could be involved in a common theme as opposed to a different one every year.

During the early 2000s in particular, the role of technology changed the way chapters communicated with their members, with other chapters, and with the national organization. Mortar Board chapter programs and service projects continued to reflect the important issues that were of interest and concern on college campuses. Service to each member's institution and its surrounding community continues to fulfill that part of the national purpose. "Advancing the spirit of scholarship and recognizing and encouraging leadership" are still central to each chapter's mission.[9] Mortar Board has not only endured for a hundred years while remaining a force on the nation's campuses, but its local chapters have also been at the heart of its success.

Centennial Celebration

The story of Mortar Board's history and evolution contained in this volume is presented as part of honoring its centennial year. Implicit in this history are three general precepts that have sustained it over the past hundred years:

The **HEART and PURPOSE** of the organization as it has been kept alive by the ideas and talents of its student members and chapters.

The **CONTINUITY** of the organization as it has been maintained through the commitment and support of alumni, chapter advisors and college administrators who have provided their time and resources.

The **CHALLENGE** of the organization as it strives to preserve its founding Ideals and standards and endeavors to create a meaningful experience for outstanding college seniors.

Embedded in this history are areas of academic and societal importance that parallel Mortar Board's evolution and development. The history of higher education, the women's movement, the impact of legislation, and the influence of cultural changes on different generations of students can be studied by scholars through the lens of this centennial history. The first chapter sets the context for Mortar Board's growth and continuity, examining the changing role and purpose of American higher education and the scope of Mortar Board's role within it. How has higher education been changed by legislation such as Title IX, for example, and how has this influenced Mortar Board's purpose and goals? Chapter 2 describes the evolution and expansion of Mortar Board as a national organization from its beginning to the present. This chapter describes major events that involved Mortar Board, Inc. and the Mortar Board National Foundation through different eras, organizational and structural changes, and important programs, projects, and traditions.

The collegiate chapters are the heart of Mortar Board, and chapter 3 records the fascinating histories of these local collegiate honor societies. The founding dates of so many of these local chapters reflect a growing need to recognize outstanding women students early in the twentieth century. These histories illustrate how activities, projects, and traditions continue to make local groups unique while maintaining an important national affiliation. Chapter 4 describes alumni members' influences and how they have provided continuity and support. Examples of specific alumni chapters' histories and programs complete this section. Finally, the last chapter speculates on future challenges and on Mortar Board's future role as it interacts with its members and college campuses. Appendices available online provide additional information about important people, programs, and milestones that have influenced Mortar Board over one hundred years.

It is hoped that this centennial history of Mortar Board can be used to not only record the remarkable journey of a national senior honor society but also engender a sense of pride in its members. This history also offers an unusual opportunity for scholars of higher education, women's studies, student life, and American history and others to use in their research. The history of Mortar Board reflects a mirror of generations of college students as they were involved in the important and even mundane issues and concerns of their day. This history is ongoing, and it is imperative that future generations of Mortar Board students and alumni continue to record their involvement in this endeavor for the next one hundred years.

Notes

1. The Ohio State University Archives, Mortar Board, (RG141/13/3), "Constitution and By-Laws, 1920."

2. The Ohio State University Archives, Mortar Board, (RG054/169/6), "National Conference, 2012." The purpose remains the same at the time of this printing.

3. William Strauss and Neil Howe, *Generations: The History of America's Future, 1584 to 2069* (New York: William Morrow, 1991).

4. Ibid., 255.

5. Samuel P. Capen and Walton C. John, *A Survey of Higher Education, 1916: Bulletin No. 22* (Washington, DC: Department of Interior, Bureau of Education, 1919), 10.

6. Ibid., 7.

7. "Women's History in America," Women's International Center, www.wic.org/misc/history.htm.

8. Alicia Notestone, "Mortar Board's Roaring Twenties," *Mortar Board Forum* (Spring 2009): 14.

9. "Bylaws of Mortar Board, Inc.," Mortar Board, Inc., www.mortarboard.org/About/GoverningDocuments/.

1

Mortar Board in the Role and Scope of American Higher Education

Susan R. Komives

Higher education in the United States is distinguished by several characteristics, including the diversity of institution type, the lack of a national university or ministry of education, a general belief in education of the whole person, and the promotion of cocurricular learning throughout the entire college experience.

Mortar Board as an honor society falls into the broad contemporary concept of cocurricular learning. To prize its position within higher education and to see how it developed as a significant factor in American higher education, a brief history of higher education and especially the development of cocurricular learning is useful. To understand its *significance* as more than a cocurricular organization, we'll take a look at Mortar Board as a capstone experience for its members and its part in providing high-impact practices.

A History of the Changing Role and Purpose of American Higher Education

The roots of contemporary American higher education began with the founding of Harvard University in 1636, 140 years before the American Revolution. For nearly four hundred years the industry of higher education has grown from this start. The mission and purpose of higher education institutions, the role of faculty, the nature of students and their experience, methods and approaches to funding, governmental intervention, town-gown relationships, and curriculum development have intertwined and changed—and continue to change.

The Early Years

Influences on the development of higher education in the colonial era through the nineteenth century came from England, Scotland, France, and Germany. Colonial institutions especially sought to develop a learned clergy by replicating the religiously centered educational models of Oxford University and Cambridge University. Harvard was founded by several men of the Massachusetts Bay Colony who were graduates of Cambridge's Emmanuel College. They adopted a classical curriculum and a residential college model, with in loco parentis (meaning "in place of the parent") defining the relationship between students (typically thirteen- or fourteen-year-old white men) and the institution. As the eighteenth century unfolded, the rise in denominationalism led to more faith-based institutions (e.g., Princeton, Brown, Rutgers, Dartmouth, Yale). However, as fewer sons of prominent community members wanted to prepare for the clergy, secular institutions also grew in number.

As early as the mid-1700s, the first cocurricular organizations emerged in the form of local campus-based and often secret literary societies that had their own libraries. Their members reveled in disputation methods and political discussions, much of which led directly to the discourse promoting the American Revolution. One of these transitioned to become the first honor society (and Greek letter–named society as well), Phi Beta Kappa, founded at the start of the American Revolution at the College of William and Mary in 1776.

The French supported the colonials in the American Revolution. French influence continued beyond the war in higher education on Thomas Jefferson in particular, with his adoption at the University of Virginia of a faculty-run institution like the University of Paris, which viewed the university as a state within a state, largely independent of government control.

The role and purpose of higher education broadened in the fledgling United States, reflecting President Andrew Jackson's assertion that the common man also wanted an education for his sons. The need for state-offered higher education became apparent. Colonial colleges, however, were private institutions that rejected government takeover. While several universities claim to be the "first" state college (e.g., the University of Georgia and the University of North Carolina), the first to have a charter, financial support, curricula, and students enrolled was "Mr. Jefferson's University" in 1825.

The first half of the nineteenth century saw an amazing diversification by institutional type and purpose. Consider the breadth of missions with the founding of institutions such as West Point, the first military academy (1802); the Rensselaer Polytechnic Institute, the oldest technical research institution (1824); Cheyney College, now Cheyney University of Pennsylvania, the first black college (1837); the Georgia Female College for Women, now Wesleyan College, the first woman's college (1836); and Oberlin College, founded in 1833 and the first, in 1841, to graduate women with a baccalaureate degree alongside men. With many different kinds of students and more of them coming to these diverse institutions, more student societies emerged, including secret fraternities for both men and women. The first men's groups of this type began in the 1820s, and the first women's groups began in the mid-1800s. Predominantly and historically black secret societies (women's and men's) began nationally just after the start of the 1900s. The popularity of the local literary societies of the mid to late 1700s began to decline.

The first direct federal intervention in higher education was the Morrill Act of 1862, which further supported the expansion of public universities through grants of land to states that had not seceded from the Union (and at the end of the American Civil War was expanded to include the former Confederate states). The Morrill Act supported institutions' liberal arts core, emphasizing the agricultural and mechanical curricula for which land-grant colleges are known even today. Their mission was to benefit the citizens of their states and provide access by diverse citizens to postsecondary education.

The second Morrill Act in 1890 required states to show that race was not a consideration in admission or else to designate a separate land-grant institution for persons of color. This resulted in separate institutions for black students, which are the foundation of many of today's historically black colleges and universities. The permissibility of this racially bifurcated system was subsequently upheld by the 1896 U.S. Supreme Court ruling in *Plessy v. Ferguson* and was not overturned until *Brown v. Board of Education of Topeka* in 1954. In practice, it took at least two more decades for race restrictions affecting admissions in American higher education to be considered discriminatory.

The end of the nineteenth century led to complexity in higher education growth. A profound innovation was the Germanic graduate research university model that emphasized freedoms of teaching and of learning and viewed the university as a workshop of free scientific research. The imposition of a Germanic graduate research philosophy and curricula on top of a largely English residential, student-centered teaching college created tension in mission and purpose that is still evident today.

Throughout higher education's early history, undergraduate faculty cared about the undergraduate student experience, and in the 1890s, college presidents began asking popular faculty to become deans of men and deans of women to capitalize on this concern. These new roles had no precedent. Stanley Coulter asked the Purdue University Board of Trustees what his duties as a dean of men would be and said that "they wrote back that they did not know what they were but when I found out to let them know." Thomas Clark, dean of men at the University of Illinois, commented on his "untried sea" and observed that "my only chart was that the action of the Board of Trustees said I was to interest myself in the individual student."[1] Regardless of uncertainty in position description, these roles evolved quickly.

Also evolving at the end of the nineteenth century were Greek-letter organizations separate and distinct from Greek-letter fraternities and sororities. The Tau Beta Pi engineering honor society began in 1885 at Lehigh University, Sigma Xi (honoring scientific investigation) began in 1886 at Cornell University, Phi Kappa Phi (superior scholarship with no limit on area of study) began in 1897 at the University of Maine, Scabbard and Blade (military officers' excellence) began in 1904 at the University of Wisconsin, and Pi Delta Phi (French) began in 1906 at the University of California–Berkeley. By 1918 more than fifteen groups, either general such as Mortar Board or discipline-specific such as Tau Beta Pi, had begun and were growing nationally. Their founding concepts emphasized the importance of recognizing excellence *in* the classroom and provided a venue for students and faculty to mix *beyond* the classroom. These were truly cocurricular organizations, and their growth would require the attention of not only the deans of men and women but also the heads of schools and departments.

Everything Expands in the Twentieth Century

The complexity of American higher education at the start of the twentieth century is mind-boggling and is chronicled well in the next chapter, which guides us through the founding of Mortar Board.

The members of Ohio State's chapter initiated in 1923 surround Dean of Women Elisabeth Conrad in this *Makio* (yearbook) photo. Front, left to right: Alice L. Lawrence, Marjorie E. Reeves, Dorothy L. Blue. Back: Marjorie E. Ferree, Kathryn H. Mathews, Miriam R. Gumble, Dean Conrad, Helen E. Cherington, K. Anita Landacre, Margaret A. Redfield. **Source:** *Makio*, 1924, 541.

As disciplines such as psychology emerged, ways of guiding youths evolved, including the guidance movement in public schools, the establishment of college counseling services, and the mental testing movement. In the vast United States, new types of institutions were needed. The first junior college was established in 1901 by William Rainey Harper, founding president of the University of Chicago, to allow students in distant Joliet, Illinois, to take their first years of study at home and then move to the university. The growth of this segment of higher education institutions has been steady over the past century.

The concept of in loco parentis, accepted practice in American higher education from the beginning, became legal doctrine in 1913 with the *Gott v. Berea College* ruling that institutions must stand in place of the parents to uphold the welfare of the student.

In the 1910s, educators such as John Dewey influenced the academy to consider education in the U.S. democracy as more than rationalistic and intellectual. His pragmatic philosophy asserted that learners be fully engaged in their communities; there was value in experiencing civil life. His work was foundational to concepts of cocurricular engagement, internship and cooperative experiences, service-learning, and the fledgling field of student affairs (begun by those first deans of men and deans of women navigating their new roles). In this milieu and era Mortar Board was founded in 1918 as the first and only national honor society for senior women. Omicron Delta Kappa had been founded four years earlier as an honorary for men of upper-division standing.

As the complexity of administrative roles grew, the American Council on Education commissioned a group to study the emerging role of student services (student affairs). The subsequent *Student Personnel Point of View,* published in 1937, one of whose authors was Mortar Board member Esther Lloyd-Jones (Northwestern University, 1922), explained that deans of men and women and their staff were committed to the development of the whole student, going beyond intellectual learning to include dimensions such as moral and religious values, vocational skills, and social relationships. Each student was unique and had dignity and worth. These concepts continue as the foundation of student affairs today.

From the beginning, student affairs deans worked closely with student leaders to influence campus culture. This is borne out time and time again in the history of nearly every early Mortar Board chapter, which recounts that the members had the ear of the dean of women, and in return they served as listening posts and sounding boards for her. Thus began Mortar Board chapters' contribution to the quality of student life—what we would call today high-impact practices.

Evolution in the Last Sixty Years

Contemporary higher education during the last sixty years shows movement from faculty, students, and administrators *internal* to the academy to entities that are *external,* such as boards of control, government, and the public at large. By the mid-2010s, higher education entered a new era of reexamination and the need to rebuild the public trust.

The 1950s through the 1970s

Following World War II and the massive influx of students, including veterans supported by the first extensive federal financial aid initiative, the Servicemen's Readjustment Act (or GI Bill), the 1950s became an era most influenced by *faculty.* Faculty developed their academic disciplines into specialties, numbers of faculty members doubled in many departments, and faculty members led the way in determining new policies for student admissions, general education, and campus governance.

The Civil Rights Act of 1964 and the Higher Education Act of 1965 supported a diversity of institutions and increased access to higher education through programs such as federal financial aid. The influx in the mid-1960s of the children of veterans dedicated to civil rights brought a loud *student* voice seeking equity by gender and race. These baby boomer activists used the campus as a platform to influence society and campus governance through protest. One of the growing concerns for them was the parietal regulations that were overly protective of women students and included curfews, dress codes, and gender-segregated housing. The concept of the student as an adult was created with the formal elimination of in loco parentis in 1969, reduction of the age of majority to eighteen years (the Right to Vote Act changed the Fourteenth Amendment in 1971), and the 1974 adoption of the Buckley Amendment to the Family Educational Rights and Privacy Act, which changed parents' rights to access their children's academic information. This required rethinking the nature of the student-institutional relationship and led to a fiduciary and contractual relationship with students.

Deans listened to their student leaders to accomplish needed societal change. At Purdue, for instance, it was Mortar Board and the Association of Women Students that encouraged Dean of Women Helen B. Schleman (Northwestern, 1923) that like men, women students did not need parietal hours. Associate Dean M. Beverley Stone (University of Arkansas, 1955) recalled that each semester these parietal hours were lessened, women's grade point averages actually *increased.* As a Society governed by its collegiate members nationally, Mortar Board treated students as adults well before this became established practice by college administrators. Collegiate members led and made policy decisions for the Society, including the decision about the way that Mortar Board would respond to Title IX, which resulted in the inclusion of men in the mid-1970s.

The rapid growth in numbers of institutions in the 1960s, including large numbers of junior and community colleges and the increase in federal laws and regulatory policies, shaped the 1970s into an era of *administrators.* States established boards of higher education to coordinate their rapidly growing systems. Campuses added administrative staff to implement numerous federal policies such as financial aid and services for students with disabilities and to manage the admission of women to previously all-male institutions such as Yale, the University of Virginia, and Johns Hopkins University.

The 1980s through the 1990s

Higher education institutions, disciplines, and other campus programs had grown rapidly in the 1970s, so by 1980 many associations and government entities called on them to examine their role, purpose, and mission and to address new needs created by campus diversity. The 1980s became an era of *senior leadership and boards of control* as presidents, provosts, senior student affairs officers, and trustees stepped up to numerous reforms that signaled the beginning of a new era of accountability. Nearly every institution revisited its mission statement to return to a focus on its core purpose, bringing renewed emphasis on undergraduate teaching, a commitment to campus diversity based on access and retention, a concern for campus community, a demonstrated need to assess everything to ensure evidence-based practice, and a new awareness of computers and the wonders of technology that would unfold past the end of the century.

The 1990s became the decade of "re-," with expectations to implement the reforms identified in the 1980s. Activities such as revisioning, reengineering, and reinvention focused on assessment of the outcomes of a college education. Technologies such as e-mail and the Internet forced everyone who delivered higher education to rethink how and where learning occurred.

The 2000s into the 2010s

For public institutions the 2000s was a decade of *increased governmental role,* as legislatures began to tie funding to outcomes. Federal involvement and intervention increased too, and the assessment of outcomes by regional and disciplinary accreditation agencies was expected. In 2006 U.S. Department of Education secretary Margaret Spellings's Commission on the Future of Higher Education became a lightning rod for higher education access, affordability, and accountability. Higher education found itself challenged to make its own case for its role in society.

In the 2010s, the public at large asked hard questions about the worth of a higher education based on perceived high costs. Higher education became strapped for revenue. Many public institutions shifted from considering themselves "state supported," then "state aided," to finally just "state located." The media and the public focused on ills of higher education in the wake of challenges to Title IX and the handling of sexual assault cases, cheating scandals, big-time college sports programs, hate speech, and ethical lapses by campus personnel. Under pressure of losing the public trust, higher education looked inward for improvement.

Student Engagement in the College Experience

The history of American higher education is a story of a student body made up initially of monocultural young men to a student body diverse in every dimension including gender, age, race, ability, religion, and sexual orientation. College students have evolved from highly controlled youths engaged in disputation and recitation pedagogies to adults engaging in experiential curricula that include a wide range of cocurricular experiences intended to create rich learning. Over its four centuries, American higher education, like its students, has become increasingly diverse, with a goal of offering distinct experiences that promote learning and development toward designated, desirable outcomes.

In recent years, many entities have defined these desirable learning outcomes for the college experience. The Association of American College and Universities (AAC&U), through its Liberal Education and America's Promise program, promotes the outcomes of

> *knowledge of human cultures and the physical and natural world* to address contemporary and enduring big questions;
> *intellectual and practical skills* such as critical and creative thinking and teamwork and problem-solving across the curriculum;
> *personal and social responsibility* such as civic knowledge and engagement and intercultural knowledge and competence; and
> *integrative and applied learning* to deal with new settings and complex problems.

The Council for the Advancement of Standards in Higher Education, a confederation of forty-two professional associations largely in student affairs, promotes six domains of outcomes:

> *knowledge acquisition, construction, integration and application* such as relating knowledge to daily life;
> *cognitive complexity* (e.g., critical thinking, creativity);
> *intrapersonal development* such as ethics and spiritual awareness;
> *interpersonal competence* including interdependence and effective leadership;

humanitarianism and civic engagement including social responsibility and global perspective; and
practical competence such as demonstrating professionalism and maintaining health and wellness.[2]

Accrediting associations for academic disciplines demonstrate common themes in the outcomes they seek, such as *management and collaborative leadership, interpersonal relations with diverse others, ethics,* and *lifelong learning.*[3] Students should demonstrate these outcomes across the whole college experience—in their major, elective course work, and employment and through cocurricular involvement in student organizations.

The assessment movement in the 1990s and 2000s sought to identify good practices that promoted desirable outcomes. Assessment gained national focus with the founding of the National Study of the Student Experience (NSSE) in 1998, which explained that

> student engagement represents two critical features of collegiate quality.
>
> The first is the amount of time and effort students put into their studies and other educationally purposeful activities. The second is how the institution deploys its resources and organizes the curriculum and other learning opportunities to get students to participate in activities that decades of research studies show are linked to student learning.[4]

Student engagement has been shown to benefit just about everything in the college experience from persistence to academic achievement, from cognitive development to leadership development, and from practical competence and skill transferability to acquisition of social capital.[5]

Years of study led the NSSE to identify projects such as service-learning, learning communities, undergraduate research with a faculty member, and applied work such as internships.[6] The AAC&U and NSSE partnered to present these high-impact practices (HIPs) to college educators. NSSE founder George Kuh wrote in 2008 that HIPs worked because they contributed significantly to all students' learning and development and were particularly helpful to those previously underserved, such as first-generation students. They include capstone courses or other culminating senior experiences.

HIPs "demand considerable time and effort, facilitate learning outside of the classroom, require meaningful interactions with faculty and students, encourage collaboration with diverse others, and provide frequent and substantive feedback. As a result, participation in these practices can be life-changing."[7]

Though the terminology is updated, Mortar Board over its one hundred years has prided itself not only on offering a capstone experience, a HIP, to its members but also providing HIPs for other students.

A relatively new arena for assessment emerged in the 2010s. How do college graduates and alumni reflect the experiences they had in college that would contribute to their after-college success, involvement, and development? The Gallup-Purdue Index, released in May 2014, observed, for example, that alumni were 1.4 times more likely to thrive in a variety of measures of well-being (such as being engaged at work) if they had been highly engaged in extracurricular activities.[8] A consistent finding across diverse institutions is that the type of institution matters less than the level of meaningful engagement a student makes within that institution. That is, what a student does is more important than where the student is. True honor societies such as Mortar Board value and honor that meaningful engagement.

Mortar Board's Ideals: Scholarship, Leadership, and Service

Over the history of higher education in the United States, scholarship, leadership, and service have been valued comprehensive outcomes for the college graduate. Woven as it has been into the fabric of higher education over the last one hundred years, it is no surprise that Mortar Board was founded on and continues to thrive because of these three factors—scholarship, leadership, and service. Mortar Board calls these Ideals, as they are always-moving targets for the highly engaged and high-achieving students who are members of the Society. The Society itself encourages its members to develop excellence in each of these three outcomes while in college and commit to lifelong excellence in the Ideals after college days have ended.

Although a fine grade point average may be an indicator of scholarship, a true scholar reflects learning at a high level of complexity, with demonstrated achievement in academic writing, outcomes of laboratory research, recitals and creative performance, publications, and conference presentations, among many other things. Mortar Board members are selected, first, on these expansive measures of a true scholar.

Contemporary models of leadership taught on campus emphasize collaboration, multiculturalism, nurturing inclusive diverse teams, being ethical, emphasizing process as well as outcome, and serving bigger purposes, particularly those advancing social justice. Mortar Board is a living laboratory where these principles are put into action. A well-advised chapter of the Society provides essential affirmation of leadership excellence and sets an expectation for collaborative, ethical leadership.

My own research in leadership identity development showed that what one thinks leadership is influences how it is exhibited. Leadership is socially constructed. The view of leadership changes over experience, with support, and through exploring oneself in the context of diverse others.[9]

College students initially appear to view leadership as behaviors of persons in authority who attempt to accomplish goals while working with others frequently but trying to do everything themselves and reluctantly delegating. This confusing and hierarchical view changes over time so that leadership is also seen as a process that can be exhibited in nonpositional roles. An awareness develops: "I can be A leader without being THE leader." This view of interdependence with others requires trust in the process of leadership and in new skills of collaboration and teamwork. Broadening the view of leadership to be both nonpositional and a process leads to the viewpoint that a positional role facilitates the active engagement of members in the work of the group.

The positional leader recognizes leadership as servant-leadership, relational leadership, and ethical leadership. Mortar Board chapters are populated by students already recognized for their *positional* leadership roles. As a group of leaders, they come to learn how to work collaboratively in the process of leadership within their chapter. They often develop a systems view of leadership that recognizes the interdependence of their organizations across their college or university and realizes their ability to leverage the capacity of their diverse organizations to benefit and change their campus community.

Recent research on leadership development affirms that a leader identity is both claimed and granted.[10] Like any identity-developing process, one may claim an identity (e.g., "leader") that is then affirmed (or not) by others in the context. In this cyclical process, one may also have leadership ability affirmed and then come to a personal awareness and claim that identity. Most Mortar Board members have already held positional leadership roles affirming both the claiming and granting dimensions of that process. On occasion, someone is seen as a

Longwood University's Geist chapter sponsors and organizes the annual Oktoberfest, a highlight of which is Color Wars, with students who began on campus in odd-numbered years, the green team, pitted against those who began in even-numbered years, the red team. The goal is to get the most color on the white T-shirts of the opposition and then come together as a campus community. **Source:** *Mortar Board Forum* 42, no. 1 (Fall/Winter 2011): 17.

leader by others but does not claim that identity, and the selection process of Mortar Board provides key affirmation to help the member internalize and claim that identity.

Many ask the question "leadership for what?" Mortar Board values leadership toward service that makes the institution holding the chapter's charter a better place. Through its purpose, Mortar Board espouses going beyond viewing service as charity to understanding that service is real engagement that identifies root causes of complex issues and applies members' excellence in scholarship and leadership in service of these causes.

Mortar Board as a High-Impact Capstone Experience

There are two predominant ways of honoring students at the culmination of their undergraduate experience. *Honoraries* select students on designated criteria usually involving academic achievement. The bestowing of the honor recognizes excellence without the student's commitment to further engagement. As an *honor society*, on the other hand, Mortar Board expects continued leadership and service to the college, the academic disciplines, and the entire campus community. Honor societies value scholarship and achievement and typically seek to select members who evidence quality in their leadership and in their service. Reciprocally, these Mortar Board members agree to actively serve in their senior year and bring great benefit to their institutions with their active engagement in enriching the culture of the institution. Over the years, wise deans of student affairs (and other advisors) worked with Mortar Board as keen observers of student life and engaged them in institutional change. The editor of the *Quarterly* asked deans of women to give their view of the role of Mortar Board

on campus. Their responses present a broad range of ideas, thoughts, and suggestions. Virginia Frobes (Utah, 1932), dean at the University of Utah, wrote that

> I resist strongly the possibility that Mortar Board is just another activity in which members "give service" and "do projects." For this special group of women, Service should become a means, Leadership a tool, and Scholarship an attitude, which all combine to achieve the objective of becoming a truly educated woman.[11]

Nora Chaffin (Vanderbilt University, 1948), dean at Vanderbilt, suggested that "it is [Mortar Board members'] responsibility to invest their personal gifts and accomplishments in furthering the welfare of their school and contemporaries." Katherine Sherrill (Hood, 1955), Hood College's dean, advised that "it is in the realm of ideas that Mortar Board can and must play its most important role."[12]

Mortar Board is a marvelous example of a senior capstone experience—a high-impact practice—that brings students together to serve their institutions and practice their collaborative leadership as a value of service. Mortar Board members become what John Gardner, former U.S. secretary of health, education, and welfare and founder of Common Cause, called "The Responsibles":

> All citizens should have the opportunity to be active, but all will not respond. Those who do respond carry the burden of our free society. I call them The Responsibles. They exist in every segment of the community—ethnic groups, labor unions, neighborhood associations, businesses [colleges]—but they rarely form an effective network of responsibility because they don't know one another across segments. They must find each

other, learn to communicate, and find common ground. Then they can function as the keepers of the long-term agenda.[13]

This cohort model of a culminating experience with peers from across the diversity of experience at an institution is a tremendous example of a high-impact practice. Mortar Board is the first experience for many students of being in Gardner's kind of network—teaching them to step up and be the *Responsibles*.

Being in Mortar Board teaches members to see a systems perspective of their institutions and value the interdependence of all parts. Being in Mortar Board with other excellent leaders promotes and models the best of collaborative servant-leadership, as members share the leadership in their service. Being in Mortar Board at the ending stage of their college career advances the leadership perspectives of generativity, seeing leadership as a process and teaching, mentoring, and guiding others toward leadership excellence themselves. This culminating experience prepares Mortar Board members to transition to their new worlds of graduate study, careers, community obligations, and family obligations as highly engaged leaders willing to assume responsibility in all of those contexts. Mortar Board members are not spectators; they engage and make a difference in their world.

Texas Tech's Forum Chapter President Gracen Daniel, like so many Mortar Boards, was engaged in her collegiate experience for reasons beyond the symbols of success.
Source: *Mortar Board Forum* 46, no. 2 (Spring 2016): cover.

Notes

1. J. R. Appleton, C. M. Briggs, and J. J. Rhatigan, *Pieces of Eight: The Rites, Roles, and Styles of the Dean by Eight Who Have Been There* (Washington, DC: National Association of Student Personnel Administrators, 1978), 14.

2. "CAS Learning and Developmental Outcomes," Council for the Advancement of Standards in Higher Education, http://standards.cas.edu /getpdf.cfm?PDF=D87A29DC-D1D6-D014-83AA8667902C480B.

3. M. B. Drechsler Sharp, S. R. Komives, and J. Fincher, "Learning Outcomes in Academic Disciplines: Identifying Common Ground," *Journal of Student Affairs Research and Practice* 48 (2011): 481–504. doi: 10.2202 /1949-6605.6246.

4. "About NSSE," National Survey of Student Engagement, http://nsse .indiana.edu/html/about.cfm.

5. Shaun R. Harper and Stephen John Quaye, eds., *Student Engagement in Higher Education: Theoretical Perspectives and Practical Approaches for Diverse Populations* (New York: Routledge, 2009).

6. National Survey of Student Engagement, *Experiences That Matter: Enhancing Student Learning and Success; Annual Report 2007* (Bloomington: Indiana University Center for Postsecondary Research, 2007).

7. "High-Impact Practices," National Survey of Student Engagement, http://nsse.indiana.edu/html/high_impact_practices.cfm.

8. "The Gallup-Purdue Index 2015 Report," Purdue University, http:// www.gallup.com/services/185924/gallup-purdue-index-2015-report.aspx.

9. S. R. Komives, J. E. Owen, S. D. Longerbeam, F. C. Mainella, and L. Osteen, "Developing a Leadership Identity: A Grounded Theory," *Journal of College Student Development* 46 (2005): 593–612.

10. Sue Ashford Sue and Scott DeRue, "Leadership—It's (Much) More than Position," *Harvard Business Review,* April 29, 2010, https://hbr.org /2010/04/leadership-its-much-more-than.

11. *Mortar Board Quarterly* 39, no. 4 (April 1963): 11–12.

12. Ibid., 14.

13. John Gardner, "You Are the Responsibles," in *Civic Partners* (Charlottesville, VA: Pew Partnership for Civic Change, 1997), 5.

2

The Centennial History of Mortar Board
National College Senior Honor Society

The Formative Years: 1918–1939

Mortar Board is a fascinating story from the very beginning. The determination and dedication of its early leaders, its stunning growth, and the enthusiasm of the first collegiate members created remarkable excitement on American college campuses. The early National Council members' resolve and matter-of-fact way of conducting business made for a good foundation to support its growth. Historical and societal events made an interesting backdrop for the many Mortar Board milestones of this time period. Chief among an astonishing array of societal disadvantages was the status of women in the United States, who did not yet have the right to vote when Mortar Board was founded. World War I, though in its final year, was still raging. The founding members, during an era when women rarely traveled alone, met in upper New York—in February! From a practical standpoint, it is equally

remarkable that for almost three years, successive classes of members of the founding chapters passed along the correspondence from senior class to senior class, keeping alive the resolve to "nationalize" a senior women's honor organization.

Although it did not become an organized national group until 1918, Mortar Board had its roots in several local honor societies that were already in existence around the United States. Even though the early chapters' stated raisons d'être were often filled with high purpose identified as "intellectual" (like the literary societies described in the first chapter of this publication), some of Mortar Board's predecessor organizations were originally secret societies with rituals filled with hocus-pocus. Cornell University's Der Hexenkreis (Circle of Witches), founded in 1892, falls into this category. The Der Hexenkreis pin, crafted by Tiffany of New York, was and still is a gold skull with red jeweled eyes and a black mystic "7" on its forehead. The

Der Hexenkreis's logo appeared on its badge and even a few rings.
Its mysteries are known only to Cornellian Mortar Boards.

symbol were in part a joke directed at the senior men's recently organized "Society of the Red Rose."

At the University of Nebraska, the members of Black Masque, founded in 1905, found more substance for their existence. The members assisted at Friday afternoon all-campus teas and "sponsored new movements and gave them [those movements] support until they were strong enough to stand by themselves."[2]

Valuing the distinct identity of each chapter was very important in the early years of the national organization and remains so today. Pamela (Pam) Pauly Chinnis (College of William and Mary, 1945) illustrates this when describing the early organizations that became Mortar Board. At Swarthmore College, "the chief activity was attendance at the public lectures of the college. Whether this improved their scholarship, tested their character, or incontrovertibly stamped their loyalty may be left to individual judgment. Suffice it to say that, from spring vacation till commencement in 1907, every lecturer at the college could count on eleven energetic ushers, and after the selection

members were forbidden to refer to or discuss anything about the organization publicly. Some of the secrecy was, in point of fact, related to the purpose that the members were to be a sounding board and a "listening ear" for the dean of women. Anonymity lent itself to this purpose.

There was frivolity on occasion. For example, the University of Minnesota's forerunner to Mortar Board was "organized solely for social purposes, and the basis for membership was simply that a girl be a good sport."[1] From its founding in 1899 and for six years after, each Minnesota group selected its own name. In 1902 the formal name was "The Society of the Green Pickle," and the members wore a free pin from the Heinz Pickle Company as their symbol. The name and

The Senior Honor Society at Colorado, founded in 1908, had a pin in the shape of a mortarboard bearing the Greek letters gamma and alpha.

of the juniors, an audience of at least eighteen."[3] A 1915 Middlebury College alumna, responding to a query about her organization's history, said that "there was nothing scholastic about us. We used to have banquets and make silly speeches and during initiation, we did all sorts of ridiculous things." The history of Miami University's Pleiade in Oxford, Ohio, established in 1916, recounts that "as a farewell to the outgoing group, the new members gave a picnic that was more famous for its lack of dignity than anything else."

Though some silliness may have been part of these early societies, all of them had meaningful reasons to exist. Camaraderie among the members was essential considering the difficulties for women, so few in number and so low in rank at their institutions. Housing and facilities for women were a major concern. The University of Wisconsin group reported that "the biggest piece of work which our chapter accomplished was the establishment of the first cooperative house for university women at Wisconsin. It was called the Mortar Board Cottage. Because of its success, several other houses were established."[4]

Penetralia at the University of Montana worked to furnish a women's restroom on campus. Visor at the University of Texas raised significant money to provide lighting for the dark walkway from campus to the women's residence. Tolo's 1910 initiation at the University of Washington was held in the Women's Building that had been built by the Federation of Women's Clubs for the Alaska-Yukon-Pacific Exposition and left on the young campus for women students. Later, Tolo would establish a residence for women whose rooms had been usurped by men returning from World War II.

Although many women's honor societies existed locally, there was no *national* organization devoted solely to honoring outstanding college senior women in the United States. It was providential when two young women shared a brief encounter on the campus of the University of Chicago in 1915. Their meeting led to the formation of Mortar

The name of Washington's Tolo Club came from a Native American word meaning "success and achievement." Founded in 1909, the club became a chapter in 1925.

The plain black mortarboard of Ohio State was selected as the national design by the national group but with the addition of the letters of the motto. The inscription on the back of this pin reads "Martha Chambers 6-5-'17."

Board. One of those women, Eliza Ulrich Ullman (Swarthmore, 1915), later recalled that meeting:

> It was on the campus of the University of Chicago in the fall of 1915 that a titian haired coed from Ohio State University greeted me by saying, "I see you are a Mortar Board." I must have looked very blank for she pointed to my pin and repeated. Now I was a member of the Senior Honor Society at Swarthmore known as Pi Sigma Chi while she belonged to a Mortar Board organization at Ohio State University, but our pins were very similar, in fact almost identical, and our methods of election, ways of working, ideals and traditions seemed to be one. I wrote back to my classmates in Pi Sigma Chi at Swarthmore telling them of this interesting coincidence, and expressing my belief there must be many similar societies and that it might be worthwhile to find out more about them and the possibility of establishing a national organization.
>
> From this casual meeting came the inspiration to organize but it was not done in a hurry. There were many discussions pro and con and the usual talk that seemed to be getting nowhere. However, the class of 1916 supplied the inspiration that led to the completion of the task by the following classes and in the fall of 1916 the first letter was framed and the questionnaire that was to accompany it.
>
> How we chewed our pencils over that first questionnaire that was sent to all Class A colleges and how eagerly we awaited their replies! However, there was not time during the last semester of our senior year for anything more than a start, so we bequeathed this work to our successors, the class of 1917. It was in 1918, nearly two years after the idea was conceived, that Mortar Board was finally born.[5]

Several organizations around the country responded to the Swarthmore students' letter (the questionnaire referred to above), and those who agreed to send delegates to a meeting to formulate plans for the "Nationalization of Honorary Societies for Senior Women" were at Cornell University, Syracuse University, The Ohio State University, University of Michigan, and Swarthmore. The first meeting was held in Syracuse, New York, on February 15, 1918, at the home of Johanna Potter. The delegates were J. Ernestine Becker of Cornell's Der Hexenkreis, Anita Kelley Raynsford of Mortarboard at Michigan, Helen Hobart of Mortar Board at Ohio State, Carolyn D. Archbold of Eta Pi Upsilon at Syracuse, and Esther Fisher Holmes representing Pi Sigma Chi at Swarthmore. Miss Holmes was elected president of the Convention[6] and was thus the first National President of Mortar Board.

The opening discussion centered on the "object of the convention which is to organize the leaders of the undergraduate and the graduate world." The first order of business was to name the society, and the main question was whether it should be a Greek-letter fraternity. Swarthmore and Syracuse were in favor of a Greek-letter name, but Cornell, Michigan, and Ohio State thought that there were "already too many Greek letter societies and one more would have no distinction and confusion might result." They also thought that "there was a broader democracy in a plain English name such as Mortar Board." Syracuse and Swarthmore delegates thought that a Greek-letter fraternity had more distinction than a plain English name and that a name such as Mortar Board "does not mean very much since [we] don't often wear a cap and gown." After much discussion, they decided to postpone a definite selection of the name until later.[7]

The next order of business was to study the constitution that Swarthmore had drawn up. The delegates "worked over this for several hours, rearranging and changing it until it stood in its present form." It could not be adopted, however, since the name of the society had not

MINUTES OF THE CONVENTION FOR NATIONALIZATION OF

HONORARY SOCIETIES FOR SENIOR WOMEN

Held at Syracuse, New York   February 15-16, 1918

   The first meeting of the Convention was held at the
home of Miss Johanna Potter, Syracuse, N.Y., at 9 A.M., on February 15, 1918. The Colleges represented were as follows:

Kexenkreis of Cornell University...Miss Ernestine Becker
Mortar Board of the U. of Michigan..Mrs. James W. Raynsford (Anita Kell
Mortar Board of Ohio State University...Miss Helen Hobart
Pi Sigma Chi of Swarthmore College...Miss Esther Holmes
Eta Pi Upsilon of Syracuse University..Miss Carolyn Archbold

   Miss Helmes of Swarthmore College was elected president
of the Convention. Mrs. Raynsford was elected secretary of the convention.

   Miss Holmes opened the meeting with a few remarks on the
object of this Convention, namely to form a National Honorary Fraternity of these various local ones, in order to get together in one
organization the leaders of the undergraduate and the graduate world.

   There was a discussion of the name of the Society. The
main question was - Should it be a Greek Letter Fraternity of not.
Swarthmore and Syracuse were in favor of a Greek Letter Fraternity.
Cornell, Michigan and Ohio State were against it. The different
representatives presented their arguments for and against as follows:

OHIO STATE: There are too many small Greek letter socieites now, so
that one more would have no distinction, and confusion might result.
Also this Society does not want to seem to copy the men.
CORNELL: Also thought there were too many Greek Letter Societies
already. We are starting here to work up to a big reputation, and such
a National Honorary Society for Senior Women should be distinctive.
MICHIGAN: Also thought there were too many small Greek letter
societies, and that such a society as we propose to form should stand
out, and not be only one of many confusing Greek Letter organizationd.
Also thought there was a broader democracy in a plain English name,
such as Mortar Board.

SYRACUSE: A name like Mortar Board does not mean very much to Syracuse
since they do not wear a cap and gown very much. Also, a number of
colleges would be likely to have Mortar Board for the name of their
Senior Honorary Society and they would be confused with a National one.
SWARTHMORE: A Greek Letter Fraternity has more distinction than a
plain English name, and a society such as this would grow to have a
reputation especially if we got together at once and took in the principal honorary societies. Greek letter societies seem to be above
the level of the ordinary.

been decided. At the second meeting held on the afternoon of that first day, February 15, the preamble to the constitution was added to more closely align with the preamble of Syracuse's Eta Pi Upsilon. A further discussion of the name of the society led to the decision to "adopt a Greek motto taken from the Greek letters meaning Service, Scholarship and Leadership to be represented by the three Greek letters Pi Sigma Alpha, which letters will appear on the pin."[8]

The pin of Ohio State Mortar Board was adopted "consisting of a black enamel mortarboard with gold edging and tassel, adding to it the three Greek letters of our motto."[9] Ohio State was appointed "Pin Committee."

The next question was the advisability of incorporating the organization. The Syracuse delegate had asked the advice of a lawyer and found that it was not necessary to incorporate at this time unless they "wanted to sue or be sued, or to hold property."[10] The delegates decided to discuss the issue further at the next convention. (It was not until 1938 that Mortar Board actually incorporated.)

The oldest national pin belonged to Lois Barrington Sharpe, the last surviving member of the founding Ohio State class of 1914. The inscription reads "Lois Barrington 5-17-14."

The form of the initiation service was discussed. Ohio State and Syracuse read their initiation services aloud. A revised version of the Ohio State service was adopted because "it was simple and would fit in with almost any local customs."[11]

The election of officers took place at the third meeting, held on the morning of February 16, 1918. Since the next convention would be in Ann Arbor, Michigan (a motion to hold the meeting in Cornell's Ithaca, New York, having failed), it was decided that the next president should be from the University of Michigan to expedite planning. Other officers were "Ohio State for Secretary, Swarthmore for Treasurer and Syracuse for Historian." It was decided that each of the five charter groups appropriate $3 "to constitute a fund to last until the next convention." The new secretary was instructed to keep Michigan's assessment and the new historian was instructed to keep Syracuse's assessment for expenses, with the understanding that they were to return any surplus to the treasurer ($3 in 1921 would be worth about $36 today). A discussion of the scholarship standard for new members led to the decision to leave the details to the various local chapters, with the recommendation that it be kept as high as possible.

The second day of the convention also found the delegates considering expansion—and "the battle of the bulge was on—as one early director of expansion who was presented with a size fifty-nine girdle would attest!"[12] A list of colleges where senior women's honor societies existed was reviewed, and a letter was drafted to be sent to twenty-two colleges, "giving them the opportunity to petition to join this national organization." The last paragraph of the letter contained the preamble to the new constitution:

Our purpose is to provide for the co-operation between these societies [the various chapters], to promote college loyalty, to advance the spirit of service and fellowship among University and college women, to maintain a high standard of scholarship, to recognize and encourage leadership, and to stimulate and develop a finer type of college woman.[13]

The minutes indicate that at the end of the convention, each delegate shared information about her group. Der Hexenkreis "worked very quietly and secretly with others unaware of their presence. The dean of women comes to them for the big things." The Michigan Mortarboards were not as secretive as Cornell except for their initiation ceremony. "The girls who are at the head of things on the campus come to Mortarboard for opinions and advice." Ohio State's initiation was also secret, but "other activities are public." They work with the dean of women and help with any "good thing that comes up" such as the student self-government asking Mortar Board to work out the point system for the campus. Eta Pi Upsilon at Syracuse was in complete charge of Women's Day in May, for which all classes at the university are suspended. "They have athletics, a big pageant, and a writing competition where they give a prize . . . and a medal is awarded to the junior girl who has the greatest number of points in activities and personality." They try to create a sentiment for seniors to wear their caps and gowns the last two weeks of college. Swarthmore indicated that there were only fifty girls in their class and that they do not push their ideas but do speak up in self-government meetings. They said that they worked quietly and abolished eating clubs because they were not democratic. "We have been working on this idea of nationalization for some time."[14]

The delegates ended the meeting with a last motion "that the sentiment of the convention go down as favoring a Greek letter name."[15] The motion carried three to two. However, National President Esther Holmes, who had voted with the majority during the convention, changed her mind—and her vote—upon her return to Swarthmore.[16]

Angered when the new majority spurned the idea of a Greek-letter name, Syracuse's Eta Pi Upsilon withdrew from the newborn society and never affiliated with Mortar Board. Mortar Board thus honors four founding chapters rather than five.

Two local groups were added before the end of Mortar Board's first year, Phi Delta Psi at the University of Illinois and Friars at the University of Missouri. The University of Minnesota was added in 1919. Other organizations invited after the first convention were located at the University of Kansas, the University of Colorado, Northwestern University, the University of Wisconsin, the University of Iowa, Washington University, the University of Nebraska, the University of Oklahoma, the University of California, the University of Washington, and DePauw University. All hastened to establish chapters.

When the second national convention convened at 9:30 a.m. in Ann Arbor, Michigan, on April 25, 1919, the world was recovering from World War I. In addition to the original four chapters, representatives from the Universities of Illinois, Minnesota, and Missouri attended. A "criticism about the lack of the name Mortar Board" in the previous convention's minutes was noted and quickly rectified. The new constitution was studied for its "theoretical policies" to determine clauses that were not practical.[17]

The national secretary was given the "power to have official Mortar Board paper printed" and to "write the Commissioner at Washington, D.C. [at the U.S. Office of Education] for a list of first rate colleges." The deans of women of these colleges were to be sent "letters explaining the meaning and purpose of national Mortar Board to tell them how they can join by petitioning." It was also decided that Mortar Board "does not send second invitations to colleges except . . . through some personal interest."[18]

Discussion about the meaning of Pi Sigma Alpha followed, since "the Greek letters on the pin did not exactly comply with the meaning of the Greek letters." The secretary was instructed to write to the secretary of the last convention to ask her for the translation of the letters "Pi.E.A."[19] A member of the present convention was appointed to look up the meaning of the letters as well.

After a break from 12:35 to 3:30 p.m., a motion that the "general sentiment of Convention was in favor of National officers being elected from Alumnae" was made and carried.[20]

After another recess, the delegates reconvened at 7:15 p.m. and elected for two-year terms Mary Mildred Logan (Missouri, 1918) as National President, Helen Dustman (Ohio State, 1918) as vice president, Marian Wash (Minnesota, 1918) as secretary, Isabel Myers (Swarthmore, 1918) as treasurer (this is Isabel Briggs Myers who with her mother was the cocreator of the personality inventory known as the Myers-Briggs Type Indicator), and Virginia Phipps (Cornell University, 1918) as historian. It was decided that *Robert's Rules of Order* would be used to conduct meetings of national Mortar Board, and the expenses of the national officers were to be paid by the national treasurer. There was $21.28 in the treasury.

An announcement was made that the Michigan alumnae of Mortar Board had organized, making it the first alumnae club, and the convention suggested that alumnae chapters pay a certain amount of their dues into the national treasury. At the close of the meeting, suggestions were made that "enthusiasm be taken back to chapters for organizing alumnae chapters."[21] The historian was instructed to send the minutes of the convention to alumnae chapters. Ohio State was selected to host the next meeting in two years. The Society was about to embark on a period of remarkable growth.

The decade that followed World War I was a time of social, political, and economic change. Women voted in elections in all forty-eight states for the first time in 1920. Greater numbers of women were in the workforce. It was the age of the automobile (the price of a Ford was $290), consumerism, prohibition, gangland warfare, and the beginning of the Great Depression. Jazz was popular, people danced the Charleston, and the first talking picture premiered in 1926. Charles Lindbergh made his famous transatlantic flight in 1927. Flappers influenced the fashions of the time (shorter skirts, bobbed hair, silk stockings). The Martha Washington Hotel opened in New York City for women only and was staffed by women "bellgirls." Its advertised purpose was to give nervous ladies peace of mind and sounder sleep, knowing that a strange man was not in the next room. Another New York hotel refused to serve dinner to ladies who "arrived unescorted after 6 p.m."[22]

Mortar Board was three years old when the delegates to the third national convention met on April 22–24, 1921, in Columbus at The Ohio State University library. Thirteen chapters responded to the roll call. The president of the convention was Anne Cornell (Ohio State, 1918).

Louise Van Cleave (Indiana University, 1921) presented her chapter's petition for membership. After a discussion the petition was accepted, and the new delegate, Van Cleave, was called back into the room to be seated. (The practice of immediately admitting a new chapter at the convention when it presented its petition was eliminated later.) Petitions from the University of Pittsburgh and the University of Idaho were accepted, but the inquiries of the University of Pennsylvania and Gamma Tau at Pullman, Washington, were delayed until formal petitions were received.

The delegates voted to accept a contract presented by a representative of Auld's jewelry store of Columbus, Ohio. In return for exclusive rights to the production of the pin, the jeweler guaranteed immediate delivery within two weeks after the order was received and a price of $3 each, reduced from $3.50. It was later decided in this convention that the price of the "fraternity" pin would be included in the initiation fees, which were set at just $3, with no cushion for other costs. Later Balfour, a growing national company that had capitalized on

the fraternity and sorority jewelry market, would undercut Auld by seventy-five cents with faster delivery.

The next order of business was to decide where to wear the pin. Several options were "at side of waist, 'v' at waist or left shoulder, and a vote of the members present fixed definitely the left side of the waist over the heart as the place for wearing the pin."[23] Also discussed were occasions when the pin should be worn, and as the minutes stated,

> No rule was laid down, but just an expression of opinion, that they should be worn on all occasions and not left at home in preference for others. It was declared that if a Mortar Board did not feel proud enough to wear the pin at all times, she was not the kind of girl that should be in Mortar Board.[24]

Wisconsin was appointed to chair a committee to find a Mortar Board "grip," although nothing came of that directive.[25] Obviously, the delegates were working through the decision making that would distinguish Mortar Board from a local secret society crossed with a women's fraternity (many Mortar Board members were also members of women's fraternities and thus were influenced by their meaningful rituals and traditions) and make it a true national honor society.

The need for a ceremony to install new chapters was discussed, and two suggested versions were read. A committee was appointed to combine them. Examination questions prior to initiation were discussed.

———————————

Anne Cornell Christensen (Ohio State, 1918) was the third National President, elected in 1921. With both baccalaureate and master's degrees from Ohio State, she was the dean of women of Franklin College in Indiana well into the early 1930s. One of the few women on The Ohio State University Alumni Board, she was also the first woman in the state of Indiana to become a licensed pilot. After her marriage and the birth of two children, she remained active in alumni activities in Columbus, Ohio.

As with any newly formed organization, the question of finances continued to be an important order of business. According to the minutes, the "treasurer's report showed great deficiency in national funds." Articles to the constitution were amended, including that the installation fee be paid before the chapter is installed and that each chapter member pay at initiation annual dues of $3. Enforcement of these financial measures was "declared imperative." Another article was amended to read "that the national treasurer shall notify any delinquent chapter at the end of each October that the dues must be paid immediately" and that it would be dropped if not paid by the following January 1.[26] It was decided that one half of each convention delegate's expenses would be paid by the national organization.

While the national organization was struggling with finances, local chapters were finding interesting ways to raise money to conduct their activities. Indiana's fund-raiser was "selling hair nets at all organized houses and dormitories." Idaho sponsored an all-campus dance, the first ever to be sponsored by a women's club on campus. The dance, called the Spinster's Skip, provided the "one chance during the year for the girls to express themselves, date the boy of their choice and show him what was considered to be an ideal date." The so-called Mortar Board grapevine must already have been in existence at this time, because Spinster's Skips began appearing on other campuses across the country soon afterward. Colorado's version was a "sunrise dance from six to eight on a spring Saturday morning. The girls asked the boys and even gave them lovely corsages of vegetables." Iowa State hosted the Mortar Board Frolic, "an afternoon of play and picnic given for freshmen at a park near the campus."[27]

The grades of chapters that took the required membership examination were printed annually in the *Quarterly* after they were administered and marked by section directors.

Mortar Board Examination Grades

By ELSIE E. MURRAY
National Vice-President

The grades of the entire active membership—463—are reported here, grouped and averaged under the forty-nine chapters and eight sections. The chairman of the examination committee congratulates the active members of Mortar Board on their fine spirit and their commendable success in attaining the highest general average ever reported: 96.48.

Special distinction goes to three chapters with the unprecedented perfect average: 100%. These banner chapters are *Indiana* and *Knox* in Section III and *South Dakota* in Section IV.

Average	Chapter	Average	Chapter
100	University of Indiana	97.81	University of Wisconsin
100	Knox College	97.75	Lawrence College
100	University of South Dakota	97.50	University of California
99.9	University of Michigan	97.4	University of Missouri
99.88	University of Texas	97.07	Pomona College
99.77	Carnegie Inst. of Technology	97.04	University of Colorado
99.53	University of Illinois	97.	University of Nebraska
99.50	Univ. of Southern California	96.61	Washington University
99.50	Westhampton College	95.83	University of Arizona
99.40	Agnes Scott College	95.27	University of Kentucky
99.30	Northwestern University	95.18	Iowa State College
99.27	University of West Virginia	94.86	Purdue University
99.09	University of Iowa	94.86	University of Oregon
99.08	University of Pittsburgh	94.75	University of Alabama
99.	Whitman College	94.71	Washington State College
98.86	Ohio Wesleyan University	94.18	University of Washington
98.44	Miami University	93.8	University of Oklahoma
98.33	Swarthmore College	93.62	Middlebury College
98.28	Florida State College for Women	92.	University of Vermont
98.20	University of Minnesota	90.85	DePauw University
98.12	Kansas State Agr. College	90.22	University of Montana
98.09	College of William and Mary	88.44	Cornell University
98.	University of Kansas	86.89	Ohio State University
98.	Montana State College	78.57	University of Penn.
97.87	University of Idaho		

Section	Averages	Rating	Highest Chapter in Section	Average
Section	I : 90.19	eighth	Swartmore College	98.33
Section	II : 97.45	third	Carnegie Inst. of Tech.	99.77
Section	III : 97.31	fifth	Indiana and Knox	100.
Section	IV : 96.16	sixth	Univ. of South Dakota	100.
Section	V : 97.37	fourth	University of Texas	97.88
Section	VI : 95.55	seventh	Whitman College	99.
Section	VII : 97.47	second	Univ. of Southern Calif.	99.50
Section	VIII : 97.54	first	Westhampton College	99.50

The newly created southern section (VIII), containing the three newest chapters in Mortar Board (Westhampton College, Florida State College for Women, and Agnes Scott College), as well as three older groups (Kentucky, Alabama, and William and Mary), is to be congratulated for holding first place.

When the fourth national convention convened at Swarthmore in February 1923, eighteen chapters answered the roll call. National President Anne Cornell gave the opening address in which she "emphasized the necessity of overcoming the problem of Mortar Board as a 'one year organization' by carrying over the spirit of this convention until the next." The policy of expansion in regard to smaller colleges was discussed, and the delegates "favored first class small schools if the local society measured up to our standards."[28] A motion was passed to admit institutions classified as first rate by the American Association of University Women (AAUW), including small schools and technical schools.

It was at this convention that "Ohio [State] suggested the plan of dividing the chapters into groups geographically, appoint directors for inspection of the section, and plan to hold annual conferences together."[29] Although it was determined then that "it was inadvisable to attempt a plan of this kind for several years," the National Council decided soon after to establish "districts" to facilitate business because of the growing size of the organization. "With the investment of one dollar in a map and pencil with an eraser, the United States, like Gaul, was divided into not three but seven parts."[30]

Then the National Council asked "seven members who would be willing to work without any reward other than the joy of service."[31] By June 1923, seven directors were at work directing their newly formed sections.

The Society continued to grow. The first East Coast chapter was the University of Vermont in 1924; the first West Coast chapters were Washington State in 1923, the University of Oregon in 1924, and the University of California–Berkeley in 1925.

Several topics were discussed without formal action, such as whether chapters should be purely honorary organizations or raise money so they could provide service to their schools. Assessing alumnae, having a national pledge pin and an official seal, and using original chapter names were other topics.

By June 1923, the National Council had divided the Society into seven sections, to be led by section directors. Five of those pictured here in 1924 were the first: (lower, left to right) Lillian Stupp (Washington in St. Louis, 1922), Irene Rems (Swarthmore, 1921), Lillie Cromwell (Kentucky, 1920), who replaced Agnes McLeaster (Indiana, 1922), and (upper) Luella Galliver (Michigan, 1923), Alline Smith (Missouri, 1922), and Eveline Broderick, who replaced Hazel Moren (both Minnesota, 1922). Hazel held the first section meeting in the fall of 1923 for her Section V, Minnesota, Wisconsin, and Lawrence.

While the national organization continued to strengthen, local chapters were continuing their own traditions and activities. Purdue sponsored the Gingham Gallop. Ohio State helped the YWCA raise money to send the dean of women to China for a conference.[32] Included in Denison's essential traditions were to "sponsor the Senior Women's All Night Party in the spring, have fresh strawberries and pineapple at the initiation breakfast, sit in chapel together in the front row, feed Granville [the town where Denison is located] schoolchildren who are needy, and chew gum at all meetings!"[33]

One of North Dakota's stated purposes was "to establish ourselves definitely against intoxicating liquors and cigarettes for both men and women." Pomona felt a somewhat similar sentiment, reporting that "we have a rather unusual problem in regard to smoking. It has in past years been regarded as taboo on the campus except in one or two places. Lately, however, it has been going on anywhere and Mortar Board felt something should be done to uphold the tradition. The consensus of opinion was that women should use discretion and good taste about where they smoke, and that they would not mind confining their smoking to the accepted places."[34]

According to "The Idea Shoppe" section of the *Quarterly*,

> the West Virginia Mortar Boards have gone in for politics, and quite successfully it would appear. The 1924–25 group sent a petition to the State Board of Control asking that an appropriation be made for a separate gymnasium for women. This petition was signed by every woman at the University. The new building is now under construction.[35]

At the fifth national convention at the University of Kentucky in November 1924, the delegates voted to have a magazine. Chapters were asked to suggest names for the publication, and eventually it was called the *Mortar Board Quarterly*. A contest to design the cover was won by Florence Dahme (Cornell, 1924); her prize was a two-year subscription.[36]

The first two issues were free to all members, and after that a year's subscription was $1. At the start it was difficult to find an editor, so National Secretary Gertrude Willis (University of Pennsylvania, 1923) volunteered for the job, and the first issue appeared in April 1925. Pam Chinnis wrote in her history that "for two years the magazine waxed and grew strong but the National Secretary found it was more than she could do to handle both jobs."[37] A full-time editor was finally appointed at the 1928 convention.

The first edition of the *Mortar Board Quarterly* in 1925 contained an essay titled "Ideals of Mortar Board" by Ethel Hampson Brewster, a charter member of Swarthmore's Pi Sigma Chi who was by then Swarthmore's dean of women. She emphasized that the Ideals of Mortar Board are "symbolized in the Greek words Pi Sigma Alpha that signify Loyalty, Scholarship, Leadership."[38] She traced the proud history of Mortar Board to that time by noting that by establishing the *Quarterly*, "another milestone has been passed and another standard raised":

> There rear proudly the first lone milestones where individual chapters sprang up in isolated spots, as one college after another, believing that it had found the open sesame to Idealism, initiated what was deemed to be unique in student life. There is the second milestone, where by accident, two of the side-lines collided. Together, then, these two traveled along a single track, in quest of others of their kind, until they set up a third milestone with the coalition of Cornell, Michigan, Ohio State, and Swarthmore. After this union the mileage rapidly increased as branch after branch tied up with the pioneers.

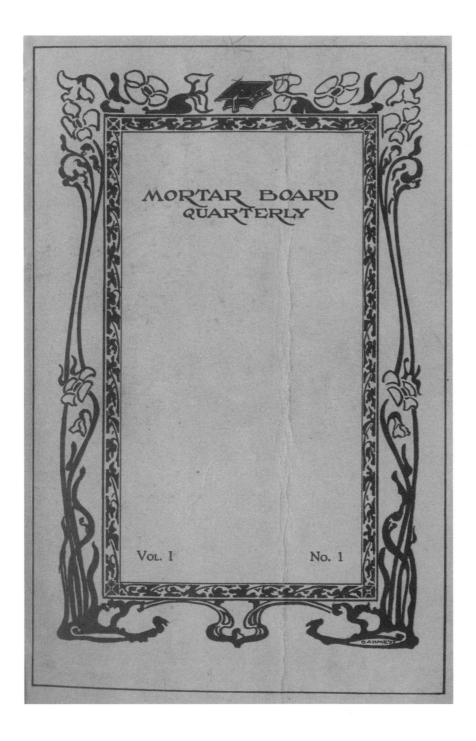

MORTAR BOARD
QUARTERLY

Vol. I   No. 1

A noticeable milestone was the institution of the Biennial Convention which give vitality and unity to the National Organization. Now the *Quarterly* marks another mile and furnishes an organ which will inform and unite all lines.[39]

The early *Quarterlies* contained articles on current topics (e.g., an article about the League of Nations or an interview with Jane Addams of Chicago's famed Hull-House), chapter reports, expansion news and descriptions of new chapter installations, biographies and photos of National Council members and section directors, national and convention news, and alumnae notes. There were also poems written by collegiate members and homey suggestions: "A careful dressmaker will not cut into a fine dress without a pattern. Neither should a Mortar Board chapter enter into its one year of national and local responsibility without careful planning."[40] A Balfour jewelry advertisement on page 97 of volume 1, issue 2, reminded Mortar Board members that "the President [Calvin Coolidge] and First Lady of the Land possess 'Balfour Badges.'"[41]

A custom among college students of the era was to sing at all types of occasions. Mortar Board members sang as a group and capitalized on this custom on their campuses. For instance, Wyoming held an impressive all-campus sing. Illinois's fall serenade was "accomplished by the cap-and-gowned girls with their cheery, haunting melodies."[42] Idaho's women enjoyed the "great privilege" of going on the Mortar Board serenade, because women students were otherwise forbidden to serenade on campus. The minutes of the 1924 national convention relayed that chapters' "suitable songs" will be collected by the

The original cover design for the *Quarterly* was used consistently from 1925 until the second issue of volume 5 in March 1929. The design is reused in the border of the charter of the MBAA, which was professionally engrossed in 2012, eighty-seven years later.

Song Committee. Members co-opted familiar tunes of the day such as "Shine On, Harvest Moon," "You're a Grand Old Flag," and even "Three Blind Mice," modifying the lyrics to suit Mortar Board. These lyrics are to the 1917 tune "Smiles":

> There are Mortar Boards from Cincinnati,
> Walla Walla and Laramie,
> Mortar Boards from sunny California,
> Pennsylvania, Utah, Tennessee.
>
> You will find the bonds of gold and silver
> Are the same wherever you may go,
> And each girl who wears our golden emblem
> Is a friend that you'd like to know.[43]

The melodies of the two musical numbers used in the Mortar Board initiation service, "Thy Ideals" and the "Mortar Board Ode," have been attributed to a songbook published in 1893. Revisions of these tunes were found in a 1933 Mortar Board songbook.

Other Mortar Board traditions were established during this time. Elizabeth Furry introduced the poem "The Torch" at the tapping ceremony of Torchbearer at Florida State University when her group was founded in 1925. The poem was adopted as part of the national ritual at the 1932 national convention and has been used at initiation and other occasions ever since.[44]

The official colors of the Society were chosen by the delegates to the tenth national convention in 1935, when they amended the constitution to read "The colors of the fraternity shall be silver and gold, signifying opportunity and achievement."

Many important decisions were made at the national conventions during the last half of the decade. Thirty-five chapters responded to

The Torch

by ELIZABETH FURRY

The God of the Great Endeavor gave me a torch to bear,
I lifted it high above me in the dark and murky air—
And straightway, with loud hosannas, the crowd acclaimed its light
And followed me, as I carried my torch through the starless night;
Till mad with the people's praises, and drunken with vanity,
I forgot 'twas the torch that drew them, and fancied they followed me.
But slowly my arm grew weary upholding the shining load,
And my tired feet went stumbling over the hilly road,
And I fell, with the torch beneath me. In a moment the flame was out!
Then, lo! from the throng a stripling sprang forth with a mighty shout,
Caught up the torch as it smoldered and lifted it high again,
Till, fanned by the winds of heaven, it fired the souls of men!
And as I lay in the darkness the feet of the trampling crowd
Passed over and far beyond me, its paeans proclaimed aloud—
While I learned, in the deepening shadows, this glorious verity—
" 'Tis the torch the people follow, whoever the bearer be."

Florida State member Elizabeth Furry is given credit for "The Torch" in this October 1932 issue of the *Quarterly*. The anonymously authored poem was actually published in a much earlier anthology.

RAILROAD FARES TO CONVENTION

The rates quoted below are based upon 1927 Summer Tourists Tickets and are, therefore, only approximately correct. However, I have had the assurance that if any changes are made in rates, they will not amount to over one or two dollars.

Merced, California, is situated between Los Angeles and San Francisco, and round trip tickets should be purchased to either place with a stop-over at Merced, Calif.

From——	To Los Angeles or San Francisco	Lower berth (round trip)
Champaign, Ill.	$ 90.00	$47.26
Chicago, Ill.	90.30	47.26
Columbus, Ohio	104.00	54.00
Detroit, Mich.	101.70	54.00
Kansas City, Mo.	75.60	39.76
Indianapolis, Ind.	95.70	51.00
Lexington, Ky.	101.35	55.00
Lincoln, Neb.	75.60	39.76
New York City	138.32	65.76
Philadelphia, Pa.	133.14	63.00
Pittsburgh, Pa.	113.01	56.26
Pueblo, Colo.	67.20	25.00
St. Louis, Mo.	85.60	45.00
Washington, D. C.	130.45	63.00
Wagoner, Okla.	83.50	

In addition to the above fare, it will cost $10.50 to go from Merced to Camp Curry by Motor stages the shortest route. The circle tours are considerably more.

KATHLEEN L. HAMMOND

---

the roll call at the 1926 national convention. The National Council was enlarged to eight members to allow for an expansion director and an editor plus two active members of "undergraduate" chapters. Section directors were included in the conventions and reported to the body. A recommendation to the convention revealed one of the decisions related to financial concerns encountered by the early Society. It was decided "that all money sent to the Mortar Board Treasury be by money order or certified check due to the large number of bad checks received by the Treasurer." Kathleen Lucy Hammond (Washington University in St. Louis, 1916) was elected National President. Her advice for electing new members was to "avoid harsh discussions of girls . . . not in the form of a popularity contest but to make Mortar Board more democratic."[45]

One of the most important decisions proposed at the 1926 convention was to adopt a national project, and "personnel work" (later known as vocational guidance) was chosen. According to one of many articles and features in the *Quarterly*,

> During their senior year, most girls are asked either once or many times by friends and members of the family, "What are you going to do next year" and nine times out of ten they answer with a rather worried, "I don't know." Personnel work, then, can aid the individual to determine what she wants her

---

Thirty-five chapters answered the roll call at the 1928 convention held in August at Camp Curry, Yosemite National Park, near Merced, California. National President Kathleen Hammond alerted delegates to the price of train fares in the March *Quarterly* so chapters could budget accordingly. **Source:** *Mortar Board Quarterly* 4, no. 1 (March 1928): 7.

work to be and by assisting her in finding a position in the line of work upon which she has decided.[46]

The article suggested ways that Mortar Board chapters could help senior women with their plans, such as securing campus speakers in different occupations and inviting large companies to interview women on campus. The author, Section Director and Personnel Chairman Mary Elizabeth (Mary Liz) Hanger Ramier (University of Illinois, 1922), who later became Mortar Board's attorney, advised that "Mortar Board is not to concern itself with all the detail work necessary to the execution of this project. Foster the idea—in a word be a leader."[47]

Helping Mortar Board members themselves find a "vocation" was emphasized throughout the rest of the 1920s and also through the 1930s. According to First Vice President Irene Rems's (Swarthmore, 1921) annual report in 1928, alumnae in four cities summarized the opportunities for college women in business and professions in Detroit, Philadelphia, Minneapolis, and Baltimore. As a result, "200 letters were sent to representative and recommended business firms in an attempt to find a number of available positions for graduating seniors."[48]

"Jobs for the Job Seekers," written by Mary Liz Ramier and appearing in the May 1929 *Quarterly*, listed contacts for some of these newfound positions. The *Quarterly*, which during this period was edited by Mary Margaret Kern (Purdue, 1926), contained interviews with and features about Mortar Board alumnae in a wide variety of occupations: ready-to-wear advertising manager Katherine L. McWhinnie (University of Nebraska, 1926), community drama director Irene Tedrow Brooks (Carnegie Mellon University, 1928), newspaper cooking school lecturer Margaret Jordan McIntosh (Florida State University,[49] 1931), dietitian Alice Mary Connolly Bustamante (University of Minnesota, 1924), and lawyer (later deputy attorney general of Pennsylvania) Ruth Forsht (University of Pittsburgh, 1924).

The photo of Mary Liz Ramier (Illinois, 1922) implies "shrinking violet," but she was anything but. She headed the Personnel Project for two years and was a section director. Elected secretary of the National Council at the 1928 convention, she had just passed the Indiana bar exam and was practicing law in Indianapolis. She became Mortar Board's legal consultant and, later in life, a benefactor of the MBNF. **Source:** *Mortar Board Quarterly* 4, no. 4 (November 1928): 7.

Before she and her mother became well known for the Myers-Briggs Personality Type Indicator, Isabel Briggs Myers (Swarthmore, 1918) aspired to write and "have a house full of babies." Writing about her dual aspirations, she teased that "by August 1928, I had achieved Peter, two and a quarter, and Ann, eight months old, [pictured with Isabel] but my writing had amounted to very little." Her award-winning mystery novel was in its seventh printing by the early 1930s.

In many issues, exposure to many different career tracks was provided by thorough coverage of several alumnae. In May 1930's issue Isabel Briggs Myers (Mortar Board's second treasurer), who had authored *Murder Yet to Come*, a detective novel that won a $7,500 Stokes-McClure prize, was featured in a section titled "Thumb-nail Sketch of Journalism," along with Ruth Elaine Wilson (Iowa State University, 1925), who was fiction and feature editor of *People's Popular Monthly*; Sunday features editor Mary Bennett (Lawrence University,[50] 1924) of the *New York World;* and Mary Meek Atkeson, the founder of Laurel Society, now Laurel chapter, at the University of West Virginia, author of plays, magazine articles, and a children's book, *The Shining Hours.*

A recommended reading list was published in the "Vocational Bookshelf" section of each *Quarterly.* Examples of book titles were *Store Management* and *The Social Worker: In Child Care and Protection* (both cost $2.50) and a study, *Earnings of Women in Business and the Professions* ($1.50). A review of the 1927 book *Occupations for Women* quoted the author's philosophy:

> Women are now beginning to realize that they cannot hope to obtain an equal footing with men in every profession, but they are gradually finding the fields for which they are best fitted, and in which they can make the greatest contribution.[51]

A vocational survey of 1928 Mortar Board graduates found that while 25 of the 165 respondents listed their occupation as housewife, most listed their fields of teaching and social service. (Teaching salaries began at $975 a year.) Some respondents were in graduate school seeking advanced degrees in medicine, music, social service, the liberal arts, and law.[52] When the stock market crashed in 1929 and the Great Depression took hold, the Society's national project of providing vocational information and placement became even more urgent.

The early growth of Mortar Board was summarized by the fourth National President, Eleanor Stabler Clarke (Swarthmore, 1917), at the completion of her term in 1926:

> Mortar Board has completed a period in her life; the first years were naturally pioneer years; they have seen the chapter roll grow from four to thirty-five chapters, the section plan worked out, a strong financial standing established, the debut of the magazine, the purchase of charters and hand books, the acceptance of an improved constitution and a new ritual. With the details of the organization fairly well established, the future looks bright for the development of interesting projects. Personnel work, section director improvement, scholarship requirement standardization, the financial stabilizing of the magazine; these and others will be the concerns of the new Council—so interesting that the problems of the past Council will seem dull by comparison.[53]

By the end of the 1920s, Mortar Board had expanded to forty-five chapters divided into ten sections that reached from coast to coast. This decade was called the Roaring Twenties, and Mortar Board roared with it.

Mortar Board in the 1930s

Mortar Boards in the 1930s were "singing 'Over the Rainbow,' reading *Gone with the Wind*, and sighing as Edward VIII abdicated his throne for the woman he loved. Mortar Boards also knew President Franklin D. Roosevelt's New Deal when it was new, Adolf Hitler when he was merely chancellor of Germany, and the end of the Spanish Civil War."[54] Fiorello LaGuardia was the mayor of New York. Country life was greatly improved by the Rural Electrification Administration.

Eleanor Stabler Clarke was the elected National President in 1923. She had been in the charter class at Swarthmore. She married soon after graduation and moved with her spouse to thirty acres called Crumwald Farm, which adjoined Swarthmore's campus. A Quaker, Eleanor ran the American Friends Service Committee, which provided clothing to children of coal miners and administered a $400,000 grant from the American Relief Administration to feed undernourished children of miners in six states. She traveled to Philadelphia three days a week, her car piled high, to deliver donated clothing. Her sister Cornelia was also a Swarthmore Mortar Board, initiated in 1920.
Source: *Mortar Board Quarterly* 14, no. 3 (May 1938): 191.

Walt Disney's *Snow White and the Seven Dwarfs* opened as the first feature-length cartoon, and the Jazz Age of the twenties became the Swing Era.

When the delegates to the eighth national convention met at the University of Wisconsin in 1930, Mortar Board expansion was an important topic, so new policies and procedures were discussed. It was decided that the rate of expansion should be "fairly conservative until the present chapters are strengthened." One of the issues debated was the use of a point system on campuses "to eliminate the same people holding all the major offices, thereby affording greater opportunities for a larger number of students to experience leadership roles." When the *Quarterly* asked whether Mortar Board should sponsor the point system of regulating activities, the chapters that responded supported the practice enthusiastically.[55]

It was at this meeting that alumnae clubs' names were changed to denote the cities in which they were located. This was done for consistency, since some were still named after the colleges or universities whose alumnae had originally formed them. National dues for alumnae clubs were set at fifty cents a year.

Mortar Board members continued to sing. Birmingham-Southern College sponsored "twilight musicales," and Michigan State members held their tapping at the May Morning Sing. The Miami University delegate to the 1930 convention moved that "the Council appoint a Song Committee to which each chapter send a song to be mimeographed by the committee and sent to all chapters."[56] The songbook that had been put together in 1924 is not mentioned.

Although the national treasurer's report in March 1930 indicated a bank balance of $156.32, the report also showed a disbursement of over $5,000 from investments. Mortar Board chapters were still facing the problem of raising money for programs and projects. According to the National President Katherine (Kay) Wills Coleman's (Nebraska,

Katherine Kuhlman was president of her chapter in 1923 at Michigan. In 1930 after serving for two years as section director, she was elected to the National Council as expansion director. She served for eighteen years, longer than anyone else. Thirty-eight chapters were installed during her tenure.

1921) annual report in 1933, the most successful means for raising money ranged from selling food, favors, programs, and senior collars to renting caps and gowns and holding benefit bridge parties, fashion shows, and dances.[57] Mum sales were blooming all over the country. Knox College sold cakes after chapel. Mortar Board teas were on the rise, and there seemed to be a tea held for every imaginable occasion. (The alumnae club section of the *Quarterly* was called "Around the Tea Tables.") The only mention of coffee was when the University of Denver's chapter served coffee and cake "to newspapermen in the press box at the half between football games."[58] The 1933 University of Kansas reaction to the need for operating funds was "our traditions are such that we cannot raise money." Tradition evidently changed, since two years later the chapter found it necessary to do so. (That year's National President's report indicated that eight chapters were not permitted to raise money because of their institutions' policy.)[59]

Some of the more interesting chapter projects of the time included the sale of secondhand gym suits at Swarthmore and sponsorship of wearing cotton dresses at the University of Texas. Whitman College's chapter began maintaining "a Kotex shop in the dormitory where the boxes are sold at any time, day or night."[60]

Many chapters sponsored "firesides" and invited speakers from the faculty to share their interests. Cleaning up campus politics was the cry across the country from Oregon State to Maryland. The National Council told chapters to "keep their skirts clean" in this regard. Whitman's most popular accomplishment of 1935 was placing the *New Yorker* in the Prentiss Hall Library, located in the girls' dormitory.

Proper etiquette commanded a great deal of attention. Michigan State's chapter sponsored a series of etiquette lectures, DePauw published an etiquette book, and Kansas composed and printed a *What's What* pamphlet on etiquette to be distributed to new women on campus. Pomona published a book of campus etiquette titled *Sagehints* that was requested by colleges from all over the country. *Your Best Foot Forward: Social Usage for Young Moderns* by Dorothy C. Stratton (Purdue, 1936) and Helen B. Schleman (Northwestern, 1923) was on the shelves of libraries everywhere.[61] As etiquette awareness continued, the authors revised their book in the mid-1950s, and it remained wildly popular.

Marriage was a hot topic that was discussed formally in conferences and bride school seminars and informally at chapter meetings. Arizona reported that "all but a few of our alumnae have taken up the time-honored career of matrimony." A Maryland chapter historian, writing about the prominent alumnae of her chapter, said that "most of our alumnae get married, a noble accomplishment in itself, but one which hardly leads to prominence, so I have left that section of the history out."[62] Michigan State's chapter was the impetus for establishing a "course in marriage relationships." The members inquired of other Mortar Board chapters about the nature of and reaction to courses such as this on their campuses and sent a questionnaire to junior and senior women on their own campus, receiving more than two hundred responses. All but two of these expressed a desire to take the course if offered "properly." They were surprised at how many men students expressed an interest.

Writing in the January 1935 *Quarterly*, Margaret Charters (Ohio State, 1929), then in graduate school, described the quandary of many women who got a college education based on the assumption that they would become financially independent contributors to society. How do they reconcile this, she asked, with the societal expectation that they marry?

> Count on the one hand the married women you know who have jobs; count on the other the married women you know who have lost their jobs or who have insecure and petty positions because their husbands work. If your tabulation is comparable with mine, it will appear that the chances of holding a good position after you are married are limited.[63]

Miss Charters gives in to the pressure of the times, unequivocally relenting that "we all decide in favor of marriage." She urges readers that the way to fill the debt to society is to become a community servant who looks "forward . . . to a life of unpaid professionalism."[64]

Bridal fairs and wedding planning were often sponsored by Mortar Board chapters. The *Quarterly* ran lists of marriages for many years, often with a request that brides notify the editor of their name change and new addresses so they could continue to receive the magazine. The wedding of the first Beloit Chapter President, Christine Croneis Sayres (center), features all the chapter members as the bridesmaids; they are seated on the Senior Bench, for which the chapter is named, in front of the campus chapel. Left to right: Audrey Liddle, Dorothy Seidenstricker Brandeau, Veronica Bunk, Christine, Marilyn Omundson Davis, Anne Knoll, Shirley Rurik. The bride's father was the president of Beloit College, her mother was made an honorary member at the 1951 installation, and her sister was initiated as a member of the second class.

The same issue of the *Quarterly* dealt with the topic of marriage differently, signaling the increasing difficulty in securing a position after marriage, in an excerpt of a study conducted by Alzada Comstock, professor of economics at Mount Holyoke, describing "the latest model in college women":

The college girl of today spends less time discussing life and its problems than her sister of the class of 1913 or 1917. Then each girl had a great socio-personal problem to settle: Marriage, or—a career! Many were the gas jets that burned far, far into the night as the alternatives were discussed. The career usually won, at least in theory. . . . But in the 1930's, the after-college-what-problem has returned. Marriage is still regarded as the natural and desirable vocation. But the question is, how is it going to be financed? There are many long years through which young people must wait for even a one-car garage. There are loans to be paid and younger children to help educate. So, without either orations or heart-burnings, the college graduate has gone job-hunting. Of course there are few jobs to be found and those that exist are poorly paid. But she has gone out cheerfully. If a girl who graduated in 1933 finds a job, she is almost sure to be more modest than the college girl of five years ago, less sure that the world is waiting open-armed for her on account of her superior education and intelligence.[65]

During the Great Depression, many chapters' minutes reflected the dreary economic situation by describing projects such as gathering and distributing clothing to needy college students, donating food, and supporting scholarships. The effects of the Depression also had a serious effect on the Mortar Board members who graduated during this difficult period. The grim unemployment problem of graduates was addressed in the content of the *Quarterly*. The editor asked Edmund Bullis, the executive officer of the National Committee for Mental Hygiene, to respond to a Michigan member's request to address "the first year of unemployment." Mr. Bullis wrote:

As long as our colleges and universities tacitly imply that their students are being prepared for privileged places that await them, I feel that the goals of these graduates are being set too high. The sudden deflation of these young people after graduation upon finding they are unwanted in the jobs for which they spent years of preparation is a most serious mental health matter. . . . Most college graduates who are finding jobs today have influence, unusual luck, or real ingenuity. Not a few instances can be cited in which students have used their ingenuity to render some service to make life easier, more interesting, or more effective for people in their communities who still had money.[66]

The article advised graduates to volunteer for services that are "fascinating and stimulating," such as helping with scouting and church leadership activities, working with literacy classes, organizing discussion groups and amateur dramatics, volunteering in day clinics for working mothers, organizing choral societies, and participating in hospital social work and political activities. Mr. Bullis suggested that "the valuable contacts and experience gained from [volunteering] are second only to the important fact that an occupation of any kind displaces withering idleness with activity that keeps both physical and mental faculties in preparedness."[67]

As though to emphasize the continuing connections that Mortar Board could build, the *Quarterly* continued with a long-running series, "Mortar Boards Are Proud Of," that showcased the careers of members such as Dempsey Creary (Florida State University, 1931); Girl Scout directors in North Carolina, Tennessee, and California; Julia N. McCorkle (University of Southern California, 1913), popular lecturer and journalist who had been the second editor in chief of University of Southern California's the *Daily Trojan* in 1913; Lois Seyster Montross (Illinois, 1918), novelist and poet; and Leona Baumgartner (University of Kansas, 1922), Yale Medical School researcher and immunologist.

Many memorable Mortar Board traditions began during the 1930s. The *Quarterly* published a few in the March 1935 issue.[68] Carnegie was in charge of a tutoring bureau that was a campus institution. Kansas sponsored interesting and popular Freshman Forums. At Wyoming the chapter sponsored Torchlight Laurels where "women students carried torches up the five walks leading to Main Hall and there sang beloved campus songs." Showing their pride, Purdue Mortar Boards wore gold flannel jackets with black mortarboards embroidered on them. They sponsored programs on vocational guidance, "since there was no such course given for the women here we thought this would be a real service to the campus,"[69] and also tutored younger students and gave $50 each year to the Office of the Dean of Women to help women "who need financial aid in small ways."[70] Knox sponsored an annual tour-the-campus party for senior high school girls and gave a Mother's Day tea. Ohio Wesleyan conducted an annual vocational guidance conference. DePauw gave awards of silver bracelets to the highest-ranking sophomore women. Montana State aided a number of university women through its loan fund. Cincinnati sponsored a faculty play, and North Dakota sponsored an annual Parents' Day.

Tapping and initiation ceremonies were rich with tradition, and this was where the greatest number of elements of the local society's customs were expressed. Arizona tapped at sunrise on the lawn between the two women's dormitories and then held a breakfast for the new members on the lawn of the university president's house. Northwestern "began with a stroll over the beautiful campus beside Lake Michigan, with frequent pauses before objects of traditional interest. After the initiation, the old and new chapters breakfasted together and then went to church in a group." Missouri held a sunrise initiation beneath the famous columns in the center of the campus. Carnegie's initiation took place at "Sky-High," a cabin high in the hills beyond Pittsburgh. Initiation at Knox was held early on the morning of Mother's Day in the garden of Whiting Hall. Washington University inducted its new members in the garden of the chancellor's home at twilight.[71] Jean Evans (Ohio State, 1933) described her chapter's tapping and initiation rituals for the *Quarterly:*

> Away in the distance of a spring night come the sounds of high, clear voices singing Mortar Board's song; and presently out of the darkness weaves a procession of caps and gowns, lighted by tapers. Slowly they make their way to your door and singing wait for you to appear to receive the symbol of your recognition, the mortarboard. The procession moves into the darkness and their song is lost. On initiation day Alumni gather to pay respect to the junior women whom Mortar Board has chosen. The old and new members make an impressive picture, in the pattern they form on the Long Walk, old in tradition while the [tower] chimes play the deep strains of the song that is Mortar Board's.[72]

Jeanne Smith (DePauw University, 1934) submitted her poem "It's Mortar Board Time" for publication in the May 1935 *Quarterly* as a way to describe the import of her chapter's tapping traditions. The poem speaks well to the feelings that members developed for the thrill of selecting new members and the honor bestowed:

T'was the night before capping
When out on the lawn
The Mortar Board members
Broke into song
With "Come out tonight, when everything's still.
See the moon come creeping o'er the hill."
And other songs too of annual fame
They sang with a thrill
At each pledge's acclaim.
But the pledges, you see, were still unaware
Of the gold-silver tassels which they were to share.
That joy was postponed till the following day
When at the breakfast, the first of May,
The people sat eager, too busy to eat,
Trying to see from the edge of their seat
Just what girls, at the surprise of a tap
Would emerge from the throng
With a big, broad, black cap.
Some call it a cap, others a board,
But regardless of that, it isn't the word,
It's the glorious symbol of service ideal
That makes the illusion of worth become real.
Then, after some weeks, our tassels are torn
The silver is tarnished; the gold it is worn.
Then finally, one day we dress all in white
Initiation is held by the dim candle light.
The service is simple, but a glorious find
To challenge the soul, the heart, and the mind![73]

The delegates to the 1933 convention recommended that Mortar Board publish a songbook. The collection that had been assembled in 1924 was enlarged, and several songs were revised. The following was included in the vice president's report for the year:

> Following the request of the convention, the music committee had the two national songs rewritten, published, and mailed to the chapters this year. Pomona chapter was responsible for the revision of The Ode and Ohio State University chapter submitted a new edition of Thy Ideals. Charles Bruning of Chicago printed 500 copies of each song with the words. One copy of each was mailed to each chapter president and each national and sectional officer. The total cost of rewriting, publishing and mailing songs was $10.[74]

The Mortar Board national project of vocational assistance for graduates took on new meaning as the Great Depression deepened. The "Vocational Bookshelf" continued in the *Quarterly,* even though the editor proclaimed that "hunting for magazine articles on women's vocations is somewhat like looking for pearls in oysters."[75] Interviews with Mortar Board alumnae in various occupations also continued in the magazine. In the May 1936 issue, Pulitzer Prize winner Marjorie Kinnan Rawlings (University of Wisconsin, 1918) was featured along with other notable alumnae. Another section noted the biographies of hundreds of Mortar Board alumnae listed in *American Women: The Official Who's Who among the Women of the Nation.*

The role of historian had not evolved as clearly as some other positions. The National Council appointed Evelyn Calhoun Miller (University of Texas, 1932) historian in 1936. Informally for some time, Hazel Moren Richards (University of Minnesota–Twin Cities, 1922) had been looking after some of these duties along with the additional job of editing the *Quarterly* (her first issue was May 1934). She described her responsibilities as keeping records of all official business

Wisconsin Mortar Board member Marjorie Kinnan Rawlings won the Pulitzer Prize for her novel *The Yearling* in 1939 and autographed "Pulitzer editions" around the country. Her book *Cross Creek Cookery* was reviewed in the *Quarterly* in March 1944.
Source: *Mortar Board Quarterly* 16, no. 4 (October 1940): 284.

I have files on all the chapters from the four founders, Cornell, Ohio State, Michigan and Swarthmore down to our newest chapter and on my shelves are all the bound *Quarterlies.* For this we built a fireproof house. Then in my workroom are many steel cabinets filled with yellowing petitions from prospective chapters, old pictures, and equally old cuts. Quite a collection for a person totally lacking in the hoarding instinct.[76]

It is because dedicated alumnae such as Hazel Richards took great pains to collect Mortar Board's early history, with *Quarterly* editor Pam Chinnis continuing her legacy, that this hundred-year history can be written. In Mortar Board's fiftieth anniversary year in 1968, The Ohio State University Archives became the repository for all the Society's historical papers. The National Office, established two years later, became responsible for monitoring and overseeing the contents of the national historical record.

Chapter visits (or inspections as they were called then) by members of the National Council and section directors were considered important for the new Society. Information sheets for section director visits in the 1930s listed how these were to be conducted. One sheet in 1935 stated that "inspection trips are paid by National (railroad fare, Pullman, and three dollars a day expenses). A tentative expense account should be sent to the National Treasurer before the trip and detailed one afterwards." The sheet also gave instructions for conducting a two-day visit, including an inspection of the chapter's black book.[77] The visitor was given suggestions for avoiding friction: "Refrain from engaging in controversies, refrain from making statements not backed up by Council, and do not break any of the school's regulations such as keeping hours and smoking on campus."[78] News of these chapter visits was shared in the *Quarterly.*

and personnel since the founding of the Society, including constitutions, bylaws, minutes of conventions and National Council meetings, correspondence, bound issues of the *Quarterly,* and other important documents. She told the delegates to the 1951 national conference that although she might be a "glorified file clerk," she considered her job very important:

Hazel Moren Richards edited the *Quarterly* from 1933 to 1945; she became the national historian in 1964 and had a special fireproof room built in her house for Mortar Board files. Initiated in 1922 at Minnesota, Hazel served our Society, regardless of formal position title, until her death in 1993.

Chapter service projects in the late 1930s continued to be described in annual reports and in the *Quarterly*. Many chapters recognized the need to improve or create common spaces for women students' comfort. Washington University furnished a recreation room in the women's dormitory, Ohio State provided a much-needed recreation room in the Women's Building, Agnes Scott outfitted sections of the student activity building on campus, Vermont furnished the library in the new women's building, and Westhampton provided the Mortar Board room in the "magnificent new Union building." Carnegie maintained a clubroom for all women's organizations.

Other chapter service was more programmatic. Leadership conferences were sponsored by Louisiana State and Iowa State. In keeping with the placement focus of the Society, Purdue brought a woman personnel director for business placement to campus, and William and Mary received a letter of appreciation from the college administration for improving the morale of women students.

Mortar Board became a member of the Association of College Honor Societies (ACHS) in 1937 with the distinction of being the only all-women's group as a member. National President Kay Coleman became a prominent leader on the ACHS Executive Board from the late 1930s and served well into the 1950s. At the meeting of the National Association of Deans of Women (NADW) in 1936, she gave a "most stimulating address" on honoraries.[79] She told the women deans that "seeing as I do the tremendous desire of so many colleges and universities to have a chapter of Mortar Board, I find it hard to realize that there is often a great deal of opposition to honoraries." She then traced the history and background of honoraries from Phi Beta Kappa in 1776 and expressed amazement at the number of honorary and professional groups (177) listed in a directory at the time:

The purposes of honoraries as stated in most constitutions are very similar ... recognition of scholarship, research, educational interest on one hand, and recognition of the ability and achievement of the individual on the other! ... What then do we stand for and what can we do? We are a company of persons educated after a fashion, and pledged to the good life dominated not by demagoguery, blind partisanship, fanaticism, excessive zeal for vague movements, but by reason and seasoned knowledge.[80]

"Membership [in an honorary] is no end in itself," Mrs. Coleman stated. "It must stand for more than a satisfied ideal; it must be a promise of growth."

In 1938, the National Council's interest in the need to incorporate was renewed when an advertisement for Block's Department Store appeared in the May 31 issue of the *Indianapolis Star:*

> Mortar Board honors may come and go but even those who aren't in the direct limelight can share the fun of receiving hosiery in clever little black Mortar Board cap boxes with bright yellow tassels. Mortar Board Gift Box, 15 cents.

A picture of the box, the hose, and the figure of a girl accompanied the words. A replica of the Mortar Board pin was reproduced. Mary Liz Ramier, as the Society's attorney, sent a letter to the department store asking that the ad be discontinued, as it "destroyed the dignity of the organization and the significance of its membership when you commercialize the name."[81] In a note to new National President Coral Vanstrum Stevens (Pomona College, 1930)[82] with a copy of her letter, Mrs. Ramier wrote that "I could not make the letter too strong because after all they have about as much right to the name as we have, inasmuch we are not incorporated."[83]

The Block's ad prompted the decision to incorporate later that year with an official document stating that "a meeting of members to form a corporation under the name Mortar Board, Inc. was held pursuant to a written waiver of notice signed by all the subscribers to the membership list."[84] Incorporation papers were filed on June 29, 1938, under the Indiana General Not for Profit Corporation Act of 1935 under the name Mortar Board, Inc., for $2.20.[85]

As a result of incorporating, Mortar Board applied for nonprofit status with the U.S. Internal Revenue Service. A March 1939 letter from the Treasury Department, Office of the Commissioner of Internal Revenue, stated that "based on the facts presented, it is held that you are entitled to exemption under the provisions of Section 101(8) of the Revenue Act of 1938, and returns will not be required for 1939 and subsequent years so long as there is no change in your organization, your purpose or your method of operation."[86]

In April of that year, the National Council explored the possibility of trademarking the Mortar Board pin but discovered in correspondence with Balfour's attorney that "since Mortar Board does not appear on the pin, the design is not registerable as a trade mark." He indicated that the Greek letters Pi, Sigma, and Alpha could be registered, however, under "Class 28, Jewelry and Precious Metal Ware." Learning that the application would cost $50.50, the National Council decided that it was "too costly for the amount of protection it would give us."[87] The logo was later trademarked.

The status of women continued to be a developing topic through the 1930s, and many important professional women offered their perspectives on women's role in society in the *Quarterly*. Marjorie Nicolson (Michigan, 1914) in 1938 wrote "a frank discussion of the present status of the college-trained woman" in an article titled "The World You Will Enter":

> If it is true that during the last decade the tide has been turning against women in the professions, how shall we explain it to those young women who follow us if we, who have had every opportunity of accomplishment, do not pass on to them the torch of opportunity.[88]

She continued, stating that many women with advanced degrees who wish to teach in colleges could not be placed. One reason, among many, was that "women scholars are in colleges which, with the best will in the world cannot offer the equipment, libraries or laboratories as the great universities."[89] She urged universities to encourage young women to train at the graduate level, give more scholarships and fellowships to women, and hire them as faculty.

In another *Quarterly* article the next year, Lillian Moller Gilbreth[90] (Purdue, 1941), the first true industrial psychologist, authored the article "Frontiers for Women: A Discussion of the Status of Women Today." In considering women's frontiers in the professional, business, and industrial world, she asked if women were holding their own:

> In the professions the answer seems to be "Yes," although women are no longer a novelty in the field and are increasing in number. . . . Are we advancing? [I]n the professions there do not seem to be many more women advancing to the top, but there certainly are many more advancing to higher levels than formerly.[91]

The growing unrest in Europe in the late 1930s was witnessed by two Mortar Board alumnae who described their experiences. Elizabeth Fackt (Washington in St. Louis, 1914) addressed the 1938 Mortar Board national convention with the speech "I Saw Europe in 1938." She had traveled all over Europe, Scandinavia, and Russia to study the area's problems. In 1936 she studied the status of the women's movement in Germany; it was there that she discovered what "drumming up a crowd" really means. She described "the brass bands with their busy drummers parading through the streets of Munich where Adolf Hitler was visiting and leading an informal parade to the huge exposition hall

where he was to speak, and then briskly turning around and going back through the streets, drawing another crowd of followers."[92]

Prof. Fackt also described the day she was in Vienna when the Anschluss (the occupation and annexation of Austria into Nazi Germany) occurred, and she "saw policemen in Austrian uniforms one day and the next in Nazi brown saying 'Heil Hitler.'" She urged the students to "use discrimination and to be watchful for bias" as they read different accounts of the war.[93]

Gene Caldwell (Southern Methodist University, 1930), a section director and president of the Dallas alumnae club, described her experiences in England while Prime Minister Neville Chamberlain was trying to negotiate with Hitler. She wrote to the national secretary that "there is a great deal of censure here of Chamberlain's procedure and of course England's stand in general."[94] She described how England was preparing for war, with trenches and sandbags everywhere. Everyone was issued a gas mask that was very uncomfortable and made her "look like a pig." When she tried to get passage home, hundreds of people were on waiting lists for each vessel. Eventually she was able to book passage on a Canadian ship.

The International Student Service (ISS) meanwhile was publicizing the problems of increasing numbers of student refugees from Europe and China. Over a third of China's colleges and universities were destroyed or used as barracks by hostile troops. After the Anschluss, the number of Austrian and German students seeking admission to American universities increased substantially. Two Florida Mortar Boards attended the ISS conference in Switzerland, where the problems of and solutions for helping student refugees were discussed. Mortar Board chapters were urged to aid in providing funds for scholarships, housing, and sustenance of these students.[95]

Throughout the late 1930s as these events took place, there were strong feelings on college campuses and across the nation against

The 1938 convention at Troutdale-in-the-Pines in Evergreen, Colorado, provided this photo, which put faces with names of national leaders. Front, left to right: Expansion Director Katherine Kuhlman, Treasurer Coral Vanstrum Stevens, Secretary and Director of Alumnae Clubs Rosalie Leslie, National President Katherine Wills Coleman, Vice President Margaret Sayres Fowler, Editor Hazel Moren Richards. Back: Historian Evelyn Calhoun Miller, Section VIII director Esther Bowman Roth, former Section V director Nell Murphy Vinson, Section II director Page Drinker, Section VI director Rosemary Lucas Ginn, Section I director Ellen Fernon, Section IV director Katherine Palmer Eichhorn, former Section III director Agnes Stump Dickey, Section VII director Evelyn Coffey Knickerbocker, Section IX director Lois Edbrooke Davis.

entering the conflict. The Ohio State chapter was a member of the campus Peace Mobilization Committee, whose purpose as described in the activities booklet was action and education on the campus toward a war-less world. Penn State members worked with the faculty and the town's Peace Action Committee in its drive for the sale of bonds. Student demonstrations against entering the war increased as the decade came to a close.

Seventy chapters answered the Mortar Board roll call by the end of the 1930s.

The War and Recovery Years: 1940–1959

When the 1940s began, Hitler had marched into Austria, partitioned Czechoslovakia, and invaded Poland. The Battle of Britain was under way. Artists and intellectuals fled Europe ahead of Hitler, many coming to the United States.

While the United States continued to declare neutrality, the first peacetime selective service law was passed, requiring men ages twenty-one to thirty-five to register with their local draft boards. The *Quarterly* printed the experiences of several Mortar Board members who wrote about their efforts to find passage home from France and Germany. Historian Pam Chinnis wrote that "Americans were dancing the Jitterbug and wearing nylon hose, Jackson Pollock was painting abstractly, and the Zoot Suit was the fashion of daring young men. While Bing Crosby sang of a 'White Christmas,' the Big Bands dominated popular music."[96] Radio was the lifeline for Americans, providing news, music, sports, children's programs, comedy and thriller series, and soap operas.

With war on the horizon, the twelfth national Mortar Board convention was held in June 1941 in Buck Hill Falls, Pennsylvania, for seventy-five delegates and fifty-one visitors, most of whom were additional participants from various chapters. A planning questionnaire had been mailed to chapters before the meeting asking what type of accommodations and program content the members preferred. The majority responded that they would rather meet at a resort, "because we are tired of campus life by the end of our 3rd year."[97] The unfolding world crisis was reflected in the topics that the delegates discussed, including "The Place of Mortar Board in Our Current Emergency," "How the Dean Hopes to Maintain Normalcy," and "Social Problems Presented by Defense Programs." The delegates changed the wording in the preamble to the Constitution, substituting "honor" for "honorary" and "society" for "fraternity."

A long-held dream of establishing a national fellowship became reality at the 1941 convention with the naming of the Katherine Wills Coleman Fellowship in honor of the retiring Kay Coleman, who had served the longest as National President—eleven years. The fellowship was designated for an "active member of a Mortar Board chapter who can qualify as a candidate for a Master's or Doctor's degree in an accepted university for graduate work. Candidates must be unmarried and not younger than 21 and not older than 25."[98] At the 1946 convention the age requirement was omitted, but the marriage clause read that the recipient had to "remain unmarried during her graduate study financed by the fellowship."[99] When one winner married before her program began, the grant was given to the alternate. The marriage clause was eliminated at the 1949 convention.

The delegates left the details of instituting the fellowship to the National Council, and a committee of three was appointed to develop the process, the criteria, the announcement, and the application forms. The committee narrowed down the applicants to ten and then formed a "Final Awards Committee" composed of deans of women from across the country to select the final winners. The original $1,000 allotted was divided into two $500 fellowships.

The convention in 1941 was at Buck Hill Falls, Pennsylvania.

The first recipients were master's candidates Barbara Wischan (Pennsylvania, 1941), with a graduate program in personnel work, and Elsie Gough (Pomona, 1941), in actuarial science. Miss Wischan wrote to the fellowship committee that her active Mortar Board experience helped her with a career direction. "Had it not been for the fellowship I could not have done graduate study.... Thank you for making it possible for me to learn, to grow, and really find my place in the world today."[100]

National President Stevens commented about the decision to create the fellowships:

Of the many fine things that were brought out on the Convention floor, there were two that I am sure will live long as outstanding projects in our history. The first was the establishment of the Katherine Wills Coleman National Fellowship which will be awarded to a Mortar Board for use in some field of graduate study. The second was the creation of a committee to gather and distribute information in the field of national defense.[101]

When the United States declared war after the Japanese attack on Pearl Harbor on December 7, 1941, American life changed dramatically. Congress extended the draft, and both men and women volunteered for military service. Women also volunteered for government service and stepped in to fill the void in industry, business, and education. During the war years, women's participation in the workforce increased from 27 percent to 37 percent. Mortar Board alumnae held many important government positions, served in the Red Cross at home and oversees, and joined the armed forces.

The *Quarterly* reported in 1940 that Eleanor Roosevelt had interviewed two Mortar Board alumnae in government positions for her radio show: Katherine F. Lenroot (Wisconsin, 1920), chief of the Children's Bureau of the U.S. Department of Labor (featured in a *Quarterly* piece in 1935), and Helen Fuller (The University of Alabama, 1932), an administrator with the National Youth Administration. Helen had been her chapter's delegate to the ninth national convention.[102]

Also featured was Lieutenant Commander Dorothy C. Stratton, a coauthor of *Your Best Foot Forward*, who had been ordered from her post in the WAVES to the Office of the Commandant of the Coast Guard in Washington, D.C., with instructions to organize the Coast Guard Women's Reserve. She developed the name SPARS, which stood for "Semper Paratus, Always Ready," and was appointed its first director. She served until 1946 and rose to the rank of captain.[103] (The U.S. Coast Guard cutter *Stratton* is named for her and was christened in July 2010 by First Lady Michelle Obama, with many Mortar Boards in the audience).

Campus life changed considerably as the number of men, both student and faculty, was reduced significantly. Women quickly filled faculty and administrative roles, and students adjusted to accelerated classes and wartime shortages. Mortar Board chapters became involved in many war-related activities and projects. Grinnell College knitted sweaters for soldiers and made care packages. Illinois joined with the United Service Organizations (USO) to invite servicemen to Sunday dinner, sponsored informal dances, and served as hostesses at the USO building. They also cosponsored a fund-raising Mardi Gras at the student union with the Red Cross to buy kits for soldiers going overseas. The University of Kansas and South Dakota State also were involved with Red Cross work. Ohio State members volunteered to help Draft Board 18 and were in charge of the students who helped with the gasoline-rationing program. West Virginia sold $648 worth of War Stamp corsages (replacing the traditional mums). DePauw

The first Katherine Wills Coleman fellowships were presented in 1942 to Barbara Wischan (left) of Penn and Elise Gough (right) of Pomona.

This photo, taken around November 1943, shows Lieutenant Commander Dorothy C. Stratton (right), director of the U.S. Coast Guard Women's Reserve (SPARS, an acronym she created), with the other three World War II service directors and First Lady Eleanor Roosevelt. Left to right: Captain Mildred H. McAfee, director of Women's Naval Reserve (WAVES); Colonel Oveta Culp Hobby, director, Women's Army Auxiliary Corps (WAACS); Mrs. Roosevelt; Lieutenant Colonel Ruth Cheney Streeter, director, Marine Corps Women's Reserve. Dr. Stratton left the deanship at Purdue, where she became a Mortar Board member in 1936, to join the war effort.

discontinued its scholarship dinner because of food rationing and instead published the names of those honored in the paper. National President Stevens reported that other chapters made blackout curtains and helped blood donors; some members acted as airplane spotters. One chapter was asked by its university to act as the committee to disseminate defense information for the entire campus.

Most Mortar Board chapters continued their traditional projects as well including programs to help freshmen, such as orientation and little sister–big sister pairings. In many cases Mortar Board served as the prime mover to secure chapters of Alpha Lambda Delta (an honor society for freshman women) on campuses. Middlebury members reported that "the project which we feel is the most worthwhile of all and which has become a tradition in Mortar Board, although no one else in college is aware of the fact, is our individual work with maladjusted freshmen." Kansas wrote that "Mortar Board is highly respected, and whether we like it or not, we are looked upon as examples of leadership to freshmen." The 1943 Illinois chapter reported that it "suffered through typhoid shots so they could work at the Union to raise money to publish *Illini Lore*, an information booklet for incoming freshmen."[104]

Correspondence between National Council members during the war years reflected the problems of communication with chapters and the lack of chapter visits because of travel restrictions. Only three new chapters were installed during the war years. Selection of new members was especially challenging. Academic acceleration and early graduation meant that previous rules for selection of new members had to be adjusted. The tradition of tapping only in the spring was no longer viable. At a special National Council meeting in June 1942, it was determined that "no two colleges were using exactly the same system of accelerating the work for the degree and consequently no two chapters had comparable problems." The National Council passed

a resolution that "since we are deep in a National Emergency the National President is empowered to decide exceptional cases."[105] Mrs. Stevens reported to the National Council that "25 chapters will need midyear elections this year." She gave her permission to all, but much to her consternation, some chapters held midyear elections and did not report doing so. She nevertheless ended her 1942 annual report on an upbeat note:

This year has brought us all a feeling of insecurity and many problems but we can remember again that there is hope and faith and that personal problems will some day seem small in comparison to the world benefits after this devastating war has ended. In our small way I hope we can continue to develop a finer type of college woman and in an infinitesimal way mold a better world to live in.[106]

An important event in Mortar Board's history during this era involved the selection of a "negro girl" by the 1942 Ohio State University chapter. Gwendolyn Brown was an outstanding student leader on the campus and president of the YWCA. Mrs. Stevens wrote to the National Council:

On the basis of a previous ruling made by Council in 1933 [The Ohio State chapter had tried to initiate a black woman in 1933, but the request had been denied.] in which they stated that election of any member other than the white race should be considered as an exceptional case, I asked Ohio State to reconsider their selection. They refused to do this and a great deal of pressure from Alumnae, Deans, and outsiders have been put on me and the rest of Council. Because our Constitution and By Laws did not bar a member of the negro race I did

Titled *The Presidential Family*, this May 1942 photo shows National President Coral Vanstrum Stevens with her husband Hamilton and son Stanley, "demonstrating war-time transportation." Coral, president for eight years, deserves a great deal of credit for the tough decision making around canceling the convention in 1944. She kept Mortar Board in forward motion in spite of the war. **Source:** *Mortar Board Quarterly* 18, no. 3 (May 1942): 180.

not believe we could definitely exclude the girl so with the approval of Council I told Ohio State that we would discuss the matter at our [summer] meeting and if the vote was in the affirmative the action would be retroactive.[107]

After Mortar Board's attorney Mary Liz Ramier advised the National Council that she did not believe they could "bar the girl," Mrs. Stevens wrote that "the matter may be decided for us automatically from the legal standpoint but the social side should be discussed such as attendance at Conventions."[108]

In spite of the National President's urging that the chapter "handle the entire matter with discretion" and wait until the National Council could meet, the chapter members wrote to Mortar Board chapters across the country asking for their support.[109] Vice president of the Ohio State chapter Jean E. Haas enclosed a list of Miss Brown's accomplishments in a letter to the National Council dated April 24, 1943:

[W]e are anticipating a reaction on the part of some alumnae members and perhaps even an advisor since our list included

Gwendolyn Brown (front, center) was president of the YWCA at Ohio State. Her selection by Mortar Board caused the National Council concern. Eventually she was initiated, and women of color formally were permitted to join.

the name of a colored girl. This girl has proven herself an outstanding leader in both the Negro and white campus communities and fully merits the distinction of membership in Mortar Board....

We [also] remember your telling us we should stand by our convictions and support at home what we are fighting for abroad. We sincerely hope you will give us all possible aid in our effort to take this one step towards true democracy.[110]

Frances Burgoon Bicknell, elected along with Miss Brown, recalled that "Gwen and I attended the YWCA Conference at Lake Geneva, Wisconsin, where most of the other Y-W presidents were also members of Mortar Board. They threatened to withdraw their chapters from National Mortar Board."[111] Many chapters and alumnae wrote to the National Council in support of Ohio State's decision. The chapter informed the National Council of their plans to hold "a modified initiation" for Miss Brown in private, and Chapter President Marjorie Sauner Pollack wrote a letter dated May 24, 1943:

You undoubtedly realize from our previous correspondence that we are desirous of holding closely to the ideals of Mortar Board. We feel that if these ideals are violated, the place of Mortar Board as a national senior women's leadership society on a democratic campus will be difficult to justify.[112]

Another member of the 1942 chapter, Marjorie Garvin Sayers, much later recalled how firm the chapter members were in their belief that Mortar Board should not discriminate. "We fought for our principles and were willing to drop out of the national organization and start our own society if national council did not let us initiate her."[113] At the first fall meeting of the 1943 chapter, the chapter president read a letter from the National Council stating that a membership policy had been established at the meeting and that "all candidates fulfilling the requirements of membership in Mortar Board as stated in the Constitution, Bylaws, and Standing Rules are eligible regardless of race, color or creed."[114]

Mortar Board celebrated its twenty-fifth anniversary in 1943, and National President Stevens noted the Society's accomplishments and challenges in a *Quarterly* article. She urged members to be "leaders of women":

Many of the changes [during Mortar Board's twenty-five years] have come about slowly and were not deliberately planned, and only in retrospect can we see the whole pattern.... As a member of Mortar Board, you are generally regarded as an intelligent leader on your campus. You, therefore, have a definite responsibility to fulfill, and you cannot complacently accept the past as perfect.[115]

After reviewing the Society's history to this date, Hazel Richards, *Quarterly* editor, asked,

What have Mortar Boards learned over these past 25 years? They have learned how to lead with enthusiasm and vision. They have learned tolerance and how to disagree agreeably. Though their thoughts turn often to world problems, they see the absurdity of condemning injustice in China and overlooking it at home. They have learned to be professional in their actions and attitudes toward volunteer work, and how to work hard and then relax. And perhaps best of all, is how they come to think of the philosophy that lies behind all service projects, all unselfish contributions.[116]

Editor Richards challenged them that "when victory comes," they should "work together for a peace that is not a timid, frightened one, but one vigorously and aggressively guarded."[117]

Although a national convention was scheduled for the summer of 1944, wartime conditions made it impossible. National President Stevens wrote to National Council members that "at the present time, I do not believe it would be practical, wise financially, or patriotic to consider holding this convention." (Most national collegiate organizations did not convene during these years, but in early 1945 the NADW held five regional meetings to which Mortar Board sent the usual representative.) A special meeting of the National Council and section directors was held in August 1944, however. After the usual business meeting, smaller groups discussed pertinent topics. These included "Is Mortar Board Democratic?" (many points were made in the affirmative), "Campus Traditions and Social Behavior" (some campuses were very concerned by what seemed to them a scrapping of all traditions and an abandoning of formerly accepted modes of social behavior), and "Campus Change in Education for Women" (that is, reeducation of war workers, reconciling vocational and liberal ideals, large numbers of single women and divorces in society after the war, and a curriculum designed to meet the real needs of women).

A summary of the meeting was sent to chapters for their black book, including the statement

> There can be no Mortar Board chapter which is not cognizant of major changes taking place on its campus. If you have been a coeducational university, you are now largely a woman's college. Are your social customs still based on the coeducational system? Wake up, and set up leisure time programs for women using the programs of the regular women's colleges as a guide. Sponsor activities where women can enjoy other

women. Don't fritter your time away at the bridge table just waiting for Johnny to come back.[118]

Chapters continued to serve the war effort in diverse ways. Washington State held monthly coffee hours for faculty and students where they discussed and formulated a postwar program. Georgia sponsored the exhibit of *British Women War Workers* and helped fill over eight hundred Christmas stockings for wounded servicemen in a nearby hospital. Another chapter was in charge of a Red Cross drive and collected more than $1,000. The University of Montana made a study of the curriculum related to women's education and "worked out recommendations." In her annual report, Mrs. Stevens relayed the concern of one of her contacts who worried about the leniency in the Dean of Women's Office at Arizona "in regard to the weekend hours that girls can leave campus with no permission necessary." The concern was that "with so many Army and Navy camps nearby there is a possibility of a serious problem arising."[119]

As the war progressed, the call for workers to make planes, ships, and ammunition was met often by young women in college. Others performed essential civilian jobs that released men for war work and filled the void in hospitals as dietitians and laboratory technicians. A former dean of women at the University of Nebraska, Helen Hosp, wrote in the *Quarterly* from her perspective as an associate in higher education for the AAUW:

> Since less than 30 percent of the 100,000 women who will graduate from colleges this June have majored in fields directly usable in the war effort, the present need for more individual and more positive direction in student advisement programs is evident. The student's appreciation of the direct relationship of the college course to the war program must be heightened. In

their choices of majors, students can be counseled to consider the fields in which shortages are serious and national needs great.[120]

She advised students who were already in unrelated majors to take courses to help them acquire the "usable skills and knowledge" that were needed.[121]

The content of the *Quarterly* throughout the war years reflected the focus on problems on the home front especially as they pertained to colleges and student involvement. Serious articles about the world situation were featured in every issue (examples included "Civilian Morale and the Colleges," "Marriage in Wartime," and "Mortar Board and the War Effort"). The magazine still contained chapter reports on war-related service, national Mortar Board news, and noted alumnae profiles. For instance, Barbara Erickson (University of Washington, 1941) described her job as a squadron commander in the Women's Auxiliary Ferrying Squadron (WAFS), ferrying aircraft from the factories to any point in the United States.[122]

The Oregon State College chapter reported a typical project that organized a Victory Center where classes in first aid, nutrition, home nursing, and other vital topics were held; scrap and salvage drives were conducted; and war bonds and stamps were sold. The chapter editor at Oregon State summed up the feeling of Mortar Boards everywhere:

Ours is a country at war and we feel we are on "borrowed time"—that we have been loaned this year by the men in the service and the men and women in defense industries for our education in order that we may be better able to improve the post-war world. But we also feel that it is our duty while we are in college to also do everything within our power to help our nation.[123]

The War finally ended in the summer of 1945. College enrollments began to increase due to the return of war workers and veterans. The U.S. Office of Education in 1944 estimated that nearly a million students' education had been delayed or interrupted by the war.[124] President Franklin D. Roosevelt signed the Servicemen's Readjustment Act, known as the GI Bill, in 1944. Money was given to veterans for college tuition, books, supplies, equipment, and living expenses. Veterans made up 49 percent of college enrollment by 1947. Three times as many college degrees were conferred in 1949 as in 1940.[125]

The effect of older, more serious students changed the campus environment and culture. Housing, classroom, and laboratory space was strained beyond capacity. Many classes were taught in temporary quarters. Many veterans with their spouses and children lived in cramped conditions. Overcrowded classrooms and housing prompted widespread improvement and expansion of college facilities and teaching staffs. New vocational courses developed skills that had previously been taught informally, including advanced training in education, agriculture, and business.[126]

One recurring issue in postwar society was civil rights and the discrimination against minorities. In spite of opposition, President Harry Truman enacted legislation that desegregated the military, federal employment, and government offices. The editor of the *Quarterly* asked Mortar Board chapters to describe the "influence of the civil rights controversy on student opinion and action" on their campuses. Southern California reported that a new article in its student government's constitution required "restrictive clauses to be removed" from all student organizations' bylaws. The University of New Mexico added an amendment to the student government's constitution that "would enable the student council to call a boycott by students of establishments which discriminate against persons because of race or color." The University of Missouri's chapter reported that although "no Negroes were allowed to enter the university up to this time," state legislators were taking action to change it. Ohio Wesleyan reported that a southern football game was canceled because one of its players, "a Negro," would not be permitted to play.[127] Other chapters reported participating in programs involving civil rights.

To raise money for scholarships for other students on campus, the Purdue chapter began in 1946 what may be the longest-running fundraising project, the Mortar Board Calendar. Originally a small date book with all events listed as well as phone numbers of all residence halls, co-op houses, and Greek housing units, the members printed enough to sell door-to-door in the residence halls for fifty cents. Several hundred dollars were raised, and the chapter contributed most of it to the Purdue general scholarship fund. The next class continued the calendar's publication, which grew from pocket-size to a sturdy five by eight inches into which class assignments and appointments could be added by the calendar's owner. Eventually the chapter started its own fund with the proceeds of the calendar, continuing to give money to support other students' graduate education. Thanks to calendar sales, by early in the 2010s the chapter had given more than $1 million to Purdue students for their advanced study or to other student organizations' programs.

The Coral Vanstrum Stevens Gift Membership was established at the 1949 convention to honor the retiring National President who had guided the Society during World War II and for four years afterward. The annual gift membership was intended for a candidate in each chapter who otherwise would be financially unable to accept membership.

The 1949 convention delegates also initiated a national project for the "education of the campus for world government."[128] This topic reflected the continuing concern with international events at the time. (The United Nations was founded in 1945, and the Marshall Plan was initiated in 1946; the Korean War started in 1950.) The delegates drafted a policy statement that chapters take responsibility "for bringing the facts of current international problems to the attention of the campus as a whole."[129]

Mortar Board in the 1950s

Historian Pam Chinnis described the 1950s as "a time of McCarthyism and bomb shelters [the Cold War was hot]; the Korean War and Geneva Conference; 'I Like Ike' and Sputnik; the Salk [polio] vaccine and 'Elvis the Pelvis' [Presley]; Davy Crockett and coonskin caps; hula hoops and 3-D movies; man making his first ascent of Mount Everest; and a Philadelphia Kelly [Grace] becoming a Monaco Princess."[130]

Most of the veterans had passed through college by the 1950s, and the number of women, nearly 50 percent of students during wartime, dropped to about a third. Postwar colleges remained male-oriented, and women students' needs were not a priority. One college president worried that "women were pursuing courses irrelevant to their futures as homemakers."[131] Along with economic prosperity, the postwar years were known for their conformity in many areas of society. There was wide acceptance of everything from uniform housing (in the new suburbia) to standards for dress. Students (later called part of the silent generation) were accused of lacking independent thought and having little interest in social and political affairs.

This was a time when Mortar Board turned inward and began questioning its purpose (although not for the first time). At the 1952 convention a general discussion topic was "Is Mortar Board a Service Group, Recognition Group or an Honor Society?" The delegates decided that it was all three and that "improper balance of the three goals of Mortar Board [scholarship, leadership and service] often results in too much busy-work and not enough constructive thinking."

WESTERN UNION

1201

JOSEPH L. EGAN
PRESIDENT

(25)=..

SYMBOLS

DL=Day Letter
NL=Night Letter
LC=Deferred Cable
NLT=Cable Night Letter
Ship Radiogram

The filing time shown in the date line on telegrams and day letters is STANDARD TIME at point of origin. Time of receipt is STANDARD TIME at point of destination

SA56 OA477 .

O=BLA214 PD=BERKELEY CALIF 16 358P=   1951 MAY 16 PM 8 15

MRS M STANLEY GINN=

43 WEST BOULEVARD SOUTH COLUMBIA MO=

BLACH, PFUND ELIGIBLE IN YOUR TERMINOLOGY DEAN SAYS WITH
CUSTOMARY GLINT SHE CONSIDERS ⬛⬛⬛ LEGITIMATE EXCEPTION
BASIS OUTSIDE WORK PRESIDENT IN JUNIOR YEAR BETTER THAN
UNIVERSITY AVERAGE RECORD=

RUTH N DONNELLY HOUSING SUPERVISOR=

National officers were very involved in every aspect of managing chapters, including approving grade exceptions such as this one from Berkeley in 1951. The recipient of this telegram, Rosemary Ginn, was National President.

One convention roundtable topic was "How May We Help Students Meet a Feeling of Insecurity?" The national historian captured the mood: "It was a time of stability—or apathy, take your pick! Were Mortar Board members apathetic? Oh, well—yes! West Virginia's project of 1954 was a study of the campus problem of apathy toward convocations." According to the Wittenberg chapter, "the fifties were a lethargic, nonactive time, marked by a return to self-perpetuation and social events on campus." A concern at Kansas was "the problem of having a satisfying experience if we had better understood our position on campus. We didn't really know if we were a 'being' or a 'doing' organization." (Incidentally, one of that chapter's budgeted expenditures was for Mortar Board paddles.) Ohio State registered "problems with lack of student participation in campus activities and with the new Speakers' Rule." Many chapters continued their traditional service projects. The University of Montana's fund-raising event in 1952 was selling "sanitary supplies to all women's living groups."[132] West Virginia members were required to present a book review once a month. Whitman sponsored a contest to see who could write the best lyrics for an old German tune.

A recurring theme during the 1950s was the role of postwar women. The image of the 1950s housewife was exemplified by *Leave It To Beaver* TV mother June Cleaver, who in her heels and pearls greeted her husband after his hard day's work. A speaker at the 1952 national Mortar Board convention discussed "Leadership in the Home" in which she defined the roles wives play including financial, recreation, nurse, disciplinarian, and example for social behavior such as moral and spiritual growth. A convention discussion was devoted to "Should I Attempt to Combine a Successful Vocation with a Career in Homemaking?" Grinnell's report in the *Quarterly* might summarize this point of view: "Mortar Board was increasingly involved in campus activities. They provided entertainment and sponsored events that helped prepare women for their future roles as housewives and mothers. Movies, teas, and bridal showers were among the most popular activities."[133]

A very conservative national expansion policy was pursued during the 1950s. The delegates to the 1955 national conference reaffirmed the policy. The type and size of the institution and the local group for membership was starting to be debated, however. In 1951, Expansion Director Rosemary Lucas Ginn (University of Missouri–Columbia, 1932), in a visit to Wayne State University, a commuter campus, stated that "if we intend to be in existence in another 50 years, we had better find out what our part can be on a campus of this nature and how we can really contribute to it."[134] As a Mortar Board historian recorded, "Many chapter histories are wrought with the trials and tribulations of local groups trying to become affiliated with Mortar Board." In some cases they waited twenty or thirty years between their initial petitions and the day of their installation. Arizona State, for example, began its petition process in 1940 and was finally installed twenty-three years later in 1963. Bowling Green State University's local group was founded in 1943 but did not become a Mortar Board chapter until 1969. Wittenberg's local group was founded in 1922; the first petition for Mortar Board affiliation was submitted in 1930, and the chapter was finally installed in 1967—thirty-seven years later.

Although the reasons for long periods of time before installation are myriad, the campuses never gave up and worked to correct defects. Iowa State petitioned Mortar Board in 1924, but "the group was not accepted that year because its membership was made up entirely of women enrolled in home economics. The following year, two women in industrial science were members and national membership as a Mortar Board chapter was granted."[135]

The Mortar Board National Foundation Fund (MBNF) was established by action of the 1955 convention at Michigan State in response

Pictured from the 1957 class of Torch at the University of Kansas are (front, left to right) Joy Yeo, Dianne Hayes, Shirley Stout, Ruth Ann Anderson, Jere Glover, Joanne Beal; (middle) Sandra Falwell, Shirley Ward, Kit Westgate, Betty Lou Douglas, Dona Seacat, Elaine Morrison; (back) Lucy Remple, Ann Johnson, Megan Lloyd, Sue Frederick, Kathy Ehlers, Mary Jo Pugh, Sheila Nation, Joyce Klemp. Absent are Marcia Goodwin, Judith Jones, Vera Stough.

to inquiries from members, alumnae, and friends who wanted to contribute to the general purposes of the organization. When tax exempt status was sought several years later, uses for the money (other than scholarships or fellowships) were still being discussed. Regulations of the Internal Revenue Service indicated that legally the MBNF could be set up as a "charitable, literary, scientific or educational" organization. Coral Stevens, now a past National President, wrote a letter to the National Council and its MBNF committee in 1957 in which she said

that it was difficult to solicit for money without indicating where it might go. She urged that they begin a "long delayed discussion" about the MBNF's mission:[136]

> What is the purpose of the Foundation? How can the money be put to use? I would like to see the money relieve the National Treasury of some of its commitments . . . to go for National Convention expenses so that we can hold them at least every 3 years; to go for more inspections, more visits; to subsidize sectional meetings. As a volunteer group maybe we need more officers to divide up the work. Probably the Foundation could underwrite the Fellowships and save that $500 for regular expenses.[137]

A solicitation letter from the trustees later reported that earnings from the MBNF's principal would be spent "for scholarships for members of Mortar Board for graduate study . . . and as our resources increase, other uses will be carefully considered."[138]

It was also during the 1955 convention that the delegates brought up the question of chapter uniforms. Wearing Mortar Board uniforms reached its peak in the 1940s, with blazers being the most popular. As pictures in the *Quarterly* attest, each chapter each year was unique in the type of uniform it chose (jackets, sweaters, jerkins, dresses, skirts, scarves). One of the first references to Mortar Board uniforms is found in the 1920s, when "Ohio State sold blazers with a Mortar Board felt emblem on the pocket for $3.50 and made a profit of 50 cents each." Purdue reported in 1938 that "all but two members wore Mortar Board jackets." The prize for longevity of uniforms must go to Montana State. In 1928 chapter members wore white jackets (or sweaters) with the Mortar Board emblem sewn onto a pocket; in 1937 it was white leather jackets; 1948 was the "basic black dress;"[139] in 1954 they wore

Iowa's 1941 class (clockwise): Miriam Katz (dark coat), Jane Nugent, Virginia Ivie, Edith Stuart, Barbara Kent, Mickey Kuever.

black skirts and blouses with white flannel jackets; and in 1970 it was black dresses with white blazer jackets (although the chapter bowed to the times by making Mortar Board T-shirts available). Perhaps to recognize individuality, in 1974 the chapter wore dresses of peach-colored material, and each member chose her own distinct pattern.

In spite of years of popularity of uniform attire, the delegates in 1955 passed a resolution that the "the high expenditure for uniforms be discouraged and that each chapter should indicate its feeling regarding the use of uniforms."[140]

It was during the 1958 national conference that a constitutional amendment was passed creating the position of second vice president. The demands of time and energy of national officers were increasing as new chapters were installed. Adding this position enlarged the number of National Council members to seven. As defined in the amendment, the duties of the national vice presidents were divided into two areas: "The first vice-president shall perform the duties of the president in her absence or disability and shall supervise the section directors. The second vice-president shall make arrangements for Council meetings and Conventions and shall establish and maintain a file on personnel."[141] Since the constitutional change was not official until the chapters voted for its approval, a person to fill the position was not voted upon immediately. National President Ruth Weimer (Illinois, 1947) appointed Helen Lang (University of Maryland, 1934), a former national treasurer, to fill the second vice presidency until the 1961 convention.

Delegates to the 1958 convention discussed the "three qualities of scholarship, leadership and service to get at the essence of our reason for being. Our ideals must be clarified in our own minds in order to permeate the campus with them."[142] A whisper campaign during orientation was suggested as a way to introduce these ideals to freshmen. Discussions of campus issues at the convention were the honor system,

emphasis on graduate work, the drinking problem, and methods of teaching.

The topic of women's education was still being discussed. The *Quarterly* printed an article titled "Coeds—Second Class Students" by Hazel Lewis (Carleton, 1953), dean of women at Carleton College, who described what a long way women had progressed by quoting Daniel Defoe (who wrote *The Life and Adventures of Robinson Crusoe* in 1719): "Want of an education makes a woman turbulent, glamorous, noisy, nasty, the devil. On the other hand, an educated woman is all softness and sweetness, full of peace, love, with grace and delight."[143] Dean Lewis relayed her observation of "an attitude among many women students that being considered 'a brain' was inconsistent with being popular." She suggested that there was a difference between women at a coed institution who were more reluctant to participate or contribute in the classroom and those at an all-women's institution. "Outside the classroom, the same attitude seems to be indicated by the fact that the president or chairman of important campus organization is typically a man, while the secretary of the organization is typically a girl." She urged Mortar Board women to "bring intellectual achievement the recognition and social approval it merits."

Although the era is remembered for its optimism and prosperity, it is also known for its conformity and conservatism. *Mortar Board Forum* editor Alicia Notestone (Ohio State, 2005),[144] summed up Mortar Board during this decade:

The Mortar Board members of the forward-thinking fifties, while constrained by direct social mores and higher education institutions completely dominated by men, made their marks as leaders and scholars and gradually dented the smooth stereotypical facades of "women's education" in the United States.[145]

The Tumultuous Decades: 1960 to 1979

The following assessment from Mortar Board's historical files points to the way the conservative and optimistic mood of the 1950s changed with the advent of the 1960s:

> While the Iron Curtain walled out the free world's heart, Dr. Barnard was transplanting those of individuals. In a short 66 years, mankind moved from its very first airplane flight to Armstrong's giant step on the moon. Rocking the "Round Table" were Beatlemania, Civil Rights, Vietnam, and Betty Friedan's *Feminine Mystique.* Woodstock and "Oh, Calcutta!" proclaimed the new knights in not-so-shining armor. The world bade farewell to John, Martin and Bobby; and "American Pie" saw Camelot die.[146]

The charismatic John F. Kennedy was elected president of the United States in 1960 but served just over a thousand days before he was assassinated, making Lyndon B. Johnson president. President Johnson promised a Great Society where poverty and discrimination would have no place. The civil rights movement impelled great changes, and violence sometimes erupted in spite of peaceful beginnings by Martin Luther King Jr. and others. The country's involvement in the Vietnam War escalated in 1964, causing massive troop buildups. The military draft was accelerated. College students organized antiwar protests, and some fled to Canada to escape the draft. Student activists grew more radical as opposition to the war increased. More than ever before, college campuses became centers for debate and protest. The counterculture changed as well, and some young people "dropped out," forming their own communities. Some positive events took place during this period, including the creation of the Peace Corps and the passing of the Civil Rights Act of 1964. Some of the ideas of the 1960s, once revolutionary, are commonplace influences in today's lifestyles, values, laws, education, and culture.

F. David Mathews, former president of The University of Alabama and secretary of housing, education, and welfare under President Gerald Ford, described the era in the *Forum:*

> The heady days of the 1950s in higher education were short lived. They gave way in the 1960s to an era of turbulence. The 1970s were essentially a defensive era . . . when higher education tried to regain its standing in the public esteem by accounting for its worth through statistics and forms.[147]

Seventy million postwar babies grew up during the 1960s, and 850,000 of them entered college as freshmen during the decade. Baby boomer Mortar Board members' experience reflected the times.

Women increasingly assumed leadership positions. Many Mortar Board members took a strong stand against the Vietnam War and actively participated in the protest movements. They turned also to intellectual and career pursuits. The structured formalities of the organization became less important as relevant activism came to the fore. Whether the chapters of this era were less fun loving or whether they just didn't find writing Mortar Board chapter histories relevant will be left to the judgment of future reviewers. In any event, the information on file is singularly lacking in, shall we say, silliness. Perhaps this is indicative of the comparative serious-mindedness of students of this period.[148]

The Presidential Commission on the Status of Women in 1963 confirmed the unequal treatment of women, giving birth to the National Organization for Women and recognition of the glass ceiling. (Later, the Civil Rights Act of 1964 was amended to include gender.) Betty Friedan's survey of Smith College women, described in her book *The Feminine Mystique,* disclosed "the problem that has no name" the widespread unhappiness of women in the 1950s and early 1960s.[149] Some Mortar Board chapters helped to sponsor a lecture by Ms. Friedan on their campuses. One Ohio State alumna vividly remembers the occasion: "I was struck by Betty Friedan's speech and proud of our chapter for helping to bring her to campus."[150] Wartime employment opportunities had proved to women that careers beyond housewife were also possible. The *Quarterly* had encouraged women's access to various professions for years, and many Mortar Board alumnae were involved in careers instead of or in addition to the role of homemaker. In one introduction to the *Quarterly*'s regular series "Vocational Opportunities for Women," the editor stressed that all women, Mortar Boards especially, should consider entering business and professional life.

Ruth Weimer was reelected National President at the eighteenth national conference in 1961 at the student union at Oklahoma State University (she was also vice president of the ACHS at the time). The delegates created a Certificate of Award in recognition "of those advisors who have exhibited outstanding service to Mortar Board chapters." The delegates also adopted a resolution that "the standard of scholarship be explored beyond the limits of grade point average in determining membership in Mortar Board" and reaffirmed that only the convention chapter delegates had voting privileges. There was a discussion of "apathy on campuses," and the delegates pondered the causes and solutions. One speculative cause was the "censorship of college thoughts and actions by political figureheads or administration." It was noted that "some students who were very active in high school failed to take the opportunity of extra-curricular programs in college." Cheating was also discussed as a problem on campuses.[151]

Ruth Weimer was elected National President in 1961 for a second three-year term. She had been a section director for ten years. She was then associate dean of women at Ohio State and would become the first dean of students there in 1968. This very popular leader's head shot appeared on the cover of the *Quarterly* three times over seven years.

The keynote speaker at the 1961 triennial convention, William Craig, Stanford University's associate dean of students, outlined five challenges: (1) rapidly changing times, (2) excellence to overcome complacency, (3) correcting deficiencies on the American scene and ignorance of social realities, (4) world affairs, and (5) making full use of your talent.

Dr. Craig urged Mortar Board members—and chapters, in turn—to establish their self-identity, be self-responsible, cultivate social sensitivity, clarify personal goals and plans, and identify their own philosophy.[152]

Chapter President Melanie Donovan (Beloit College, 1961), on a reactor panel after the keynote, commented that "womanpower is one of our nation's most valuable yet unexploited resources. Cooking, bottle washing, diaper changing and other domestic chores should not be woman's primary occupation. Men and women will have to accept the changed role of women."[153]

The Lawrence chapter decided to "deal with the issue of woman's potential and its place in our society." The chapter editor quoted the president of Radcliffe College: "The college girl of the classes of '62 [to '65] is a creature of high emotions, originality, beauty, freedom and wisdom. Notably missing are the 'apathetes' of the 50s—the 'silent generation.'"[154]

The theme of the section meeting hosted by Ohio State in November 1961 was "The Educated Woman: Companion or Competitor?" Chapter editor Mary Kay Evans reported that fifty members from seven chapters tackled questions such as "Do educated women want to be men's equals, do men want them to be, what are some of the difficulties women encounter in men's fields, and how do men influence women's educational and social plans?"[155]

Elizabeth Cless of Claremont College, internationally known pioneer in women's continuing education, reflected on women's education for the *Mortar Board Forum* at the end of the decade:

At no time in human history has there been such a conflict between what was, what is, and what will be. Women suddenly control their own biology. This fact alone has destroyed what was. Woman's search for a new definition of herself constitutes

the painful present. We can only guess that the future must hold feminine expectations and potential unlike anything with which we are familiar.[156]

Quarterly editor Pam Chinnis noted that with the advent of the 1960s, students' concerns were also with the outside world. The delegates to the 1961 convention moved that a study examine how Mortar Board could "include colleges and universities outside the national borders of the United States." In 1961 the Albion chapter editor, Nancy Hilts (1961), wrote of Mortar Board's participation in Eleanor Roosevelt's visit to campus. Mrs. Roosevelt, who had been the U.S. delegate to the United Nations General Assembly, stressed the urgency of understanding other people of the world and said that "this country of ours has met crisis after crisis . . . because we have the courage and belief in all things that established it. We have to work harder in the present crisis than we've ever had to work before."[157]

Westhampton sponsored "raft debates" during which professors of physical science, social science, and humanities debated their disciplines' importance to the world. After a vote, the debaters decided among themselves who should jump off the raft and who should remain, thus "existing alone to revitalize the world." Kansas heard a guest speaker who "told of his experience with a part in the testing of the new atomic bomb in New Mexico."[158] The University of South Dakota chapter initiated programs for the foreign students and sponsored a series of cultural foreign films. The University of California–Berkeley editor wrote about one of her chapter's programs in 1962:

Our main project, incorporating all the Mortar Board ideals[,] is extremely complex. As a result of ignorance and fear, many people in the State feel that the University is dominated by Communists, and therefore, that free expression should be curtailed, funds restricted, etc. . . . Mortar Board is eager to help change this situation and has been meeting with members of the administration for advice, information and help. We will be having "discussions" with prominent leaders and businessmen and arranging for speakers at the meetings of some local service organizations. We hope the solution to a very serious problem will lay the foundation for the future, taking the initiative in an area where the University needs help in educating the people.[159]

The University of California–Los Angeles (UCLA) hosted Mortar Board's section meeting in December 1962 with the keynote by Chancellor Franklin D. Murphy, who asserted that the Russian attitude toward using the brainpower of educated women was much better than that of the United States, which was shelving 50 percent of its badly needed brainpower by allowing women to "vanish into the seclusion of the home."[160]

Chapters continued to initiate programs that served the needs of their campuses. Kansas sponsored a program that was "designed especially for the liberal arts major who often feels useless and helpless as she approaches graduation." Grinnell held coffee hours with professors to discuss research projects and career possibilities. Agnes Scott College studied the academic life of campus, including evaluating campus attitudes toward the intellectual aspects of college and the college's independent study program. Some chapters became involved in the effort to extend or abolish women's curfews on campus (see chapter 1). Ohio State's chapter developed and distributed a pamphlet titled *Freshmen . . . You* Can *Be Someone.*

Many chapters viewed Mortar Board as a clearinghouse for the discussion of problems in areas of concern in which they were involved individually elsewhere on campus. Editor Chinnis opined that "some

chapters became introverted and self-development oriented."[161] Perhaps this was a reflection of the student culture at a time when judging other students' behavior was off limits.

Tradition was still valued. Local tapping and initiation ceremonies that had existed for so long on each campus had not lost their power to impress. As one historian commented, many chapter histories actually begin to "glow" when these events are described. "Indiana's initiation is always held outside early in the morning, usually 6:30 on a Sunday morning. There is something infinitely wonderful about an early spring morning—and, of course, we always order sunshine!" Wittenberg's chapter name was Arrow and Mask, and its initiation ceremony centered on the white robe, the arrow, and the mask. "The white robe symbolized purity. The arrow was given to each member, symbolizing keenness of insight. The mask was thrice symbolic: it represented the spirit of play, the mystery of life, and the screen which a woman of culture and refinement throws up between her sorrows and the world."[162] Many chapters passed physical items to new initiates as a part of their tapping ceremony. Early Florida State chapter members bore torches to present to newly chosen members (Torchbearer had been the name of the local group). Northern Arizona chose the less dangerous option of red roses.

The MBNF, which had been established in 1955, continued to pursue tax exempt status in hopes of increasing donations. Mortar Board attorney Mary Liz Ramier drew up an amendment to the trust agreement in 1961 "to show the Foundation's method of operation which is required by Form 1023—Exemption Application." To prove to the Internal Revenue Service that the MBNF was "operating," Attorney Ramier urged that at least one $100 scholarship be given at once ($400 had been collected for the MBNF up to this time). The MBNF was declared exempt from income tax by the U.S. Treasury Department's Internal Revenue Service on June 29, 1961, in a letter stating that the

MBNF had shown that it is "organized and operated exclusively for educational and literary purposes."[163] The first donors were listed in the *Quarterly*. These included a few members, several alumnae clubs, the University of Louisville chapter, and the national Chimes Honor Society.

As the MBNF mounted an effort to encourage donations for fellowships, Mortar Board, Inc.'s need for funds increased as the Society expanded. Sparse funds to hold national conventions changed annual meetings back to the former triennial pattern. This lack of resources for programming, scholarships, and conferences can be found throughout Mortar Board's history. The financial report for the fiscal year ending August 31, 1965, submitted by National Treasurer Joy Wade Moulton (California, Berkeley, 1949) shows that the largest expenditures had been for the *Quarterly* at $8,901 and pins at $6,875. Clerical center expenses were $3,633 (typewriter fees for section directors would be increased from $3 to $5), and National Council meetings and convention came in at just over $2,000.[164]

The report shows an excess of cash receipts ($45,623) over disbursements ($31,425) with $17,942 cash on hand, more than $14,000 better than the previous year.

The financial footing at the end of fiscal year 1965 is directly related to tireless efforts by the treasurer. Reading between the lines of her matter-of-fact report points to the effort it took to secure all 112 chapters' $35 convention fund fee (four months from the due date to get them all) and members' initiation fees of $7.50 each (a total of 2,110 members). She personally examined 117 chapter financial reports (including some alumni chapters, no doubt), prepared the national budget, submitted the report for audit, placed the pin orders, and worked to improve the accuracy of the membership role. On top of these expected duties for a volunteer treasurer of a national organization, Mrs. Moulton made a site visit to the State University of New York at Buffalo and was the installing officer for the 115th chapter of Mortar Board at Augustana College in Rock Island, Illinois.

In spite of the seemingly positive cash flow in 1965, Treasurer Moulton's report underscored the perils of a group whose revenue generation is based solely on the vagaries of membership and convention fees. After one year as treasurer, she consulted a financial advisor who recommended, among other measures, that reserves be placed in savings and loan associations, since they were "equally as good as bank savings accounts and in some cases give better rates for a year's period."[165] When she followed this advice and shifted some money to a savings and loan account, she was accused of "risky investments" by a former National Council member.[166]

Many chapters shared the frustration about the lack of funds to promote and initiate programs. National Treasurer Emily Large Fuhs (University of New Mexico, 1949) offered some advice in the *Quarterly* with the article "Mortar Board's Change Purse—A Guide to Money Raising."[167] In answering the question about why chapters need to earn money, she gave five reasons: (1) for operating expenses; (2) to support special scholarships given by the chapter; (3) to fund service projects; (4) to support other projects that advance scholarship, leadership, and service; and (5) for contributions to the MBNF. She suggested that chapters study the local campus situation and establish a goal, limit moneymaking to one major project that takes a minimum amount of time, avoid busywork, and not be bound by tradition.

Some of the common chapter moneymaking projects during this period were book exchanges, ushering, selling calendars, mum sales, silver or china displays, donut days, bridge parties, and on-campus clerical assistance. The keynote speaker at the 1964 conference at the University of Nebraska–Lincoln, Betty Cosby, director of the graduate program in student personnel at Syracuse University, remarked (rather dismissively) that "[selling chrysanthemums] is justified on

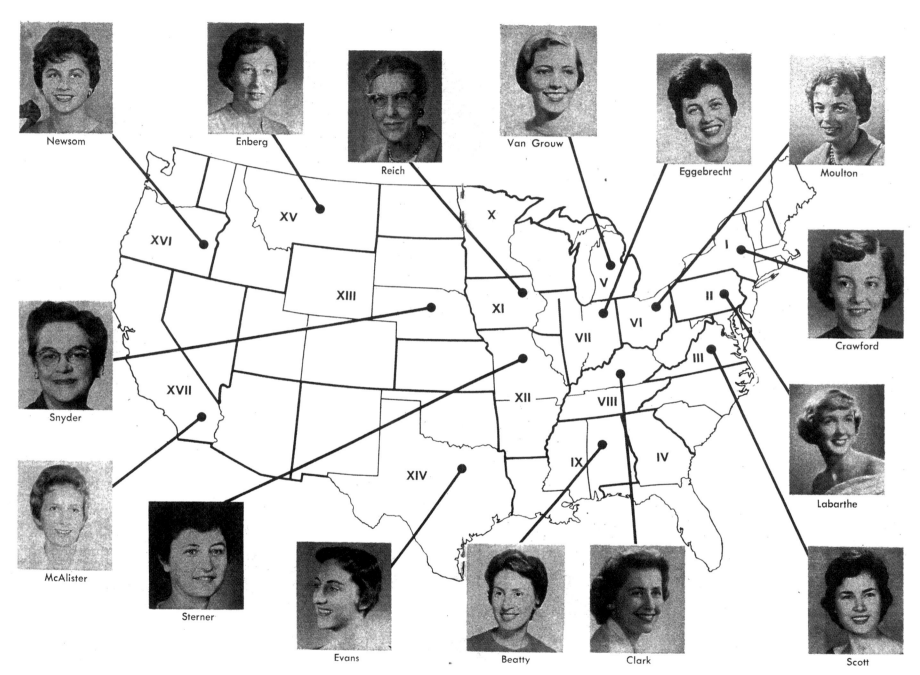

Section directors in the December 1963 *Quarterly*.

most campuses, I suppose, by the need to provide the chapter with an independent income for campus service projects and scholarship awards. I begin to wonder, rather, whether a unique group—such as Mortar Board—with its tremendous potential for *real* service can justify the expenditure of energy on projects of this kind when there is so much to be done."[168]

Editor Chinnis asked chapter editors in 1963 to comment on the most serious problem their chapters encountered during the year and how they had attempted to solve it. As expected, there were the usual problems that seem inherent with an organization such as Mortar Board—finding time for meetings, overactive members, and the over-organized campus. There were problems that "some chapters should not have," such as poor orientation or static programs resulting from a failure to evaluate campus needs and update chapter projects. A few chapters listed communication problems due to lack of campus awareness of what Mortar Board is and does or lack of communication within the chapter group itself. There were also problems over which the chapter had no control, such as dwindling numbers of members due to student teaching, studying abroad, or accelerated programs.[169] The editor was pleasantly surprised, however, at the small response to her request, since most chapters indicated that they had few problems.

Starting in the early 1930s, Mortar Board had developed a close relationship with the NADW (which changed its name three more times to reflect its members).[170] The National Council regularly sponsored a social gathering at the NADW conference, and a close relationship became a tradition. National President Ruth Weimer[171] praised the continued support of the deans who offered their time and resources to Mortar Board on their campus. They responded with glowing commentary in the *Quarterly* on the role of Mortar Board and its value to campus.

Christine Y. Conaway (Ohio State, 1922), dean of women at Ohio State, urged "Don't underestimate your power as members of Mortar Board. As a group and as individuals you have a responsibility to interpret the role of women on your campus."[172] Marna V. Brady (Cincinnati, 1924), the first dean of women at the University of Florida on whose watch Mortar Board was chartered there, reminded Mortar Boards that "each campus is unique, and each chapter should best serve its own university within the outlines of Mortar Board's ideals."[173] (Interestingly, during this time the position of dean of women was sometimes replaced with a dean of students or vice president, who was most often a man.)

The delegates to the 1964 national conference debated a proposal to add "character" to the three original membership criteria of scholarship, leadership, and service, and after lengthy and sometimes heated debate, it was rejected. Discussions about adding character as one of the three established criteria can be found from the earliest years of Mortar Board. "Pi, Sigma, and Alpha" were translated in "Article II, Object" in the 1920 Mortar Board Constitution as "Character, Scholarship and Service." Some of the early local groups listed "character" as a criterion for membership before becoming Mortar Board chapters. There was always a problem, however, with how to define the word. It is interesting that collegiate members in 1964 were still discussing character.

Hazel Moren Richards was appointed national historian at the 1964 conference and was authorized to prepare a written history of the Society in preparation for the fiftieth anniversary to take place in four years. A clerical center was established in 1964 to assist with the increasing burden of secretarial-type duties on the part of National Council members. The national secretary was authorized to spend a maximum of $5,000 to "purchase an electric typewriter, telephone, desk and chair, a worktable and supplies." After one year, the National Council decided that the clerical assistance office was not cost-effective, and it was closed. It would take another five years before a national office would be established.

Dean of Women Helen Snyder (serving pizza to Mortar Boards about 1965) was active in the NAWDC and was a popular dean and s spirited advisor at Nebraska. She was initiated at Lawrence in 1932 and was National President from 1967 to 1970.

A historic first took place in April 1965 when the Swarthmore College chapter gave notice of its intention to withdraw from the national organization. In their letter of resignation to National President Margaret Stafford (Kansas State University, 1946), chapter members indicated that "we have considered this decision carefully, and would like to assure you that it does not in any sense represent a disagreement with the goals and purposes of the national organization."[174]

The Swarthmore chapter had been on probation "due to its failure to accede to national policies" (failure to respond to correspondence or send reports). The National Council accepted the resignation reluctantly, especially because of Swarthmore's historic contribution as a founding member. The mechanics for resignation were not covered in the constitution or bylaws. The consensus of the National Council was that "it was not the desire of Mortar Board to force a group to remain." It was decided to list the chapter as "inactive" in case it ever decided to return to the national organization.[175] Almost fifteen years later, a procedure for disaffiliation was developed.

Mortar Board installed 5 new chapters in 1965, the most in one year since 1923. Included was the most distant, the University of Hawaii. The national roster showed a total of 166 chapters. In the late 1960s national Mortar Board experienced a "crisis" in expansion resulting in a policy change whereby the emphasis moved from the prestige of a given institution to the strength of the local chapter. Treasurer Joy Moulton wrote a position paper urging that when considering a petition for a charter, the National Council should look not just at the amount of service projects but also at how the group functions as campus leaders who generate ideas, promote scholarship, and identify and help solve the problems of their campus.[176] Prompting this discussion was the situation of a few newly installed chapters that were not fulfilling "their role as campus leader and innovator." Since the delegates to the 1967 convention voted unanimously to continue the

The most distant installation was of Hui Po'okela at the University of Hawaii on April 21, 1965, at the Kaimana Hotel overlooking Waikiki Beach. The charter members were (left to right) Patricia Awamura, Maria Hart, Jean Yorita, Elsi Ota, Kathleen Kau, Diana Kuwana, Linda Sakaue, Bette Yamaski, Patricia Young. Beneath their robes the members wore their "formal dress" uniform, a white cotton brocade sheath muumuu.

concept of Mortar Board as an "honor society" rather than a "recognition or honorary society," the need to clarify the purpose and expectations of Mortar Board to petitioning groups before accepting them as new chapters was emphasized.

As Mortar Board continued to expand, the need for a central office became more pressing. National officers were overburdened with the many responsibilities connected with their positions, particularly with the detailed correspondence, checking of reports, and coordination and proper functioning required of a large organization. Each National Council member estimated that she spent an average of ten hours a week on office and secretarial tasks alone.[177] A committee was appointed to investigate the feasibility of establishing an office. To prepare for discussing the topic at the next national conference, a questionnaire was sent to chapters for their input.

As a reflection of the times, the charge that honoraries were elitist organizations was renewed in the late 1960s and early 1970s. National President Jayne Wade Anderson (Nebraska–Lincoln, 1951) noted that actions of the delegates to the 1973 conference were "a concern for others in a social sense."

The buzz words were "elite" and "relevant"—delegates did not wish Mortar Board to be an elite organization in the snobbish sense, and they had a desire for all of our activities to speak to the times on each campus. This was accomplished by broadening the expansion policy.[178]

An ad hoc Justification Committee was appointed to examine how Mortar Board was "meeting the changing attitudes of college students and answer some of the charges that have been laid against selective organizations."[179] The report stated that

> we are in the midst of a dramatic reversal of the "join-a-club" trend that was so prevalent on college campuses ten short years ago. College students now question the relevance of joining any group that is not actively and openly rendering a service to either the college micro-society or the world as a whole.[180]

The report reiterated that Mortar Board is an honor society and that "mere recognition makes it meaningless in view of the high potential of its membership." The report outlines certain steps that Mortar Board should take to ensure its survival and stresses the responsibility of each retiring chapter to convey the Society's purpose and uniqueness to its new members so that continuity is maintained. In addition, the report refers to a convention resolution that "Mortar Board become a voice for non-violent efforts for equal rights for all people." Although one purpose of Mortar Board is to recognize outstanding collegiate women, it is also a "pool of the resources of talented young women" that provide a unique service to their institutions.

This pattern of questioning Mortar Board's objective or purpose emerges at many points throughout its history. The issues and concerns prevalent at a given time often prompted self-examination. The most pressing concerns in the early years were related to establishing a framework for operations (for instance, name, officers, finances, badge—even where to wear the pin!) and the very important task of expansion. Although the intent was to honor outstanding senior college women, the early members held an idealistic view of how the Society could serve local colleges and universities and immediate communities. The preamble to the earliest constitution describes the "object" of the Society:

> We, the undersigned, recognizing the advantages of a national union of Senior Honorary Societies for women, do hereby bind ourselves together to form a national fraternity whose purpose shall be to provide for the cooperation between these societies, to promote college loyalty, to advance the spirit of service and fellowship among university women, to maintain a high standard of scholarship and to recognize and encourage leadership, and to stimulate and develop a finer type of college woman.[181]

Editor Chinnis in 1962 reminded members that the primary reason a national union was formed was for "similar organizations on campuses throughout the country to cooperate with one another in pursuing their common ideals." An article in the first issue of the *Mortar Board Quarterly* in 1925 defined the Ideals of the society—scholarship, leadership, and service—and then suggested that

> after all, honor comes through service, does it not? The three ideals we cherish furnish quite ample opportunities for the enthusiasm and energies of senior girls, and due honor comes without thought or need of seeking other glories of a more shallow splendor.[182]

A 1973 initiation address at Ohio State by Naomi Meara (Ohio State, 1957), a psychology professor, was typical of this self-questioning. She asked, "Can an organization such as Mortar Board survive the de-personalization and frustration that have become a part of organizational life? . . . We will survive if we can find the strength in our womanhood and our collective ability to achieve and use this strength to bring cooperation and compassion, as well as individual excellence, to this already over-competitive world."[183]

Even Mortar Board alumnae clubs examined their purpose over the years. In the *Quarterly* Pam Chinnis asked,

> What do you think about the problem of having a purpose, as requested by (alumnae clubs in) Ithaca, Los Angeles and Manhattan? Has your Club discussed whether it should have a function other than purely social? If so, what is it doing thus to justify its existence? We shall be glad to hear the program that Los Angeles is working out. . . . What have you found to do to help your active chapter? The rest of us want to know the demands that it makes, and how you answer them.[184]

During the 1960s many important movements or events affected politics, education, economics, and social and cultural areas, but three stand out: international events, including the Cold War and the Vietnam War; the civil rights movement' and the women's movement. (Rachel Carson's 1962 book *Silent Spring* helped set the stage for the environmental movement, which would emerge later.) Many Mortar Board chapters' programs and activities reflect the influences of these events. In her 1970 three-year report, National President Helen Snyder (Lawrence, 1932), who was dean of women at the University of Nebraska–Lincoln, summarized the new directions she had seen on campuses in the late 1960s: "fewer parietal rules, more student participation, broader and more flexible curricular patterns, phasing out of traditional activities and the embracing of broader social concerns by students."[185]

The late 1960s were the harbinger of the "national identity crisis" of the 1970s, when death, violence, and corruption assaulted the senses and sensibilities.[186] (Kent State, the Munich Olympics, My Lai, and Watergate are examples.) President Richard Nixon's visit to China, the first unelected U.S. president (Gerald Ford with Nixon's resignation), the victory of Russian writer and dissident Aleksandr Solzhenitsyn, and a tension-producing shark called "Jaws" also were part of this period's history.[187] National Council member (and later National President) Catherine Nelson Evans (Texas Technological University, 1957) reflected what she saw as the state of the Society at this time:

> Mortar Board must be considered within two contexts: the outside world and the higher education world. Initially, Mortar Board operated only within the world of higher education; in the late 60s, it began to look outward.[188]

The 1970 triennial convention was held a little over a month after the killings at Kent State. The National Council briefly considered canceling the convention but decided that there were too many important issues to resolve. The mood of the convention is reflected in the words of National President Shauna Adix (University of Utah, 1952), who was a higher education professional: "Mortar Boards shall function in whatever ways they can on their respective campuses to help create the climate for communication in which people can talk, relate, explore, and dissent without having to kill each other in the process."[189] The delegates adopted this statement later as a conference resolution.

Many resolutions passed at this convention committed each Mortar Board chapter to involvement in local issues engendered by national concerns. Kay Thoreson (University of Washington, 1970) remembered that "it was a convention concerned with the driving concerns of the day: student dissent, the gap in communication between campuses and the surrounding communities, national polarization and the causes behind these problems—war, poverty, discrimination, pollution, despair. This was very much a 1970 convention."[190]

Barbara I. Wood Cook (University of Arkansas, 1950), a former National Council member and MBNF trustee, also recalled the mood of upheaval and change of the late 1960s when she spoke at the 1979 national conference:

> Many of the delegates [to the 1970 Mortar Board convention] had recently experienced the closing of their institutions that were wracked by disruptions caused by a very unpopular war and by the government's recent decision to send troops into Cambodia; and all were fresh with the memory of the tragic student deaths at Kent State and Jackson State. . . . It was a period in which erosion of faith and trust among segments of the academic community was intensified. The goals and purposes of individual institutions seemed unclear and unarticulated. The very survival of higher education seemed in question.[191]

The 1970 convention will be remembered for several significant decisions. One of the most important was the establishment of the National Office. The Committee on National Office–Finance had made a careful study of the costs and benefits of a central office, and The Ohio State University had offered free space in its new continuing education building, the Center for Tomorrow. (Mortar Board's historical files had earlier been placed into Ohio State's archives.)

When the doors to the National Office opened on September 1, 1970, a dream of many years was realized. The office's general functions were a central location of records, a clearinghouse for information, a coordinator of national affairs, and a facilitator for more efficient operation. The National Office's existence released volunteer officers for other duties such as planning and programming and eliminated excess reports and duplication of effort. To fund the office, each chapter paid $2 for each initiated member. The estimated cost was between $17,200 and $19,200, although a few years later the office would be moved from its free quarters on campus to an off-campus office building with monthly rent charges. A full-time executive secretary-treasurer was responsible for running the office and reporting to the National Council.[192] Donna Walls (Ohio State, 1968) was the first to fill the post.

Almost immediately after the office opened, there appeared a need for additional help because expansion was exploding (fifty-one chapters were added in the 1970s). Elaine Thomas Barnum (Ohio State, 1948) was hired part-time and became an indispensible part of the office. She served eighteen years. A gift from her estate in 2016 created a handsome endowment in the MBNF to support the Society.

Another important decision made by the 1970 delegates was to include student advisors to the National Council. Their role was to help "in making appropriate decisions on behalf of collegiate members by

Donna Walls
(Ohio State, 1968)
became the first executive
secretary-treasurer of
Mortar Board in 1970,
taking the burden of
secretarial tasks from the
volunteers on the
National Council.
She was highly regarded
for her thoroughness
and kindness.

"convention" to "conference," and changing the title "section director" to "section coordinator."

The 1970 delegates also changed the national mode of communicating with members. Due to the increasing cost of publishing the forty-four-year-old *Mortar Board Quarterly* and some criticism about the timeliness of its content, the delegation voted to replace it with a new tabloid format publication called the *Mortar Board Forum*. The first editor, Mary Dawn Bailey Liston (Utah, 1958), advised that recycled paper would be used, warning that although its appearance would "look dirtier, we may save a tree a year." She envisioned a "quasi-academic publication with a very free exchange of ideas." By the second year, she worried about lack of response to announcements, whether she editorialized too much, and how much time was spent rewriting.[194] She was very complimentary of the support provided by Executive Secretary-Treasurer Walls.

The most important issues that the delegates to the 1973 national conference would confront were outlined in the preconference copy of the April 1973 *Forum*. Chapters were asked "For what purposes shall Mortar Board exist and what goals should be pursued for the years 1973–1976?" Some questions raised for the delegates to ponder included "Do honor societies have a place on today's campuses? Has their function changed? What makes the composition of a Mortar Board chapter unique, and what is its potential for acting as a force on the campus?" Since it was not clear at the time how Title IX of the Education Amendments of 1972 would affect college honor societies, the delegates were asked to consider the issue of "who should Mortar Board members be and how should they be selected?" Another question was "Should Mortar Board membership include men?"[195]

After much debate, delegates to the 1973 national conference reaffirmed their belief in the Ideals and purpose of Mortar Board as

insuring that the changing needs and interests of those members are communicated in such matters as membership, expansion, programs, conventions, policies and other issues of concern and by reflecting the changing image of Mortar Board."[193] National President Adix appointed the first three student advisors "on the basis of expression of interest and recommendation," and they participated fully at the next National Council meeting. Other modifications made at the convention were adding "Inc." to the Mortar Board name wherever it appeared in the constitution, changing the title "national treasurer" to "director of finance," changing the name of the national meeting from

MORTAR BOARD FORUM

VOL. 1, NO. 1   FALL 1970

President's Letter

It is 3 a.m. That is not particularly significant except that I have found myself in times past often starting to write Mortar Board messages at that hour. It seems that is when, finally, for me, there is time to crystalize my thinking and get at the myriads of waiting tasks without a hundred interruptions. TIME is what this message is all about.

For three days last week, the National Council met to finalize and put into motion the action plans distilled over the summer from the decisions, directions, and dictates of the Convention in Lincoln. We had many of the same problems each chapter has as it begins its work: limited time in which to "get to know each other" and decide on ways to work and what the work meant to and for each of us. There were decisions to be made and tasks to be completed. Much of our work you will see — in this and subsequent issues of the Forum, in Black Book materials, in the reporting and operational system we hope to use to make your membership as satisfying and simple as possible. Some of the work is yet to come, as we all left with a lengthy "TO DO" list. This letter was on the top of mine.

Some impressions seem clear to me as I begin to reflect on where we are. Let me try to summarize to save space.

1) The call to action for Mortar Board is clear: We are committed to work as chapters to do something of value to humanity. The particular something is up to each chapter's discretion. This is most clearly enunciated in Barbara Cook's article regarding Convention Resolutions in this issue of the Forum. The important thing, I think, is that the Convention has proclaimed a sense of commitment for us all which, to my knowledge, has not been done before. As a Council, we see one of our roles as helping make that commitment visible to others. To that end, letters will be sent (No. 4 on the TO DO's) to President Nixon, HEW Secretary Richardson, the Commissioner of Education, the governors of your states, and the presidents and deans of students at your institutions, advising them of the Convention resolutions and inviting them to contact you regarding implementation. The letters should be out by the time this reaches you. A copy will be in the next Forum. That action says, I think, that it is imperative that you know, as a chapter, how you want to respond to the resolutions and how aggressive you want to be in finding ways to implement them. Hopefully, all Section Meetings will consider this, and the next Forum will detail specific ideas for implementation from any and all chapters and individuals who send their ideas to the National Office.

2) Even though the Constitution ratification is needed to make it official, we have already acted upon the Convention delegates' decision to establish a national office in space generously offered by The Ohio State University. All mailings will be sent from there, and all official correspondence should be sent there. We expect it will take time to make it totally functional, but we have a great gal as an Executive Secretary and expect to see the benefits in coordination within a matter of weeks.

(Continued on page 2)

The Survival of Higher Education

Every three years, collegiate members of Mortar Board meet to decide the direction of Mortar Board for the next triennium. The students at this time also elect a National Council which is charged with implementing the decisions made by the collegiates.

At the 1970 Convention, student delegates concerned themselves with many of the real issues facing higher education. Indeed, it is not overstating the case to say that the major focus of the resolutions discussed and debated in Lincoln was **the survival of higher education.** The resolutions call for clear thinking and commitment from not only the 136 Mortar Board chapters throughout the country, but from each individual member as well.

The Convention was convened in June of 1970, with the events following the decision to enter Cambodia fresh in each delegate's mind. Kent State and Jackson State stood as tragic reminders of the consequences of violence. Many of the delegates had recently experienced the closing of their institutions and the ensuing confusion and uncertainty of the future. The erosion of faith and trust among segments of the campus community was intensified, resulting in greater polarization between the academic and civic communities. The goals and purposes of higher education seemed to be unclear and unarticulated.

The survival of higher education is a critical challenge, and perhaps no collegiate organization ever before has stated a determination to constructively and non-violently play an important role in actively seeking methods and programs which will assist in the quality and continuation of our educational institutions. This is the urgent message, the challenge, and the important commitment made by the student delegates at the 1970 Mortar Board Convention.

The resolutions from that Convention are written here with some suggestions of interpretation and implementation. These resolutions give a clear direction for programming, for purpose, for action. Each individual chapter will know best what the problems are and what the needs are on a particular campus and will, therefore, have other ideas for interpretation and implementation. The order of the resolutions has been changed for continuity in ideas.

I.   BE IT RESOLVED THAT MORTAR BOARD ENDORSES THE STATEMENT OF MRS. SHAUNA ADIX AS A GOAL FOR THE COMING TRIENNIUM:
"Mortar Boards shall function in whatever ways they can on their respective campuses to help create a climate for communication in which people can talk, relate, explore, dissent, without having to kill each other in the process."

DISCUSSION: This powerful resolution relates directly to the crisis in higher education which we all face currently. This statement reflects forcefully the real purpose of Mortar Board as it has always existed. The creation of Mortar Board chapters allows for a functional group, well versed in a particular collegiate situation, to analyze, criticize, and to make suggestions for needed change so that the educational environment may continue to improve and remain flexible to the needs of the students and the community. No group is better able to accomplish this sort of critical analysis than Mortar Board.

Communication is also fundamental here — communication which includes understanding, bridging schisms, acting from facts and objective analysis. Too often, concerned students refuse to be involved, refuse to try to bring people and points of view closer together. If our concerned stu-

(Continued on page 2)

The first issue of the *Mortar Board Forum*.

MORTAR BOARD QUARTERLY

SPRING 1970

21st Triennial Convention

The last issue of the *Mortar Board Quarterly*.

a women's honor society by voting to remain open only to women. To emphasize this purpose, an addition was made to Article II of the constitution: "As a society of women, each chapter of Mortar Board, Inc. shall contribute to the self-awareness of its members and shall concern itself with the status of women in the college or university and community of which it is a part."[196] The delegates passed other related resolutions, especially about the treatment of women athletes:

> Whereas the inequities in the caliber of competition, funding, and facilities offered to men and women athletes on campuses underscores the traditional inequities in the treatment of men and women in general, be it resolved . . . that Mortar Board, Inc., encourage and promote adequate funding and upgraded facilities for women athletes, promote athletic scholarship aid to intercollegiate women athletes, and promote the status of women's athletics in general.

The 1973 delegates established the Mortar Board National Citation for persons "who have made outstanding contributions to the status of women nationally within the ideals of scholarship, leadership, and service." The first National Citation was awarded to Congresswoman Martha Griffiths of Michigan for her involvement in steering the Equal Rights Amendment toward passage in the U.S. House of Representatives. The delegates recommended that in the future the MBNF take over the responsibility for awarding the Katherine Wills Coleman Fellowships. All references to "girls" in the constitution and other documents were changed to "women," and "chairman" was changed to "chairperson." In 1971 the National Council had switched to referring to national leaders in minutes and reports by their own first and last names instead of their husband's first name. So, "Mrs. Vern Adix" in the 1970s directory was "Shauna Adix" in the 1971 directory. This shift happened in Mortar Board much earlier than many other all-women's societies (blessedly for historians trying to track down the first name of a member to place into a print publication such as this one!).

Most chapters during this period could be characterized by a need for "relevancy" and reluctance to continue so-called traditional projects. The name of the Baylor chapter's "Bride School" was changed in 1973 to "Choice Expressions," a symposium for opportunities for all women. Bradley sponsored a tea for faculty women where the changing role for women was discussed. Eastern Michigan sent questionnaires to Mortar Board alumnae for an independent study to see whether women students of higher academic achievement found more satisfaction with their lives than an average sample (they did). Perhaps the University of Miami summed up the burning question of the decade with the title of the chapter's panel program in 1974, "What's a Woman For?"

The Utah State chapter must have had at least one idea as to a woman's purpose, as the members instituted PHT Awards (Putting Hubby Through)![197] Wittenberg saw Mortar Board members as "working within the campus as a microcosm of society at large." The 1970s placed emphasis not only on the particular concerns of women but also, according to the historian, on "the rights and needs of all peoples." Chapter histories described programs "with and for racial and ethnic groups, the elderly, the incapacitated, the fighting men, and the needy. These bear witness to Mortar Board's concern with all the facets of human life."[198]

Even the sacred rituals of tapping and initiation faced some changes during the 1970s. Bowling Green reported that "the once-traditional secret early morning tapping had given way to a more open kind of ceremony which attempted to combine the element of surprise with the hectic, relatively unstructured schedules of today's coeds." The changing lifestyles of the 1970s could probably not be better documented than by the story that emanated from New England when one chapter, following its normal procedure of night-time tapping, found that one of their tappees was not alone in bed. Seems the debate is still going on as to who was more surprised: The tappee, the Mortar Board members, or the man![199]

The somewhat new leadership role for women that was assumed in the 1960s provided the groundwork for the militant women's movement of the early 1970s. Mortar Board chapters sponsored leadership workshops, career planning workshops, and lectures on how to cope as a woman in a man's world. At a time when the women's movement and the Equal Rights Amendment to the U.S. Constitution were headlining the national news, the ramifications of just how Title IX of the Educational Amendments of 1972 might affect Mortar Board as an all-women's society were unknown.

Title IX is a comprehensive federal law that prohibits discrimination on the basis of sex in any federally funded education program or activity. After its passage, the U.S. Department of Health, Education, and Welfare (HEW) began writing the regulations that would be used to implement the law, so for a great deal of time interpretations of Title IX continued to be speculative. Would sororities and fraternities, typically single-gender organizations, have to become coeducational? What about honor societies with long traditions of single-gender success? Correspondence between National Council members reflects the frustration and confusion about the ramifications for single-sex honor societies.

Not content to sit and wait, national leaders took action in several forms. National President Catherine Nelson Evans wrote letters to the president of every institution where there was a Mortar Board chapter indicating the Society's awareness of and concern about the potential ramifications of the legislation. She was surprised at the

Catherine Evans presided over the special national conference at which delegates voted to extend membership to men in October 1975. She corresponded with legislators; the Department of Health, Education and Welfare; lawyers; and ODK, which was facing the decision to admit women to its ranks.

large response from college and university presidents to her letter indicating their degree of support for Mortar Board. There were also letters of support from other organizations and members of Congress. In a letter to the National Council, Mrs. Evans wrote that "we truly have more friends than we give ourselves credit for."[200]

Continuing to seek clarification of Mortar Board's status, she also spent a great deal of time contacting people who were involved with the legislation. Representative Edith Green, who along with Representative Patsy Mink drafted the language for Title IX of the Education Amendments of 1972, replied to her letter about Mortar Board's status:

It was never my intention nor do I believe it was the Congressional intent, to include sororities and fraternities. The conferees [at a meeting of the Labor-HEW appropriations bill for 1975] are agreed that this is an absurd interpretation of the law and direct that none of the funds appropriated in this bill be used to enforce the provisions of Title IX with respect to such organizations. The conferees also are agreed that *none* of [the] funds in this bill are to be used to enforce the integration of physical education classes by sex.[201]

The regulations for enacting Title IX were finally made public in June 1974 and entered into the *Federal Register.* Information about Title IX was presented at regional meetings around the country throughout the summer, and members were urged to attend the meeting closest to them. Cheryl Lightfoot (Missouri–Columbia, 1973), student advisor to the National Council, attended the HEW hearing in St. Louis. There she asked if under the guidelines college honor societies could have separate but equal leadership societies.[202] She communicated the response to the National Council: all decisions would be on a "case by case" basis. National President Evans pointed out that this meant that Mortar Board might be violating Title IX at one institution but be in full compliance at another.

To illustrate the continuing frustration with conflicting information, an article in the *Chronicle of Higher Education* was circulated among national leaders. The article described how the Casey Amendment, attached to the Education Appropriations Act of 1975, might exempt Mortar Board:

> The House amendment . . . also would forbid the use of funds in a fiscal 1976 appropriation bill to force the sexual integration of such organizations as the Girl Scouts, Boy Scouts, Y.M.C.A., Y.W.C.A., and social, service, and honorary fraternities and sororities from the coverage of Title IX. The Casey amendment would extend that exemption to physical

education classes and honorary and service-oriented fraternities and sororities.[203]

This offered some hope, since a contact in Representative Casey's office indicated that indeed, this language would exempt Mortar Board. Another letter-writing campaign was mounted to support this amendment. Unfortunately, "honorary and service-oriented fraternities and sororities" were not exempt in the final regulations.

In June 1975 Mortar Board's attorney Huntington Carlisle submitted "official comments" to the HEW secretary "relative to Subpart D of Section 86.31 of the Proposed Regulations in implementation of Congressional Enactment of Title IX." He offered an amendment suggesting that the subpart was inconsistent with the congressional enactment itself and therefore was inappropriate and a nullity: "(d) Nothing contained in this Sub-part shall apply to admissions to programs and activities not operated wholly by such recipient, which are involved in actions by one sex, designed to create equality with the other sex, where inequality exists."[204] His comments were acknowledged as received by the chair of the Subcommittee on Postsecondary Education of the Committee on Education and Labor, who indicated that they would be part of the subcommittee's Title IX hearings.

As events progressed and it became increasingly clear that Mortar Board would not be exempt from Title IX, National President Evans asked for attorney Carlisle's opinion about the advisability of a lawsuit. He responded:

> It is our opinion and you are accordingly advised, that an attack upon the validity and enforceability of the regulations on the basis that they are beyond the intent of Congress presents a complex series of legal issues. The initiation of such an action

would be the beginning of a protracted and expensive effort under circumstances that leave the outcome in doubt.[205]

Although the National Council wanted to abide by the vote of the delegates to the 1973 conference to remain a women's honor society, the pressure from Title IX legislation and the expanding challenges to chapters from their institutions was inescapable. Mortar Board chapters in state institutions in Florida, Iowa, Washington, and other states were being challenged for discriminatory practices. The Florida system's chapters were told that they could not "participate in projects on behalf of the University."[206] The president of the Ohio State chapter received a letter typical of state universities stating that "we are a *probationally* registered [campus] organization. This means that if the final vote is to exclude men, the University could deny us the use of campus mail and unions."[207]

Finally a decision about the Society's future could no longer be delayed, so a special national conference was called to consider the appropriate response. It was the first special conference ever called, and prior to it the *Mortar Board Forum* provided the delegates with information about the regulations of Title IX and detailed background information about five possible alternatives as developed by the National Council and an attorney:

Alternative I: That Mortar Board, Inc. cease to exist as a national
    organization.
Alternative II: That Mortar Board, Inc. exist as a private honor
    society, separating itself from the institution and severing any
    formal affiliation or relationship with colleges and universities.
Alternative III: That membership criteria be altered in the
    Constitution and Bylaws to enable Mortar Board chapters to
    have male members.

Alternative IV: That Mortar Board, Inc. consider a merger with a
    traditionally male honor society or honorary group.
Alternative V: Court Action.[208]

Delegates from 167 chapters met for two days in October 1975 in Kansas City, Missouri. A speaker from the Higher Education Office of Civil Rights of HEW, the agency responsible for enforcing Title IX, told the delegates that although she did not find it a pleasant experience to bring bad news to "the membership of such a fine organization," their "tradition of female-only membership, may have to cease. Although it could be argued that some discrimination—such as that of Mortar Board—is not invidious, it is difficult, if not impossible to codify such distinctions."[209] Small groups carefully studied and discussed the ramifications of each alternative before the greater body convened. A motion to "explore the legal recourse against H.E.W. concerning Title IX and/or legislative exemption" lost. After much discussion and debate, Alternative III was approved as amended:

Resolved, That membership criteria be altered in the Constitution and Bylaws to remove references to the sex of the candidate as a criterion for membership and to strengthen the purpose of Mortar Board as stated in the Constitution.[210]

National President Evans remembers that as the paper ballots were distributed and voting on the resolution began, "You could literally feel it in the air—a little tension as the discussion wound down, but primarily an intensity and concentration on making a decision that the delegates knew would have a dramatic impact on the future of the organization."[211] The resolution carried but not unanimously. Seventeen delegates cast "no" votes. Following the special conference, the

Kathy Kuester Campbell (Nebraska–Lincoln, 1968), who in her National Council role as director of conferences and alumni had planned the special conference, recalled the mood after the motion carried: "Actually the reaction was quite positive, and we saw chapters admitting men the first year. . . . [A]n effort to have every chapter represented at the special meeting and hear the discussion probably was a key factor in how smoothly the decision was incorporated into practice."[213]

Barbara Cook, who in 1974 helped author a position paper that attempted to make a case for some women's organizations (e.g., the Association of Women Students, Alpha Lambda Delta, the Society of Women Engineers) remaining single sex, said that "it became clear to me that equality is somewhat finite—it either exists or it doesn't exist and one has to be careful about any area singled out for special exception."[214] She recalled

issue would be ratified by all chapters through mail ballot by a vote of 135 to 32. The process of admitting men began.

When the conference ended, delegates revealed their impressions of "the exciting but exhausting thirty-six hours." One said that "I feel sadness that Mortar Board as a senior women's organization has ceased after so many years, but I feel the step we have taken will be in the best interest for all involved." Another said that "I came to this conference against admitting men. My entire attitude changed as a result of bringing bright minds together. We are living in a country now where an effort to gain equality for all is in progress. If we choose to ignore, or even deny that we are living in a constantly changing world, we are not facing reality."[212]

Barbara Cook, then associate dean of students at Purdue, where she was also chapter advisor, led the process through which Mortar Board articulated its position on Title IX. She declared that the delegates' refusal to "vote [Mortar Board] out of existence, recognizing the advantages of diversity and exchange of ideas that a national organization affords, was the only rational choice." **Source:** *Mortar Board Forum* 6, no. 2 (January 1976): 4.

leaving that Conference in 1975 thinking that if it is ever possible for men and women to enter into a full partnership where there is equal respect for what our society deems masculine qualities and feminine qualities, Mortar Board is surely the place where this can happen. That October day I felt a great sense of optimism about the future of Mortar Board and the attitudes held by our collegiate members. . . . [I]t takes strong women to work in a man's world; it also takes strong and understanding men to work in a woman's world. Perhaps this association together in such a group of equal peers may help us all learn to work someday in a human world where talent, ability, responsible behavior, and creativity are the only required prerequisites for opportunity.[215]

Alumnae reaction to the transition from an all-women's honor society to a coed organization was mixed. Past National President Evans recalled that "after the Constitutional change to accept men had been made, I was amazed at the local attention it received in the next several months. I was not surprised at the disappointment in losing our single-sex status, but I was surprised at the hostility."[216] Some alumnae were not pleased with the change and were vocal about their disappointment.

As could be expected, it took a while before men realized that Mortar Board was open to them. The president of one chapter reflected what many chapters experienced in the first year after the change: "In spite of publicity, only a few men were nominated. They were either not interested or didn't realize they were eligible. Our chapter needs to make a greater effort in making men aware they are now eligible for membership in Mortar Board."[217]

Many years later past Mrs. Evans recounted that

during my term as President I met the most outstanding women; they were courageous, fearless, bright beyond belief, and dedicated to Mortar Board. I never thought Mortar Board would cease to exist, but I was concerned about the challenge of maintaining an organization with a stellar history as a single-sex organization now coping with a totally different composition.[218]

In an article titled "The Challenge of the Future" in the April 1976 *Forum*, National Director of Expansion Marylu McEwen (Purdue, 1968) called the "decision to delete sex as a criterion for Mortar Board membership the most significant event in the history of Mortar Board." She discussed the concept of sacrificing what "we are for what we might become." Dr. McEwen offered challenges for the future:

To maintain the purposes of Mortar Board, especially those relating to the advancement of the status of women as set forth in the Preamble and Article II of the Constitution;
. . . to provide a unique organization on the campus . . . and to communicate the uniqueness and purposes of Mortar Board to the academic community;
. . . to be open to Mortar Board's evolution . . . specifically to be open to a new mode of chapter functioning while maintaining the tradition and purposes of the organization; and
. . . a hope that we might develop through Mortar Board new and creative ways for women and men to work together, replacing stereotyped modes which have done little to build on commonalties or separate strengths.[219]

Marjorie Lasko first learned of the opening for executive secretary-treasurer at a meeting of the Columbus alumnae, where her husband coincidentally was the guest speaker (on the topic of the new Columbus Convention and Transportation Center). She asked him right there if he would mind if she applied for the job. She cancelled a planned trip to Ireland to tour Georgian Manor Houses and Castles to tackle the job.
Source: *Mortar Board Forum* 7, no. 1 (November 1976): 8.

Reacting to the decision by the delegation, Donna Walls resigned as executive secretary-treasurer of the National Office, and Marjorie Erskine Lasko (Ohio State, 1948) assumed the post. In the *Forum* she welcomed new members and urged them to use the office for a variety of needs. She shared the lighter side of her job, describing a phone call to the National Office one day by a man asking for the requirements for concrete in Ohio. She patiently replied that the office was for a collegiate honor society for seniors and the name referred to the caps worn by graduates, not cement. The caller replied "Oh, isn't that cute," and hung up.[220]

The regularly scheduled 1976 national conference took place in June at Colorado State University. Men were present for the first time in an official capacity as delegates (18 men out of 170 attendees). One of the first men to register at the convention was Roger Levesque (Carleton, 1976). He commented that the reason he joined Mortar Board was to be in a position to encourage women to engage in more campus activities. The newly elected president of his chapter, Clancy Wolf (Whitman College, 1976), revealed that "I was apprehensive at first [to attend the national conference]; I felt I might be scorned, but my concerns were not warranted."[221] National President Jayne Wade Anderson remembered that

the major issue on the floor of the conference was dealing with that portion of the preamble to our constitution that supports the status of women. Many delegates felt this aspect should be deleted and that Mortar Board should not single out one sex; others felt that this aspect was not only the very backbone of Mortar Board historically but also part of the uniqueness of the society. Many of our male delegates took the floor of the business meeting to share with the delegates their personal reasons for selecting membership in Mortar Board. The unique background and reputation

Less than a year after Mortar Board's historic vote, men's faces appear in the conference photo taken at Colorado State in June 1976. **Source:** *Mortar Board Forum* 7, no. 1 (November 1976): 5.

of Mortar Board attracted their interest and they were emphatic about maintaining this tradition. Bless their hearts!!![222]

A resolution passed by the delegates acknowledged that since "student involvement in university and community activities is decreasing," chapters were challenged to "become catalysts to stimulate increased student involvement in campus and community concerns."[223] The 1976 conference keynote speaker was Martha Peterson, president of Beloit College, who was awarded the National Citation. Congresswoman Barbara Jordan of Texas was also awarded the National Citation that year.

Four years older than Mortar Board, the historically men's honor society ODK also changed its constitution to accept women in March 1974.[224] The two organizations decided to discuss their common concerns and exchange information. (Each organization had chapters on seventy-seven campuses at the time.) Members from both national councils met in September 1977 to share information, including expansion, selection of new members, financial concerns, conferences, and alumni chapters. The two groups agreed to continue contact, exchange publications, and "correspond or call our Council counterpart at any time."[225] The president of the Mortar Board chapter at Augustana College reported that "the alliance of both [of our groups] has served, not to blend, but rather to strengthen the individual identities of each. By combining for certain activities we are able to draw interested people from both groups and our base of cooperation becomes bigger and more functional."[226]

A study of collegiate Mortar Board members who attended the 1976 conference was published in the *Journal of NAWDAC* in the spring of 1980. The purpose of the study according to Dr. McEwen, then a faculty member at Auburn University, was to "examine a national sample of members of Mortar Board selected on the basis of scholarship and outstanding leadership and service to the college or university and community." The study hoped to gain knowledge of student leader

Marylu McEwen (front), pictured with Catherine Evans, Ruth Weimer Mount, and Barbara Cook, was national director of expansion when she conducted a study of Mortar Board members' majors and career aspirations for publication in the *Journal of NAWDAC*. In addition to many roles, she also is a fund founder in the MBNF.

characteristics to acquire a better understanding of advising student leaders and student organizations as well as suggesting implications for leadership and student development. She and coauthor Earl B. Higgins found that friends and family appeared to have the greatest effect on students' involvement in extracurricular activities. The housing unit, counselors, and student personnel staff had the least impact. As could be expected, Mortar Board members exhibited high grade point averages, broad college experiences, and clearly defined future plans. The study revealed major differences between the 1976 and 1973 initiates' interest in academic majors and long-term career aspirations; 1976 students were more interested in business and law and had a decreased interest in education and the liberal arts.[227]

The delegates to each national conference over the years have been responsible for the direction of the Society until the next conference. When the delegates to the 1979 meeting met, conferences were held every three years. Part of their responsibility was to update the Mortar Board constitution, bylaws, standing rules, and resolutions to reflect current needs and issues. Unfortunately, over time these changes and rewording had caused these documents to appear rather irregular and in need of streamlining. In a preconference message to the delegates of the 1979 conference, National President Anderson wrote that

> Mortar Board has retained an attorney to assist us throughout this year and during the National Conference with efforts directed toward the revision of our Constitution. The goal for this project is to provide Mortar Board with a document that will stand up through the years, one that does not appear to be a patchwork quilt following each conference.[228]

At the conference, the attorney who had assisted with the revision explained the process and stressed that "you have an obligation to change what needs to be changed and not what does not need to be changed."[229] The revision committee carefully went over the revisions and presented them to the delegates, and each was voted on after debate.

It was at this conference that the problem of chapter resignation from the national organization, which first appeared when the Swarthmore chapter withdrew in the 1960s, reappeared. The vice president for student affairs at George Washington University sent a letter to the National Council stating that its chapter was no longer functioning or viable. He indicated that since ODK tapped both juniors and seniors, "they are fulfilling the role that both Mortar Board and ODK filled in the past." Since no procedure for disaffiliation from Mortar Board was established after Swarthmore resigned, National President Anderson concluded that "for the first time in Mortar Board history this [procedural] action will be taken, so we are indeed plowing new ground without some very specific guidelines." (After some debate, the delegates to the 1982 conference would approve a revision of Article V of the constitution indicating that chapters on the inactive list could be disaffiliated by a two-thirds vote of the delegates attending the national conference.)

Mortar Board and the Age of Technology: 1980–1999

The 1980s will be remembered for the fall of the Berlin Wall, the massacre in China's Tiananmen Square, the space shuttle *Challenger* disaster (on whose crew was Judith Resnik [Carnegie Mellon, 1970]), and the assassination of Beatle John Lennon. President Ronald Reagan declared a war on drugs. The computer age began in earnest with the rise of the personal computer and the Internet. There was the "me" generation, and the expression "shop 'til you drop" trended. It was a

time of floppy shirts, shoulder pads, leg warmers, big hair, and Rubik's Cube. Cabbage Patch dolls flew off store shelves. Pac-Man (and Ms. Pac-Man) video games were wildly popular in arcades, malls, and bars. By the end of the decade, the average yearly income was more than $27,000; gasoline was less than a dollar a gallon. The television show *M*A*S*H** ended after eleven seasons.

The Cooperative Institutional Research Program Freshman Survey by the Higher Education Research Institute found that college freshmen were more interested in status, power, and money than they had been at any time during the previous fifteen years. The most popular major was business management. The doctrine of in loco parentis was vestigial, and colleges and universities had all but let go of the complicated rules regulating students' behavior.

Higher education in the 1980s could be called a time of "retrenchment to recovery," when "the drive for both quality and prestige prompted institutions to spend generously."[230] This spending came to an end with a stock market crash and a drop in state revenues late in the decade.

The Family Educational Rights and Privacy Act, Title IX, and other legislation contributed to a change in students' relationship with their college or university. The president of the National Association for Women Deans, Administrators, and Counselors, Jane McCormick Lewis (Penn State, 1980), wrote a guest article in the *Forum* about the effects of decreased campus rules and increased government regulations.

Tau Iota Omega members cleared a three-quarter-mile section of path on a trail near the Colorado State Arena on a sunny Saturday in April 1980. Marshaling the efforts of many other student organizations and also members of the Epilepsy Task Force, the chapter raised $500 and contributed to the community good. They called the event Epicology Day—for *epi*lepsy and *ecology*. **Source:** *Mortar Board Forum* 11, no. 1 (Fall 1980): 4.

She urged Mortar Board chapters to "look at what is happening to the woman student on campus," including "the effects on women on the elimination of internal regulations and changes affecting them as a result of increased governmental legislation and guidelines."[231]

The delegates to the 1979 national conference had requested a study of "the need for computers and their possible use by Mortar Board." Executive Secretary-Treasurer Marjorie Lasko solicited advice from The Ohio State University's computing services to determine how word processing could meet the National Office's needs. In addition to a system for maintaining membership records, other uses were projected to improve the efficiency of office operations, expand the list of potential staff, facilitate research, provide sources of alumni contact, and allow for individual mailings, especially the *Forum*.[232] Ms. Lasko and National Director of Finance Dorothy (Dottie) Moser (University of Cincinnati, 1970) met with various computer company representatives to determine the need for service, training, and financing. When the system was in place, the National Office requested that collegiate chapters send lists of their alumni for the national membership database. Later there was a plea in the *Forum* from the office asking chapters to stop submitting these lists with married name only, since the old lists in the office were by maiden name and no match could be made. The cost to buy and maintain the DECmate word processing miracle in 1983 was $6,162 plus $3,847 for data entry employees' wages.

National Council members' annual reports in the early 1980s reflected the Society's agenda at that time. National President Anderson called for a full examination of selection criteria, mainly grade point average, to ensure that Mortar Board's selection criteria remained consistent with the constitution of the ACHS. A report by Sharon Sutton Miller (Miami University, 1954), national director of elections, urged a "serious investigation of our scholarship requirement." Although 22 percent of chapters used a higher grade point average than the required

3.0, it was not certain that Mortar Board's minimum requirement satisfied the ACHS standard that those selected rank in the highest 35 percent of their class in scholarship. Since over half of chapters were located at middle- and larger-size campuses, she asked "how realistic is our current selection process to the majority of our chapters?"[233] (The problem of determining grade point eligibility has emerged at many points in Mortar Board's history, especially at larger institutions.) There was a question also about how grade inflation might be increasing the number of eligible persons.

Other items on the National Council's agenda were to study how to charge a national conference registration fee and a list of topics to discuss with ODK at an upcoming meeting. National Citation recipient Barbara Bush, spouse of then U.S. vice president George H. W. Bush, held a coffee at the vice president's residence on the grounds of the Naval Observatory in Washington, D.C., for Mortar Board National Council members and section coordinators who met in the summer of 1981. National President Anderson presented Mrs. Bush, who had written an article about volunteerism for the *Forum*,[234] with the citation.

A resolution by the delegates of the 1982 national conference established the concept of Mortar Board Week during which each chapter should "actively promote scholarship, leadership and service"[235] in February to coincide with the dates of Mortar Board's founding. The delegates to the 1987 conference later clarified this and set the week containing February 15, the founding date, as the time for the annual celebration. Chapters celebrated this special week in many creative ways and gained visibility in the process. At Oregon State University, a Mortar Board member in cap and gown passed out balloons and free apple cider, while other celebratory activities included speakers, musical events, and a basketball auction. The new University of Toledo chapter celebrated with its annual People in Motion Lecture.

Barbara Bush hosted a coffee at the vice president's mansion for Mortar Board national leaders during their 1981 summer meeting. Here National President Jayne Wade Anderson presents a National Citation to Mrs. Bush as National Council members and student advisors look on.
Source: *Mortar Board Forum* 12, no. 1 (Fall 1981): 7.

Some chapters promoted the national project (AIDs awareness, organ donor awareness) during the week. The University of Texas at Austin held Applause for Excellence Week by displaying a beautiful banner on the main mall and presenting "applause for excellence" buttons to thank dedicated professors.[236] Like many others, Eastern Kentucky created a Mortar Board display in the student union and took shifts to answer students' questions about Mortar Board. The University of Redlands "designed and sewed a large flag in Mortar Board's bright yellow and black"[237] and flew it by the student center. Baylor sponsored a lecture by Doris Kearns (later Goodwin), history scholar and author, whose topic was "The Presidency: The Men and Women It Involves and Where It Is Going."[238] She urged students to "strive for a balance between work and play in their quest for success." Many university and college presidents as well as mayors and governors recognized the Society's special week through official proclamation.

The delegates to the 1982 conference changed the language in the constitution to clarify that members who did not graduate in four years could continue active membership and that the initiation of tapped students studying abroad could be delayed for up to two years from the date of tapping. The delegates added to the discrimination article in the constitution to read "No candidate shall be discriminated against in regard to race, ethnic origin, creed, age, sex, affiliation, marital status, alternative life-style or *disabling condition*." The members at the University of Massachusetts at Amherst wrote to the *Forum* editor in 1988 with concern about the outdated language in this clause and urged that "alternative lifestyle" be changed to "sexual orientation" and that "disabling condition" be changed to "any physical disability." These terms continued to be debated and changed over the years depending on the language that prevailed at the time. By 2008 the nondiscrimination clause of the *Bylaws of Mortar Board, Inc.*, contained the terms "sexual orientation" and "physical challenge." The phrase "gender expression, or any other affiliation or protected class" was added at the Society's first virtual special national conference in April 2012.

The interest and confusion about the transliteration of the Greek letters Pi, Sigma, and Alpha in Mortar Board's motto reemerged in the 1980s. Marcia Moxley (Swarthmore College, 1932) wrote to the National Office in 1986 with this question: "I am now living in a retirement home and there are several of us here who have been members of

CONVENED 9:30 P.M.

A motion was made to accept the installation ritual as drawn
up by the committee with the insertion of the Greek words PISTOS , SOPHIA,
? archais
ARCHAE, as the words of our letters Pi Sigma Alpha. The installation
service was thus accepted by the convention vote.

An excerpt from page 4 of a draft of the minutes of the third national convention shows some definition of the Greek letters
in our motto, Pi Sigma Alpha. The corresponding page of the final version of the minutes is missing!
The yellowing of this document is evidence of its age.

Mortar Board in the distant past. In conversations among us the question arose as to the meaning of those letters [Pi Sigma Alpha]." Diane Selby, executive secretary-treasurer of the National Office, responded that "the founders' intent is not exactly clear but we think the three Greek letters are a loose translation of scholarship, leadership and service."[239]

This question of a transliteration of the Greek letters was not a new one. The minutes of the second convention in 1919 reflected this uncertainty when the secretary was instructed to "write to the secretary of the last convention, asking her what the exact letters Pi. E. A. [spelling is original] stand for and appoint a member of the convention to look up the meaning of the letters."[240]

A draft of the minutes of the third national convention, which took place April 22–24, 1921, describes a motion made to accept the installation ritual as drawn up by committee "with the insertion of the Greek words PISTOS, SOPHIA, ARCHAE, as the words of our letters Pi Sigma Alpha. The installation service was thus accepted by the convention vote." The word "ARCHAE" is outlined in pencil, and handwritten in cursive above it (with a question mark before it) is the word "archais."[241]

A present-day transliteration of the word "pistos" means "faithful" or "reliable," which could be related to the concept of character. The constitution in 1920 ascribed the meaning of "pi" as character:

ARTICLE II OBJECT
Section 1: The object of this fraternity shall be service, scholarship and leadership.
Pi, character
Sigma, scholarship
Alpha, leadership[242]

Since many of the old original local honor societies used "character" as a selection criterion, this interpretation is not surprising. Adding the criterion of character has been considered at many times during Mortar Board's history. The delegates to the 1964 conference considered adding character to the three established criteria but rejected it. The National Council discussed a character requirement in 1994, believing rather hyperbolically that "Mortar Board is the only honor society that does not have a character requirement."[243] It was concluded that character is a part of leadership, and "this is discussed in the membership manual." (The difficulty in designating character as a requirement for membership was defining it.)

This quest for a literal translation of the three Greek letters persisted over the years, and Nick Genovese (San Diego State University, 1994), a classics professor and Mortar Board advisor at San Diego State, offered a translation from the ancient Greek that, regrettably, was lost. In a letter to the National Office in 1983 a meaning of Pi Sigma Alpha was offered by Grace Beede (University of South Dakota, 1928), head of the Classics Department and longtime advisor at South Dakota, who had a version in her files:

Pi stand[s] for pistotes, a Greek word that means good faith; Mortar Board takes it to mean service. Sigma stands for sophia, a Greek word that means wisdom; I believe that Mortar Board takes it to mean scholarship. The Alpha stands for archal, which in Greek (it is a plural word, here, oddly enough) means authorities, powers or dominions; Mortar Board takes it to mean leadership.[244]

Considering the time (1920s) and the reliability of the source, this transliteration of the Greek letters seems plausible. It is very similar to what is reported in the minutes of the 1921 convention.

The most recent translation of the Greek letters was offered in 2012 by Hood College Chapter Advisor and Dean Ted Chase and Hood College librarian Jan O'Leary: Pi, scholarship (*polymatheya*); Sigma, service (*servis*); and Alpha, leadership (*arkheegya*).

Glenda Earwood (Auburn University, 1973) explored another historical marker in 1983. She conducted a study on the effect of Title IX on members, officers, and faculty advisors in Mortar Board,

ODK, Alpha Lambda Delta, and Phi Eta Sigma. A survey instrument was mailed to the 676 presidents and advisors of chapters located at coeducational institutions. The survey data revealed that Title IX had a significant effect on the membership practices of honor societies. Women students held an average of 59 percent of the membership in these four honor societies. In formerly all-women's societies, women were 53 percent of the membership and men 35 percent. In Mortar Board, men made up 35 percent of the membership, while 34 percent of the advisors were men. Dr. Earwood indicated that this finding was consistent with the research positing that men who engage in female sex-stereotyped activities are perceived as seeking downward mobility. Although it was feared that women would not be allowed to be leaders in the coeducational setting, women held a higher percentage of officer positions than men across all four honor societies.[245]

Dottie Moser, who was the first honorary member of Mortar Board to be elected National President, remembers the 1980s as a time of active and involved Mortar Board students. Jane Dobbs Brechin (Pittsburgh, 1950), national director of programming who was also associate dean of students at the University of Tulsa, asked chapters in the 1980s to name the factors that influenced their programming decisions. The most frequent influences on chapter activities were based on tradition, campus needs, and national conference resolutions, followed by visibility, financial need, and chapter development. Trinity College's chapter held a wine and cheese fireside for Jimmy Carter's visit to the campus, providing the opportunity for honors students and distinguished faculty to interact with the former president. Oregon State members were assigned a foreign student "buddy" and assisted a professor with a new course, "American Ways of Life for Foreign Students." Ball State published a brochure to inform the student body about various honor societies and their criteria. Colorado State sponsored a "fishing day" for veterans from the army hospital in Denver in cooperation with a local hunting and fishing organization. Kansas State assisted the university administration with the problem of student retention (of great concern nationally in the 1980s) by gathering advisor evaluations.

Wisconsin opened a "Mortar Board jail" for local celebrities who were taken into captivity; the "prisoners" had to solicit money for multiple sclerosis to "be sprung." Westhampton College assisted at a battered women's home, and Bowling Green sponsored a Christmas party for Easter Seal children. So that library hours could be extended during finals week, the University of North Dakota chapter worked at the university library monitoring floors and assisting staff. Cornell held a fund-raiser offering to "tuck in" a friend with milk and cookies and a bedtime story or a song for $2.

Bucknell held a wine tasting lecture, and Tennessee Tech held a "dress-as-your-major" party. As a prelude to their annual football rivalry, the South Carolina and Clemson chapters teamed up to raise money for graduate scholarships for graduating seniors who planned to continue studies at their universities. Troy State held an autographed football raffle as part of homecoming. Monmouth and Ohio State (and probably every other chapter with a fall homecoming) held traditional mum sales at football games to raise funds for scholarships.

Southern California sponsored an innovative program in 1984 through a talk show format called "Meeting of the Minds." The program featured Socrates, Joseph Goebbels, and Richard Nixon (portrayed by professors) in a lively discussion addressing the issue of freedom of information. In addition to assuming the ideology and mannerisms of the historical figures, the talk show participants wore period costumes and were ushered into the auditorium and onto the stage by Mortar Board members costumed as Secret Service agents. After the discussion segment of the program, members of the audience were able to question the "imposters." The event was so popular that the chapter scheduled another program featuring portrayals of George Orwell, B. F. Skinner, and Leonardo Da Vinci in a timely discussion of *1984*.[246]

Indiana sponsored a National Issues Forum that was held in the county library and open to both the campus and the community. The topics ranged from national defense and nuclear arms to the federal budget and the deficit. The University of Wisconsin–Eau Claire presented Chancellor's Roundtable discussions once a month that were open to all students, faculty, and administrators and provided an opportunity to question the chancellor on any topic.

Proving that beauty and brains go together, two Mortar Board alumnae from the same Troy State chapter in Alabama were finalists in the 1982 Miss America Pageant, one representing Tennessee and the other Ohio. Two more Mortar Board members competed in the 1985 Miss America pageant, one from Nebraska's chapter and the other from the University of Tennessee's chapter. A surprising number of Mortar Board members have competed in the Miss America contest; Marilyn Van Derbur (University of Colorado, 1959) won the title in 1958. The proliferation of pageant syndicates has diluted some of the spotlight of the single pageant of days gone by. Mortar Board members participate still. Boni Yraguen (University of South Alabama, 2014) holds two titles in the state of Alabama and is also the recipient of two national Tau Beta Pi Engineering Honor Society scholarships.

Long-range planning was an important agenda item in the 1980s. An ad hoc long-range planning group presented a report at the 1980 summer meeting of the National Council. Broad goals were proposed as the basis for a "ten-year plan." In addition to continually reviewing the purpose of Mortar Board as set forth in the constitution, other areas were development (including chapter workability and membership size); structure (including National Office staffing, computerization, and alumni); meeting the mutual needs of the MBNF and Mortar

Board, Inc.; and visibility (ensuring the development of a viable image at the national and local levels).[247] The National Council meeting in 1981 noted that good information on which to make informed decisions was not available, so the first steps would be to collect it. Important factors considered were declining membership and expansion, chapter minimum standards, a 12 percent rate of economic inflation, the relationship with ODK, and an increasing difficulty in finding volunteer section coordinators.[248]

The long-range planning committee that met in the summer of 1983 published thirty-six recommendations.[249] This long-range planning continued through 1985, as these recommendations continued to be concerned with chapter procedures, financial operations, National Council structure and responsibilities, national conferences, and the National Office. The delegates to the 1985 triennial conference voted to adopt many of the recommendations, and most were implemented later.

Other issues of concern were revealed in National Council reports in the mid-1980s. One was addressing the programming needs of "commuter campuses with their increasing numbers of non-traditional students and the increasing fiscal constraints on all students as it affected the use of the limited free time available to them." Also expressed was concern for the competition on some campuses "between like honor societies."[250] This issue evolved from the Title IX–inspired transition from single-sex to coed societies, which continued even into the 1990s.

In her 1985 annual report, National Vice President Phyllis Dohanian (University of Massachusetts at Amherst, 1972) stated that "the role of Section Coordinator has changed during this triennium. Section Coordinators are currently viewed as a proactive resource and chapter consultant. They take initiative to help chapters rather than wait for problems to come up. This role is far more rewarding than the role of policing. The goal is to help chapters develop their leadership abilities and strengths and to work with them to overcome personal and chapter weaknesses."[251] She also noted the critical role of chapter advisors, their need for "support from national," and the difficulty sometimes faced by chapters in identifying new advisors.

A letter of congratulations from President Ronald Reagan was read to the delegates at the 1985 conference held in Columbus, Ohio. National Citation award winner and keynote speaker for the conference was U.S. Supreme Court justice Sandra Day O'Connor, and a luncheon was given in her honor. Award-winning syndicated cartoonist Milton Caniff, a famous Ohio State graduate, was also made an honorary member of Mortar Board that year. Mr. Caniff gave a "chalk talk" to the conference participants, and his drawing was raffled off to raise funds for the MBNF.

The 1985 delegates changed the number of years between national conferences from three to two. The constitution was changed to accommodate this biennium, with National Council positions lasting two years. David Coleman (Bowling Green, 1982) was the first man to be appointed a section coordinator.

The Society's financial health was continually monitored. After the 1985 national conference, Bette Swilley (Auburn, 1968), director of finance and records, was concerned about the cost of holding the national conference every two years. She wrote to the National Council that "I see us spending an unbelievable amount of money. We must tighten our expenditures if we expect to stay liquid over the next several years. We cannot overspend our income year after year by 20 or 40 thousand dollars and expect to survive. I am working on a financial presentation that will hopefully reflect our financial status and future predictions."[252]

Executive Secretary-Treasurer Lasko also noted the need to make some important financial choices because of the additional cost of biennial conferences. "The Long-Range Planning Committee proposed a package of suggestions with a composite of ideas that made

Marjorie Lasko handed the National Office operation over to Diane Selby in the summer of 1986. Diane had been a section coordinator and held all the offices in the Greater Columbus Alumni chapter, making her a good fit to command the Society's headquarters. Marjorie accepted a volunteer assignment as section coordinator after moving to Charleston, South Carolina. **Source:** *Mortar Board Forum* 17, no. 1 (Fall 1996): 5.

more frequent conferences possible. They [the delegates] adopted only the idea of a biennial conference without incorporating the money-saving ideas of controlling costs of airfare, shortening the length of the conference, and eliminating some section meetings."[253]

Director of Finance and Records Swilley listed the costs for each item required to support a collegiate member for one year (e.g., section allocations, fellowships, the National Council, section coordinators' operating expenses, and membership pins). As in the past, the two largest costs were the national conference and the National Office expense. To cover the deficit, an additional $6.32 would be needed from each new member.[254] Dues were raised again at the 1989 conference to $41, "since the national organization was forced to use interest on savings to meet current expenses."

After ten years of outstanding service, Marjorie Lasko resigned as executive secretary-treasurer in 1986 when her family moved out of Ohio. After a brief search, Diane Miller Selby (Ohio State, 1961) was hired as executive secretary-treasurer. The National Office continued to update its computer storage and retrieval needs. A toll-free telephone line, which had been suggested by previous conference delegates to improve communication, was not installed because the cost would exceed that of continuing to accept collect calls. The toll-free line was eventually added.

The delegates of the 1987 national conference passed a resolution to commemorate the bicentennial of the U.S. Constitution. A request by the Commission for the Bicentennial to develop a "living legacy" across the nation prompted Mortar Board's "200 chapters on 200 colleges and universities" to participate in the "Plant a Living Legacy to the Constitution" project. The delegates resolved that "each chapter plant a 'Constitution Tree' on its campus, accompanied by an appropriate ceremony, to celebrate the Bicentennial of the United States Constitution, completed by the third year of the Commemoration in the year 1989."[255] Many campus trees were planted as a result of this resolution. Midwestern State University planted thirteen bur oak trees developed by the biology department, and a time capsule was buried in the grove with instructions for it to be opened in the year 2037. Oklahoma State celebrated Mortar Board Week with a Constitution Tree planting and provided bookmarks for the occasion. Valparaiso combined tree planting with a reception to welcome new faculty. The university president led the ceremony by breaking ground for the sugar gum tree that had been donated by a local nursery.

Western Michigan and the Mortar Board alumni of Kalamazoo planted a twenty-two-foot Norwegian spruce in front of the student center. U.S. Supreme Court chief justice Warren Burger helped the chapter at South Carolina plant a fourteen-foot oak tree on the historic campus Horseshoe.

Another 1987 conference resolution reflected the growing concern about higher education funding. Students were increasingly reliant on loans, as the cost at both public and private institutions was well ahead of inflation. Student loan default was also mounting.[256] National President Catherine (Cathy) Johnson Randall (Alabama, 1971) recalled that the lack of funding for student financial aid "was the strongest issue that emerged from the students at the conference." The delegates reaffirmed a previous resolution stating that "Mortar Board, Inc. continue to encourage individual colleges, universities and public officials to increase financial support for higher education through current and alternative sources for funding student financial aid."[257]

Mortar Board sent a letter to every U.S. senator and representative urging an increase in funding for federal student aid.[258] Senator Sam Nunn replied that he appreciated Mortar Board members' "interest and concern" and then listed the "large" sums of money provided under the FY88 Continuing Appropriations Bill that was just signed into law.

A major goal of the National Council in the late 1980s was to incorporate a greater student voice in the governance of the Society. The 1987 delegates created the position of student-at-large as a full voting member of the National Council. Although previously students served as advisors to the National Council, they had no vote. The first student-at-large elected was Billy Earnest (Midwestern State, 1987), who established an outstanding track record for the student representatives who succeeded him. He recalled being welcomed by National Council members, who picked him up at the Atlanta airport before his first meeting: "Mortar Board introduced me to Atlanta; we forged as a group, and I found my time on the National Council to be collaborative and inclusive."[259]

Other actions were to create the concept of a national award for chapter excellence and to add a chapter officer for alumni relations. The national change in the legal drinking age to twenty-one resulted in another conference resolution that encouraged institutions to provide alcohol-free programming on campuses.

David Coleman became the first man to be elected to the National Council, as director of programming. He had been president of his chapter, a student advisor, and a section coordinator (the first man).

Queens College (now University) of Charlotte, a women's college in North Carolina, was installed as the two hundredth chapter in 1987.

National Council Elected

The newly elected National Council is (left to right): Esther Williams, Marilyn Wirtz, Bette Swilley, Dave Coleman, Cathy Randall, Billy Earnest, Kay MacKenzie, Gail Harrison, and Dottie Phillips.

Billy Earnest filled the first student representative position on the National Council. He became a Mortar Board fellow and now, as a faculty member at St. Edward's University, is a reader in the Mortar Board fellowship application process each year. **Source:** *Mortar Board Forum* 18, no. 3 (Spring 1988): 4.

The first man on the National Council, David Coleman continues his support for Mortar Board as a speaker at national conferences. His program "Making a Community of Leaders" is a stimulating and fun icebreaker to start our conferences the right way.

An agenda item that had been recurring from the 1950s was the possibility of Mortar Board expanding internationally. The delegates to the 1987 conference recommended that National Director of Expansion Bette Swilley investigate "the feasibility of the establishment of or inclusion of Mortar Board in an international union of honor societies." She pointed out that "we must first investigate the university standards in each country before we can evaluate applications for affiliation fairly." The National Council decided to begin the process by "contacting our alumni in foreign countries beginning in Canada."[260] After a search of the database, the National Office found Mortar Board alumni in eighty countries. Countries with the most alumni were the Bahamas, Canada, France, Hong Kong, India, Japan, Malaysia, Mexico, Saudi Arabia, Singapore, the United Kingdom, and West Germany. Contacts were made with alumni in these countries encouraging them to form alumni clubs. At the 1988 summer meeting of the National Council and section coordinators in Toronto, Canada, Mortar Board alumni in the area were invited to participate in a discussion of development in foreign countries. A representative from the University of Western Ontario expressed interest in membership and was given information on how to start a comparative local group.

The National Council made a change in the title from "executive secretary-treasurer" of the National Office to "executive director" in 1991. This change was prompted by the need to keep up with national Greek-letter groups and other honor societies that had already elevated or were in the process of elevating the job title. As National Office employees are technically employees of Ohio State, there was an expectation that Mortar Board's nomenclature equate with the position descriptions of similar jobs on campus.

The question of forming a national alumni association was discussed. Members of the MBNF "did not feel a national association is a good idea since it would be redundant because all memberships are for a lifetime." They were concerned that this might detract from alumni clubs raising money for local scholarship projects (there were fifty alumni clubs at the time, and almost all gave a local scholarship).

The National Council expressed a concern when MBNF trustees explored the possibility of adopting an affinity card to raise money. At the time, almost all honor societies and Greek-letter groups as well as alumni and civic associations were using these cards to raise funds through trailing revenues that the cards generated. Many companies were contacted to see which might offer the most benefit. National President Randall informed the trustees that the 1989 delegates had "rejected every proposal dealing with the use of their names on a mailing list."[261] A compromise was reached when the MBNF solicited only alumni for the card and not collegiate members. (This changed several years later when the delegates opened the door to an affinity card.)

Dr. Randall remembered that one of the challenges during her years as National President was the issue of duplication among honor societies that arose after Title IX. After gender barriers were set aside, some eligible students joined several honor societies. There was also some confusion about the role and purpose of the various honor societies and honoraries that students were invited to join. Delegate discussions at the national conference reflected the concern that students were overextended and that subsequent time constraints caused a lack of engagement in chapter activities. Since this problem seemed to take different forms on different campuses, no solutions were proposed.

Long-range planning was emphasized once more as Dr. Randall urged that a framework for a plan for "Mortar Board in the 21st Century" be developed. This was prompted partially by the anticipation of Mortar Board's seventy-fifth anniversary and the desire to set goals and plan for the society's role and purpose into the next century. At the 1988 summer meeting, five areas were incorporated into the plan: (1) position Mortar Board as the most distinguished and

During her presidency, Cathy Johnson Randall urged that Mortar Board position itself for the twenty-first century. Gracious and organized, she charmed and encouraged delegates and national leaders alike as section coordinator and director of communications. Now she is a generous donor to the MBNF's Centennial Campaign and a fund founder.

State University Archives, where Mortar Board's historical documents had been stored since 1968. Underlying many of the changes in Mortar Board in the 1980s was technology's impact on the Society's modes of communicating and operating. Mortar Board installed 18 new chapters during the 1980s, bringing the nationwide total to 204.

Mortar Board in the 1990s

The 1990s will be remembered as the age of electronics. The Internet grew at an astounding pace, and the World Wide Web dramatically changed how the world communicated. Operation Desert Storm, starving children in Somalia, mad cow disease, the bombing during the Olympics in Atlanta, and the increase of AIDS in Africa and other parts of the world are a few of the historic events that marked the decade.

The Americans with Disabilities Act was signed into law in 1990. Social security reform and health care were debated, and a gun control bill (which expired later) was passed in 1994. The federal program No Child Left Behind was intended to assist disadvantaged students. Large numbers of children were diagnosed with ADD (which later became ADHD). Grunge and preppie were both fashionable dress. A sheep named Dolly was cloned, and stem cell research and genetic engineering were in the news. *Titanic* was a hit, *Cheers* ended in 1993 after eleven seasons, and *Seinfeld* and *Friends* were popular whether in first-run or reruns. Video games were hot, and kids played with Furby, Tickle Me Elmo, and Beanie Babies.

Mortar Board had 151,134 members in 1991. By the end of the decade the Society had added 10 more chapters, increasing the total to 214. Longtime outstanding National Office staff members Elaine Barnum and Alice Thomas were recognized with special onetime Mortar Board fellowships named in their honor upon their retirement.

enriching college honor society, (2) emphasize the service component of membership, (3) emphasize the leadership component of membership, (4) improve services to chapters by streamlining operations, and (5) improve financial support for the organization. The plan was presented to the delegates at the 1989 national conference and adopted.

The delegates to the 1989 national conference also increased the upper limit of members in a collegiate chapter from thirty-five to forty (now it is a percentage of the junior class). "Environmental Awareness" was chosen as the national project for the next biennium. Chapters were encouraged to include environmental issues in their programming. Minimum standards were approved for chapters on probation. National Citation recipients were automatically made honorary members. An agreement was renewed and signed in 1989 with The Ohio

New part-time employees who replaced them were Twilo (Twi) Kegler (Hanover College, 1976) and Nancy Long (Denison University, 1954), who took charge of merchandising for the MBNF.

During the 1990s Mortar Board's expanded use of computers in the National Office was student driven. Delegates to almost every conference passed resolutions to increase the use of electronic devices to add to operational efficiency and student communications. When Diane Selby began to run the office in 1986, there was one yellow dial telephone with a long cord that reached all of the office's three rooms. One old copy machine took forever to heat up. Finally, a toll-free phone line and a fax machine were installed. Many official report forms were set up so they could be submitted via e-mail.

Lloyd Stambaugh (Missouri–Columbia, 1989) developed a national computer bulletin board for Mortar Board members in 1990. For the first time, Mortar Board "implemented a mail distribution system available to everyone through BITNET, a national computer network and LISTSERV, a mail distribution system." Each chapter was "urged to find one active member familiar with electronic mail ... who can 'get on line' and educate others on its usage." Student Representative-at-large Tracy Johansen (University of California–Santa Barbara, 1989) reminded chapter presidents of the flyer with detailed instructions on how to use the electronic mail that was sent to them and added that "we might be having our own student teleconference before long!"[262]

The National Citation was to be presented to former president Jimmy Carter and former first lady Rosalynn Carter at the 1991 national conference in Atlanta to recognize them for their efforts on women's issues and conflict resolution. Their representative accepted the award. The delegates also chose literacy as the national project for the next biennium. The delegates heard that "one out of every three Americans over the age of sixteen cannot read or write well enough to be considered fully literate." The delegates agreed that literacy complements the very tenets of Mortar Board and encouraged chapters "to reach out to assist those in need." Mortar Board officially adopted the San Diego State chapter's medallion design. The medallion was offered for sale by the MBNF to be worn for "alumni events and other special occasions."[263] Members of many chapters began wearing the medallion at commencement.

In anticipation of Mortar Board's seventy-fifth anniversary, the delegates to the 1991 conference passed a resolution marking the founding of Mortar Board stating that "Mortar Board chapters across the nation will prepare to celebrate our 75th Anniversary by highlighting Mortar Board's continuity, by uniting with and honoring our alumni and honorary members, and by planning campus and section activities." They also resolved that "the 1993 national conference will serve as both a celebration of Mortar Board's distinguished and proud past and a preparation for Mortar Board's challenging and promising future."[264] Past National President Ruth Weimer Mount and her spouse John Mount (Ohio State, 1981) agreed to chair the celebration to be held during the thirtieth national conference in Columbus, Ohio, in 1993.

In conjunction with the seventy-fifth anniversary, National President M. Kathryne MacKenzie (Oklahoma Baptist University, 1969) urged chapters to update their local histories and highlight their own founding date along with the national celebration. Most of the early Mortar Board chapters emerged from local women's honor societies founded in the nineteenth and early twentieth centuries. Chapter 4 details the fascinating histories of many of these groups before and after they joined the Society.

Throughout Mortar Board's history, the preamble that expresses the Society's purpose has been slightly altered by the delegates to national meetings, but the core emphasis on advancing the status of women has remained. The delegates to the 1991 conference submitted for ratification by chapters an amendment to the constitution that would change the preamble's wording from "emphasize the advancement of the status of women" to "acknowledge the historical emphasis on the advancement of the status of women." The amendment was defeated. Mortar Board national leaders continue to emphasize the advancement of the status of women as an important way that chapters can contribute to the quality of student life on their campuses. Delegate Sarah Spiegelman (Tulane University, 2014) proposed a resolution at the 2014 conference in Atlanta that encouraged conference programming to explain how to advance the status of women. The motion carried, and in addition to "Purpose Sessions" at the 2015 conference in Phoenix, the Capstone Leadership lecturer Betty M. Nelson (Purdue, 1988) was enlisted to explain to chapter leaders how they might recognize and do something about the gender inequities they see on campus. A delegate to the 2015 national conference commented in a postconference electronic survey that

> I also really would like to start a dialogue about what it means to be a male leader in an organization that is about promoting the advancement of women. I want to be able to have a conversation with [my] chapter and it would be nice to get some advice from the conference. Maybe that could be a breakout session next year. I think it's important that I am aware of my privilege as a man and based on the number of men in the organization, this is a meaningful conversation to have.[265]

At the July 1993 National Council meeting, National President Dorothy (Dottie) Buchanan Phillips (Texas Tech, 1975) appointed a committee to study "servicing large urban campuses." Another committee was formed to "look at how higher education views Mortar Board."[266] An Alumni Career Network was formed in 1993 to provide Mortar Board graduates with names of alumni in different occupations who were willing to offer information about their areas of expertise. Within two years it had seven hundred alumni in its database. This first network was the beginning of an expanded data bank.

Ruth and John Mount chaired the seventy-fifth anniversary celebration in Columbus in 1993.

The 1993 national conference was special because the delegates were involved in the celebration of the Society's seventy-fifth anniversary. It was held in Columbus, home of one of the founding chapters at The Ohio State University, around the theme "Share the Tradition . . . Shape the Future." Evaluations showed that highlights were a mock initiation on the Ohio State campus, a meeting with U.S. attorney general Janet Reno, the Mortar Board choir, the special Candlelight Ceremony, and "the buzz of brilliant minds working during the business sessions."[267] The positive effect of the conference on the delegates was summed up by Chapter President Teresa Shaffer (Northern Illinois, 1993):

> The experience of the conference gave me something I will hold on to this year and in future years. It gave me the reassurance that I am not alone. We worked together to do many things. We celebrated 75 years of a tradition we are only beginning to comprehend. As we embark on what has the potential of being our best college year yet, I hold a feeling of reassurance given to me by all of you and I am driven by the 75 years of tradition that preceded us.[268]

National President Phillips challenged members after the anniversary celebration to think about the future of Mortar Board and how it must "adapt to changes in technology, communications and the economy."[269] She reflected on the Society's historical heritage and how future directions were implied in the purpose revised in the summer of 1994:

> Mortar Board, Inc., a national honor society that recognizes college seniors for the achievements in scholarship, leadership and service; creates opportunities for continued leadership development; promotes service to colleges and universities; and encourages lifelong contributions to the global community.[270]

The global community was added to signify the contemporary mission of the society. The national service project chosen for the next biennium was "Substantive Women's Issues," and chapters were encouraged to become involved in related projects such as supporting rape crisis networks, women's literacy, and prevention of sexual harassment. National President Phillips appointed a committee to study possibilities of moving to an annual conference. The pros and cons of this move were outlined in the *Forum* so that delegates to the 1995 conference would be prepared to vote.[271] (Ten years earlier it was decided to move from a triennial to a biennial conference in spite of the cost of that decision.) Once more the financial burden of an annual conference was debated, and the advantages of bringing chapter representatives together every year were viewed as outweighing the cost.

For its part, the MBNF launched the campaign "A Million in the Millennium" to increase its endowed funds. The MBNF continued to focus on raising funds for fellowships. During this special push, twenty additional graduate fellowships were funded along with a chapter project grants program. The grants provided "an exciting and challenging opportunity for Mortar Board chapters with financial assistance to attempt new and creative projects."[272]

Gail Harrison Corvette (Ohio State, 1980) was the president of the MBNF Board of Trustees and spearheaded the Millennium Million idea. As she ended her term of office, she created the first endowment in the MBNF that was not connected to a fellowship. Her Gail Harrison Corvette Leadership Endowment would provide funding for national conference leadership initiatives. In spite of the prod from Ms. Harrison Corvette, it would take the MBNF more time to shift its focus away from fellowships to building endowment funds that could be used for broader purposes affecting groups of members through programming.

The seventy-fifth celebration was an opportunity for National President Kay MacKenzie to recognize her predecessors (front, left to right) Shauna Adix, Catherine Evans, Dottie Moser, Margaret Parker Stafford; (back) Kay, Jayne Wade Anderson, Cathy Randall, Ruth Weimer Mount.

Mortar Board chapters across the country continued to serve their campuses with helpful and innovative programs. In conjunction with their Mortar Board Calendar project, the University of Louisville held a "Curious Quotes Contest" where quotations from "famous and not-so-famous authors as well as original quotes" were solicited. Winners' names and their quotes were used throughout the calendar. Purdue developed campus-wide interest in the calendar by soliciting inspirational quotations to be placed as headers for each week of its extremely popular date book-style calendar. New Mexico State chose a professor of the month and honored all winners at a reception at the end of the school year. Eastern Kentucky celebrated Cultural Awareness Week and received a grant from Mortar Board, Inc., to create "unity bracelets" to be worn during the week. Members braided black, white, brown, yellow, and red bracelets representing the major races of the world. UCLA held Cultural Diversity Day, bringing high school students to campus to "address cultural issues concerning the development of dialogue and leadership in communities."[273]

In part because of their great interest in literacy, the University of Texas at El Paso inducted Laura Bush, wife of the governor (who was in the audience) and her mother Jenna Welch, a Texas at El Paso graduate, as honorary members. University president Diana Natalicio (Texas at El Paso, 1994) participated in the ceremony.

South Carolina elected author, poet, and activist Maya Angelou, Reynolds professor of American studies at Wake Forest, as an honorary member in 1993, and she was additionally presented with a National Citation. The University of California–Berkeley organized a Student Community Service Center that offered assistance to students who wanted to organize community service projects and needed advice about raising money, office space, facilities, publicizing an event, and how to recruit volunteers. Northern Colorado sent birthday cards to residents of a nursing home. Texas Christian created a thirty-six-page freshman handbook titled *Mortar Board Presents: What We Wish We Knew When We Were Freshmen* that included essays about college life written by chapter members. They marketed the booklet to parents of incoming freshmen. The Mary Washington College helped sponsor a campus talk by Ralph Nader, a spokesperson for consumer issues and a presidential candidate. Mortar Board members continued to be finalists in the Miss America contest, with one active member from the Mississippi chapter and two alumnae from South Carolina and Oklahoma competing.[274]

The Mortar Board National Office celebrated its twenty-fifth year as Mortar Board's administrative center in 1995, and the National Council formally recognized Mortar Board's twenty-five-year affiliation with The Ohio State University. Amira N. Ailabouni (Ohio State, 1994), the undergraduate student representative to the university Board of Trustees, presented the acknowledgment at a board meeting.[275] Mortar Board, Inc., granted sole rights to sell Mortar Board merchandise to the MBNF in 1996, with the profits used to fund fellowships and chapter projects.

Delegates to the 1995 conference proposed that national conferences be held every year, and the article in the constitution dealing with the election of National Council members was amended to read that office terms should be for two years, with no more than three consecutive elected terms in any one office. A second student representative-at-large position was created by the 1995 delegates so there would always be two collegiate members on the National Council. The delegates chose "Children's Concerns" as the national project for the next biennium. Chapters were encouraged to create projects around children's issues—hosting speakers or bringing children to campus for an event or a meal in a residence hall were suggested.

The delegates passed a resolution to form a national association of Mortar Board alumni with a lifetime membership fee. National

In October 1995 under the leadership of Chapter President Ruben Nevarez (left), Texas at El Paso initiated Laura Bush and her mother
Jenna Welch (who had gone to the School of the Mines, now the University of Texas at El Paso) to honor their work in literacy.
Also initiated were research professor Lillian Mayberry (right of Ruben) and President Diana Natalicio. Governor George W. Bush was in the audience.

President Phillips appointed a committee to study this. National Director of Alumni Emma Norris (Alabama, 1959) remarked that "we will need to customize it for our own purposes and not limit ourselves to old models of alumni associations we have known."[276] The 1995 delegates changed the name Alumni Club, which had been used for seventy-seven years, to Alumni Chapter. The feeling was that the word "club" was "outdated and sounded too much like a women's organization."

The National Council began an intensive effort in 1995 to formulate a plan for the future of the Society. A Strategic Planning Task Force was appointed in July 1996 with the task of "developing new approaches to maximize the organization's purpose with particular emphasis on the internal operations of Mortar Board, Inc."[277] The task force was charged with formulating a clear definition of the responsibilities of the National Office, developing a financial plan, improving chapter continuity and diversity, stating a clear definition of the purposes of the national conferences, and changing the volunteer leadership structure. Conducting a SWOT[278] analysis, the task force would examine current services provided to collegiate and alumni members and chapters.[279] Goals were set for addressing each of these issues.

The 1997 delegates emphasized the need for more electronic communication from the National Office. A resolution designated that chapters "develop, promote and maintain electronic communication with current and perspective members, alumni, sections and chapters, the National Office and National Council." Each chapter was to develop, implement and maintain a chapter web page, chapter electronic mailing list, and electronic distribution list. The resolution recommended that the National Council establish standards for chapter and section websites and seek corporate sponsors to help fund the establishment and promotion of the national Mortar Board website. National President Mabel Gilbert Freeman (Ohio State, 1965) commented that "at the time we were living in two worlds—using the old

Mabel Freeman has been advisor, section coordinator, National Council member, and National President and now is vice president of the Board of Trustees. She, with her daughter Kirsten Freeman Fox, has endowed the Freeman-Fox Chapter Revitalization Fund. The Ohio State chapter was named in Mabel's honor in 2004.

ways of communicating and the new world of communicating through technology."[280]

Vickie Reed (Spelman College, 1996) was elected to fill the recently created second student representative spot on the National Council in 1997. She joined Jefferson Hancock (University of Georgia, 1995), who had been elected the year before.

The strategic plan adopted in 1997 by the National Council was designed to eventually add four permanent full-time positions to the National Office. The plan focused on (1) implementing leadership structural changes by 1999; (2) increasing revenues; (3) ensuring that collegiate chapters be vital, visible, and diverse with a strong local and national support system; (4) developing a national conference plan, including a financial strategy to ensure student leadership, chapter development, and Mortar Board governance; and (5) developing programs to maintain ongoing contact with alumni members. National President Freeman pointed out that by 1999 "the National

Council will have a slightly different look and the National Office will have a slightly larger staff."[281] A suggested change not adopted was replacing the section coordinator model with a chapter development team model.

Mortar Board celebrated its eightieth anniversary in 1998. The national conference that year emphasized planning for the future as well as remembering the Society's "impressive and meaningful past." Dr. Freeman emphasized the challenges that the organization faced as the new millennium approached, acknowledging that "this isn't your Mother's Mortar Board any more." She addressed the new challenges of operating a people-dependent voluntary organization in a constantly changing technological environment. The previously adopted 1997 strategic plan addressed the need for a new national organizational structure and the "issue of sufficient and involved advisors for the next millennium."[282]

The makeup of the National Council and position titles changed to national president, president-elect (a new position), vice president, secretary-treasurer, and four members-at-large (two student representatives and two alumni representatives). The executive director, the MBNF president, and the chair of the Conference Committee served as nonvoting, ex officio members of the National Council. This structure would remain for a while until the National Office took over the planning of the conference and the Conference Committee was disbanded, eliminating that position from the National Council. In February 2015 the immediate past president position was added to the National Council (the president of the MBNF was given vote as well as voice after a bylaws amendment adopted in February 2013).

The duties of the National Council shifted to a board with responsibilities for determining policy, and many of the tasks of volunteer alumni leadership positions were shifted to the expanding, though still small, staff of the National Office. Also sharing responsibility were several standing committees for alumni, chapter leadership, conference, expansion, finance, governance, membership, nominations, publications, and technology. Dana Viglietta (Otterbein University, 1995), coordinator of communications at the National Office, said that

the Strategic Plan recognizes Mortar Board's strong history and image as a respected honor society with a large alumni constituency. It addresses the challenges of nonprofit organizational budget constraints, a desire for increased visibility on campuses on a national scale, as well as a need to assess structural issues that will result in a better support to national and chapter levels.[283]

A new Mortar Board website was created in 1998 by Guy Ram (Ohio State, 1998), a National Office intern.[284] The website was "a resource for chapters to receive information and ideas as well as download and print off important forms that are due throughout the school year." It included a chapter directory, chapter resources, annual conference information, alumni information, publications awards, grants, and merchandise. All chapters that had a Mortar Board website of their own were encouraged to link their site to the national site. A resolution at the 1998 national conference urged every chapter to "make every effort to develop, promote, and maintain electronic communication with current and prospective members, Mortar Board alumni, Mortar Board sections and chapters and the National Council."[285] Chapters were also asked to develop a chapter web page, develop and use a chapter electronic mailing list and an electronic distribution list, and use electronic mail for the distribution of chapter meeting minutes. The National Council was asked to seek corporate sponsorship in establishing and promoting Mortar Board websites with a target of 50 percent of active chapters with a website by the year 2000.

Mortar Board Week took on special meaning as the eightieth anniversary took place in 1998. Alabama celebrated the week by publishing a sexual harassment brochure and placing it in all residence halls, cafeterias, and fraternity and sorority houses. Hope College celebrated by honoring its favorite professors with poems of appreciation and provided cookies and punch for academic departments across campus. Otterbein sponsored a roundtable discussion of Mortar Board alumni and raised money for Habitat for Humanity. Central Michigan celebrated Mortar Board Week by raising academic awareness throughout the campus community, posting a list of graduating seniors in the top 10 percent. The chapter also organized a "Guess the Average CMU G.P.A." competition, challenging students to identify the grade point average of all undergraduate students at the university. MacMurray College members wore their Mortar Board shirts and gave all faculty members a certificate of appreciation. Chatham College assisted alumni with a "Car Care for Women" workshop that was open to the entire Pittsburgh community.

In response to several past conference resolutions and recommendations to form a national alumni association, all alumni were contacted for the first time in Mortar Board's history. This was nicknamed the "Postcard Project" for the cost-saving (but not inexpensive) method of outreach. As responses came in, National Office staff updated the member's address and phone number and tracked willingness to participate. E-mail addresses were not collected. With an influx of connections with alumni, the National Alumni Sustaining Membership program was developed, and promotions blanketed Mortar Board and encouraged that membership was an opportunity to support "your collegiate chapter, a local chapter, or an alumni chapter."[286] The membership fee ($25 annually or $300 for a lifetime membership) was split among Mortar Board, Inc.; the MBNF; and the collegiate or alumni chapter of the member's choice. The program was intended to be especially attractive to alumni who resided where an alumni chapter did not exist.

The 1999 delegates replaced the previous national project, Learning Knows No Boundaries, with Reading Is Leading. The national project conference committee hoped that it would "serve as an umbrella over the tenets of community and campus involvement, and academic integrity"[287] as chapters sponsored programs to serve and increase visibility. As the millennium approached, Executive Director Selby reflected on the 1990s:

> Change has been the watchword of the '90s. It has been the only constant we have! A social climate now means fewer volunteer hours available to serve community or extracurricular organizations. There has been a roller-coaster ride for invested funds with a growth of 30% in 1999 and a decline of 6% in 2000. An explosion of electronic communications has almost made the art of letter writing obsolete and created an expectancy of instant response. The momentum of the millennium is clearly showing that people are our most important product.[288]

During this decade the size of the fellowships given by the MBNF grew, as did new funds for leadership development and service initiatives. A full-time financial development position was added to the National Office staff. The Career Network added over five hundred new graduate school or career mentors. It was clear that technology had revolutionized how the organization functioned. The computerization of records and other documents in the National Office and the change in communication methods and patterns were significant. There were 208 collegiate chapters, and the Society looked forward to its thirty-sixth national conference in the year 2000.

The early 2000s were filled with memorable events. The world stood still when hijacked airliners crashed into the World Trade Center, the Pentagon, and a field near Shanksville, Pennsylvania, on September 11, 2001. The same year, Apple computer unveiled the first iPod. The space shuttle *Columbia* broke apart during reentry, killing the seven astronauts on board. In 2004 one of the largest earthquakes ever recorded caused a tsunami that devastated South Asia, leaving over 230,000 dead. Young people were reading J. K. Rowling's first book of the Harry Potter series and listening to music by Justin Timberlake, Lady Gaga, and the Black Eyed Peas. Popular television shows in the early 2000s were the *West Wing* and *The Sopranos,* and later reality TV was trending. The *Twilight* movies broke box-office records. Facebook, created in 2003, and Twitter, created in 2006, quickly became popular methods for social networking.

After September 11, Mortar Board chapters across the nation showed their support. National President Barbara J. Arnold (Penn State, 1981) wrote in the *Forum:*

> I encourage you to take leadership roles in providing service to those affected by our national tragedies, in establishing forums where knowledge can be exchanged and ideas can be debated, and in embracing the diversity of our campus and communities where we live, study, work and pray.[289]

Mortar Board, Inc., and the MBNF cooperatively launched renewed efforts to further develop Mortar Board alumni and corporate support for chapter leadership programs and alumni benefits. The MBNF decided to retain an attorney to "look at the issues involved in corporate sponsorships, including the process to secure corporate sponsors and fundraising beyond charitable contributions and website restrictions." The Postcard Project initiated earlier reconnected over fifteen thousand alumni with Mortar Board. As Board of Trustees president, Gail Harrison Corvette announced in 2001 that "taking into account the value of the National Foundation funds plus new donations and pledges, the 'Million in the Millennium' milestone was passed!"[290]

Two new awards were announced at the 2001 national conference. The Ruth Weimer Mount Chapter Excellence Award was established to serve as the ultimate recognition in chapter achievement. Intended to memorialize past National President Ruth Weimer Mount (also past president of the MBNF Board of Trustees and of the ACHS), the annual award would be given to a chapter that lived up to her legendary service to Mortar Board. Student Representative Mark Kratina (Nebraska–Lincoln, 2000) worked with National Office staff member Julie Saker to draft the criteria of an "ideal" chapter, such as conducting an activity for the national project with at least 75 percent of chapter members participating, effective communications within the chapter, a current chapter website, and good financial standing.[291]

New website awards (Best Web Site, Most Improved Web Site, Best New Web Site) were added to the already established Outstanding Web Site Award to encourage chapters to use the Internet to publicize Mortar Board on campus. (The website awards were eliminated at the July 2008 National Council meeting, as the Internet as a showcase tool had become commonplace.)

At the 2001 conference the first Outstanding Alumni Chapter Award was presented to the Metropolitan Denver Alumni Chapter, which had celebrated its fiftieth anniversary in 2000 by raising over $6,000 for graduate fellowships for students in the Denver area. Two individual alumni awards were also established. The Alumni Achievement Award honored members who had demonstrated outstanding achievement in their profession or their career or were noted for outstanding community service, had shown a continuing commitment to Mortar Board's Ideals, and were outstanding role models for collegiate members. Eligible alumni must be between five and forty years from their undergraduate degree. The Distinguished Lifetime Membership honored alumni who had retained collegiate or alumni connections or contacts with Mortar Board, demonstrated outstanding community or campus service on a national or international level, and epitomized the true meaning of "lifetime of service." The only age requirement was that "substantial years had passed" since graduation.

Mortar Board engaged in long-range planning many times during its history in an attempt to identify and anticipate changing needs. An ad hoc committee on long-range planning had proposed a ten-year plan in 1980. This led to the thirty-six recommendations of 1983, and the delegates in 1985 adopted many of them. Another strategic planning effort was mounted in 1996 to develop new approaches to maximize the Society's purpose with particular emphasis on the internal operations of Mortar Board, Inc. This plan was adopted in 1997 and eventually led to the implementation of a new national organizational structure that included the creation of the president-elect position on the National Council. The new position of president-elect provided by the new plan made the transition to the next president smoother and more efficient. Dr. Arnold remembered that "I served as the first president-elect under the new leadership structure so there was no question that I would become president. I think that the idea of a term as president-elect and a term as president is much more manageable for a volunteer structure. I felt the need to begin to define the role of president-elect."[292]

When National Council members met at the beginning of the new decade, they continued to debate some of the issues that had been identified by past strategic plans. Some of the issues in the 1997 plan were put into recommendations for the 2001 national conference agenda. These included removing the position of conference chair from the National Council and placing the responsibility for planning the national conference in the National Office; removing certain standing committees except Nominations and Governance from the constitution, bylaws, and standing rules; and hiring a development officer for the MBNF. Increases in the National Office staffing reflected the need to centralize the increasing volume of work and to transfer daily tasks from volunteers.

Thirty members of Mortar Board, Inc., and the MBNF met in Columbus, Ohio, in January 2002 for more planning. Six issues were identified, and small groups developed action plans to "guide initial response to these significant issues." The issues were a consistent national project, alumni development, conferences and timing, sustaining the quality of Mortar Board chapters, National Office staffing, and conference design, content and purpose.[293] By 2003 the goal was "to position Mortar Board as the premier honor society for college students whose members, both past and present, want to be actively involved." Increasing the number of new members, alumni participation, funding, and visibility were identified as ways to achieve this goal. A chart was developed outlining how these objectives were to be met that listed who was responsible, when they were to be completed, and the success measures needed to accomplish the objectives. One result of these actions was to emphasize the need to strengthen chapters by funding chapter projects and by concentrating more time at national conferences in leadership development. Chapter advisors were strongly encouraged to attend national conferences, and special programming was initiated for them.

The use of technology increased significantly in many areas of Mortar Board operations in the early 2000s. The website was enlarged and updated, and the latest applications were used to make it easier for collegiate chapters to fill out reports. All National Council members and section coordinators now communicated electronically. The National Council met monthly by conference call, and this increased the efficiency of transacting the Society's business and led to more timely and productive decision making. National funds were conserved, since travel was reduced.

This increase in electronic connections made the need for a national privacy policy apparent, and a policy was adopted in 2002 to "protect members and visitors using the Mortar Board web pages." The privacy policy stated the type of information Mortar Board collected and included other ways in which information could be gathered (such as clicking on the links included on the site). The policy also clearly described how the information was used.[294]

The 2002 national conference was held in Tampa, Florida, where Purdue's Barbara Cook chapter became the first to be awarded the newly developed Ruth Weimer Mount Chapter Excellence Award.

The national project that began in 1932 (with the theme of personnel, or vocational guidance) continued throughout the years so that all chapters nationally could engage in a program that had a common theme. Subsequent themes such as educating the campus for world government (1946), AIDS (1989), children's concerns (1995), and literacy (1998) are examples of topics that concerned collegiate members over time. The practice of designating a different topic at each conference, however, decreased the time available to search for project funding. Delegates to the 2003 conference in Columbus, Ohio, adopted Reading Is Leading as the national project and made it permanent so that long-term funding could be sought. Chapters began organizing service projects associated with the new national project. The requirement that a chapter conduct a Reading Is Leading project each year was reduced to an encouragement in January 2015 by vote of the delegation at the special national conference.

Michigan members read to children of married housing students to allow parents a night of Christmas shopping. Duquesne collected books on campus and from businesses in the downtown Pittsburgh area and distributed them to urban schools. The University of Tennessee at Chattanooga involved the entire campus in its book drive by holding a competition among various campus organizations and educational departments. The group donating the most books was rewarded with a plaque, a pizza party, and considerable recognition. Patricia Vasquez (Monmouth College, 2001) used Reading Is Leading as a basis for her senior honors project. She held a community book fair for over two hundred children who had their photo taken with Clifford the Dog, and more than $4,000 in books were donated to a local library. The national organization formalized a partnership with the Library of Congress, joining eighty other nonprofit organizations that focused on reading and literature programs.

Other chapter programs and service projects reported during the first part of the decade represented a variety of interests. Illinois State started an organ donation campaign and volunteered with Habitat for Humanity. The Purdue chapter celebrated its seventy-fifth anniversary at its annual Mortar Board Leadership Conference, which the chapter hosted for three hundred students on an icy Saturday in January. Faculty, staff, and local community leaders were the speakers. Stetson University completed a service project at a home for recovering drug-addicted mothers and their children. To help local foster children with their transition from home to home, Western New England College provided gently used suitcases, duffel bags, and totes packed with toiletries, stuffed animals, and children's books. Converse College regularly sponsored a symposium called PROBE where a topic relevant to the college community was explored. The 2001 chapter selected the issue of domestic violence and "hoped these efforts would help recognize the problem, identify the resources to escape from the problem, and provide the incentive to prevent the problem from perpetuating."[295]

The chapters that received chapter project grants from the MBNF in 2003 were involved in a wide array of outstanding service initiatives. Many chapters focused on Reading Is Leading. Northern Arizona hosted the Holiday Book Drive, which had campus residence halls competing to donate the most books; the winners earned a pizza party. The Rowan chapter invited campus and community members to participate in the Walk for Literacy, with participants donating a book. Michigan State charged admission of one children's book for a benefit concert to support the local hospital's pediatric ward. The South Florida chapter created a storybook forest for elementary students in the botanical gardens. Drama and educational clubs performed stories in the setting. The San Diego State University chapter received the Ruth Weimer Mount Chapter of Excellence Award in 2003.

The national news in the early part of the decade publicized the unacceptable behavior on the part of business executives, politicians, clergy, and others. A Gallup poll in 2004 indicated that over 80 percent of Americans thought that the country's moral values were fair or poor. Educators were calling for an active dialogue on the issue of increasing academic dishonesty on campuses. An important topic at the 2004 national conference was how to reduce cheating and plagiarism through a new honor code movement. In response to this issue, the delegates voted to join a national project, "A Matter of Ethics," led by the ACHS, and the "Matter of Ethics" statement proffered by the ACHS was adopted in 2005. A three-year effort "to promote, encourage and strengthen our commitment to ethical behavior" was detailed in a conference resolution:

> Mortar Board supports and encourages promising students as they strive to meet their full potential as future leaders, and knows that such potential is found not on the surface of a person, where the worthy goals of achievement and knowledge shine brightly for all to see, but rather can only be reached by building upon the core of one's character, by encouraging honesty, trustworthiness, integrity . . . [and] ethics.[296]

Denise Rode served as National President and as president of the Board of Trustees of the MBNF and continues as chapter advisor at her alma mater. A fund founder, she has also inspired her chapter to create an endowment in the MBNF.

Chapters were urged to promote ethics on their campuses, and examples of activities to incorporate into their programs were detailed in the *Forum*.

National President Denise L. Rode (Northern Illinois, 1971) recalled the changing nature of college students and the influence on Mortar Board:

There was a broader mix of students [in higher education], including growing numbers of transfers, nontraditional, and commuter students. Also, fewer faculty and administrators were willing to advise chapters. . . . More demands on students, increasing costs of higher education, students working more so they could afford school, students perhaps not seeing as much value in an organization such as Mortar Board, and perhaps not as willing to make a commitment to active membership in an honor society like Mortar Board—all of these were issues we faced in the early years of this century. A proliferation of other types of honor societies, ones that you could just join and not really have to be active, also influenced higher education at that time.[297]

This decline in interest in honor societies was universal (even the acceptance of membership in Phi Beta Kappa declined). The National Council's response to this issue was to examine what made Mortar Board unique and what value it had for each student member. (This had also been an issue in the 1970s, when students questioned the value of college activities in general.) Several actions were taken, including a move to strengthen chapters through the Leadership Initiatives Fund.

The MBNF's relationship with Mortar Board, Inc., was strengthened at the 2004 conference when it specifically located its "fundraising and grant programs" at the National Office. This was done to give credibility to the MBNF and for legal and tax purposes. The Outstanding Member Award was established at the suggestion of Student Representative Chris Sandles (Texas Tech, 2002). The award was created to "honor one member from each chapter who has given exemplary service to the chapter and has upheld the ideals of scholarship, leadership, and service in a manner that merits recognition at the national level." Dr. Rode hoped that the chapter member selected for this award would embody the concept of "servant-leader," a selfless leader rather than a self-aggrandizing one.[298]

Mortar Board chapter annual reports in 2004 showed that 5,988 collegiate members contributed nearly thirty thousand hours of service to their communities. Members dedicated the greatest number of hours to Reading Is Leading projects, followed by participation in national cancer research benefits and Hurricane Katrina relief.[299] Grinnell collected books, supplies, and money to send to a remote village school in South Africa. Ohio University, Purdue, and Wisconsin–Eau Claire raised funds for the Hurricane Katrina disaster. Ohio State attempted to break the world record for the largest pillow fight to raise funds for pancreatic cancer. Evansville contributed eighteen gift boxes to the Operation Christmas Gift Boxes for Children program. SUNY at Buffalo[300] worked with a local runaway/homeless shelter to provide youths in need with warm blankets and donated fifteen hundred books to the shelter library. Hood College provided children from the community with an opportunity to participate in a safe Halloween, with games, snacks, and a costume contest. The children were also escorted through the dormitories for trick-or-treat and enjoyed a reading corner where Mortar Board members read scary stories. Kansas State was awarded the Ruth Weimer Mount Chapter Excellence Award that year.

The MBNF celebrated its fiftieth anniversary at the 2005 conference in Columbus, Ohio, and was recognized for its outstanding contributions to collegiate members and the Society. Over the years its purpose broadened from providing fellowships to Mortar Board alumni pursuing graduate and professional degrees to granting funds to active chapters for special projects that enhanced their campus and community. The 2005 delegates voted to lower the allocation of new member dues to the MBNF fellowship fund from 6 percent to 2 percent, with the other 4 percent remaining in the Mortar Board, Inc., Leadership Initiatives Fund. The delegates also elected the first man,

William (Bill) Niederer (Indiana State University, 1983), as National President. Oklahoma State won the Ruth Weimer Mount Chapter Excellence Award.

The Historical Planning Committee was created by Executive Director Selby in 2005 to raise awareness of the impending centennial of Mortar Board, encourage chapters to collect and maintain their own local histories, and begin collecting historical information about Mortar Board that would later be put into a commemorative book. The original committee consisted of Ohio State members Martha Nichols Tykodi (1951), Mary Lou Nichols Fairall (1956), and Joan Slattery Wall (1988). As the years progressed, members were added to and left the committee. The vision materialized that there should be a book that would not only detail the history of the organization but also serve as a reference for those interested in how the growth of an honor society reflected historical issues and events and influenced higher education. The name of this committee would adjust over time until it became known as the Historical Publication Steering Committee. This book is its product.

In keeping with this historical perspective, past National President Niederer summed up his twenty years of working with Mortar Board:

There have been many changes—the advent of the National Office's fax machine, toll-free telephone number, first computer, the establishment of the Web site and National Office email, the restructuring of the national leadership positions and the National Office staff, and of course, all the exciting new faces in our chapters who are now alumni members.[301]

The 2006 delegates, meeting in Columbus, were urged to update their chapter histories in anticipation of the coming centennial publication. The University of San Diego, the first private institution, was awarded the fifth Ruth Weimer Mount Chapter Excellence Award.

Bill Niederer was the first man to serve as National President. His term began in 2005, and he brought a vast amount of experience as section coordinator and National Council member. Bill is known for his attention to detail and for running meetings effectively. He is a lifetime member of the MBAA and a generous donor to the MBNF.

A committee was appointed to address the "current selection model endorsed by Mortar Board nationally." A survey at the 2007 national conference found that only 50 percent of the chapters used the "Selection by Consensus" method for selection. Other chapters used a combination or something completely different. It was considered important to make the selection process as uniform as possible from chapter to chapter so that the strong values and standards of Mortar Board would be upheld. The committee observed that the selection process should be "stronger, more agreeable to chapters, more uniform, and more inclusive."[302] Five "enhancement" recommendations along with supporting reasons were offered: (1) reduce the required percentage for candidate approval from 80 percent to 60 percent, (2) expand the current role of the membership selection committee, (3) allow for a blind selection process, (4) create a mandatory selection instruction document, and (5) adjust the time schedule for voting. A task force was appointed to study how to simplify the process.[303]

The retirement of Diane Selby as executive director in 2007 marked an important milestone for the Society. After twenty years, she was the longest-serving paid staff person in Mortar Board. Her contributions and dedication of talent are legendary and were celebrated with a special program at the 2007 conference. The MBNF named a fellowship fund in her honor.

The University of Nebraska–Lincoln was the 2007 recipient of the Ruth Weimer Mount Chapter of Excellence.

The new executive director, Jon Cook, who had relocated from Texas, was hired by a search committee of volunteers. He told the *Forum* that a goal was advancing Mortar Board technologically so that the "ease and frequency of sharing information with current members, advisors, alumni and partners can build on the capacity of what the society is already valued for—actively involved people." The *Forum* editor noted that "although not monumental in the eyes of the rest of the world, [it is monumental for Mortar Board that] the first male national president completed his term in July 2007 and the first male executive director was hired in January 2007."[304]

As required by the new federal Sarbanes-Oxley law, a conflict of interest statement was approved in 2007 indicating "that all staff and volunteers scrupulously avoid any conflict of interest (perceived or actual) between the interests of Mortar Board, and their personal, professional, and business interests."[305] This policy required that all Mortar Board professional and volunteer participants sign a conflict of interest statement every year. Discussions about a memorandum of agreement between Mortar Board, Inc., and the MBNF about the way the two nonprofits would manage investments and resources were begun in 2008. This agreement was completed and signed by National President Daniel (Dan) J. Turner (Northern Illinois, 1994) in January 2010. A new Chapter Endowment Program was established in 2009 in the MBNF for donors or chapters to create an endowment in the MBNF to benefit a collegiate chapter.

The University of Wyoming was awarded the Ruth Weimer Mount Chapter Excellence Award at the 2008 national conference. A task force was appointed to follow a 2008 conference resolution for a national alumni program to "consistently involve alumni at all levels of leadership and service and develop an executable plan to support such an initiative."[306] The 2009 conference was held in Chicago, where the MBNF awarded forty-seven chapter grants and also twelve fellowships totaling $40,000. A new initiative, "Ten in Ten," was announced by the National Council with a goal of increasing new member applications by 10 percent in 2010. "Membership 101" sessions were held to make chapters stronger and more viable. The University of Washington became the Ruth Weimer Mount Chapter Excellence Award recipient.

Jon Cook resigned as Mortar Board's third executive director less than two years after his hiring, and the responsibilities for maintaining the National Office in the interim were placed in the capable hands of Associate Executive Director Megan McGough Stevens (Ohio State, 2003).

Alumni Representative Jane M. Beyer (University of Wisconsin–Milwaukee, 1980) chaired the committee conducting a nationwide search for a new executive director. After interviewing candidates at

Jane Hamblin became executive director following the short tenure of Jon Cook. Jane brought with her to the position experience as a student affairs professional, a Mortar Board advisor, and an association executive.

the National Office, the committee recommended that the National Council hire Jane A. Hamblin (Purdue, 1973), who became Mortar Board's fifth executive director in November 2009. National President Turner said that "Jane has a rich understanding of higher education, nonprofit organizations, fundraising, team-building and Mortar Board. She brings to her new role a mix of practical experience in and joyful enthusiasm for Mortar Board." Ms. Hamblin had been advisor to the Barbara Cook chapter at Purdue for fifteen years and had both student affairs and higher education association backgrounds.

Mortar Board in the 2010s

As the second decade of the new century dawned, Mortar Board chapters continued to create their own unique approaches to service and leadership. To celebrate Reading Is Leading, Bowling Green gave a living book presentation by acting scenes from the book while children read along with enlarged words on projection screens. Colorado College tutored students at a community middle school. Los Angeles mayor Antonio Villaraigosa honored UCLA for its "devoted service and outstanding contributions to the Los Angeles community."[307] Hood College sponsored a fund-raising dodge ball tournament and was able to donate two hundred books to needy children in the community. Ohio Northern recognized faculty with a Favorite Professors Dessert. Hope College hosted a Thanksgiving dinner for international students. Northern Illinois helped form a new local alumni chapter. Kansas State worked with members from other chapters in the section to assemble more than twenty-five hundred bags of food to be given to needy local grade school students. Many chapters wrote letters to U.S. military personnel stationed abroad or in the United States, created care packages for them, or stuffed backpacks for children of active-duty service members.

The National Council, section coordinators, the Board of Trustees, and National Office staff held a strategic planning session in January 2010 in Chicago, facilitated by Kathy Cleveland Bull (Bowling Green, 1982). National President Turner indicated that the five-year strategic plan would lead Mortar Board to its centennial in 2018 and urged chapters to create their own strategic plan. The national plan included five main goals:

1. Create a unified culture of lifetime membership.
2. Develop a long-term strategy for financial stability at the local and national levels.
3. Enhance governance, administration, and operations.
4. Build strong relationships and enhance connections by observing and adapting to generational and demographic trends
5. Establish recognition, enthusiasm, and loyalty for the Mortar Board brand.[308]

Executive Director Hamblin, Section Coordinator Kathryn E. (Katie) Chick (Hood, 2006), and Alumni Representative Bridget Williams Golden (Purdue, 1997) were declared "Keepers of the Strategic Plan" with the responsibility of reviewing roles and monitoring the path forward. Current and former national leaders were appointed to a planning team for each of the goals, and timelines were set for five years.

A new training program for chapter advisors, Leadership Excellence and Advisor Development (LEAD), was introduced at the forty-sixth national conference in Chicago in 2010. Past National President Sally Steadman (University of Wyoming, 1968), an advising award winner and a member of the LEAD faculty, said that

during that time honor societies began to face the challenges of decreased membership, declining chapter numbers, and rising financial obligations. To help chapters meet these challenges we established the Leadership Excellence and Advisor Development (LEAD) training that recognizes the critical role that advisors play in the success of a collegiate chapter.[309]

LEAD is a certification program that helps advisors effectively advise the collegiate chapter's leadership team by learning, for example, the "best practices in student organization advisement with topics including fundraising, member motivation, conflict resolution, and risk management." The program is held during the summer national conference and includes a course of instruction and a workbook as well as access for a year to the LEAD website. Initiating this program emphasizes Mortar Board's support "for the important role of advising and helps give advisors the tools to make their advising experience a rich and rewarding one."[310]

Hope College was awarded the Ruth Weimer Mount Chapter Excellence Award at the 2010 conference.

An important tradition in Mortar Board's history was brought up to date in 2011 when the National Council approved a change in the poem "The Torch" to make it gender neutral. The change had been suggested by former National Council member and past MBNF president Barbara Cook, who always read "The Torch" at the Purdue chapter's initiation (a chapter that was named for her in 1987) with a gender-neutral substitution in the second stanza. So,

Caught up the torch as it smoldered, and lifted it high again,
Till, fanned by the winds of heaven, it fired the souls of men.

became

Caught up the torch as it smoldered, and lifted it high and tall,
'Till fanned by the winds of heaven, it fired the souls of all.

Concerned by intimations of typical postinitiation conduct at one chapter, the National Council, with Alumni Representative Bridget Williams Golden taking a lead role, adopted the "Policy on the Dignity and Worth of Members and Prospective Members" in March 2011, which declared expectations for chapter behavior:

> As leaders on their campuses and in their communities, Mortar Board members are expected to model civil behavior that is always congruent with Mortar Board's ideals of scholarship, leadership and service. Implicit in Mortar Board's Purpose is an emphasis on the dignity and worth of every person. Consequently, it is incomprehensible that a chapter or a subset of chapter members would conduct an activity that might demean, endanger, embarrass, or debilitate a member or prospective member regardless of the person's willingness to participate. In the unlikely event that this kind of activity occurs, the Mortar Board National Council shall: Declare the chapter to be below minimum standards for operation, place the chapter on probation for one year, and subsequently after review, may recommend the chapter for disaffiliation. The National Council may consider only the recommendation of the college or university's president, chief student affairs officer or chief academic affairs officer to forestall this course of action.[311]

The 2011 national conference began with an emergency when the manager of the Chicago Marriott O'Hare met Assistant Executive Director Stevens at the curb of his completely darkened hotel on the early evening of the day before load-in. He revealed that flooding caused by torrential rains had made the property uninhabitable. Fortunately, the Marriott organization had arranged to "walk" Mortar Board to the just-opened J. W. Marriott Hotel in Chicago's Loop! Unfortunately, there had been no time to notify Ms. Stevens, much less anyone else.

The National Office staff, under Ms. Stevens's instruction, flew into action while they themselves were traveling to Chicago. Through e-mail, text, and phone calls, nearly everyone learned of the new—and very upscale—location (the Lincoln Suite was rated at $5,000 a night). Almost everyone else was intercepted at the O'Hare bus/shuttle center or the drowned hotel and redirected downtown at the Marriott's expense. (One presenter who had a cell phone but didn't believe in turning it on could not be reached. He eventually found his way.) Remarkably, the opening of the conference was not delayed or interrupted.

The University of California–Los Angeles was awarded the Ruth Weimer Mount Chapter Excellence Award at this memorable conference.

National President Turner had appointed a small group of National Council members to explore Mortar Board's practice of paying for all conference delegates' travel. President-elect Susan Herndon Caples (Alabama, 2006) chaired the committee of MBNF Representative Sally Steadman, Student Representative Vicente (Vinny) Gonzalez (Cornell, 2010), and Ms. Stevens. At the National Council meeting during the conference, their initial findings were presented, including that no other honor societies paid for conferees' travel. Concerns were that attendance would be reduced, chapters farther away from a conference site were hit harder, not all institutions could supply travel support from the dean's office or student government, and chapters were already paying a conference fee of $225 (it had been raised from $200 just the year before).

By the September 2011 meeting section coordinators had been invited to give their opinions, and the National Council fleshed out a plan to provide travel hardship stipends in larger measure to help chapters that needed time to budget for the travel expense. In October, with Susan Caples as National President, the National Council voted (by e-mail) to increase the conference fee by $25 to $250 and place a limit per delegate on travel funds to the 2012 conference of $250 for air travel or $100 for mileage, bus, or train. Chapters were encouraged to fund travel without asking for this subsidy. Vice President Brian Bock (Valparaiso University, 2004) and Ms. Stevens conferred with section coordinators to discuss the ways they could promote this information to chapter leaders. In spite of worry over the decision to cap travel funding, the number of delegates registered was up two over the previous year. Requests for travel reimbursements were manageable. Conference travel expense at the end of the 2012 fiscal year was $19,348, compared to $73,834 the previous year.[312] Clearly, the National Council had made a good decision.

A special use of Mortar Board's history was made in 2012 when Judy Wu, professor of history and women's studies at Ohio State, used the Society's collection in the university archives as a basis for a class assignment. After hearing a presentation by Executive Director Hamblin and historian Virginia N. Gordon (Ohio State, 1948), Prof. Wu's students were oriented to the university archives and specifically the Mortar Board collection. The course assignment asked students to take a period of history of interest to them and record the entire content of each issue of the *Mortar Board Quarterly* during that time. In addition to teaching the students how to use the archives, a comprehensive, searchable index of the *Quarterly* was created.

Chapters sponsored many interesting service projects during this time. Kansas State hosted a potluck dinner for the residents of a government housing unit that partnered with the city's mental health facility. Northern Michigan participated in a living history project at an assisted living residence by interviewing individual residents so that memory books could be organized and published for their families. The University of Tennessee at Knoxville logged many hours of reading for Recording for the Blind and Dyslexic, Inc.

To create more opportunities for meaningful program delivery, the National Council held Mortar Board's first special national conference virtually by telephone conference call in April 2012. The special national conference was viewed as a way to redirect precious time at the physical national conference to optimize the programming for new chapter leaders. Governance issues and elections of National Council members (except the student representative) would be stripped from the physical conference and moved to the special national conference. The conference was also an opportunity for chapter leaders who had met face-to-face at the national conference to get reacquainted—if only by phone.

Ms. Caples, the second honorary member to be National President, convened the special national conference with a discussion about three proposed amendments to the bylaws that had been made available to chapters earlier by e-mail. The proposed amendments concerned removing the membership fee from the bylaws, deferring active service by collegiate members such as those who were studying abroad or otherwise off campus, and adding the term "gender expression" to the nondiscrimination clause. The special national conference was held in three sessions on a Thursday night, a Saturday afternoon, and a Sunday night in April; a chapter need only be represented at one of the sessions, as the content was repeated three times. Attendance was greater than had been anticipated. Altogether, more than one-third of collegiate chapters were represented on the call, which was promising for a first try at a virtual gathering. (The second special national conference saw just under half of chapters participating, while the third saw 64 percent participation, the fourth in 2015 67 percent, and the fifth 66 percent.) Following the last session, one delegate from each eligible chapter

could vote on the amendments electronically (using SurveyMonkey). The results were declared through the *LeadingLeaders* e-newsletter.[313]

In spite of the ease of voting online and with nearly two weeks to cast a ballot, the number of chapters failing to vote remained of concern to the National Office staff. A low of 79 chapters actually cast a ballot in the first year, 2012; the high was 110 in 2014. This does not appear to be issue-driven. To counter the potential problems wrought by failing to secure a majority of votes, the authors of the *Bylaws of Mortar Board, Inc.,* in 2008 had added "The lack of a vote counts as an affirmative vote."[314]

The removal of the actual amount of the membership fee from the bylaws was momentous, as it allowed the National Council to set the fee instead of waiting for a vote of the delegation. It is considered a best practice of nonprofit organizations that decisions on membership fees or dues be the purview of the governing board, and this change, while not favored by all delegates, passed with a comfortable majority. The fee was $75 at the time, and the National Council raised the fee to $80 but not until nearly two years had passed.

The MBNF, coming off a successful challenge opportunity supported by Gail Harrison Corvette, who had matched all donations to the Gail Harrison Corvette Leadership Development Endowment up to $5,000, decided to start a challenge of their own, each pledging their own funds to match gifts to the MBNF. On a motion by Trustee Martha (Marty) L. Starling (Kansas State, 1965), the board voted that for "every $2 donated there will be a $1 match made" from trustees'

National President Susan Herndon Caples presides over her first conference in 2012. Chapter advisor and honorary member, Susan is the mother of two Mortar Boards, Jay (Vanderbilt, 2006) and Rob (Auburn, 2008) Herndon. Susan is a fund founder.

Since beginning it in 2010, Mortar Board members have presented LEAD eleven times and certified more than 170 advisors from twenty honor societies, institutions, and programs with the Certified Organization Advisor credential.

personal gifts, up to $10,000.[315] The funds would be used to support advisors to attend the national conference and otherwise participate in advisor sessions and the LEAD program. All in all the Trustee Challenge raised $15,000, which allowed for advisor scholarships for the next four conferences.

During the presidency of Sally Steadman the MBNF was beginning to formulate its role as a backer for the long-term success of Mortar Board, Inc. The generosity of the trustees during this time was never more needed or appreciated by the staff of the National Office—and by the chapter operations that benefited directly.

The Mortar Board Alumni Association (MBAA) was launched in 2012 at the national conference, again in Chicago, with the purpose of "connecting alumni distinctly and formally." The MBAA's intent was to extend "the legacy and tradition of the society beyond the collegiate experience to encompass Mortar Board's quarter-of-a-million alumni."[316] The purpose of the MBAA is displayed on a beautifully engrossed charter that hangs in the National Office:

Whereas, Mortar Board alumnae and alumni have led the Society since its founding in 1918;

Whereas, the value of Mortar Board extends beyond college;

Whereas, members deserve a network for making meaningful worldwide connections with one another throughout their lives; and

Whereas, we desire a means to encourage members to demonstrate the Society's Ideals long past initiation and to ensure the endurance of the Mortar Board experience for future generations;

Now be it known, that we, the Charter Members, on this Twenty First day of July, Two Thousand Twelve do hereby establish the Mortar Board Alumni Association.

One hundred six charter members' names, listed according to the time of entry, appear on the scroll. Fifty-one chapters are represented among the charter members; Purdue had the most, with eighteen. Charter member no. 1 is Doris Finnie (University of Denver, 1940), whose Alumni Committee made headway on the idea of an alumni association in the late 1990s.

The first chapter to become a repeat winner of the Ruth Weimer Mount Chapter Excellence Award was San Diego State University in 2012.

The second special national conference was held in January 2013, with National President Caples presiding. Collegiate chapter representatives along with members of the National Council, section coordinators, and National Office staff reviewed nine proposed amendments to the bylaws. Among the proposed amendments were those concerning the MBAA and timing for future bylaws amendments.[317] Another amendment proposed giving the MBNF president a vote on the National Council based on the rationale that the two Mortar Board, Inc., representatives could vote on matters before the MBNF Board of Trustees.

The MBAA was launched in 2012, with 106 charter members whose names appear on a beautiful scroll framed in the National Office.

A new alumni award, the Emerging Leader Award, was established in 2013 to recognize extraordinary Mortar Board alumni who are within fifteen years (later twenty) of their graduation, have demonstrated exceptional achievement in their careers, and are noted for outstanding community service.

In August 2013 in a discussion led by National President Marty Starling about declining revenues from paid initiates, the National Council discussed in earnest an increase in the membership fee from $75 to $80 (ODK's fee was $70, and Phi Kappa Phi's fee was $50). Student Representative Christopher Shulman (Texas Tech, 2013) reported that he and his class were "surprised" at the size of Mortar Board's fee compared to the fees of similar institutions. Alumni Representatives Clay Mingus and Paula Stuettgen (Wisconsin–Eau Claire, 1976) debated the possibility of spreading out the fee over the member's active year. MBNF representative (and past National President) Sally Steadman shared that the Society had been forced to increase fees the last time by $15 (from $60 to $75) because the National Council had waited too long to get the delegates to vote for smaller incremental jumps. Paid initiate numbers declined the next year.[318] At the September meeting, National President Starling said that "based on the 2012 consumer price index it would appear an increase in dues to $80.06 would be appropriate."[319] The motion to increase the membership fee from $75 to $80 passed unanimously.[320]

Service projects continued to be an important part of Mortar Board chapter programs. Louisville volunteered for an event that encouraged members of the community with disabilities to participate in different sporting events (power soccer, basketball, rowing) after watching paralympians demonstrate them. Hawaii volunteered to assist with the

Honolulu Pet Walk and help with the Zen Pet Massage Booth, the Pet and Pet-Parent Photobooth, and parking for three thousand pet-parents.

A continuing concern expressed at National Council meetings was about declining member numbers and chapters that were experiencing problems. The number of students declining offers of membership led to a discussion about the current generation of students and how they are different from those in the past. There was a discussion about the relevance of Mortar Board in this time of digital students, a decline of campus life, and a "new tribalism." Chapter advisor and section coordinator support was emphasized, as were ways to strengthen these ties. National Council and section coordinator visits were assigned to particular problem chapters. Since declining numbers had a negative effect on the amount of revenue received, generating solutions for making up the shortfall was viewed as imperative.

A related topic concerned "defunct chapters" that were inactive for a long time and campuses where Mortar Board had lost contact over the years. President-elect Abby Diehl (Penn State, 1995) conducted a detailed study. She determined that of the 230 chapters that Mortar Board installed, 43, or nearly 19 percent, were no longer active. These included 9 whose charter had been revoked by Mortar Board, 1 that had withdrawn, 6 that were inactive, and 27 that were defunct. Among the causes for chapters to become inactive were lack of institutional support, poor advisor support, weak student leadership, lapse in selection of new members, and a poor institutional fit with Mortar Board (such as a commuter campus where students do not attend evening meetings or do not have a strong culture of participation in student organizations).

Important factors to examine when considering efforts to reestablish a defunct chapter were discussed and included reviewing the chapter's history, its previous success, and institutional fit with Mortar Board. The best results when trying to revitalize an inactive chapter had come by working through the student affairs staff on a campus. The defunct chapters to be targeted for revitalization were identified, and a team to work with each chapter was formed, with each team's progress monitored regularly.

Another concern was the uneven number of chapters in the twenty-five national sections that made the work of section coordinators uneven (one had four chapters while another had fifteen, for example). To rectify this disparity the sections were reorganized to twenty-one, with ten chapters in most sections.

In 2010, the National Office staff researched and, with special approval of the National Council, purchased web-based software that would help manage the operations of the Society. Through patient development by manager of data and member services Tracey Fox, this software (netFORUM Pro) allowed for more than a quarter of a million member records, formerly in Access, to be stored and manipulated for other office functions. The staff used the software to sort addresses for development and publication mailings and online registrations for the national conference. In 2013, the software had been massaged to the point that new members could pay their membership fee online with a credit card. Sophisticated communications sent by e-mail to newly tapped members presented the link to the payment site. This improved the promptness and efficiency of payment, since it eliminated the need for chapters to collect the initiation fees as a group.

From small gifts to Mortar Board, Inc., by chapters and others, Executive Director Hamblin created a "Pay It Forward Fund" that could be used to help additional delegates attend national conferences. Hawaii offered a donation and suggested that the name be changed to the Kokua (helping or pitching in) Fund. This was approved by the National Council.

The forty-ninth national conference was held in August 2013 in Atlanta with 266 registrants, who included collegiate participants,

The 2013 national conference saw the first Emerging Leader awards go to public relations expert Maureen Kaiser Richmond (far left, Purdue, 1996) and community activist Joseph Lee (far right, Northwestern, 2008) and the Alumni Achievement Awards to (center, left to right) marketing consultant Steven Biondolillo (Boston University, 1976), actor Marion Ross (San Diego State, 1965), and marketing expert Julie Eddleman (Purdue, 1991). Julie also presented the Capstone Leadership Lecture.

advisors, national leaders, and alumni. Since the purpose of the annual conference changed from governing the Society to a program for leadership development of collegiate members, slimmed-down governance was the choice of the National Council. The MBAA Alumni Summit was held concurrently again with the conference, and lively discussion and valuable programs were well received, although the numbers were small. The Ohio State University chapter was awarded the Ruth Weimer Mount Chapter Excellence Award at the 2013 conference. John Mount had seconded the chapter's nomination.

The 2014 special national conference was conducted by National President Starling via conference calls to review eight bylaws amendments. The first was to clarify that any member who was still working on a baccalaureate degree was eligible to continue as a collegiate member. Other changes were made to clarify the membership status of alumni and that honorary members must have at least the baccalaureate degree. Chapter participation in the national project Reading Is Leading was made optional. The term "audit" was removed to allow for an annual financial review that cost less, and the procedure for transferring funds when a collegiate or alumni chapter became inactive was clarified. With 110 chapters voting via SurveyMonkey over a two-week period, all amendments carried.

Since its last revision was in 2007, the section coordinator's job description required changes. A draft to update the position included a deliberate ordering of responsibilities and the use of broader categories to make it easier to fix when specific components of the role changed. The new document gave guidance on reasonable time frames for responding to and communicating with chapters. Benefits to section coordinators were also noted, such as the opportunity to continue professional development through a national leadership role and to support and contribute to the success of some of the most dedicated and talented college students in the United States. A mentoring program by experienced section coordinators was developed to orient and bring on board new coordinators as part of their initial training. The title of section coordinator emerita/us was established to honor those section coordinators who served in that capacity and other offices for many years and were retiring permanently from it and other formal national positions. Other criteria cited were being a role model for other section coordinators as well as donating generously to Mortar Board.[321] Glenda Guyton (Carson-Newman University, 1974) was retiring from the national scene after forty years of involvement and so was named section coordinator emerita (she remains an advisor at Alabama).

A brief message was approved by the National Council in June 2013 to be used as a guideline whenever a brief description of Mortar Board was needed. The approved language was

Mortar Board is the premier national honor society for college seniors. Every year new members are selected on the ideals of scholarship, leadership and service. With over 200 chapters across the nation, Mortar Board encourages members to develop leadership skills and take advantage of their newfound connections while serving their alma mater. Membership in Mortar Board is life-long with an alumni association where members network and provide leadership opportunities on campuses and communities that impact society both locally and globally.[322]

Student Representative Brandon Caten (South Alabama, 2010) offered a more "youthful" version to the National Council as well.

The fiftieth national conference was held in Atlanta in August 2014 with 280 participants. The awards program included those for chapter, advisors, and alumni. The delegates elected the new student representative to the National Council, and the chapters at the University of Nebraska at Kearney and Purdue University (which had been the first recipient in 2002) tied for the Ruth Weimer Mount Chapter Excellence Award.

The stated purpose of Mortar Board that is defined in Article II of the bylaws was discussed by the National Council in terms of the need to improve its visibility to chapters, alumni, and university administrators and the importance of integrating its tenets into chapter programming. Chapters were encouraged to use the Mortar Board purpose as a framework or guide for planning their yearly program by implementing one or more of the goals stated within it:

- To contribute to the self-awareness of its members;
- To promote equal opportunities among all peoples;
- To emphasize the advancement of the status of women;
- To support the ideals of the college or university;
- To advance a spirit of scholarship;
- To recognize and encourage leadership;
- To provide service; and
- To establish the opportunity for a meaningful exchange of ideas as individuals and as a group.[323]

"Purpose sessions" at the 2015 conference were held to help chapter delegates brainstorm ways to incorporate the goals into their future chapter programming.

Dr. Starling called the fourth special national conference to order via a January 2015 webinars and conference calls. After giving a brief history of the special national conference, she outlined the meeting agenda, including a review of bylaws amendments and an introduction to the slate of candidates for the National Office. This was the first time that National Council members would be elected outside of a physical national conference, a plan that had been approved by the delegates voting after the 2013 special national conference.

Five proposed amendments to the bylaws were reviewed. The first amendment changed National Council elections from one member in even years and four members in odd years to two and three members, respectively, allowing for more continuity. Other amendments included adding the immediate past National President to the National Council, with the duty of running the Standing Nominations Committee, and clarifying how candidates for student representative would be nominated and how the conference Nominating Committee presents the candidates. Various topics of interest to chapters such as selection, tapping, visibility, and fund-raising also were discussed during the three sessions of the special national conference. The amendments carried, with ninety-one chapters voting. Five National Council officers were elected, some for one-year terms so as to begin the planned-for balance in the number of new officers.

The strategic plan of 2010 expired in 2015, and after an evaluation of how its goals and objectives were met, a new plan was established after an energizing winter meeting hosted in the National Office. Three new goals were set:

Goal 1: Improve the financial position of Mortar Board.
Goal 2: Increase membership and enhance the membership experience.
Goal 3: Define and communicate a clear vision of the Mortar Board brand and value proposition.[324]

Action steps to accomplish each goal were identified, and subcommittees or task forces were appointed to work on the objectives. Some frameworks were suggested to help accomplish the goals: Become a data-driven organization, beta-test with selection in the fall of the junior year with full spring to transition, strategize more effective

Delegates on the last day of the 2014 conference in Atlanta are excited to lead their chapters.

and concise ways to communicate between chapters and the National Office, and revitalize content and delivery of the conference to maximize technology and learning preferences of today's students. As part of improving communication, the Mortar Board website was updated after much input and work. The redesign cost $4,500.

The *Handbook for National Leaders* that was developed in 2011 by vice president of the Board of Trustees Sally Watlington (Purdue, 1958) and trustee (and past National President) Marty Starling, with help from Jane Hamblin, was again reviewed and revised, adding changes necessitated by the 2015 special national conference. A mentoring program consisting of former officers and coordinators was created to assist new section coordinators. The program was intended to make the coordinator transition more efficient and to have experienced leaders fill the gap when positions are vacant. The MBNF, now presided over by past National President Denise Rode, increased the number of trustees from a maximum of seven to eleven, so the trust agreement was re-signed by the trustees. The MBNF took a broader look at the overall financial health of the organization and its role in being the financial stewards of the Society.

The fifth special national conference was called to order by National President Abby Diehl in January 2016 by telephone conference calls and webinars. Four amendments to the bylaws were proposed and discussed. The first amendment clarified that one may not stand for elective chapter office unless membership fees and local dues were paid. The second amendment proposed that there be no co-office holding in a chapter. The delegates discussed the intent of this proposed amendment at length, particularly the chapters that used co-officers. The last two amendments clarified the language about the length of service of a collegiate member. In the time that remained, conference participants shared the activities and projects in which their chapters were involved. After nearly three weeks during which balloting was conducted online,

Kay Moore (Ohio State, 1964), here with her husband Dan and past National President Mabel Freeman, presented the Capstone Leadership Lecture "Wine, Women and Winnie the Pooh" at the 2014 national conference. Kay also received the Alumni Achievement Award for her internationally recognized work on women's leadership in higher education and intercultural competence.

the tellers reported that all amendments had carried and that the two candidates for national office had been elected.

The idea of establishing a virtual Mortar Board chapter was discussed in 2016, since several universities with Mortar Board chapters were offering four-year baccalaureate degrees globally online (Carnegie Mellon and Penn State, for example). A virtual or online chapter would be composed of students matriculating in these degree programs if all requirements were met. The idea was considered interesting enough to pursue further.

Chapters continued to contribute to their campuses and communities in the latter part of the decade through creative service projects. The Ruth Weimer Mount Chapter Excellence Award was given to Alabama at the 2016 national conference, the first time a chapter in the Southeast had received the honor. The chapter had set its sights for service on three groups: incoming freshmen, international students, and elderly members in their community. They started with the *Legacy of Lessons Learned* video of tips for new students, partnered with the English Language Institute for several programs, and sponsored programs at a retirement home.

Carnegie Mellon hosted the "Family Math Fun—How to Get to 100" event, where children tried different ways to get to the number one hundred (for example, predicting the volume of one hundred water drops, doing one hundred exercises, making snacks with one hundred pieces, or drawing self-portraits of themselves at age one hundred). Florida State raised money for childhood cancer research, and San Diego State once again sponsored its magnificent tree-planting ceremony honoring distinguished faculty.

A long and growing concern for Mortar Board, as is the case for many other national honor societies, continued to be the insecurity of revenue based on membership fees alone. The decline of membership fees and constant rising costs, plus the former practice of paying the full cost of each delegate to the national conferences from 1985 to 2012, had depleted reserves. Although many stop-gap measures were instigated to slow the process, Mortar Board's financial future continued to be precarious, and finding ways to reverse the trend was considered essential. An eight-member Futuring Task Force was appointed in 2016 and chaired by Robert S. (Bob) Sorensen (Purdue, 2000) to study the problem and suggest solutions. National President Diehl charged the task force with addressing the issue of long-term financial viability and how Mortar Board can prepare staff and national leaders to improve the situation.

After reviewing nine years of financial summaries, the task force found two items most significant: the decline in collegiate membership fees and the amount needed to cover conference activity every year. These two factors constituted the primary reasons for the net income of Mortar Board, Inc., to be negative for eight of the nine years reported. Two basic possibilities resulted from the task force's analysis of trends: (1) add juniors-to-be to collegiate membership and (2) hold the national conference every two years. The recommendations were reported at its preconference meeting in 2016, and National Council voted to accept the recommendation about biennial conferencing. Dr. Diehl appointed a work group, chaired by Vice President Katie Chick to examine the juniors recommendation, and two additional work groups. The first, led by Alumni Representative Clay Mingus, would study organization structure, both volunteer and staff; the second, led by President-elect David Whitman (Wyoming, 1998), would study implementation of the biennial conference decision and interim training activities.

The second charge to the Futuring Task Force was to consider the question "Is Mortar Board relevant to college seniors?" After perusing the current literature on higher education, millennial students, and other honor societies, members discussed the value of honor societies in general and Mortar Board's purpose in particular. The consensus was that the time-honored Ideals of the Society are as relevant and important today as they were for students in the past. The task force also urged Mortar Board's national leaders, chapter advisors, and alumni to help today's students understand what it can mean to be part of such a group and the value of belonging to an organization that upholds these Ideals.

The role of new alums in conference planning has been significant over the last thirty years. Here Shawna Johnson (Northern Illinois), Taylor Hand (Drury), and Michelle Olson (Minnesota-Duluth), all 2015 initiates, carry the torch and much more in their work on the Conference Advisory Board at the 2016 national conference.

Notes

1. Pam Chinnis, an early editor of the *Mortar Board Quarterly*, wrote a history of Mortar Board for its fiftieth anniversary, and much of the early information in this section is quoted from her account (hereafter Chinnis's History).

2. National Council Historian: Report of 1932, 1938, 1950–1957, 1961, Mortar Board: National (RG 50/a-1/5/21), The Ohio State University Archives (hereafter Historian Reports).

3. Chinnis's History. It was Chinnis who used the term "hocus-pocus."

4. It is unclear how long these housing groups remained in existence.

5. *Mortar Board Quarterly* 3, no. 3 (October 1927): 11–12.

6. Conference and Convention: Minutes, 1918–1919, Mortar Board: National (RG 50/a-1/2/30), The Ohio State University Archives (hereafter Conventions: 1918–1919).

7. Conventions: 1918–1919.

8. Ibid.

9. Ibid.

10. Ibid.

11. Ibid.

12. Historian Reports.

13. Conventions: 1918–1919.

14. Ibid.

15. Ibid.

16. National Historian Hazel Moren Richards wrote in the April 1967 *Mortar Board Quarterly* that Esther Holmes Jones "once told me that . . . after she returned to Swarthmore, it came to her very forcefully that the name must be Mortar Board."

17. Minutes of the Second National Mortar Board Convention, April 25, 1919, 2.

18. Ibid., 1.

19. Ibid., 2.

20. Ibid.

21. Ibid., 3.

22. Script of the 60th Anniversary Celebration of Mortar Board at The Ohio State University, 1978.

23. Ibid.

24. Ibid.

25. Conference and Convention: Minutes, 1921, 1923–1924, 1926–1928, Mortar Board: National (RG 50/a-1/2/30), The Ohio State University Archives (hereafter Conventions: 1920s).

26. Conventions: 1920s.

27. Historian Reports.

28. Ibid.

29. *Mortar Board Quarterly* 2, no. 1 (February 1926): 3.

30. Historian Reports.

31. Instead of "national officers" or some other designation, the term "Council" or "National Council" began to develop in the fourth or fifth year of existence. "National Council" is the terminology still used today.

32. Before her appointment as dean of women, Elisabeth Conrad was an assistant professor in romance languages at Ohio State. She became a Mortar Board honorary member in 1918.

33. Historian Reports.

34. Ibid.

35. *Mortar Board Quarterly* 3, no. 1 (February 1927): 20.

36. The prize-winning drawing for the first *Mortar Board Quarterly*'s cover was replicated as an engrossed border on the charter of the MBAA, which was launched on July 21, 2012.

37. Historian Reports.

38. The origin of Ethel Hampson Brewster's interpretation of the motto of Mortar Board is not known. Her 1917 University of Pennsylvania doctoral dissertation "Roman Craftsmen and Tradesmen of the Early Empire" shows a vast knowledge of Latin. Possibly her abilities in Greek might also have

been strong, leading to her transliteration. The meaning of her own chapter's name, Pi Sigma Chi, might also have influenced her understanding of the words relating to pi, sigma, and alpha.

39. *Mortar Board Quarterly* 1, no. 1 (April 1925): 8.

40. *Mortar Board Quarterly* 2, no. 2 (May 1926): 65.

41. Ibid., 97.

42. Historian Reports.

43. Ibid.

44. H. M. Richards, "Historian Report," 1951, Mortar Board: National (RG 50/a-1/15/21), The Ohio State University Archives. The author of "The Torch" is anonymous, but the poem can be traced to a poetry anthology of the early 1900s.

45. Historian Reports.

46. *Mortar Board Quarterly* 3, no. 2 (June 1927): 6.

47. Ibid.

48. National Council Annual Reports, 1928–1947, Mortar Board: National (RG 50/a-1/5/29), The Ohio State University Archives (hereafter National Council Annual Reports).

49. Carnegie Institute of Technology and Florida State College for Women at that time.

50. Then Lawrence College.

51. *Mortar Board Quarterly* 7, no. 1 (January 1931): 13.

52. *Mortar Board Quarterly* 6, no. 3 (May 1930): 180–181.

53. *Mortar Board Quarterly* 3, no. 1 (February 1927): 19.

54. Chinnis's History.

55. *Mortar Board Quarterly* 7, no. 2 (March 1931): 47.

56. Minutes of the Eighth National Convention of Mortar Board, June 24–27, 1930, 6.

57. National President Annual Report, 1933, Mortar Board: National (RG 50/a-1/5/29), The Ohio State University Archives (hereafter National President Annual Report, 1933).

58. Historian Reports.

59. National President Annual Report, 1933.

60. Historian Reports.

61. Dorothy C. Stratton and Helen B. Schleman, *Your Best Foot Forward: Social Usage for Young Moderns* (New York: Whittelsey, 1940).

62. Historian Reports.

63. *Mortar Board Quarterly* 11, no. 1 (January 1935): 3. Margaret Stafford married Ralph M. Lyon in 1935. They were distinguished educators at Livingston College, later the University of West Alabama, and Lyon Hall there is named in their memory. Margaret was a professor of educational psychology, among many other roles, until her retirement in 1977.

64. Ibid., 7.

65. Ibid., 11, 64.

66. *Mortar Board Quarterly* 10, no. 3 (May 1934): 169–170.

67. Ibid.

68. *Mortar Board Quarterly* 11, no. 2 (March 1935): 102–103.

69. Ibid., 110 (Mary Weinland reporting).

70. Ibid. This fund eventually became known as FSBIT, an acronym "For Small But Important Things (For Which No Other Funds Are Available)." Giving emergency loans was a common duty of all staff members in the Office of the Dean of Students (previously the Office of the Dean of Men and the Office of the Dean of Women), who drew "drop-in" duty.

71. *Mortar Board Quarterly* 12, no. 2 (March 1936): 130–131.

72. *Mortar Board Quarterly* 10, no. 3 (May 1934): 177.

73. *Mortar Board Quarterly* 11, no. 3 (May 1935): 191.

74. First Vice President: Annual Report: 1928–1947, Mortar Board; National (RG 50/a-1/5/12), The Ohio State University Archives.

75. *Mortar Board Quarterly* 7, no. 2 (March 1931): 49.

76. Historian Reports.

77. The black book was a leather embossed binder, supplemented each year by new information. Each member of a chapter was to read the book

and was tested on its contents so as to demonstrate knowledge of Mortar Board.

78. National Council Annual Reports, 1935.

79. *Mortar Board Quarterly* 13, no. 1 (January 1937): 6.

80. Ibid., 8.

81. Attorney Correspondence: 1938–1965, Mortar Board: National (RG 50/a-1/2/1), The Ohio State University Archives, (hereafter Attorney Correspondence).

82. Coral Stevens was a "postgraduate initiate," meaning that she was a member of the earlier local organization at Pomona that joined Mortar Board in 1930. Mortar Board accords the installation year of the chapter to all members who preceded the granting of the charter.

83. Attorney Correspondence, June 4, 1938.

84. Attorney Correspondence, March 27, 1939.

85. Attorney Correspondence, June 27, 1938.

86. Attorney Correspondence, March 27, 1939.

87. Attorney Correspondence, April 8, 1939.

88. *Mortar Board Quarterly* 14, no. 4 (October 1938): 231.

89. Ibid., 232.

90. In addition to being a famous and sought-after industrial psychologist (for example, she was hired by Johnson and Johnson in 1926 to do marketing research on sanitary napkins), Dr. Gilbreth was also famous as the wife of Frank Gilbreth, who began the time and space movement in industrial engineering, and as the mother of their twelve children, portrayed in the book and movie *Cheaper by the Dozen*.

91. *Mortar Board Quarterly* 15, no. 1 (January 1939): 11.

92. *Mortar Board Quarterly* 14, no. 4 (October 1938): 228–230.

93. Ibid.

94. *Mortar Board Quarterly* 15, no. 1 (January 1939): 6–8.

95. Ibid., 3–5.

96. Historian Reports.

97. The Ohio State University Archives, Mortar Board: National (RC 50/a-1/5/29) "President: Annual Report: 1933–1955" (hereafter President's Annual Report).

98. The Ohio State University Archives, Mortar Board: National (RG 50/a-1/4/2), "Fellowship Correspondence, 1942" (hereafter Fellowship Correspondence).

99. Ibid.

100. Fellowship Correspondence, 1942.

101. *Mortar Board Quarterly* 17, no. 4 (October 1941): 259.

102. *Mortar Board Quarterly* 16, no. 1 (January 1940): 76–77. Eleanor Roosevelt, the wife of President Franklin D. Roosevelt, was one of the early women radio commentators. She had her own radio show from 1936 through the war years.

103. Dr. Stratton had taken a leave of absence from her post as dean of women at Purdue to join the WAVES in 1942. After leaving the SPARS at the end of the war with the Legion of Merit, she became the director of the International Monetary Fund and later the executive director of the Girl Scouts of the U.S.A. She returned to West Lafayette, Indiana, in retirement and lived to the age of 107.

104. The Ohio State University, Script from the 60th Mortar Board anniversary celebration, September 1978.

105. The Ohio State University Archives, Mortar Board: National (RG 50/a-1/5/26), "National Council Meeting Minutes, 1923–1959" (hereafter National Council Meeting minutes).

106. President's Annual Report, June 1944.

107. President's Annual Report, July 1942.

108. The Ohio State University Archives, Mortar Board: OSU Chapter (RG 44/1/23), "Racial Equality Issue: 1933, 1943" (hereafter Racial Equality Issue).

109. Ibid.

110. Ibid.

111. Personal communication, February 14, 2014.

112. Racial Equality Issue, May 24, 1943.

113. Personal communication, Marjorie Garvin Sayers, November 4, 2011.

114. Racial Equality Issue.

115. *Mortar Board Quarterly* 19, no. 4 (October 1943): 247.

116. Ibid.

117. Ibid.

118. National Council Meeting Minutes, 1944.

119. Ibid.

120. *Mortar Board Quarterly* 18, no. 4 (October 1942): 227.

121. Ibid.

122. *Mortar Board Quarterly* 19, no. 4 (October 1943): 252.

123. *Mortar Board Quarterly* 19, no. 1 (January 1943): 46.

124. *Bulletin of the American Association of University Professors* 30, no. 4 (1944): 525–554.

125. See "The GI Bill," Wessels Living History Farm, http://www.livinghistoryfarm.org/farminginthe40s/life_20.html.

126. See "FDR Signs GI Bill," History.com, www.history.com/this-day-in-history/fdr-signs-gi-bill.

127. *Mortar Board Quarterly* 25, no. 2 (March 1949): 64.

128. Minutes of the Fourteenth National Convention, June 21–25, 1949.

129. Ibid.

130. Historian Reports.

131. Linda Eisenmann, "The Impact of Historical Expectations on Women's Higher Education," *Forum on Public Policy Online* 2007, no. 3: 11.

132. Minutes of the Fifteenth National Convention of Mortar Board, Round Table Discussion Notes, June 22, 1952.

133. *Mortar Board Quarterly* 29, no. 2 (March 1953): 91.

134. The Ohio State University Archives, Mortar Board: National (RG 50/a-1/24/51), "Wayne State University Correspondence, 1947–1951."

135. Report of the Expansion Director, 1925.

136. Historian Reports.

137. Fellowship Correspondence, 1957.

138. Historian Reports.

139. Ibid.

140. Minutes of the Sixteenth National Convention of Mortar Board, July 1–4, 1955.

141. The Ohio State University Archives, Mortar Board: National (RG 50/a-1/2/31), "Conference and Convention: Minutes: 1941–1958."

142. Appendix A of the Minutes of the Seventeenth National Convention of Mortar Board, June 28–July 1, 1958.

143. *Mortar Board Quarterly* 24, no. 2 (January 1958): 47–49.

144. The *Mortar Board Forum* was edited from the National Office.

145. *Mortar Board Forum* 41, no. 1 (Fall 2010): 10.

146. The Ohio State University Archives: Mortar Board: National (RC50/a-1/11/34), "History of Mortar Board, 1963–1965, 1978" (hereafter History, 1978).

147. *Mortar Board Forum* 11, no. 1 (Fall 1980): 1.

148. The Ohio State University Archives: Mortar Board: National (RC50/a-1/4/16), "History, 1970, 1971, 1973" (hereafter History, 1973).

149. Betty Friedan, *The Feminine Mystique* (New York: Dell, 1963), 63.

150. Personal communication, Anne Craig Droste, September 24, 2012.

151. Appendix A of the Minutes of the Eighteenth National Convention of Mortar Board, July 2–6, 1961.

152. *Mortar Board Quarterly* 28, no. 1 (1961): 7.

153. *Mortar Board Quarterly* 28, no. 1 (1961): 11 (Melanie Donovan, Beloit chapter president and delegate to the eighteenth national conference).

154. Ibid.

155. *Mortar Board Quarterly* 38, no. 2 (1962): 13–14.

156. *Mortar Board Forum* 1, no. 3 (1971): 1.

157. *Mortar Board Quarterly* 38, no. 2 (1962): 5–7.

158. *Mortar Board Quarterly* 39, no. 2 (January 1963): 59.

159. *Mortar Board Quarterly* 38, no. 2 (1962): 14.

160. The Ohio State University Archives, Mortar Board: National (RC 50/5/1), Chapter Reports, 1962.

161. History, 1973.

162. Ibid.

163. Tax determination correspondence, U.S. Treasury Department, Internal Revenue Service, June 29, 1961.

164. *Mortar Board Quarterly* 42, no. 1 (1965): 32.

165. The Ohio State University Archives: Mortar Board: National (RC50/a-1/6/21), "National Council: Treasurer: Correspondence: 1965."

166. History, 1973.

167. *Mortar Board Quarterly* 37, no. 1 (1960): 32–33.

168. *Mortar Board Quarterly* 41, no. 1 (October 1964): 15.

169. *Mortar Board Quarterly* 39, no. 4 (1963): 7.

170. The organization began as National Association of Women Deans and then became the National Association of Deans of Women; the National Association of Women Deans and Counselors; the National Association for Women Deans, Administrators, and Counselors; and finally the National Association for Women in Education.

171. Weimer Mount would later become president of the National Association for Women Deans and Administrators.

172. *Mortar Board Quarterly* 39, no. 4 (April 1963): 24.

173. Ibid., 22.

174. Correspondence from the Swarthmore chapter to the National Council.

175. The Ohio State University Archives: Mortar Board: National (RC50/1-a/2/33), "National Council Minutes, June 27, 1965."

176. The Ohio State University Archives: Mortar Board: National (RC50/a-1/15/21), "Chapter Programs, 1967."

177. The Ohio State University Archives: Mortar Board: National (RC50/a-1/6/12), "National Office Correspondence, National Secretary Letter to Chapters, 1969."

178. *Mortar Board Forum* 13, no. 1 (Fall 1982).

179. National Council Minutes.

180. The Ohio State University Archives: Mortar Board: National (RC50/a-1/4/25), "Justification Committee: 1970."

181. The Ohio State University Archives: Mortar Board: National (RC50/a-1/3/24), "Constitution and By-Laws: 1920."

182. *Mortar Board Quarterly* 1, no. 1 (1925): 1.

183. *Mortar Board Forum* 3, no. 4 (1973): 2.

184. *Mortar Board Quarterly* 16, no. 4 (1940): 13.

185. The Ohio State University Archives: Mortar Board: National (RC50/a-1/3/7), "President's Triennial Report, 1970."

186. History, 1978.

187. Ibid.

188. Personal interview, Catherine Nelson Evans, 2011.

189. The Ohio State University Archives: Mortar Board: National (RC50/a-1/2/33), "National Conference Minutes, 1970" (hereafter National Conference Minutes, 1970).

190. *Mortar Board Forum* 1, no. 1 (Fall 1970): 2.

191. *Mortar Board Forum* 10, no. 1 (October 1979): 5–6.

192. National Conference Minutes, 1970.

193. National Conference Minutes, 1970.

194. Annual reports of national editor, 1970–1971 and 1971–1972.

195. *Mortar Board Forum* 3, no. 4 (April 1973): 7.

196. The Ohio State University Archives: Mortar Board: National (RC50/a-1/2/33), "National Conference: Minutes: 1973."

197. History, 1978.

198. Ibid.

199. Ibid.

200. The Ohio State University Archives: Mortar Board: National (RC50/a-1/18/30), "Title IX, 1974–1976" (hereafter Title IX, 1974–1976).

201. Title IX, 1974–1976.

202. *Mortar Board Forum* 5, no. 2 (November 1974): 5.

203. *Chronicle of Higher Education,* April 28, 1975.

204. The Ohio State University Archives: Mortar Board: National (RC50/a-1/18/31), "Attorney Correspondence, June 19, 1975" (hereafter Title IX Attorney Correspondence).

205. Title IX Attorney Correspondence, September 5, 1975.

206. *Mortar Board Forum* 5, no. 2 (November 1974): 1.

207. *One Hundred Years History: Mortar Board History, The Ohio State University, 1914–2014,* 39. Available at http://osumortarboard.com/blog/history/.

208. *Mortar Board Forum* 6, no. 1 (October 1975): 1.

209. *Mortar Board Forum* 6, no. 2 (January 1976): 4.

210. The Ohio State University Archives: Mortar Board: National (RC50/a-1/13/32), "National Conference Minutes: 1975."

211. Personal interview, Catherine Nelson Evans, 2011.

212. *Mortar Board Forum* 6, no. 2 (January 1976): 1.

213. Ibid.

214. Ibid.

215. Ibid.

216. Personal interview, Cathcrine Nelson Evans, 2011.

217. Ibid.

218. Ibid.

219. *Mortar Board Forum* 6, no. 3 (April 1976): 1, 5.

220. *Mortar Board Forum* 8, no. 1 (November 1977): 7.

221. *Mortar Board Forum* 7, no. 1 (November 1976): 4.

222. *Mortar Board Forum* 11, no. 1 (Fall 1982): 9.

223. The Ohio State University Archives: Mortar Board: National (RC50/a-1/14/1), "National Conference Minutes: 1976."

224. Michael Nichols, *The Laurel Crowned Circle,* Omicron Delta Kappa (2014), 48.

225. *Mortar Board Forum* 8, no. 2 (February 1978): 1.

226. Ibid., 9.

227. *Journal of NAWDAC* (Spring 1980): 15–23.

228. *Mortar Board Forum* 8, no. 2 (February 1978): 1.

229. The Ohio State University Archives, Mortar Board: National (RC 50/5/15), Attorney correspondence, 1979.

230. John R. Thelin, *A History of American Higher Education* (Baltimore: Johns Hopkins University Press, 2004), 341.

231. *Mortar Board Forum* 11, no. 3 (Spring 1981): 1.

232. The Ohio State University Archives: Mortar Board: National (RC50/a-1/8/52), "Correspondence: Computerization: 1980."

233. Report of National Director of Elections, 1982.

234. *Mortar Board Forum* 12, no. 1 (Fall 1981): 1.

235. Minutes of the Twenty-Sixth National Conference of Mortar Board, 1982.

236. *Mortar Board Forum* 18, no. 3 (Spring 1988): 7.

237. Ibid.

238. *Mortar Board Forum* 11, no. 3 (Spring 1981): 2.

239. The Ohio State University Archives, Mortar Board: National (RC 50/5/15), Executive Director Reports.

240. Minutes of the Second National Mortar Board Convention, April 25, 1919, 2.

241. Minutes, Mortar Board National Convention (early draft with handwritten notes in margins): Archives (50a-1/9/14).

242. The Ohio State University Archives: Mortar Board: (RC44/17/1), "Ritual of the Mortar Board Fraternity: 1920–1921."

243. Minutes of the National Council Meeting, July 27, 1994.

244. Personal communication from Brent Froberg, advisor to the University of South Dakota chapter, May 9, 1983.

245. *Mortar Board Forum* 4, no. 1 (Fall 1983): 5.

246. *Mortar Board Forum* 14, no. 3 (Spring 1984): 5.

247. *Mortar Board Forum* 11, no. 1 (Fall 1980): 6.

248. The Ohio State University Archives: Mortar Board: National (RC50/a-1/9/10), "Council: Long-Range Planning Committee: Washington, D.C.: April, 1981."

249. *Mortar Board Forum* 4, no. 1 (Fall 1983): 3.

250. Report of National Director of Expansion, 1985.

251. The Ohio State University Archives: Mortar Board: National (RC50/a-1/9/4), "Council: Annual Reports: 1984–1985."

252. The Ohio State University Archives: Mortar Board: National (RC50/a-1/9/3), "Council: Annual Reports (1985–1986)."

253. The Ohio State University Archives, Mortar Board: National (RC 50/5/15), Report of Long Range Planning Committee, 1985.

254. *Mortar Board Forum* 17, no. 2 (Winter 1987): 4.

255. Minutes of the Twenty-Eighth National Conference of Mortar Board, 1987.

256. "National Student Loan Two-Year Default Rates," Federal Student Loan Aid, https://www2.ed.gov/offices/OSFAP/defaultmanagement/defaultrates.html.

257. Ibid.

258. The lobbying restrictions on 501(c)(3) organizations were far less in the 1980s than at the time of this writing.

259. Personal communication, June 27, 2016. Earnest was also an MBNF fellow and now is a reader for fellowship applications.

260. *Mortar Board Forum* 18, no. 3 (Spring 1988): 11.

261. The Ohio State University Archives, Mortar Board: National (RC 50/5/15), National President Correspondence.

262. *Mortar Board Forum* 21, no. 1 (Fall 1990): 3.

263. The Ohio State University Archives, Mortar Board: National (RC 50/5/15), MBNF merchandise brochure, circa 1990.

264. Minutes of the Thirtieth National Conference of Mortar Board, Inc., July 17–21, 1991.

265. The Ohio State University Archives, Mortar Board: National (RC 50/5/15), Postconference Evaluations, 2009–2015.

266. National Council Minutes, July 19, 1995, 2.

267. *Mortar Board Forum* 24, no. 1 (Fall 1993): 8.

268. Ibid., 6.

269. Ibid., 2.

270. *Mortar Board Forum* 25, no. 1 (Fall 1994): 2.

271. Ibid., 4.

272. Ibid., 11.

273. *Mortar Board Forum* 23, no. 3 (Spring 1993): 5.

274. *Mortar Board Forum* 21, no. 2 (Winter 1991): 11.

275. Minutes of the National Council, January 20, 1995.

276. *Mortar Board Alive! A Newsletter for Mortar Board Alumni* 2, no. 1 (1995): 1.

277. *Mortar Board Forum* 26, no. 2 (Spring 1996): 3.

278. Strengths, weaknesses, opportunities, and threats.

279. Mortar Board, Inc., Strategic Plan, December 1996.

280. *Mortar Board Forum* 29, no. 1 (Fall 1998): 3.

281. *Mortar Board Forum* 28, no. 2 (Spring 1998): 10.

282. *Mortar Board Forum* 29, no. 1 (Fall 1998): 3.

283. *Mortar Board Forum* 29, no. 2 (Spring 1999): 4–5.

284. *Mortar Board Ink* 4, no. 1 (September 1998).

285. National Conference, Mortar Board, Inc., Transcript, July 25, 1998, 62.

286. *Mortar Board Forum* 29, no. 2 (Spring 1999): 11.

287. *Mortar Board Forum* 30, no. 1 (Fall 1999): 7.

288. *Milestones in the Millennium,* Mortar Board Annual Report, 2000, 3.

289. *Mortar Board Forum* 32, no. 1 (Fall 2001): 3.

290. The Ohio State University Archives, Mortar Board: National (RC 50/5/15), Foundation correspondence.

291. Minutes, January 20, 2001, National Council Meeting.

292. Personal correspondence, July 2, 2010.

293. Report of Strategic Planning Work Session, January 26, 2002.

294. Mortar Board Privacy Policy, Adopted by the National Council July 25, 2002.

295. *Mortar Board Forum* 32, no. 2 (Spring 2002): 18.

296. *Mortar Board Forum* 35, no. 1 (Fall 2004): 5.

297. Personal correspondence, July 2, 2010.

298. *Mortar Board Forum* 34, no. 2 (Spring 2004): 2.

299. *Mortar Board Forum* 37, no. 1 (Fall 2006): 17.

300. Now the University at Buffalo.

301. *Mortar Board Forum* 37, no. 2 (Spring 2007): 3.

302. Report on proposed enhancements to the current Mortar Board selections process, June 28, 2007.

303. National Council Minutes, January 26, 2008.

304. *Mortar Board Forum* 38, no. 2 (Spring 2008): 6.

305. National Council Minutes, May 24, 2007.

306. National Conference Resolution, July 2007.

307. *Mortar Board Forum* 41, no. 1 (Fall 2010): 13.

308. National Council Minutes, January 31, 2010.

309. Personal correspondence, October 18, 2016.

310. "LEAD: Leadership Excellence and Advisor Development," Mortar Board, http://www.mortarboard.org/Advisors/LEAD/.

311. National Council Minutes, March 23, 2011.

312. Mortar Board, Inc., Profit and Loss Budget Overview, December 31, 2012

313. Special National Conference Minutes, April 26, 28, 29, 2012.

314. Bylaws of Mortar Board, Inc., 2012.

315. Minutes of the MBNF Meeting, April 26, 2012, 2.

316. *Mortar Board Forum* 42, no. 3 (Autumn 2012): 12.

317. Special National Conference Minutes, January 24, 26, 27, 2013.

318. Membership fees were $50 from 1998 through 2001, $55 in 2002, $60 from 2004 through 2009, $75 from 2010 through 2013, and $80 from 2014 until the time of this writing.

319. National Council Minutes, September 9, 2013.

320. Only one member was absent from this meeting.

321. National Council Minutes, May 22, 2013.

322. National Council Minutes, August 27, 2013.

323. "About Mortar Board," Mortar Board, www.mortarboard.org/About.

324. Mortar Board National Council Minutes, February 10, 2015.

3

Collegiate Chapters

The Heart of the Society

Although Mortar Board became a national society in the early 1900s, there was already in existence a surprisingly large number of local honor societies for college senior women. The founding chapters, Cornell (1892), Syracuse (1898), Swarthmore (1898), Michigan (1905), and Ohio State (1914), were well established locally when they united in 1918 (recall that Syracuse dropped out in 1919 when a Greek-letter name was not selected). Other established local groups that quickly joined the national organization (before 1920) were state universities in Nebraska, Illinois, Missouri, and Minnesota. DePauw University in Indiana also joined. Thirty-five delegates from fourteen chapters attended the 1921 national conference at Ohio State just three years after the founding, a sign that Mortar Board was on to something.

Preserving Chapter Identity and History

It was important to the founders of Mortar Board that the local identity of each chapter accepted into the national organization be preserved. There was an expectation that each would remain true to its distinct origins and honor its unique history, role on campus, traditions, and projects and programs. This individuality was emphasized as local names were preserved. It is interesting that two of the founding chapters were named Mortar Board (Ohio State was Mortar Board, and Michigan was Mortarboard).

Perusing local Mortar Board chapter names is a fascinating study and offers insight into the times and the groups' origins. Cap & Gown (or Cap and Gown) is the name for seventeen chapters, with

Northwestern (1922) as Cap and Tassel and Boston University (1974) as Cap and Crown. Tassel features itself in some variation in thirteen chapter names: Idaho State University (1972) as Silver Tassel and Illinois State University (1976) as Red Tassel. The University of Southern California (1929) is the Torch and Tassel chapter. "Torch" in some variation is used in six chapter names, with the oldest to lay claim to it the University of Kansas's Torch, which started in 1911 and became Mortar Board in 1924.

Some chapter names are unique: Nebraska's Black Masque, Cincinnati's Mystic 13, and Denison University's original name, White Nun, now one of the Cap & Gowns. Bradley University's chapter name, Wakapa, is an Indian word meaning "to excel"; Butler University's Scarlet Quill was named after a poem about the Bird of Knowledge named Scarquill.

Other chapter names have distinctive, even complex origins. The chapter name of the University of Texas at El Paso is Chenrezig. The university's buildings are based on architectural forms from the Kingdom of Bhutan (located between India and Tibet) that embraces Chenrezig and is also related to the practice of Buddhism. The chapter chose the name in the 1960s because "we felt that the single motivating force that causes people to do extraordinary things is compassion,"[1] a tenet of Chenrezig.

The origin of the Drake chapter name, Fuller/Sieve/Shears, is related to the Margaret Fuller Club, established in 1896, whose purpose was to study literature, art, and science, and the 1912 Sieve and Shears, which reflects the college group it sprang from, home economics majors.

Beloit College's Royal Order of the Senior Bench began in 1929, when the group's name was placed on a stone bench at the entrance to the college. When the total number of senior women reached more than eighty (one of Mortar Board's expectations was that the number of women in the senior class sustain a high-quality chapter), Dean of Women Elizabeth Stanton, who had inherited a previous dean's wish that Beloit have Mortar Board, "vigorously corresponded with Mortar Board" to ensure that the chapter's petition would be accepted.[2] It was installed in 1951.

Two early chapters, the University of Arizona (1926) and Montana State (1927), used Pi Sigma Alpha as their name, probably after Mortar Board's motto. Sigma Lambda Sigma at South Dakota State University (1972) and Virginia Polytechnic and State University (1977) picked up on the motto too but in English. Purdue's precursor group was just S.L.S.

Other Greek-letter names often marked the local organization's origins and so were retained. Phi Delta Psi at Illinois came to Mortar Board in the first year. DePauw University's Gamma Sigma Delta was invited to join in 1919. University of Pittsburgh (1923) is Alpha Lambda Nu, Berea College (1973) is Alpha Sigma Chi, Grove City College (1972) is Alpha Theta Mu, and Duquesne University (1976) is Sigma Lambda Delta. Colorado State University (1961) is Tau Iota Omega, and Monmouth College (1972) is Tau Pi.

As even a quick glance at the list of chapters will show, many chapters are named for women who influenced a given chapter. None of them started out that way, but with one exception they required a name change approved by the National Council. Indiana University's Mrs. Granville Wells chapter is named for the mother of former president and chancellor Herman B Wells, Anna Bernice Harting Wells. She died in 1973, and it is unclear when the name got traction or if it was approved by the National Council. In 1987 Purdue sought approval to name itself the Barbara Cook chapter for longtime advisor and Mortar Board national leader Barbara Cook.[3] Bowling Green followed in 1989 when Mortar Board champion Fayetta Paulsen (Bowling Green,

Martha Scott Trimble was selected to Tau Iota Omega at Colorado State around 1935. After teaching there, doing graduate work at Iowa, and then joining the WAVEs, she returned to campus to teach English in 1961, about the time that the local society became a member of Mortar Board and she along with it.

1969) retired as vice president. The Colorado chapter honored long-time advisor and matriarch of the Boulder community Virginia Patterson (Colorado, 1945) in the mid-1990s, and in 2004 Ohio State collegiate members renamed the chapter for advisor and past National President Mabel G. Freeman. Maryland's chapter is named after the famed dean Adele H. Stamp, who brought Mortar Board to campus. The Jane K. Smith Cap & Gown chapter at San Diego State University was renamed for its tireless advisor and national leader in 2008.

In 2014 the University of Findlay chapter renamed itself in honor of Catherine Moore Freed (University of Texas at Austin, 1947), who had been a Mortar Board champion wherever her spouse's presidencies had taken her. In honor of her extraordinary advising capabilities and soaring enthusiasm for Mortar Board at Hope College, the Alcor chapter surprised its long-term and retiring advisor Dianne Portfleet by adding her name to the chapter's name—Dianne Portfleet Alcor chapter at Hope College—in 2016. South Alabama's Azalea chapter, recognizing

Jane K. Smith, who earned Excellence in Advising with Distinction status in 2012, has loyally advised the Cap & Gown chapter at San Diego State for thirty years, and it was renamed for her in 2008. The chapter was the first to win the Ruth Weimer Mount Chapter Excellence award for a second time.

Past National President Sally Steadman has also been president of the Board of Trustees. The advisor of two chapters (her own at Wyoming and at South Alabama), she has earned an Excellence in Advising with Distinction award and was surprised to find that the South Alabama chapter renamed itself in her honor in the spring of 2017.

the long service of past National President and president of the Board of Trustees of the Mortar Board National Foundation Fund (MBNF) became the Sally Steadman Azalea chapter in April 2017.

Tapping Traditions

Another aspect that makes chapters unique is their method of tapping new members. Many tapping (or "pledging" as the very early chapters called it) ceremonies sprang from the traditions of the original local group. The tapping methods used by some western chapters were described by former vice president turned Section VIII director Esther Bowman Roth (University of Montana, 1930) in 1941:

Idaho tapped at the May Fete on Mother's Day, Whitman at the May Queen crowning ceremony, and Montana State at the Honors Day Assembly. Wyoming tapped following the "Torchlight Sing after which the [current] girls in caps and

Nebraska's tapping during Ivy Day is meaningful for the new members of Black Masque; this shot is from 1940.

gowns call on each girl at her home and tap her. This takes place about 11:30 at night and is followed by a formal announcement [the next day] at honors assembly."[4]

Washington State "went to the houses at 5 in the morning, took the girls to breakfast, and had them wear caps and gowns that day."[5] Tapping at night in the early decades was a common practice, with the current chapter members going to houses (sorority or "town girl" or commuters' homes), often by candlelight while singing "Thy Ideals." Some chapters continued this practice into the 1960s. Tapping also occurred at honors banquets and assemblies and in lecture halls.

In the Mortar Board of today, chapters work hard to maintain their personal tapping tributes, realizing that this form of recognition not only adds to their visibility but is also an honor to the candidate elected, not to mention fun.

Even though it is sometimes virtual, a personalized tapping is memorable and important to a candidate's enjoyment of the capstone experience that is Mortar Board. YouTube contains videos of tapping ceremonies of candidates who are studying abroad or are otherwise off campus for internships or research.

The Push and Pull of Expansion

When the founders of Mortar Board met in Syracuse, New York, on February 15, 1918, representatives had been corresponding with each other for almost two years. (The archives contain letters from Swarthmore dating from 1916.) The representatives agreed that the meeting's objective was "to organize the leaders of the undergraduate and the graduate world," and the first order of business was to name the Society, adopt a constitution, and decide on an initiation service. The

second day of the convention, however, found the delegates already considering other local women's honor societies for expansion. A letter was sent to twenty-two colleges and universities inviting them to "petition to join this national organization."[6]

A first "Procedure for Investigation of Groups" that was used for inquiries from local groups interested in Mortar Board was established in 1920.[7] The procedure listed certain requirements for the college or university as well as the applying group. Requirements for the institution included accreditation by the Association of American Universities (later the preferred group was the American Association of University Women [AAUW]), a chapter of Phi Beta Kappa (later this was a preference rather than requirement), a certain type of institution with certain policies and ideals, a high rank and standing of its faculty, and total enrollment of at least fifty women.

Requirements for the petitioning group itself included that it have been organized for at least five years, meet the requirements of the Mortar Board constitution, be an "outstanding and influential group on the campus," and have a "program of service."[8]

Conservative or Liberal Expansion Debates

Many local groups (such as city colleges and municipal universities) inquiring about membership in the 1920s were discouraged or put on a waiting list for a variety of reasons. The type of institution and geographical location were primary considerations. Some institutions, such as San Jose State University and Wichita State University, were placed on the waiting list because they "were not accredited by the AAUW." Another issue was the status of "pioneer" state institutions that were still in the "development" stage, such as the Universities of Nevada, New Mexico, North Dakota, and Pennsylvania State. Around the middle of the decade, however, Mortar Board was "lacking representation" in twenty-five states, so a resolution was proposed at the 1926 national conference that "Mortar Board favor expansion in state institutions that possibly have not entirely passed the pioneer stage in their development." A conservative policy was still being followed in 1928 when the expansion director, Lillian Stupp (Washington in St. Louis, 1922), wrote that "no ambitious expansion policy should be taken until present chapters are strengthened."[9] In spite of this, there were forty-five chapters by the end of the 1920s, located from Vermont to California.

It was at the end of the 1940s that Expansion Director Rosemary Ginn queried the quality of interested schools:

I would like to raise the question whether by individual consideration we are getting the very best schools that are interested. I hope there will be some discussion as to our ultimate goal. Are we planning simply to grow without a plan? Most collegiate groups of our size maintain varying officer staffs, all of which are larger than the National Council and working directors who maintain Mortar Board. Whatever is done in the field of expansion adds to the burden of the present officers and I feel that we should make our plans so that our whole organization grows together.[10]

Mortar Board had 131 chapters, and the time involved in reading petitions, visiting prospective chapters, and installing them was a real concern. Director Ginn recommended in 1949 that "Mortar Board continue a conservative policy of expansion."[11]

That policy began to be questioned in the 1950s when Expansion Director Mildred Rader (Ohio State, 1945) urged the National Council "to re-examine the conservative policy of expansion with a view to

Rosemary Lucas Ginn was National President from 1949 to 1955 and had been expansion director for roughly two years before that. Her view of a conservative expansion policy prevailed.

the ultimate size of Mortar Board, its distribution in various types of schools as well as geographically." In her 1953–1954 annual report, Director Rader reported that "interest in having a Mortar Board chapter is getting stronger every year and with the colleges expecting expansion and staggering enrollments within a few years, I recommend that we again re-evaluate our very conservative expansion policy."[12] She estimated that there were 170 interested schools in the files that were not eligible for a variety of reasons. She urged the National Council to "give consideration to the many small schools that have been carried in our files for many years with some positive suggestions for their future ... and to give schools definite answers wherein they lack the necessary standards for acceptance."[13] She suggested that the National

These delegates arriving in Lincoln for the 1964 convention carry their "black book," a necessity for each chapter's leadership. Passed down from president to president, the book contained everything one needed to know to pass chapter examinations and lead a chapter. Refreshed pages were sent each year by the national officers with the expectation that each president would insert them into the binder in place of outdated ones.

Council also needed to establish a policy in relation to chapters in teacher's colleges and schools of agriculture.

The next expansion director, Margaret Stafford, weighed in as well in the 1960s and suggested that the National Council

> discuss the trends in higher education that influence the area of expansion, including the influence of heightened academic interests, enrollments in institutions of higher education, governmental loans to institutions, economic stability of states, costs of education and endowment standards, and the role of women in higher education.[14]

Dr. Stafford reminded the National Council that "the developments in higher education are not a mirage. New institutions are being developed to take care of the mass demand for higher education. In all this development Mortar Board is being labeled as having an anachronistic expansion policy." She emphasized that this eager demand for chapters required decisions, saying that "this is our heritage which I say should be utilized, not stifled."[15]

An example of the fallout from this traditional conservative expansion policy is illustrated in a report by national secretary Betty Carol Pace Clark (University of Kentucky, 1951), who was the first to visit Fort Hays State College in 1968. She provided an insight into the situation that a few long-petitioning schools experienced:

> They asked me why they have waited fifteen years for a visit after carefully fulfilling every request and suggestion each year; why was I making this visit when there had been little change in the college and the chapter; why I had come after they had one time been told that they could never have Mortar Board because they were one time a teacher's college.[16]

Another example is found in the close association that Mortar Board had with the National Association of Women Deans and Counselors (NAWDC) for many years back to its founding as the National Association of Deans of Women. Since many of the deans of women were members of this professional association and also Mortar Board, Mortar Board began holding a reception at its convention in the 1930s. This provided a structured opportunity for the expansion director and the National President to talk about Mortar Board to interested schools and answer questions. Dr. Stafford commented in 1961 that

> much time was spent by the Director of Expansion at the N.A.W.D.C. convention discussing the expansion policies and procedures with deans and other institutional representatives. This was a very exhausting period of time because of the pressure for answers and the numbers eagerly searching for recognition. The expansion director is sometimes introduced in a friendly manner as the Mortar Board Director of NON-expansion.[17]

She then described a situation that exemplified the society's dilemma:

> One example seems pertinent at this point. This year a college president and his wife called for an appointment before the convention was in session because the president came with the specific purpose of making an official appointment with the representative of Mortar Board. He brought his wife for assistance as she was a member of Mortar Board and an advisor of the local honor society. The materials they brought were placed in exquisite leather binders which they use for special college presentations and asked to have returned when Mortar Board was finished with them. I returned them

acknowledging their receipt and asked to have all papers sent to me. The materials arrived boxed with the questionnaires in individual binders, shipped registered mail at a cost to the college of approximately $7.00. From my experience with institutions I would hasten to add that their eagerness is not atypical. This poses what I judge to be one of the urgent problems facing Mortar Board at the present time, the expansion policies.[18]

Sponsoring these receptions at the National Association of Deans of Women (and later the NAWDC and the National Association for Women Deans, Administrators, and Counselors) continued for many years. National Director of Expansion Marylu McEwen reported in 1976 that more than one hundred persons attended each of the three "Hospitality Hours" that were held that year.

When the national conference met at Nebraska in 1970, there were 182 chapters. At the conference the delegates passed a resolution stating that the expansion policy of Mortar Board should be liberalized. Over fifty chapters were added in the 1970s, the largest number in one decade. Mary McAlister (Utah, 1950), the expansion director at the time, cautioned "open the windows but do not remove the screens."[19] The liberalization meant that the types of colleges expanded, including many former teachers' colleges. Another concern was forming a policy about commuter campuses. Expansion Director McAlister's recommendations in 1971 included the following:

> While there are inherent problems and concerns about the commuter campus that cause increasing difficulties and stress on the chapter itself, because the institution is serving a particular need in the area and because the honor society is probably serving the campus in a unique fashion, it may be even

more imperative that these campuses be considered for possible expansion.[20]

An Expansion Task Force was formed in preparation for the 1973 conference for the purpose of studying the "implications and ramifications of expansion in the future." A position paper written by a delegate summed up the society's expansion policies at the time and described the different opinions about expansion with which the National Council was struggling.[21] On one hand it was feared that growing too large would continue to increase operating difficulties both financially and administratively. Considerable debate centered on how the demands of future large numbers of chapters could be met. (The National Office had opened in 1970 with only one staff member, and the burden of time and clerical duties on volunteers was not expected to decrease. National Council members were assigned no fewer than seven petitions to review at a time.)

The author continued, stating that nevertheless, "the preservation of existing structures cannot be a rationale for limiting expansion. Gradual expansion should not be employed merely to stave off the inevitable reorganization which Mortar Board now faces because of its size." There was concern also about being perceived as "elitist" for not accepting more institutions. The position paper urged that the "prestige or class" of the petitioning school not be a factor in expansion.[22]

The final report of the Committee on Expansion was presented to the 1973 delegates. The first consideration was why Mortar Board should expand at all, asking "what can Mortar Board offer a new chapter and what can it offer us?" The committee members recommended some basic guidelines and some changes for admitting new chapters. In addition to simplifying the process of admission, they felt that

> there is strength in diversity and that, in this day of expanding horizons for women, Mortar Board should not be concerned

with deference to the liberal arts. We also feel that chapters and Section Coordinators play an increasingly greater role in the direction of expansion.[23]

Reference to "the liberal arts" pertained to the debate about the types of institutions to which Mortar Board should expand.

Constitution and bylaws changes eliminated the former unanimous vote of the National Council that was necessary to visit an institution. Unanimous approval of the petitioning campus by the other chapters in the section was retained, because

> we feel that what the students have to say is an important indication of how well the petitioning school fits the students' idea of Mortar Board (and we are confident it will rise above rivalry and snobbism). And since one of the main advantages of Mortar Board membership is the opportunity to work with other schools, Section cooperation is important.[24]

The task force also brought up the cost of expansion. "If we liberalize expansion, national Mortar Board will have to bear the expense of more first visits." They proposed raising the installation fee (of new chapters) to $250, applying the increased revenue to first visits to schools "without adding a huge drain on the treasury."[25]

In the 1980s, eighteen chapters were installed. The back-and-forth about opening to institutions of many different types had abated within the National Council and was seldom an issue for the delegates. Site visits remained an important part of the expansion routine. In 1987, official regalia (academic hoods for installing officers) had been made. In 1988 Diane Selby and and Director of Expansion and Alumni Jane Baur Merrill (Purdue, 1963) were examining the possibility of an alumni directory.

In the 1990s, there were ten chapters installed. Emma Norris was director of expansion and alumni after having served as director of communications. Director of Finance and Records Dolores Rogers (University of Idaho, 1953) signaled her concern about finances and conference costs early in this decade, and a deficit budget was approved in 1995. The conference fee was still $100. Chapters that were not selected or that didn't participate actively were reviewed by the National Council, and various strictures around "probation" were placed on them as motivation.

This was a decade when the National Council faithfully attempted to follow the resolutions that had been adopted by the delegates meeting in conferences while at the same time realizing that more was being demanded of the Society externally. Higher education was changing rapidly. More and more expansion efforts were being handled by the National Office, and in 1996 Director Norris proposed that the title of her position have the word "expansion" eliminated because of this.

Late in the 1990s National President Mabel Freeman responded to Diane Selby's request for an ad hoc committee to study expansion, especially as it related to dual-campus and international campus situations. The references to expansion during the late 1990s took less of a center stage in the National Council's discussions; much of the work being done related to the strategic plan and to conference planning. The National Council also worked on chapter development and spent time on those not represented at the national conference, newly installed or reestablished chapters that needed assistance, and chapters with fewer than fifteen members.

Executive Director Selby visited two campuses for expansion possibilities in November 1999, Western New England College and the University of Texas at San Antonio. She reported that three more were planning to submit petitions and that there were inquiries from forty-two other institutions. She planned to increase the work of the

Expansion Committee to a more aggressive state, reporting to the National Council that "a strong case must be made for having a Mortar Board chapter on campus."[26]

As the society moved to the decade of the 2000s, it would see eighteen chapters installed but only four in the 2010s (at the time of this writing). The National Council continued to consider expansion an issue and passed a recommendation in 2005 to "fully utilize current chapters, section coordinators, and alumni in expansion efforts" and to establish a website link for prospective campuses. It was also agreed that there must be no other senior honor society on the prospective campus that had purposes similar to those of Mortar Board.[27]

The National Office staff urged a very willing Expansion Committee in the mid-2010s to help with reinvigoration of chapters as well as identifying new chapters. In 2013, Jane Hamblin shifted part-time telecommuting staff member Bridget Williams Golden's role from alumni engagement specialist to expansion specialist. At the end of 2016, Ms. Williams Golden gave this assessment: 177 active chapters, 52 inactive chapters, and 2 reinvigorated chapters. A newly constituted Expansion Committee in 2016 sought to locate alumni to find out the effect of Mortar Board on recent alumni members' professional lives. Feedback was positive, with more than three hundred members responding to a five-question electronic survey. The committee plans to relay this information to influential college presidents and student affairs vice presidents to increase interest.

The 231st chapter of Mortar Board, the Black and Gold chapter, was installed at Pacific Lutheran University in April 2014. The institution had proposed an exceptionally tight plan to use Mortar Board as the culmination or capstone for its four-year leadership development program. The level of institutional support, including an installation conducted before the Board of Regents, showed the institution's commitment. President Thomas W. Krise (Pacific Lutheran, 2014), writing in support of the petition, stated that

it is an honor to support a petition for Pacific Lutheran University to join an honor society as prestigious as Mortar Board. Student leadership programs at PLU have been nationally recognized for their rigor, content, and impact on the student experience. A partnership between PLU and Mortar Board is a win-win for both organizations that share a mission for scholarship, leadership, and service.[28]

At the time of this writing, installation for the Oregon State University Cascades is impending. Much of the impetus for the desire of this youthful campus to secure Mortar Board is to help its development and season its student life, providing both a capstone for its senior leaders but also marshaling Mortar Board's efforts to create high-impact programs for other students. The student government has been heavily in favor and supportive of Mortar Board.

Installations: Getting Off on the Right Foot

The installation of new chapters that began in the 1920s was conducted with a carefully planned ceremony. Instructions to the early national officers installing the new chapters were carefully laid out. They were told to conduct a private conference before the ceremony with the dean and advisors and an informal meeting "with the girls." Installing officers were also advised "to check to see if all the accessories were gathered, the room arranged, caps and gowns ready, etc." It was suggested that they also check the social arrangements ("hopefully they have already told you if you have to give a speech at the banquet!").[29]

After the installation ceremony, a two-hour business meeting was to be held where the constitution and the work of the National Council and the section director were explained. An installation fee of $25 was to be collected from the institution by the installing officer. Half of her expenses were paid by the national organization (the other half were paid by the school). Each initiate was charged $3 for her pin, $3 for national dues, and $1.50 for a year's subscription to the *Quarterly*. There was considerable concern about how to collect installation expenses from some schools, since a few lagged in payment. The wording of today's installation ceremony is very similar to the original ritual.

Installations were conducted in the 2010s with as much of the ceremony as can be expected. At Illinois Wesleyan University in 2009, National President Dan Turner found that a classroom setup was arranged, and the advisor and new members were the only ones present to witness the installation. The installation in 2013 of the Epignosis chapter at Alcorn State University took on grand proportions, with robed initiates and faculty and a procession onto the stage of the chapel by the university president alongside installing officer National President Susan Caples. The Alcorn Glee Club performed several pieces,

New initiates at Alcorn State enjoy the Glee Club's performance during installation in 2013.

including "Thy Ideals." A luncheon preceded the affair, which was also attended by other Mortar Board national representatives: Dr. Sally Steadman, Dr. John Steadman (Wyoming, 2000), and Mr. Brandon M. Caten.

The cost of installation had risen over the years from $250 to $500. In 2011 the National Council voted to increase the fee to $2,500, which would cover the costs of the site visit and travel of the installing officer. This was comparable with other national organizations' installation costs.

The evolving nature of expanding Mortar Board over its one hundred years reflects a culture of conservatism in the beginning that gave way to more liberal policies as higher education changed and the type of institution accepted became more diverse. An attitude of exclusion changed to one of openness and a desire for diversity.

The strength and sustainability of Mortar Board is in its chapters individually and collectively. The common vision and purpose that chapters have shared for nearly one hundred years, however, is also its strength. One of the purposes of Mortar Board is "to establish the opportunity for a meaningful exchange of ideas as individuals and as a group." Generations of collegiate members have experienced this vividly during their active year. They carry this with them as they leave their campus as Mortar Board alumni, secure in the links forged among them because of the growth they have experienced together and the understanding they have reached.

Chapter Founding Histories

A history of Mortar Board would not be complete without accounting for the start of each chapter. After the centennial history committee was formed in 2005, alumni and collegiate historians were asked to submit their chapter's local history or provide a copy of the one used during the initiation ceremony. A surprising number of chapters could not find their history, while others researched and found it in paper files, on a USB disk, or with their advisors. Some chapters, however, had preserved either a complete or partial history of their founding and had recorded significant programs or events as well as beloved traditions. Many of the descriptions that follow are taken from these histories. More about each chapter can be found at the Mortar Board website.

Adrian College, 1989

The Golden Gavel Leadership Honor Society was established in March 1983 to recognize outstanding student achievement in campus scholarship, leadership, and service. With this recognition comes the commitment to continue to collectively and individually serve our campus. In 1985 Golden Gavel reviewed literature from three well-known and respected honor societies. A survey of administrators, staff members, and faculty fully supported the students' belief that Mortar Board's reputation, Ideals, and organization would best serve Adrian and its deserving students.

The members of the Golden Gavel chapter coordinated the Student Leadership Conference that brought Adrian students together to learn and study leadership theory and practice, coordinated the annual Student Life Awards Banquet that recognizes outstanding student leadership, sponsored an aid station for the CROP walk that raised funds for meals for the elderly in Lenawee County and for the needy in Africa, coordinated the Advisor of the Year Award that recognizes the leadership and service contributions of an Adrian faculty or staff member to a student organization, and sponsored a reception after the

Festival of Lights Christmas celebration where people from Adrian and the surrounding community celebrate the holiday season.

Champion: Vice President and Dean of Students Robert Turek.

Installing officer: National Director of Programming David Coleman, assisted by Section Coordinator Julie Prohaska (Eastern Michigan University, 1981).

Agnes Scott College, 1931

The Honor Organization of Agnes Scott College (HOASC) was formed in 1916 by 11 women who felt the need for an organization of seniors with similar high ideals and interest in the college. The purpose of HOASC was to stimulate effort along the lines of college activities, further the development of the college by supporting new significant movements, and serve as a clearinghouse for student and social activities. According to a 1938 history, the order of the meeting began with the reciting of the pledge, followed by the roll call by number. Each member when initiated was given a number. By 1938 there were 279 members.

In 1927 HOASC conducted a survey of campus conditions at the request of the president of the college. "This survey included a careful estimation and criticism of physical equipment, such as dormitories, appearance of the campus, personal relations of students and faculty, day student and boarders and boarders with each other, extracurricular activities, curriculum, and ability of professors. This survey was handed to the president to be looked over and later discussed with him."[30] Another project was sponsoring annual parties for sophomores so they could meet boys of Decatur and Atlanta.

In 1930 members of HOASC, realizing that its aims and Mortar Board's were quite similar, began petitioning to become a chapter of the national organization, and in October 1931 the HOASC chapter

was installed. The old service activities and traditions of HOASC were combined with the national Mortar Board traditions and Ideals. In 1938 the chapter sponsored a class for seniors on marriage and hosted a week of vocational guidance with speakers and a bureau to help students choose vocations.

Petition: 1930.

Installing officer: Expansion Director Katherine Kuhlman (Michigan, 1922).

University of Akron, 1964

Pierian, the senior women's scholastic honorary, was founded in 1923. Professor of ancient languages Joseph Rockwell (a faculty member of the original Buchtel College) spearheaded the group. He suggested the name Pierian, referring to well of learning in Greek mythology, and urged the members to excel in activities, scholarship, leadership, democracy, and character. The purpose of the first Pierian chapter was "to recognize outstanding women leaders, to maintain a high standard of scholarship, to advance the spirit of service and fellowship among university women, and to stimulate higher standards in extracurricular activities." On April 24, Pierian was installed.

The University of Alabama, 1929

In February 1921 the women of the Senior Honorary Club, which was founded in 1914 as the sister organization of the Jasons, organized the Hypatia Honorary for outstanding senior women. The name Hypatia was adopted from the Greek mathematician and philosopher of Alexandria, a very broad-minded and progressive Greek woman famous for her lectures in philosophy. The Hypatia Honorary chose her colors of white and gold and the yellow rose as its flower, and the honorary's first pin was a gold profile of a Greek woman against a black enamel background, symbolizing wisdom, beauty, and fame. The recognition of new members was held on Jason Tap Day; Hypatians wore solid white and tapped their new initiates by pinning on them the yellow rose.

In 1922 Hypatia established a silver loving cup to be awarded at the end of each year to the girl who contributed the most to the university's welfare.

The chapter was installed on May 11.

Albion College, 1941

The first senior honor organization at Albion College was founded in May 1930 when eight senior girls were chosen by a faculty committee. The name Chevron was chosen because it was a mark of distinction and honor. The purpose of the group was to maintain a high standard of scholarship, recognize and promote a spirit of service and fellowship among college women, and honor the college women who embody these ideals of culture. Members who have received the unanimous vote of the active chapter and are passed upon by a faulty committee were chosen. Chevron members were tapped at the May Morning Breakfast, an all-college event. Service programs included the sponsorship of at least one cultural program a year; the formation of a new freshman women's honorary, Alpha Lambda Delta; the sponsorship of the "comrade" system between the dormitory and town girls; and the publication of a campus etiquette booklet, *When in Doubt*.

Champion: Dean of Women Marian Gray.
Installing officer: Expansion Director Katherine Kuhlman.

Alcorn State University, 2013

Shortly before installation in 2013, President Christopher Brown chose Epignosis, the Greek word for knowledge, as the chapter name. A description of the installation appears earlier in this chapter.

Petition: 2012.
Champion: Director of Preprofessional and Honors Programs Thomas Sturgis and Assistant Director Wandra Arrington.
Installing officer: National President Susan Caples.

American University, 1969

Cap & Gown was founded on January 8, 1937, by eight women who chose the name because it was often used by local chapters aspiring to become Mortar Board members. The custom of presenting the blue and gold stole from the old members to the newly elected members was established. Roses and cornflowers were chosen as flowers for the society. Qualifications for candidacy were a B average, active and unselfish participation in school activities, and in general service to the college community. One project in 1965 was to hold a small seminar with faculty on the subject "Why Student Demonstrations?"

Petitions: 1956, 1961, 1966.
Installing officer: Editor Pam Chinnis, assisted by Section Coordinator Pam Carew.

Arizona State University, 1963

Pleiades was founded in January 1934 by six original members who chose the name after the cluster of stars in the constellation Taurus.

The purpose was "to render altruistic service in the interests of Arizona State Teachers College."[31] Faculty members began inquiring about establishing a chapter of Mortar Board in 1940. (The 1963 petition gave the name of the chapter as Senior Honor Board, founded in 1957.) After submitting a series of petitions, Pleiades became the 108th chapter of Mortar Board on March 23.

Petitions: 1955, 1963.

Installing officer: National President Ruth Weimer.

University of Arizona, 1926

The local organization, Pi Sigma Alpha, had been organized in 1923 to promote interest and service in university activities, uphold high scholastic standards, maintain worthy ideals of womanliness, and create a spirit of democracy among university women.

Two silver cups were presented to the freshman and sophomore women who had attained the greatest "all around womanliness."

Five collegians and fifteen alumnae were initiated at the March 20 installation at 6:00 a.m. Mortar Board was the highest honor on campus with the exception of the Freshman Medal, which went to one woman.

Installing officer: Field Representative Pauline Wherry (Texas, 1918).

University of Arkansas, 1940

On November 19, 1929, Octagon was approved by the Student Affairs Committee. One woman from each of the women's houses on the campus, seven sororities and one dormitory, was chosen by a two-thirds majority of the existing group. Candidates must have held at least a 3.5 grade point average and were unanimously selected on the basis of scholarship, leadership, and personality. The new members took an oath of truth, honor, friendship, loyalty, fidelity, dependability, courage, and charm.

Octagon sponsored Sigma Epsilon Sigma and gave a cup to the sophomore with the most outstanding scholarship and ability. The group annually assisted the dean of women during orientation and sponsored lectures for personal improvement of all women students. Octagon became the seventy-second chapter.

Over the years, the Octagon chapter has had many notable accomplishments. In 1964, members of Mortar Board were instrumental in the establishment of Dead Day so that students would not have to end classes one day and begin finals the next. Mortar Board also issued a resolution stating its opposition to racial discrimination in university housing and intercollegiate athletics in 1964. In 1976, the chapter admitted its first male member. Some of the Octagon chapter's various projects have included donating books and other items to underprivileged children, fund-raising for buildings in Fayetteville and on campus, conducting activities to recognize outstanding students, and assisting during new student orientation.

Petition: 1939.

Installing officer: National President Katherine Wills Coleman.

Auburn University, 1955

In the spring of 1932, eight women students at the Alabama Polytechnic Institute became interested in forming an honor society for women. This group organized as a chapter of Cardinal Key, with its objective to study, discuss, and strive to further the best interests of the college. This organization was open to junior and senior women. In 1935 another organization, Sphinx, was established as an honor society only for senior women by six girls who had high standards of achievement in scholarship, activities, and leadership; were loyal to high ideals; and realized the importance of worthy recognition.

One of the purposes of Sphinx as stated from its beginning was to achieve recognition by Mortar Board. Through the years the two organizations were active, and in 1949 they believed that affiliation with Mortar Board would give them expanded opportunities for service on their campus, association with similar groups on other campuses, and honor and prestige. In 1952 the two merged and adopted the name Sphinx to meet the Mortar Board requirement that there be only one honor society for senior women. A formal petition was submitted in June 1953. Installation was held in the Faculty Club on November 13, with dinner in the Banquet Room of the student union.

Petition: 1953.

Installing officer: National President Jane Klein Moehle (Cincinnati, 1941).

Augustana College, 1955

Aglaia was founded in April 1940 by nine junior women. Aglaia, symbolizing brilliance, was traced to one of the three graces of Greek mythology, and her three symbols were the rose (devotion to the beautiful), to inspire one to rise above the commonplace in life; the myrtle leaf (ever alive and growing), exemplifying growth in all worthy human endeavor; and the lyre (harmony of sound), symbolizing every utterance entirely harmonious with one's inward thoughts. The purpose of Aglaia was to foster scholarship, develop leadership, promote service, and strengthen character by recognition of outstanding achievement by senior women. Aglaia sponsored the all-school Christmas event, Swedish Smorgasbord, every year. Dressed in traditional Swedish costume, Aglaians provided festive entertainment. Aglaia also participated in the total counseling program for new women students.

Installation was at the Weyerhaeuser Estate, with a buffet supper afterward.

Installing officers: National Treasurer Joy Moulton and Section Coordinator Helen Reich (Iowa, 1936).

Ball State University, 1971

Four outstanding senior women founded Clavia in 1950 and tapped the first members in 1951. The term *clavia* means "key," which was chosen as the insignia. From Clavia's beginning, the charter members hoped to become a chapter of Mortar Board and began sending annual reports to the national society in 1967. The group sponsored a leadership workshop for high school students who were in the upper 10 percent of their graduating class and active in extracurricular activities and also sponsored a drug symposium with speakers from the Muncie community and Ball State faculty. Clavia was installed as a chapter of Mortar Board on April 18 in the West Lounge of the art gallery. Esther Ebrite Ball and Thelma M. Hiatt (both Ball State, 1972) were significant in the life of the chapter.

Petitions: 1950 and around 1967.

Champion: Assistant Dean of Students Martha J. Wickham (Ball State, 1972).

Installing officers: Second Vice President Barbara Cook and Section Coordinator Dottie Moser.

Baylor University, 1971

In the spring of 1961 a faculty-administrative committee met to organize a senior woman's honor society. Its constitution was written with the long-range goal of obtaining a chapter of Mortar Board. Nine senior women were selected. The committee went to the dormitory rooms of the women who were chosen, tapped them with a laurel wreath, and assembled the group for breakfast. A major project was to sponsor Woman's Day each spring to emphasize women's potential and achievements. The Laurel Society was the first student organization to hold a fund-raising drive to promote the new library and received permanent recognition on a bronze plaque on the Garden Level of Moody Memorial Library. They also sponsored a Bride's School annually, open to all Baylor women. Laurel was installed as a Mortar Board chapter on April 4.

Petition: 1969.

Installing officer: Expansion Director Mary McAlister.

Beloit College, 1951

A local group of senior women called the Golden Taper was established in 1926 by the dean of women with the expressed purpose of petitioning Mortar Board. When that dean left, the group disbanded and another group, the Royal Order of the Senior Bench, was formed in 1929. When the secretary of Senior Bench in 1938 asked for information about Mortar Board, she was told that the local group did not fulfill the requirements for membership, as it was a "secret society" and the number of senior women did not reach the required fifty.

The group's secretary responded that the Golden Taper was a secret society because "the men have a powerful senior committee which is also sub-rosa, so all activity of the Senior Bench is done under another organization or in the name of a committee of senior women."[32] During World War II the chapter sponsored a bandage-rolling course and the College Canteen. Later chapters gave an annual tea for faculty women, chaperoned dances, sponsored "senior tables" in the dorms, and presented all-college convocations in the chapel.

When the dean of women wrote about petitioning Mortar Board in the early 1940s, the number of senior women was still only forty-four. New dean of women Elizabeth B. Stanton vigorously continued correspondence with Mortar Board during the late 1940s, and when the number of senior women reached eighty-four, she filed a petition for membership on December 19, 1949. After a visit by National Secretary Jane Klein and a vote of the chapters, Beloit was installed on May 26 as the eighty-fourth chapter in the home of President Carey Croneis, whose spouse was made an honorary member along with new dean of women Eleanor McGranahan.

Champion: Dean Stanton.

Petition: 1949.

Installing officer: National President Rosemary Lucas Ginn.

Berea College, 1973

Alpha Sigma Chi was founded on the watch of Dean of Women Ann Marshall in 1965. The constitution of Mortar Board was used as a basis for Alpha Sigma Chi's with the idea that in five years the group would apply for Mortar Board membership. The name was formed from the initial letters of the motto: Excellence Benefits Wisdom. Alpha Sigma Chi was installed as Mortar Board's 159th chapter.

Alpha Sigma Chi has always been an active group, with service to the campus and community. Many activities were annual events, such as hosting the president's ice cream social for freshmen and sponsoring the Faulty Follies in the spring. Alpha Sigma Chi sponsored an auction where faculty members donated various items, such as dinners, movie tickets, and trips, and students bid on them. The profits went to various charities. Women's Day was the biggest event, with a convocation speaker in the afternoon and a banquet honoring outstanding students in the evening where Alpha Sigma Chi members were tapped.

Petition: 1971.

Champions: Dean of Women Ann Marshall and Associate Dean of Students Ruth Butnell.

Installation: May 12.

Installing officers: Secretary Betty Boyd and Section Coordinator Susan Bowling (later Susan Bowling Komives, the author of the first chapter of this book).

Birmingham-Southern College, 1935

The Scroll Honor Society was formed in 1928 by eight senior women who felt the urgent need for a senior honor society for women that would recognize leadership, service, character, and outstanding scholarship. The ultimate aim of the organization was to petition Mortar Board, and the petition signed by the women was presented on April 2, 1929, to the faculty of Birmingham-Southern for approval. The faculty gave its hearty approbation to the new organization. "The title of Scroll was chosen because each young lady honored with membership was permitted to sign her name on a permanent scroll, thus pledging herself to adhere to the high traditions of Birmingham-Southern College."[33]

The guidelines for the new honor society were drawn up by the college's president, Guy E. Snavely, who was instrumental in bringing the Scroll Honor Society and Mortar Board together. Some traditional service programs during the early 1930s included sponsoring career guidance programs for both high school girls who "were beginning to think seriously of their life work"[34] and for the women on campus, tutoring women students who were falling behind in class work, helping with freshman orientation, and sponsoring a homecoming banquet for alumni before a football game.

The petition to join Mortar Board was accepted in 1935. The installation date, October 26, was chosen because it was President Snavely's birthday. In the 1940s a book sale became the Mortar Board Textbook Exchange, and in the 1960s the chapter "renovated its Career Day for women and developed a new Graduate Forum for the college community as interest shifted to graduate work."[35] According to a history written in the early 1970s, "Scroll is always striving to be not only an honorary organization but to contribute significantly in campus affairs."[36]

Petition: 1935.

Champion: President Guy E. Snavely.

Boston University, 1974

Cap and Crown was founded on May 11, 1966, by the Association of Women Students (AWS) to honor those women students who showed outstanding qualities of scholarship, leadership, and service. To be eligible for membership, one must have attained a cumulative grade point average of at least a 3.0 and have had a 3.0 the semester prior to tapping. Also, she must have demonstrated leadership in at least two major activity areas. One outstanding goal of Cap and Crown was the attainment of official membership in Mortar Board. The chapter was installed on May 5.

Petitions: 1967, 1973.

Installing officer: *Forum* editor Mary Dawn Bailey Liston.

Bowling Green State University, 1969

The Cap & Gown senior honor society for women was founded on May 20, 1943, by Dean of Women Audrey K. Wilder (Albion College, 1952) with the assistance of ten Mortar Board alumnae who lived near Bowling Green. Cap & Gown was structured from its beginning after the pattern of Mortar Board with the hope that eventually an application for membership might be submitted. Associate Dean of Students Fayetta Paulsen (Bowling Green, 1969) was "instrumental in the petitioning process by compiling volumes of material to be submitted for inspection and coordinating national visits."

Several Cap & Gown traditions developed over the years, including a breakfast at homecoming to honor alumnae and cosponsoring a campus leadership conference. The 1967 group sponsored a speaker on the topic "Are You Ready for Marriage?" and assisted with the new library's open house.

Cap & Gown was installed on April 20. Former deans Wilder and Florence Currier (Ohio Wesleyan, 1930) were among the honored guests. In addition to the twelve active members, more than one hundred Cap & Gown alumnae were initiated as postgraduate initiates. The chapter became the Fayetta Paulsen chapter in 1989 upon Dr. Paulsen's retirement as vice president.

Petition: 1966.

Champions: Dean of Women Wilder and Associate Dean of Students Paulsen.

Installing officer: National President Helen Snyder.

Bradley University, 1967

The Wakapa chapter was founded on April 13, 1948, by sixteen senior women for the purpose of establishing a society to honor senior women displaying superior scholarship, leadership, and service. The founders patterned the criteria for membership and the constitution after Mortar Board. Traditional service activities included speaking at orientation meetings with freshmen, presenting at high school career programs, and sponsoring a leadership conference. The changing role of women was discussed at a tea with women faculty. At the installation on April 15, which was held in Neumiller Chapel, twenty-six collegiate members and sixty-seven alumni became Mortar Board members.

Petition: 1965.

Installing officer: National Second Vice President Helen Reich.

Bucknell University, 1941

A chapter visitor reported in the 1930s that a local group, C.E.A., was founded as an intersorority group but was reorganized in 1935 as an honor society, Gamma Beta. It was then that the group began a correspondence with Mortar Board. To meet the requirements of Mortar Board, the members patterned their constitution after Mortar Board's and strengthened their program. They were instrumental in establishing a chapter of Alpha Lambda Delta.

After the required five years, Gamma Beta petitioned Mortar Board for a chapter and was accepted. The installation was on Mortar Board's twenty-third birthday, February 15.

During World War II, the members acted as registrars for male students who had to register under the conscription law. The chapter organized the campus's first public debate on Vietnam. Later programs included raising money for the formation of a women's library, holding a tea for students who had spent their junior year abroad, and holding a tea for the League of Women Voters after the voting age was changed to eighteen.

Petition: Around 1940.

University at Buffalo, 1993

UB LAUNCH (Leaders As Undergraduates Noted for College Honors) was founded in August 1990. Through 1967 there had been two senior honor societies, Bisonhead and Cap & Gown. As these no longer existed, it seemed appropriate to establish an organization on campus that would promote and recognize excellence and reward a group of exceptional students. On April 25, the chapter was installed in the Student Union Theater with nineteen new members, twenty retiring members, and thirty-seven alumnae of Cap & Gown initiated.

Installing officers: Student Representative Steve Schortgen (Trinity University, 1991) and Section Coordinator Barbara J. Arnold.

Champions: Assistant Dean of Women Ann Hicks (Buffalo, 1993), Vice President Robert Palmer, Associate Vice President and Dean of Students Dennis Black (Buffalo, 1997), and Director of Student Life Barbara Ricotta (Buffalo, 2005).

Butler University, 1956

Scarlet Quill was founded at Butler College in October 1921 "as an honor group of senior women whose goal was to petition National Mortar Board which has corresponding ideals of Scholarship, Leadership, and Service."[37] Its insignia was a black felt hat with a scarlet feather across the front. A service project was to "maintain a scholarship for a girl who by the end of her sophomore year had made herself outstanding in scholarship and school activities."[38]

In 1926 Scarlet Quill inquired about petitioning Mortar Board but was told that certain requirements must be met in the growth of the college before a petition could be granted. In 1954 Scarlet Quill contributed financially to the building of large stone marker benches placed at the two main entrances to the campus. This gift was recognized with the permanent inscription of the society's name there.

After meeting all requirements, Scarlet Quill petitioned for membership in Mortar Board in 1953 and was installed on May 6. Eight collegiate members, three honorary members, and eighty-three alumnae were initiated at the Garden House, with a banquet following. College president M. O. Ross and Dean of Women Elizabeth Durflinger spoke.

According to a 1975 history, the outstanding service activity of Scarlet Quill was the annual cosponsorship with Blue Key (senior men's honorary) of homecoming activities. The chapter also helped support women's athletics that were underfunded.

Petitions: There is correspondence asking for petition information in 1922, 1924, 1926, 1933, and 1951 by the deans of women and officers of Scarlet Quill.

Champion: Dean Durflinger (Butler, 1956).

Installing officer: National President Jane Klein Moehle.

California State University Channel Islands, 2011

The team assembled to petition Mortar Board for a chapter consisted of twelve faculty and staff and at least as many student leaders. The chapter, which would be named the Four Pillars on which the institution's purpose rested, would bring meaning to leadership development for this relatively new campus. Mortar Board would give California State

University Channel Islands (CSUCI) the chance to recognize students and hone their leadership skills for the betterment of other students.

Petition: 2010.

Champion: President Richard R. Rush (CSUCI, 2012), Professor Andrea Grove (Georgia, 1991), Interim Associate Provost Dennis Muraoka, Vice President for Student Affairs Greg Sawyer.

Installing officer: National President Dan Turner.

California State University Long Beach, 1972

Cap & Gown was founded in 1964 with the intent of petitioning Mortar Board and so was patterned after Mortar Board's structure. The group began a child daycare center on campus that was badly needed to allow mothers of young children to continue their studies. There were foreign student dinners and leadership seminars. Moneymaking projects involved the sale of food, since there was a need on this commuting campus. The installation was at noon on December 10, followed by a luncheon attended by Dean of Students John W. Shainline. Sixteen collegiate members and twenty-nine alumnae representing each previous class were initiated. Ten advisors were listed in the program.

Petition: 1970.

Installing officers: Expansion Director Mary McAlister, assisted by past National President Coral Vanstrum Stevens and Section Coordinator Hedy Kirsh (University of Southern California, 1961).

University of California–Los Angeles, 1939

Agathai was organized in 1922 by Dean of Women Helen Matthewson Laughlin to serve the university and help build tradition and loyalty, qualities that would be essential to the growing institution that started on the old campus. The members ware tapped every year at the Women's Activity Banquet. Agathai became the seventieth chapter of Mortar Board on October 18.

Champion: Dean of Women Helen Matthewson Laughlin (University of California–Los Angeles, 1922).

Installing officer: National Treasurer Coral Vanstrum Stevens.

University of California–Santa Barbara, 1965

Crown and Scepter was founded in 1937. A constitution was written by the next year's chapter, with the preamble "WE, as members of Crown and Scepter, do hereby organize ourselves as a senior women's honor organization for the purpose of maintaining and furthering high standards of conduct, unquestionable character, scholarship, willing service, leadership, cooperation and University loyalty."[39] At the time of installation in 1965, the chapter sponsored the Senior Torchlight Farewell, which followed the baccalaureate service. Since 1938 the group had presented at this event a scholarship award to the senior woman with the highest grade point average.

Crown and Scepter also sponsored surveys and studies that provided information for student body or administrative action, sponsored faculty-student dinners, presented a panel titled "The Role of the Woman College Graduate in the World," and worked to establish Alpha Lambda Delta.

The installation on May 16 was at the home of the chancellor, which had a beautiful view of the Pacific Ocean. There was a reception in the Women's Residence Hall lounge and a banquet later at the El Encanto Hotel in Goleta.

Petition: 1965.

Installing officers: Expansion Director Betty Jo Palmer, Section Director Mary McAlister, past National President Coral Vanstrum Stevens, and Dean of Women Ellen E. Bowers (Pomona College, 1930).

Carleton College, 1951

Correspondence concerning Carleton students' interest in Mortar Board dates back to 1935. The Carleton Women's League cabinet believed that there was a need on campus for a women's honorary organization and patterned its creation after Mortar Board. "A society such as Mortar Board with a national structure encourages and provides a certain stability and traditionalism to any campus community."[40]

The Senior Women's Honor Board began in 1945. The group's first project was to give students on probation reading tests to determine their possible difficulties and then provide aid in reading, outlining, and general methods of study.

In 1948 the group held a Careers Conference and awarded a Carleton Spirit Cup to the freshman girl who best exemplified honor, friendliness, steadfastness, and courtesy. In writing the group's first constitution, group members noted that they had difficulty with Mortar Board's requirement with the unanimous vote for selection of a new member.

The expansion director sent them a copy of the affirmative plan of voting, and since that plan was similar to the one they had been using, they adopted it. The group filed a petition for membership in Mortar Board in 1949 and was installed two years later on November 4. Attending were seven collegiate members, the dean of women, two advisors, and two alumnae. In spite of a raging blizzard, four members of the chapter at the University of Minnesota attended and assisted with the initiation ceremony. A very simple banquet followed the initiation, and the installing officer spoke about the "nature, meaning, and organization of Mortar Board."[41]

In April 2014, the National Council granted the chapter's request to change its name to Golden Schiller. This petition reflected at least two years of extensive discussion and progress. The chapter name was changed, with approval, in 2017 to SERV for Senior Engagement through Rewarding Volunteering.

Petition: 1949.

Carnegie Mellon University, 1923

In the winter of 1920, the feeling that an honorary society for women would promote the aims of Carnegie Tech grew into actuality. At a meeting of the junior and senior classes of the Margaret Morrison Carnegie College and the College of Fine Arts, certain girls were chosen by their classmates as most nearly approaching the ideal college woman. A list of these girls was then taken to the directors of the colleges and to the president so that the first generation of Sphinx was composed of the choice of both the students and the administration.

The standard upon which Sphinx girls were chosen was threefold: personality, activities, and scholarship. The "identification of the local group with Mortar Board"[42] took place in 1923, and Sphinx became the nineteenth chapter. Some of the early achievements were to establish the Women's Club Room for a central meeting place of women's organizations, standardize the Women's Point System, hold a tea dance for transfers, and bring the women's sophomore honorary Cwens to campus in 1928.

Among the traditions cited in the 1937 history was to plant an Oriental plane tree each year for new members on the Cut, a broad grassy stretch that connected the campus proper with the rest of the city. New and old members formed a circle around the hole dug in the ground, and after a short service the tree was planted, with each member placing a shovelful of soil over the roots.

Another tradition then was the initiation ceremony, which was held at a retreat in the mountains outdoors at sunrise. "Whether it is the magic of the early hour or the quiet freshness of the morning air, or the strange sweetness of bonds of friendship being knit into the fabric of a secret society, this sunrise initiation has an unusual loveliness that makes it a deeply moving and ever-remembered experience."[43]

The chapter goes by the name Eta.

Carson-Newman University, 1974

Panathenees was founded in 1958 by two faculty members for the purpose of recognizing and stimulating achievement among the women at Carson-Newman College and to serve the college and community in any capacity in which its members are capable. The intent was also to petition Mortar Board. The name was derived from the Greek words *pan* (many) and Athena, the goddess of wisdom. The insignia was an olive branch representing goodwill and peace in a gold on black oval background.

Projects of chapters in the 1970s included sponsoring sessions on finance, automobiles, income taxes, securing a job, and how to find a home. The group sponsored a graduate school seminar and held a tea in honor of sophomore and junior women with a grade point average of 3.0 or better.

Installation was on March 23. New members had been tapped at 4:00 a.m. the day before, and recognition was held in the chapel later that morning. The installation was held at the First Baptist Church, followed by a reception at Sarah Swann Hall and a dinner at the Morristown Country Club.

Petitions: 1965, 1966, 1968, 1971.

Champions: Academic Dean Walter R. Guyton, Assistant Dean of Students Janelle Hederman, associate professor of foreign languages Rosemary Edens, and assistant professor of education Kay Wilson Shurden.

Installing officers: Expansion Director Marylu McEwen and Section Coordinator Janis Pierce (Mississippi, 1955).

Case Western Reserve University, 1952

Lux Honor Society was organized in the spring of 1941 by Mather student government members in the hope that the society might someday become a chapter of Mortar Board. Taking the Latin name for light from the seal of the university, Lux stated as its purpose as being "to recognize outstanding attainments in both scholarship and leadership." In the fall of 1941 Lux Honor Society received official approval from the Student Activities Committee as a service group on the Mather campus as well as an honorary organization. Lux members undertook as their first service program a study of the major and minor campus offices to be used in the new election system. They also planned to administer the Student Activities Calendar. In 1948 Lux added sponsoring the Big-Little Sister Program in cooperation with the dean of admissions.

Petition: 1952.

Central Michigan University, 1973

Installation: April 15.

Installing officers: Editor Mary Dawn Bailey Liston and Section Coordinator Wendy Raeder.

This is the insignia used by the local society Tassels before becoming a Mortar Board chapter at Central Missouri in 1984.

University of Central Missouri, 1984

Tassels was founded on October 23, 1967, with the intent of eventually petitioning Mortar Board for membership. A name and a pin were selected, and a constitution was completed. In 1968 Tassels was accepted by the college administration as the only senior women's honor society on campus. The first service project was working with the university archives. Later groups initiated Women's Week on campus and gave an annual award to the outstanding sophomore woman.

Petition: 1971.

University of Central Oklahoma, 1978

Bronze Key was organized at Central State University in October 1968. Its purpose was to promote college loyalty, advance a spirit of service and fellowship among college women, promote and maintain a high standard of scholarship, recognize and encourage leadership, and stimulate a finer type of college woman. Its first campus projects were sponsoring "Graduate Emphasis" speakers and providing a list of fellowships and scholarships in the graduate dean's office.

The group also promoted the organization and establishment of Sigma Delta, an honorary for freshman and sophomore women.

Petitions: 1973, around 1976.

Chapman University, 2007

Chapman sought a chapter of Mortar Board "to reward the best and brightest seniors in all disciplines in a more significant way."[44] The chapter was named after Albert Schweitzer, whose "reverence for life"[45] was central to the university's purpose.

Champion: Dean Emerita Barbara Mulch (Chapman, 2009).
Petition: 2007.

Chatham University, 1957

Hood & Tassel was founded in 1941 by seven senior campus leaders under the sponsorship of senior class advisor Dorothy Shields and with the approval of the dean of the college Mary Helen Marks. At the 1941 Moving-Up Day exercises, the last all-college convocation of the year, the founders announced the establishment of Hood & Tassel and tapped seven juniors whom they had selected for membership on the basis of character, leadership, service to the college, and scholarship.

The group was founded for a twofold purpose: first, that students who had demonstrated their principles and ability should be organized for leadership in greater service to the college, and second, that in due time the society should gain membership in Mortar Board. Throughout the years the members have helped to maintain high standards of scholarship on the campus and provided other special services in the interest of the college community.

Petitions: 1942, 1955.

Installing officer: Editor Marianne Wolfe.

University of Cincinnati, 1932

On November 13, 1912, three women met in McMicken Auditorium for a lecture by a "boring speaker." They decided to do "something exciting and be of service to the university" and organized as a university service group. They met later in the rear of Westwood School, where they wrote a constitution and a ritual. The purposes of the organization were "the betterment of women, further the ideals of the university, a closer understanding of college women, an advisory board to the dean of women, and band together and stand up for what they think is right."[46] The original seven members chose six more members to equal the thirteen who were initiated.

The Mystic 13 kept its connection to its local origins by attaching the original skull and crossbones to the Mortar Board badge. These are Mary Kathryn Barber's (1963) pins.

Dues were fifty cents a month, with twenty-five cents for nonattendance and ten cents for tardiness. The initiation fee was $13 plus the cost of the pin, which was a gold skull with a "13" on the forehead along with "emerald eyes (for secrecy) of a cat—ever watchful, with a ruby mouth for warmth, love, and fire. Colors were black for death and eternity and white for youth and purity." The Oriental poppy stood for mysticism. Invitations were written on rice paper with egg white (invisible), which had to be held over a flame to be read. Replies for acceptance for membership had to be made by phone at the stroke of midnight. For a week pledges had to wear ridiculous clothes or the same clothes in which they were tapped.

In 1919 the dean of women urged the group to "go national Mortar Board." They petitioned but were turned down because they would not "throw out their mystic ritual."[47] Mystic Thirteen did much to break down sorority barriers and to start Panhellenic on a frank, open basis of friendly cooperation.

Eventually, the chapter was admitted to Mortar Board on the third try.

Petitions: 1919, 1924, 1932.

Installing officer: Expansion Director Katherine Kuhlman.

Clemson University, 1977

The Order of Athena, which began in April 1968, concerned itself with the status of women on campus and their expanding role in society. In the beginning the organization worked closely with the Blue Key Honor Fraternity, which was a men's group at the time. Selection for the Order of Athena was based on scholarship, leadership, and service to the university. The major project of the organization was the annual Miss Clemson Pageant. The Order of Athena began accepting men in 1976.

In February 1976 National President Catherine Evans visited campus to determine if it was suitable for Mortar Board. During her visit, she met with university president Robert Edwards and Associate Dean of Students Susan G. Delony. Mrs. Evans found Clemson to be a first-class institution and stated that Mortar Board would be well served by adding the chapter to its roll. New members were tapped on February 9 at the Miss Clemson Pageant. The installation took place on February 26 in the Edgar A. Brown University Union Ballroom, followed by reception and dinner.

Throughout the 1980s and 1990s, the chapter at Clemson University was involved in projects including T-shirt sales, Habitat for Humanity volunteering, and continuing the pageant.

Petition: 1975.

Champion: Dean Delony (Clemson, 1977).

Installing officers: Expansion Director Marylu McEwen and Section Coordinator M. Kathryne MacKenzie.

Coe College, 1985

The Crescent Honor Society was formed in March 1925 and petitioned Mortar Board in 1965, but the college's petition was not accepted until 1985. Installation was on April 14. After that point the Crescent Honor Society chapter was noted in the *Forum* in 1985 for a workshop titled "Women and Issues," a faculty-staff-student breakfast, a luncheon for U.S. representative Shirley Chisholm, open forums with the dean and students, and recognition of an outstanding sophomore woman.

In 1987, the chapter hosted Mortar Board's first Constitution Tree planting as part of Mortar Board's national project, and Gladys Eddy (University of Denver, 1937), former national director of programming, attended.

In the winter of 1990, the chapter started a memorial fund for fellow student Brian Schappert, raising $1,000 from donations and recycling of aluminum cans.

In 1992, the chapter assigned each member an area in which to promote literacy, such as a day care center or retirement home. Adopting the freshman honor society Alpha Lambda Delta as a special project, the members became role models for younger students.

Petitions: 1965 and later.

Colorado College, 2002

Twenty-six members were initiated on April 24. The chapter was nameless until 2011, when it requested that the National Council approve Pikes Peak as its name.

Champions: Dean of Students Mike Edmonds (University of Mississippi, 1983) and Assistant Dean of Students Jeff Cathey (University of Tennessee-Knoxville, 1995).

Installing officers: National Secretary-Treasurer Sally Steadman and Section Coordinator David Whitman.

Colorado State University, 1961

Four senior women founded the senior women's honorary Tau Iota Omega in 1936 at Colorado Agricultural and Mechanical College. The English translation of their Greek motto is "We honor knowledge and achievement." The purpose in their constitution stated that "the object of the organization shall be to recognize and to promote scholarship, leadership, and character and to render service on the campus." The history of Tau Iota Omega reveals many and varied service projects: orienting new women to the campus by holding a tea for transfer women, founding Counselettes in 1939, a big sister group for new women students, and sponsoring it until 1956, when it became independent. Tau Iota Omega founded the campus chapter of Alpha Lambda Delta in 1955. Other projects have included parliamentary law classes for new officers in student organizations, a study-aid program for students, and faculty-student coffee hours. As of 1961, Tau Iota Omega gave the Freshman, Sophomore, and Junior awards. All three awards recognize high attainment in scholarship, leadership, and service. Tau Iota Omega was installed on March 19 in the auditorium of the student union. A brunch had been held at President William E. Morgan's home before the ceremony. An initiation banquet was held later that day.

Petitions: 1956, 1960.

Installing officer: National Vice President Eleanor Knoll Swanson (Nebraska–Lincoln, 1946).

University of Colorado, 1924

The Senior Honor Society was founded in 1908 by ten girls of the senior class for the purpose of furthering democracy, good fellowship, and scholarship. A constitution was adopted with the provisions that the badge be a mortarboard bearing the Greek letters Gamma Alpha, that the flower be the pink sweet pea, and that the colors be pink and white. The group built its traditions for fifteen years, and the membership was limited to ten girls from the junior class who were "bid" on May Day.

On December 10, the chapter was installed by Vice President Sarah G. Blanding (Kentucky, 1922). The chapter was renamed with approval of the National Council in 2011 for longtime advisor and community leader Virginia Patterson (Colorado, 1946).

University of Connecticut, 1949

In the spring of 1938 Mildred Haglund, class of 1939, was selected by the faculty of the School of Home Economics as the most outstanding student leader and was recommended for a Danforth Foundation fellowship. While in St. Louis and at a leadership camp in Michigan (probably Camp Miniwanca), she found that many of the students present were members of Mortar Board. She returned to the university in September of that year anxious to have a chapter. A faculty committee selected the first group of six senior women. The organization gave itself the name Laurels. The main purpose was to help foster good relations among students, faculty, and administration and to act as a service group on campus in whatever capacity and in whatever manner seemed advisable.

The motto of the society is a reminder and a standard: "Nothing wilts Laurels as much as resting on them." One of the most valuable programs undertaken by the Laurels was the supervision of the Student to Student Counseling Program. Student counselors were selected in their junior year and assigned to each entering student. Other early programs included teas for commuting students and arrangements for them to receive the college newspaper and to have ample locker space. Working with the administration, Laurels helped speed up the sale of books at the beginning of each semester. They sponsored a war bond auction during the war and helped with a program sponsored by the armed forces for the purpose of recruiting medical aides. With the increasing number of married veterans on campus (after World War II), Laurels entertained their wives.

Petitions: 1946, 1949.

Champion: Mildred Haglund and Dean of Women Mildred French.

Installing officers: National Secretary Ellen Reisner (Swarthmore, 1930) and Section Director Helen Lang (Maryland, 1934).

Converse College, 1967

The Order of the Gavel was founded on October 9, 1944, when the two senior leadership organizations, Alpha Sigma Sigma and Senior Order, merged into one honorary organization. The ten charter members of Gavel felt that Converse was too small to support two senior honoraries, and the purposes of the two groups were essentially the same. The purpose of the Order of the Gavel was to promote scholarship, encourage and recognize true leadership, and bring tangible benefits to the entire campus through a service program.

Gavel awarded a scholarship to a "rising senior chosen on the basis of need, scholastic standing and general fine qualities of character."[48] Other service projects included distributing the academic hoods to seniors at graduation, assisting with freshman orientation, and providing a student tutorial service. Gavel was installed on April 9 in Hartness Auditorium. Sixteen students and thirty-two alumni were initiated after the installation. A reception was held in Carmichael Lobby following the program. Gavel was the first chapter to be installed in South Carolina.

Petition: 1963.

Installing officers: National Secretary Jacqueline Sterner Douglas (Indiana University, 1949) and Section Coordinator Lynn Rountree Bartlett (California–Berkeley, 1927).

Cornell College, 1943

The Torch honor society for senior women was organized on January 9, 1923. The purpose as defined in its constitution "shall be to uphold standards in general, to promote high scholarship, to encourage participation in worthwhile activities upon the campus, and to promote leadership and service in the college community." The service program was adapted to campus needs, including the training of Big Sisters, vocational questionnaires, sponsoring speakers on vocations, special attention to the adjustment of transfers, and a used book exchange. In February 1968 a special event was held to celebrate the fiftieth anniversary of Mortar Board and Torch's twenty-five years as a part of Mortar Board.

The 1974 group ushered at commencement, sponsored voter registration for students with the League of Women Voters, and held a used book sale on campus.

Petition: 1940.

Champion: Dean of Women Alice Betts (Cornell, 1943).

Installing officers: Vice President Margaret Sayers Fowler and Section Director Miner with Iowa assisting.

Cornell University, 1918

The senior society Der Hexenkreis was founded in October 1892 by six members of the class of 1893. The name means "Circle of Witches," and it was a secret society.

According to a 1938 history, the object of the society was to maintain a high social standard among the women of the University, by example and influence to create a proper sentiment on those questions which concern the good of all, and to represent the best element among the women students with regard to both social and intellectual qualities. The society was entirely secret, and members were not permitted to refer to it or anything concerning it and "to ignore the allusions of others."[49]

The society asked Tiffany of New York to secretly design the "badge," which was a gold skull with red eyes and bore the mystic number 7 in black on the forehead. In February 1918, Ernestine Becker was elected to represent Der Hexenkreis at a gathering at Syracuse University of delegates from senior women's honorary societies of five universities. At this meeting Mortar Board as a national senior women's honorary society was born, and Cornell thus became one of the four founding members.

In 1922 for the first time, the new members were tapped the night before the big spring mass meeting, where elections to membership were announced. A house party was held on a weekend soon after initiation, with both old and new members attending. "Mortar Board has always tried to raise the standard of conduct of the women. The class of 1937 circularized the women students to ascertain their ideas about etiquette and dress of the Cornell women. The class of 1938 assembled this material into a booklet which was sent to all women entering the University in the fall." The 1950s chapters worked with freshman orientation and "helped with a new set-up for our student government." In the 1960s the chapters established a "basic reference library" in the women's dorms and proposed "University Standards of Academic Integrity" to students and faculty that led to an honor code. A national visitor to the chapter in 1970 reported that the University "was in turmoil." She indicated that two years earlier the students voted out of existence the student government and found "a resistance to and lack of need for honoraries."[50]

In 1996 Jessica R. Cattelino authored and published an extensive history of her chapter. In 2010–2012 Chapter President Vinny Gonzalez served on the National Council as student representative.

University of Delaware, 1960

The senior honorary for women was discussed in the fall of 1949 by Mortar Board alumnae, whose names had been supplied by the National Council, and a small group met with Dean of Women Amy Rextrew to discuss how to establish an honor society that would recognize and promote scholarship, leadership, and service to the university. The deliberations of this initial meeting resulted in a decision to form an informal Mortar Board alumnae group that would sponsor the new honorary.

The organizational meeting was held on May 11, 1950, at the home of one of the members. Eighteen members representing eight chapters attended. Also among those present was Elizabeth T. Worth (Swarthmore, 1937).

The alumnae selected the five charter collegiate members of Tassel, chose its first advisory committee, and conducted the first initiation ceremony. These alumnae, all outstanding leaders in the area, continued to maintain an active interest in Tassel once it was established. Supporters in the early years also included the university president's wife, two women deans, and several faculty wives, all of whom were members of Mortar Board. A few of the programs of Tassel in the early years were Listening Parties (for the benefit of students who remained on campus during away football games); an I.Q.T. Party, a tea given in honor of freshman and sophomore women who were on the deans' list; a survey for the University Parking Committee; and a student opinion poll.

The May 15 installation was held in the student center, with a reception and a dinner at an alumna's home.

Petitions: 1956, 1960.

Champion: Dean Rextrew.

Installing officers: National Second Vice President Helen Lang and Section Director Pam Chinnis.

Denison University, 1936

Eight senior women met on April 11, 1921, to "formulate plans for establishing a Senior Honorary Society." They felt that "there was a crying need for some group which would stand ready to help the school in any way possible and encourage in women students responsibility and an attitude of service. The name White Nun was chosen because it signified the highest possible achievement and the purity of purpose in attaining it. Its main purposes were to further the very best interests of Denison, to uphold in the highest degree the ideals of the university and to exemplify through the individual members beauty of character and womanliness."[51] Other qualifications were scholarship in the upper quarter of their class and actual accomplishments in the way of campus activities.

During the spring of 1927, White Nun was more or less put out of existence due to some very unwise actions of the members in the matter of selecting their successors (they could only agree on two). That fall White Nun was reorganized as Cap & Gown. The standards of this society were womanliness, tolerance, and depth of character as well as a cooperative, democratic spirit; good scholarship (B average); and leadership and service to the university. The chapter was patterned after Mortar Board, since there was an "earnest desire"[52] to secure a charter from the national organization. The chapter was officially accepted and on March 28, 1936, was installed.

The essential traditions at that time were to sponsor the Senior Women's All Night Party in the spring, feed Granville School children who were needy, sponsor the Dad's Day Banquet, honor underclassmen excelling in scholarship with a dinner, have fresh strawberries and pineapple at the initiation breakfast, sit in chapel together on the front row, and chew gum at all meetings. Later chapters in the 1930s arranged for talks in the women's chapel on vocational guidance, sponsored etiquette week, and conducted a survey concerning smoking among the girls in an effort to solve the smoking problem on campus. In the 1940s and 1950s, chapter projects included creating an orientation program for transfer students, sponsoring a dinner for high-achieving freshmen, monitoring the honors day convocation with ODK, and sponsoring a marriage clinic.

Helping to disseminate graduate school information, holding a picnic on pledging night for unaffiliated women, and sponsoring a Last Lecture Series and an Ugly Man contest were a few of the projects in the 1960s. In the 1970s the chapter held leadership and job interview seminars and sponsored the Bloodmobile on campus.

Petition: 1935.

Installing officer: National Expansion Director Katherine Kuhlman, with support from members of Ohio Wesleyan and Cincinnati chapters.

University of Denver, 1937

Kedros was organized at the University of Denver in 1913 by four students. The purpose was to foster high scholarship among all students, serve the University of Denver and its women students, interest the students in the activities of the university, and encourage the development of leadership among women students. Kedros's tapping was an exciting yet impressive ceremony held at the annual Honors Convocation.

The Kedros bell was first rung on March 19, 1923, in the belfry of Old Main. It was used for Kedros tapping and initiation and was rung after every athletic victory. For the first game or two, all the girls went up into the belfry and pulled the rope. The real fun came after the night games, when the building was dark. One girl waited at the

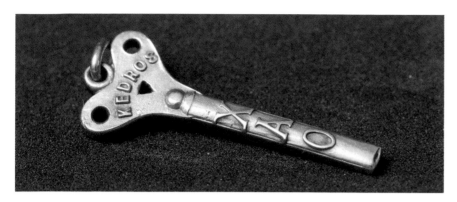

The key belonged to Gladys Shellabarger Eddy and bears the date of her initiation, 5-18-36. Mortar Board came along shortly after she became a member of Kedros. Gladys became a noted educator, national Mortar Board leader, and longtime advisor at Colorado State; she also became a distinguished lifetime member in 1999.

telephone for the report of the game's outcome while the other girl climbed the creaky stairs of Old Main to the belfry. All fears of the dark were forgotten when the ring of the phone broke the silence and the voice from the press box said "We've won." When the new Mary Reed Library was completed, it became necessary to have some means to dismiss the classes, so Kedros gave the bell to the university for this additional purpose.

The formal petition to become a Mortar Board chapter was put together with great care. Soft green suede binding with a gold-outlined print of the Library Tower held a book that medieval monks might have been proud to produce. The pages of the book were parchment, every word hand-lettered with beautiful art. So beautiful was the original that the girls could not let it go without providing a duplicate for themselves. The second copy of the formal petition is an exact replica

of the first book except for a dedication page whereon are honored the names of the Kedros founders. It rests in the Treasure Room of the university library. An original copy is also in the Kedros chapter file in the Mortar Board National Archives.

Some early Kedros service programs included a Christmas tea for all senior women and their mothers, a presentation to the library of books of contemporary biography that were appropriately labeled and placed in the Renaissance Room, and the sponsoring of a series of lectures titled "Women in World Affairs," including subjects about the opportunities for women in various occupational fields; "Responsibilities of Women as Citizens and Consumers"; and "Women's Emotional Adjustment to the Modern World." Kedros also was responsible for bringing a chapter of Alpha Lambda Delta to campus.

The installation was January 23 in the Renaissance Room, with a banquet after; a candlelight tea was held the night before.

Petition: 1936.

Champion: Dean of Women Gladys C. Bell (Denver, 1937).

Installing officer: National President Katherine Wills Coleman, with the assistance of Colorado.

DePauw University, 1919

The DePauw chapter of Mortar Board originated with Gamma Sigma Delta, a senior women's honorary founded in 1918. The purpose of the new organization was "to further good fellowship between the girls on campus, to arbitrate difficulties which might arise, and to emphasize scholarship." The group was chartered on May 9, 1919, becoming the eighth chapter of Mortar Board. Correspondence in 1925 indicates that the original charter was "framed and in the archives" and included the names of the charter members. Much of the correspondence in

1920s reflects concerns that any newly founded organization might anticipate, especially those that involve selection (grade point average, junior standing). An "inspection"[53] report by National Treasurer Rhea Walker (Purdue, 1926) in 1933 encouraged the chapter members to include a brief history of their local group in their initiation ceremony, since their chapter was among the first to receive a Mortar Board charter. Miss Walker's visit was overshadowed by a fire that morning in Mansfield Hall, a women's dorm, which was completely destroyed.

The chapter's service program was a tea for transfer students in the fall and a dinner for "an upper group of sophomores" who tended to be neglected. This certainly parallels the current times, when research shows that the sophomore year is a tough year for students. The effects of the Great Depression were evident when the college's investments "proved to be bad," causing faculty layoffs.[54]

In the spring of 1944, an awkward situation was created when the president of the university, Clyde E. Wildman, sent a telegram to National President Coral Vanstrum Stevens complaining that Mortar Board was too "exclusive," since the chapter had tapped only nine junior women and more had been eligible. President Wildman's daughter was one of those not chosen. There is voluminous correspondence in the file from this president to and from Mrs. Stevens in which he disagrees with the society's election policies and procedures and threatens to take action if they aren't changed. He continued this tirade against Mortar Board for several years at the expense of the newly elected members, who were not privy to the original problem.

A 1968 chapter visit report by Section Director Barbara Cook (and then assistant dean of students up the road at Purdue University) discussed "the distance, particularly with the seniors, between the students and administration." She noted that "the DePauw Mortar Board chapter reflects the problems at DePauw itself. It is a difficult period with student leaders under pressure to commit themselves to change

and the administration seen as a barrier to change." Although there was some discussion about disaffiliation from national Mortar Board, subsequent chapters have been active.

Petition: 1918.

Champion: Dean of Women Katherine S. Alvord (DePauw, 1930).

Drake University, 1954

The Margaret Fuller Club was founded in 1896 to study literature, art, science, and current topics. Margaret was a "famous American writer and defender of women's rights." Membership was made up of students, faculty, and alumnae. Student membership was not to include more than fifteen women each year.

Sieve and Shears was founded in 1912. Its purpose was to provide recognition for scholarship, character, personality, and campus activities. The two groups functioned side by side, overlapping membership to some extent. On February 4, 1949, the two combined with the purpose of forming one senior women's group that would be eligible to petition Mortar Board.

In November 1951, a national officer of Mortar Board visited and determined the club and the campus to be suitable and deserving of a Mortar Board chapter.

Some of the projects of the group at the time included the Margaret Fuller Scholarship Fund, a Scholarship Tea to honor all women who attained a B grade average, freshman orientation, the May Breakfast to honor graduating seniors and alumnae, and sponsoring Honors Day and convocation.

Ten members of Margaret Fuller–Sieve and Shears petitioned Mortar Board in 1953. In the 1960s and 1970s, some of the projects of the chapter included the Mortar Board Book Exchange, the

Scholarship Luncheon, writing for the school paper, meeting with the vice president of student life, and selling a cookbook.

Petition: 1953.

Champions: President H. G. Harden, Dean of Students Robert B. Kamm, and physical education professor Ruby A. Holton (Drake, 1959).

Drury University, 1966

Skiff (for "Scholarship, Knowledge, Ideals, Faith, and Friendship") was founded by eight senior women on December 9, 1914. It endeavored to promote better standards for women by stimulating underclass women, standing for high ideals in all campus activities, and performing and promoting service to the college. The initiation was traditionally held in the spring on a Sunday at 7:00 a.m., with a breakfast following. Some of Skiff's projects included a handkerchief sale and Mother's Day, which involved a chapel service, a luncheon, and a tea in a women's dormitory.

After petitioning Mortar Board a few years earlier, the chapter was installed on April 23. The day involved a meeting of the outgoing and incoming group, initiation in the Congregational Church, a luncheon at a local motel, an installation ceremony, and a reception in the president's home. There were twenty-three collegiate members and ninety-seven alumnae initiated.

Some popular projects of the chapter over the years included new student orientation, homecoming, a scholarship luncheon, the round-robin newsletter sent to alumnae of Mortar Board, Penny Nights, and one of the most significant annual events, Mother's Day.

Petition: 1961.

Champions: President Earnest Brandenburg, dean of the college Frank Clippinger, head of humanities and fine arts Robert L. Wilhoit,
Dean of Women Mildred Schrotberger (Drury, 1966), and professor of biology Lora Bond.

Installing officers: National Secretary Jacqueline Sterner and Section Director Patricia Herminghouse (Knox College, 1961).

Duquesne University, 1976

In the spring of the 1969–1970 academic year, Dean of Women Patricia E. Watt proposed the establishment of Mortar Board. A selection committee composed of deans of the colleges and the director of the Career and Placement Center was asked to submit three names of current senior women who in their opinion had demonstrated high scholastic attainment, leadership, and a high level of interest in fostering the university. Nineteen names were submitted, and all were sent letters requesting their presence at a meeting for senior women that was held on March 4, 1970. Each woman was asked to reply in writing to the Office of the Dean of Women stating her acceptance or rejection of the invitation to join the society. Twelve students responded in the affirmative. Decisions were made to repeat the initial selection process, to name the group Sigma Lambda Delta, to wear the colors dark blue and gold signifying truth and faithfulness, and to identify service projects for the coming year. When the selection process was repeated, twenty-nine women accepted the invitation to join the new honor society. A constitution committee was formed along with membership and fund-raising committees. Early service projects included the establishment of the Focus on Women program, the Senior Mentor Program, and the Transaction orientation program for transfer students. March 27 was the installation.

Champion: Dean Watt.

Installing officers: National President Catherine Evans and Section Coordinator Catherine Bush.

Eastern Illinois University, 1992

The Tassels chapter was installed on September 21. The local group had been founded in May 1983.

Eastern Kentucky University, 1983

The first senior honor society, Collegiate Pentacle, was founded in 1948 on the campus of what was then Eastern Kentucky State Teachers College. "Collegiate" denoted "environment," and "Pentacle" denoted the "top students on the college campus." The purpose of the organization was designed to recognize and foster leadership, scholarship, and service. The first meeting was held on September 23, 1948, in Burnam Hall, and the group discussed publishing a handbook to be distributed to incoming freshmen on campus points of interest, such as the bookstore, the library, dorm curfew, and dress codes. In 1961, members instituted a scholarship for a deserving student with high academic qualifications and meeting the characteristics reserved for Collegiate Pentacle members. In 1966 when Eastern Kentucky State College became Eastern Kentucky University, Collegiate Pentacle members expanded their quality of service. With the impending reality of Title IX and the effect it would have on organizations and activities, Collegiate Pentacle opened its membership to men in 1975. In 1976 the organization began thinking beyond the bounds of the university and central Kentucky and started an investigation about what would be necessary to become a member of a national organization. The group studied several honor societies and found that Mortar Board was most closely aligned with Collegiate Pentacle's principles and purpose. Initial groundwork began in 1979. The 1980–1981 members dedicated their year to researching and completing the application for affiliation. The chapter was installed on March 27.

Petition: 1981.

Installing officers: National President Dottie Moser and Section Coordinator Dorothy Bryson (Carson-Newman University, 1977).

Embry-Riddle Aeronautical University, 2003

Alpha Lambda Omega became a chapter on March 5, with forty-six new members initiated.

Champions: Chapter Advisors Deb Myers and Fred Cone.

Installing officers: National President Denise Rode and Section Coordinator Angela Eicke Schrader (Wyoming, 1998).

Emory University, 1969

On April 4, 1954, six girls met for the purpose of forming an honorary organization for women students in the upper division. A temporary charter was granted to the Women's Honor Organization on May 12. Membership in the organization was the highest honor an Emory woman could receive, since it required excellence in scholarship, leadership, service, and character. By its mere existence, the Women's Honor Organization encouraged Emory women to set lofty goals and strive to attain them. The organization recognized that these ambitions and goals were consistent with those of Mortar Board. The Women's Honor Organization encouraged students to attend intellectual and cultural events in Atlanta and on campus. Two annual events held at the time of installation into Mortar Board were to sponsor a weekend on campus for high school leaders and to hold a tea for the Board of Trustees. The chapter name became Omega Epsilon.

Petition: 1969.

Installing officer: National Secretary Betty Carol Pace Clark.

University of Evansville, 1975

Cap & Gown was begun in 1961 by ten senior women chosen by Director of Women's Counseling Virginia Grabill for their scholarship, leadership, and service. The organization was established with the aims of Mortar Board. The first project chosen by the group was to provide suitable distinguishing markings for seniors graduating with honors. This project was first financed by personal contributions of the members, who rented cords for the designated seniors. Other service projects at that time included organizing lectures to provide information about graduate education and financial help for women students and helping the admission staff with projects for welcoming freshmen to campus. The group sponsored a tea for outstanding high school senior women, and over the years the rather formal tea was changed to more informal Coke parties with skits and singing. Cap & Gown published a pamphlet titled *Something Borrowed–Something Blue: Reflections for Women* that examined women's role in modern life. Cap & Gown was installed on April 20.

Petitions: 1967, 1968, 1969, 1973.

Champions: Dean of Women Luise F. Schnakenberg (in the 1960s) and Dean Grabill (1973).

Installing officers: National Director of Elections Hedy Kirsh and Section Coordinator Mary Sue Harrington.

University of Findlay, 2008

Twenty-four members were selected in the first chapter at Findlay, and on March 25 an impressive installation ceremony was held in the Ritz Auditorium in Old Main, complete with an academic procession led by Faculty Marshall Don Collins, a harp prelude by instructor of music Nancy Glick, and a welcome by President DeBow Freed (Ohio Northern, 1989), who had supported Mortar Board at other campuses where he had been president. The invocation was given by associate professor of pharmacy Marc Sweeney (Ohio Northern, 1991). At least eleven Mortar Board alumni were also present to observe the ceremony, including President Freed's spouse Catherine Moore Freed (Texas, 1947) for whom the chapter was named in 2014.

Petition: 2008.

Champions: Assistant professor Cheri Hampton-Farmer, Dean of Undergraduate Education Marie Louden-Hanes (Findlay, 2009), professor of English Diana Montague (Valparaiso, 1982), and assistant professor of business Daniel Yates.

Installing officers: Executive Director Jon Cook and Assistant Executive Director Megan McGough.

Fisk University, 1975

Gold Key was established in February 1961 to serve a five-year probationary period before applying for a chapter of Mortar Board. The founding advisor was Dean of Women Anne S. Pruitt. Twelve women were selected as members. Although Gold Key was an honor society, its primary function was service to the Fisk community. Service projects included sponsoring the annual Awards Day Convocation, presentation of the Teacher of the Year Award, tutorial services, orientation activities for freshmen, and community projects. Installation took place on March 22 in the Memorial Chapel, with a reception afterward in Jubilee Hall.

Petition: 1973.

Champion: Dean Pruitt.

Installing officers: Expansion Director Marylu K. McEwen, Editor Mary Dawn Bailey Liston, and Section Coordinator Janis Pierce.

Florida International University, 1996

Golden Panther Honor Society was installed at 6:00 p.m. on March 29, and President Modesto Maidique received the charter from Director of Conferences Margaret E. King (Alabama, 1968) and Section Coordinator Tara Bowers.

Florida State University, 1931

At the Florida State College for Women three prominent seniors realized the need for a senior honorary society, and on December 16, 1925, thirteen seniors chosen from a group of thirty who had been suggested to a faculty committee began Torchbearers, whose ideals would be leadership, scholarship, and service—to conform with the standards of Mortar Board. Professor of history Kathryn Abbey was elected sponsor of that first group and continued in that capacity, reelected each term by the new members until she married and left the university in 1941. Each spring the outgoing members tapped a group from incoming seniors at an impressive ceremony—the old members carrying torches that are given to the new members. The installation was on March 7 at the home of "Mrs. Richards, an alumna of the Wisconsin chapter."[55] There were eight active members and then twelve alumnae members initiated. There was a banquet at the Floridian Hotel.

In 1997 Shirley Rodgers Tellander (1947) wrote to members of the chapter from the 1940s and 1950s:

> Do you remember how exciting it was to be tapped for this prestigious organization? I was on the verge of turning blue from holding my breath while robe-clad seniors walked slowly up and down the aisles looking at everyone but me. One by one, my junior classmates were chosen—the tension was almost unbearable. Finally, and thankfully, I was selected. What an honor and privilege to belong to Mortar Board.[56]

Champion: Professor Abbey.
Installing officer: National President Katherine Wills Coleman.

University of Florida, 1960

The University of Florida became coeducational in 1947, and Trianon, the honorary for women students, was founded on March 28, 1950. The charter members were chosen from the outstanding women students on campus by a committee composed of the deans of women and men, the president of the student body, and representatives from Florida Blue Key, the Women Students' Association, the student government, and the faculty. The name Trianon was chosen as representative of the three-part basic code of the organization: scholarship, leadership, and service. These aims were exemplified by the girls, who wore the three-sided Trianon Key embellished with a capital "T" and two stars for fields of service.

Newly elected members were tapped in the spring in a surprise postmidnight pinning ceremony at their residences. The following day, a more formal private initiation ceremony was held. From the outset the members of Trianon prepared and corresponded with Mortar Board hoping to be accepted, because Mortar Board represented the highest in ideals and achievement for college women. The aims of Trianon were to promote student activities and to promote service projects throughout the year. Early service projects included providing information during Orientation Week from booths around campus, sponsoring a coed tea, and serving as official hostesses for all official university functions. Later chapters continued to participate in the traditional Christmas Tree Lighting on campus, held a party for women junior transfer students, gave a Woman of the Year award to an outstanding woman on campus, organized a petition to extend the hours of the infirmary services, and printed a pamphlet for freshmen listing all the organizations on campus.

The installation of active members and then alumnae was on April 30 after an organ prelude and an invocation. A reception at the university president's home was held afterward.

Petition: 1956.

Installing officers: Fellowship Chair Daisy Parker and National Historian Hazel Moren Richards.

Fort Hays State University, 1971

The Women's Leadership Organization was interested in Mortar Board for some time, but Mortar Board was reluctant to give the go-ahead since it was felt by some on the National Council that Fort Hays State College was not of the caliber to merit Mortar Board. The dean of women was Jean Stouffer, a Mortar Board member from Kansas. She was discouraged as was the very patient and gracious advisor, Alice McFarland, assistant professor of English. Finally, after much wrangling and excuse making on the national level, a national visitor was assigned by the expansion director, and National Secretary Betty Carol Pace Clark conducted a visit in 1968. She wrote a thoroughly supportive and in some cases glowing report.

Meanwhile, the Women's Leadership Organization went about its business giving scholarships to other students, supporting Alpha Lambda Delta, and being a vibrant part of the growing campus of 4,700 students.

A second visitor, Second Vice President Lynn Rountree Bartlett, went to Fort Hayes in 1969 to find that the Women's Leadership Organization was working with the orientation of new students, tutoring, ushering, and giving scholarships.

The chapter, which took the name Gold Cord, was installed with Secretary Clark, Vice President Bartlett, and Treasurer Joy Moulton beating the drum for the establishment of a chapter at this fine institution.

Georgia State University, 1972

The Crimson Key Honor Society was founded in 1934 as an organization for senior women who had attained high scholastic achievement and made a distinguished contribution to the activities of the university. The organizational meeting was held in the Frances Virginia Tea Room on Peachtree Street and was formed by President George M. Sparks, Dean Nell H. Trotter, and Dean T. M. McClellan. The purpose of Crimson Key was to promote a closer understanding between students, the administration, and the faculty. Crimson Key also encouraged high standards of leadership, scholarship, and service to Georgia State and the city of Atlanta. The principal activity was its annual seminar cosponsored with the Georgia Commission on the Status of Women that attracted participants from all over the state. The seminar was concerned with education of women for political, social, and economic leadership. Crimson Key sponsored a series of dialogues with the dean of student life at Tuskegee Institute and conducted a citation ceremony for graduating seniors at commencement.

The installation was held at noon on February 5 in the Student Activities Building, along with a luncheon and a reception at President Sparks's home.

Petitions: 1964, 1965, 1966, 1970.

Champion: Dean Trotter.

Installing officers: Secretary Virginia N. Gordon and Section Coordinator Cheryl Wilkes.

University of Georgia, 1939

The first senior honor society for women was the Gold Quill Club, founded in January 1929. The requirements for membership were the completion of three years of college work with high average, high character, acceptable personality, and participation in not less than one major nonsorority activity for each year of college life.

Gold Quill was active until 1932, when a reorganization of educational institutions within the university system took place, resulting in the consolidation and coordination of certain colleges and such preoccupation of thought that Gold Quill was forgotten. It lapsed for two years. Feeling that this lapse was one of the most unfortunate results of the reorganization, which otherwise had been a notable success over the entire state, considerable thought was given to its reestablishment.

Accordingly, on April 10, 1934, Gold Quill was revived and its name changed to Parthenians. The constitution and the ritual were slightly changed, but the purposes, the requirements for membership, and all points of distinction remained the same. The first group was chosen from the class of 1933–1934, and included in this group were some students who had been as outstanding in scholarship and character as any women in the university. Parthenians promoted many cultural and artistic functions and were a potent force in the life of the university. Service projects at that time included assisting the dean of women during Freshman Week, entertaining faculty and presidents of student organizations at a formal reception, being "big sisters" to Alpha Lambda Delta, assisting the Personnel Office in the counseling

program, and entertaining all visitors with a tea during the Annual Music Festival.

The chapters in the 1950s participated in freshman orientation, held a Smarty Party for outstanding junior women, and sold sandwiches and Coca-Colas each Sunday night in the freshmen dormitory. Later chapters sponsored lecture series, held a Mortar Board Fair to introduce freshmen to cocurricular activities, served as ushers for Honors Day, and were trained as peer group counselors to make women aware of the opportunities available to them.

Petition: 1938.

Installing officer: Editor Hazel Moren Richards, with assistance from the entire collegiate membership of Agnes Scott.

Grinnell College, 1937

Cap & Gown received its grant of power from the faculty in February 1918. Plans for the organization had been worked out by a small group of women from the faculty and from the senior class, and a list of the senior women ranking in the highest fifth of the class had been prepared. On February 19 all the women of the faculty and of the senior class voted on those girls in this group who seemed to have the most outstanding powers of influence and leadership. As a result of this election, four young women were declared charter members of Cap & Gown. The constitution was adopted, faculty and advisory members were chosen, and formal initiation services were held.

From time to time distinguished visitors were guests of the organization. Money was raised for national work in World War I and for the college endowment, and official representatives have served on various college committees of importance. In 1933 Cap & Gown established the Quadrangle browsing library to supply books and magazines for leisure-time reading in the women's dormitories. Later it organized a college course in orientation, vocational roundtables for freshman women, and the state leadership conference where deans of women and student leaders from all Iowa colleges carried on a discussion of freshman orientation problems.

Installation was held in February 1937 at the home of the president, with a tea afterward. A formal dinner was held during a blizzard.

Petition: 1923.

Installing officer: Vice President Margaret Sayers Fowler.

Grove City College, 1972

Alpha Theta Mu was founded in 1944 with twelve members selected by Dean of Women Marguerite Appleton and her assistant, Mabel Hood. At the May Pageant, these twelve tapped the next members. Orientation assistance was a big service, and the members organized an honor society for sophomore women called Crown and Scepter, which became Cwens in 1951.

After two visits, one in 1962 and the next in 1971, Alpha Theta Mu was installed as a Mortar Board chapter on February 5.

Petitions: 1951, 1960, 1970.

Installing officers: First Vice President Melanie Hodge (Beloit, 1962) and Section Coordinator Betty Boyd (West Virginia, University 1942).

Hanover College, 1976

Tassels was founded in February 1967 to recognize senior women who had proven themselves outstanding in areas of scholarship, leadership, and service to the college community. Fellowship among the members was important. Tassels sponsored several programs that were of value, such as the Last Lecture Series and a three-day program in 1972 titled "The Feminine Dimension," which focused on the role of women in society. A similar program was given the next year titled "Miss, Ms. or Mrs." that included lectures delivered by faculty, community leaders, and past presidents of Tassels. To reach the campus community on a more personalized level, Tassels shared advice about college with freshman women in the residence halls.

The chapter was installed on April 11 on the Point. A reception was held at the college president's home, followed by a banquet later at the J. Graham Brown Campus Center.

Petition: 1974.

Installing officers: National First Vice President Constance Wallace (West Virginia, 1963) and Section Coordinator Patricia Slavens (Purdue, 1970).

University of Hawaii at Manoa, 1965

The Hui Po'okela (meaning "the chosen ones") Senior Women's Honor Society was founded in 1928. It was so christened by Princess Abigail Kawananakoa in recognition of its high aims and especial qualities of its women. Its members proudly wore the maile lei, formerly a badge of royalty, as the official flower of Hui Po'okela. The purposes of the society were to promote scholarship, recognize and encourage leadership and service to campus and community, foster fellowship among women students, and help to extend the hospitality of the campus. Each year Hui Po'okela honored undergraduate women of superior scholastic attainments at a Smarty Party and a Recognition Tea. The group presented the Outstanding Freshman Woman Award each spring, basing selection on scholastic and service criteria. A tuition scholarship for an outstanding sophomore woman was given in 1963 and 1964. Hui Po'okela sponsored and nurtured the formation of Hui Na'auao, a scholastic honorary that pledges freshman women in their second semester. Hui Po'okela members acted as hostesses for a reception honoring a visiting artist in the Music Department, ushered for productions in the Drama Department, and served as guides for campus tours offered by the Office of University Relations. In addition, Hui Po'okela contributed to the local community as well as to the academic community. Each week members aided the visually handicapped and blind students at the university by reading and tape-recording required books for their courses. Later chapters assisted with commencement exercises, helped with advising during fall registration, held a tea for "bewildered women transfer students,"[57] and sponsored a secondhand book sale.

The installation ceremony took place at the Kaimana Hotel on April 21. Nine actives and seventy-two alumni were initiated. A dinner was held after the ceremony.

In 2013 the chapter contributed to the national Pay-It-Forward Fund and asked that the fund be renamed Kokua, which means "to help."

Petitions: 1949, 1955, 1965.

Installing officer: Second Vice President Gen DeVleming.

Hood College, 1948

Upon the recommendation of the dean, the Keystone Honor Society was established by a faculty committee in March 1922. The purpose of the organization was "to bring together the students in the upper classes of Hood College who are preeminent in scholarship, leadership, and loyalty to the college, so that they may work together for the coordination of the activities of the various organizations and, through their personal influence, may improve the attitude of the student body toward every important phase of college life."[58] Some of its first projects were encouraging attendance at college functions, helping to make the dining room atmosphere a more gracious one, and assisting with the orientation program for freshmen.

Keystone sponsored chapel programs for the purpose of explaining the origin of and the requirements for academic honors and encouraging student interest in the attainment of honors. Keystone also sponsored an annual spring leadership conference, with a follow-up conference in the fall. The Student Committee on Academic Affairs was established by Keystone to meet with the dean for the purpose of discussing student opinion of the curriculum and other phases of academic life. Although Keystone has aided the college community in many specific ways throughout the years, the society has always felt that its greatest and most enduring contribution is an intangible one: the ideal of scholarship, leadership, and loyalty manifested in the various campus activities by the members of Keystone.

Installation was held on April 29 in the Meyran Reception Room, with a banquet afterward in Coblentz Hall.

Installing officer: National Secretary Ellen Reisner.

Hope College, 1961

Alcor was founded in the fall of 1937 and organized to give recognition to outstanding senior women and an opportunity for more effective campus service. The name Alcor is an Arabic word meaning "a test," symbolic of the high requirements for acceptance in the society. Alcor is also the name of a star in the constellation, Ursa Major. The

Dianne Portfleet (Hope, 2011) learned that the Alcor chapter would be renamed for her at Hope's commencement ceremony in 2016. She earned Excellence in Advising with Distinction in 2013 and was honored by National President Susan Caples (right).

a cultural program with a film series each year and a program with Hope's foreign students to promote a closer relationship. Alcor also sponsored International Night, where programs, exhibits, and a menu of different countries' foods were offered. Alcor members were selected to serve as counselors of freshman houses and received commendations from students and administrators for this work.

The installation was on March 18, and in addition to the seven charter members, twenty-seven postgraduate initiates were welcomed.

In 2016 the chapter added the name of its outstanding retiring advisor, Dianne Portfleet (Hope, 2011), to the chapter's original name; an announcement was made at the college's honors day, surprising Dr. Portfleet.

Petition: 1956.

Installing officers: Expansion Director Margaret Stafford and Section Director Margaret Foster.

University of Houston, 1970

On May 29, 1959, ten senior women who had shown excellence in scholarship, leadership, and service met at the invitation of Dean of Women Bessie M. Ebaugh and with the approval of President Clanton Williams to consider the establishment of a local honor society for senior women. These women chose Cap and Gown as a name, elected officers, and modeled a constitution after that of Mortar Board. Their first service project was to give recognition and an award of $50 to the outstanding freshman woman student at the annual University Awards Day. Cap and Gown also has given a reception for new faculty members, completed a survey of freshman attitudes for the director of the counseling center, and planned a tutorial project for freshmen in the residence halls. Cap and Gown also presented a panel titled

star was adopted as insignia for the organization. The "A" of Alcor symbolized the three qualities of scholarship, leadership, and service. Alcor's purpose was to discover specific needs of the campus, take the initiative in supplying leadership and ideas, and when the problem was met discover other needs. Throughout its history, Alcor has been dedicated to its founding ideals and standards. Early projects included

"Woman's Role in the Urban Environment" during the annual university Spring Festival.

Installation was held at 2:00 p.m. on May 10 in the A. D. Bruce Religion Center Chapel. A reception followed at the University Center.

Petition: 1968.

Idaho State University, 1972

To satisfy the need for a senior women's honorary on the campus of Idaho State College, Silver Tassel was founded under the sponsorship of Flora Smith Carlile and Mrs. Carl Isaacson. The first twelve members were tapped during Mothers' Weekend in 1953 by five senior women graduating with high honors. Each member was chosen on the basis of leadership, scholarship, loyalty, service, and citizenship. The members drew up a constitution that included the motto "Wisdom is the principal thing, Therefore, get wisdom and with thy getting, get understanding."[59]

The first dozen girls and their sponsors began the task of building an organization suitable for Mortar Board acceptance. From 1953 to 1972, Silver Tassel members ushered at university functions; sold concessions at games, dances, and movies; sold corsages for Parents' Weekend; and helped with various teas and socials. Community activities included helping with various drives and marches and assisting with Red Cross blood drive. Silver Tassel members became student advisors with the Student Curriculum Advising program and sponsored a tutoring service.

On March 11 a rehearsal and brunch were held at the home of the university president, and the installation began at 4:00 p.m., with a dinner in the Student Union Ballroom.

Petitions: 1964, 1968, 1970.

Installing officers: National President Shauna Adix and Section Coordinator Valeria (Val) Ogden (Washington State, 1945).

University of Idaho, 1923

The Mortar Board Society was founded in 1920 when the Idaho delegates to the Women's Intercollegiate Conference at Washington State College in Pullman found that they were the only institution represented without a senior women's honorary society. The women of the senior class took action at once. A committee of five was appointed and empowered to formulate a constitution and define the eligibility and standards of the organization. Idaho first sent a petition to national Mortar Board during its third convention in 1921, but it was not accepted until the fourth convention at Swarthmore on February 3, 1923. The chapter was installed in April 1923 with the distinction of being the first chapter of Mortar Board in the far western part of the country. (Annual reports of the chapter to the national organization go back to 1928.)

Early programs included sponsoring an all-campus dance, the first ever to be sponsored by a women's club on campus, that came to be known as the Spinster's Skip. Another early tradition was to take charge of the May Fete during which Mortar Board led the May Day procession and tapped its new members. Early chapters raised money with a bridge tea and a reception and later a Fashion Tea with the cooperation of Moscow merchants. According to the 1938 history, "Mortar Board occupies a peculiar position of respect on the Idaho campus. It is the one organization that is entirely free from politics, members being chosen for their merit alone."[60] Later chapters sponsored an information booth for freshmen during orientation, held the Narthex Table where they honored outstanding junior women, sponsored a panel on graduate schools, awarded scholarship plaques to outstanding freshman and sophomore women, and helped foreign students by holding small conversation groups with them each week.

Petition: 1921.

Illinois State University, 1976

The senior women's honorary Red Tassel was organized in October 1968 with the assistance of Associate Dean of Student Services Miriam Wagenschein. The first members were selected and the first constitution of the organization was written at that time. In the early 1970s Red Tassel members established a tutorial service in the residence halls, cosponsored a Women's Career Workshop, acted as campus hostesses for the president's office and Parent's Day, and volunteered for the Student Book Exchange.

Installation was April 10 in the Prairie Room of the Union, and a reception and banquet followed.

Petition: 1973.

Installing officers: National Director of Elections Hedy Kirsh and Section Coordinator Virginia Danielson (Lawrence, 1970).

Illinois Wesleyan University, 2009

From the inception of Egas in 1937, one of its goals was affiliation with Mortar Board. The purpose of Egas as stated in its constitution is to recognize and unite those women who have attained a high scholastic standing, have shown qualities of leadership and cooperativeness, and have demonstrated the ability to distinguish themselves in service to the university.

Egas, perhaps as much as any other chapter, fell into the push and pull of expansion described in chapter 2. Egas petitioned Mortar Board in 1941. National Expansion Director Rosemary Lucas Ginn visited in 1948 and extolled the relationship between faculty and students, but inexplicably no action was taken. A second visit took place in 1957 by National President Jane Klein Moehle, and Egas was set up for special observation by the National Council. Nothing happened. A petition was made in 1965 but was continually deferred.

Egas finally ceased to exist as an active student organization, but when National President Dan Turner learned of the protracted history of the petition after he became a staff member at Illinois Wesleyan University, he reinvigorated interest, and Egas was installed on November 8 as the 228th chapter. Sue Stroyan (Illinois State, 1976) was the advisor. Several former members of Egas requested pins and certificates after the installation, becoming postgraduate initiates.

Petition: The first formal petition was in 1965.

Installing officer: National President Dan Turner, assisted by Executive Director–elect Jane Hamblin.

University of Illinois, 1918

Mortar Board chartered its fifth chapter at the University of Illinois two months after its founding. The group of women who were "active members of the local senior women's honorary, Phi Delta Psi, were elated to have this privilege. They realized that they owed more to the courageous coeds who had been working since 1905 to make Phi Delta Psi worthy in every respect of being a chapter of Mortar Board than to their own peculiar abilities." The Mortar Board charter contains the names of the members of the classes of 1918 and 1919 and is dated April 12. An early service project included a survey about the installation of a university course on marital relations and exactly how the students wanted such a course to be conducted. A homecoming breakfast for Mortar Board alumnae was a tradition (a 1928 invitation shows the breakfast cost $1 and was held in the Marigold Tea Room). The chapter sponsored an Annual Interactivity Dinner to which all outstanding junior and senior women were invited. During Vocational Week in 1931, Mortar Board members were hostesses at the Women's League Tea and ushered at the evening lectures. The 1938 chapter historian reported that "a lovely and impressive tradition is the fall serenade when the squeal of brakes and the rush of footsteps announce the cap-and-gowned girls with their cheery, haunting melodies." The 1950 chapter members acted as hostesses for an informal tea for the representative from *Mademoiselle* and made money from selling Mother's Day corsages. Some chapters in the 1960s gave scholarships to junior and senior women who "showed financial need and had a 4.00 grade average or better."[61] The 1970s chapters sold sandwiches in the dorms, fraternities, and sororities to raise funds; organized Noon Hour Programs at the student union with speakers on heated campus issues; and sponsored the Women's Career Development program to familiarize women with career possibilities.

The original charter was signed by National President Esther Fisher Holmes and National Secretary Anita Kelley Raynsford.

Indiana State University, 1982

Pamarista, founded on December 12, 1937, was a senior honor society whose purposes were to promote college loyalty, to advance the spirit of service and fellowship among university students, to recognize and encourage leadership, and to stimulate and develop a finer type of college woman. In 1978 six men were initiated, and by then Pamarista had already petitioned Mortar Board.

The chapter sent bookmarks to academically outstanding freshmen and had a scholarship program for an outstanding sophomore and also held a Junior Tea. Pamarista was installed on March 26.

Petition: 1972.

Installing officers: National Director of Elections Sharon Sutton Miller and Section Coordinator Jane Baur Merrill.

Indiana University, 1921

Believing that an organized effort on the part of the most representative senior women would further the spirit of service, scholarship, and womanliness on the campus, the women of Indiana University expressed their desire to establish a local chapter of Mortar Board. A committee formed to organize a local honor society was chaired by Dean of Women Agnes Wells and consisted of women faculty and the presidents of the three largest campus organizations. Names of prospective members were suggested to this committee by upper-class women at a mass meeting. Eleven girls were elected on the basis of scholarship, campus activity, and womanliness, and the new members were announced on November 17, 1920, at convocation. The group aimed to promote interest in scholarship and to be a factor in college life and campus activities. Louise VanCleave carried the petition to establish a national chapter of Mortar Board to the 1921 national conference in Columbus, Ohio, and the charter was granted on April 23, 1921, which is considered the date of installation.

A tradition established early was "to pack all available automobiles with bedding, luggage, food, phonographs, etc. and drive the twenty miles to Brown County for an inspiring weekend where the retiring girls advised the new members concerning the coming year's privileges and duties, as well as a chance for a rollicking good time."[62]

The chapter name, Mrs. Granville Wells, was the name of the mother of Herman B Wells (the beloved president and chancellor of Indiana University), Anna Bernice Harting Wells. She died in 1973, and it is unclear when the name was adopted and if it was approved by the National Council.

Petition: 1921.

Installing officer: National President Anne Cornell.

Indiana University of Pennsylvania, 1997

In March 1995, President Lawrence K. Pettit began a discussion about establishing a Mortar Board chapter. Assistant to the president Ruth Riesenman and Director of Annual Giving Mary Moore moved forward with the petitioning process, assisted by Director of Student Activities and Organizations Terry Appolonia and grad student Elizabeth Sechler (West Virginia Wesleyan College, 1993).

It was the organizers' vision that the Sutton Society become a well-respected organization to which students would strive to belong. The Sutton Society was begun on January 17, 1996, the date of the petition to Mortar Board. An official visit was made by Director of Communications Barbara J. Arnold, and by November the chapters in the section had voted to accept the new chapter.

On March 16 of the following year, the installation was held at the University Lodge with eighteen outgoing members and thirty-seven new members.

The chapter name was taken from that of John Sutton, the first president of the Board of Trustees in May 1875.

The institution surrendered the charter of the chapter in 2013, while members were still active, over repetitive disagreements with Mortar Board's selection policies.

Petition: 1996.

Iowa State University, 1925

The only women's honorary on Iowa State College's campus until 1914 was Jack O'Lantern. Several outstanding girls believed that this organization was not sufficiently discriminating in its selection of new members as representative of the college, so they founded the local Mortar Board group. The group took a few faculty members into their confidence, and Frederica Shattuck, who founded the Iowa State Players (and since her death in 1969 has reputedly haunted Shattuck Hall, which was named for her, and then Fisher Hall after Shattuck was razed), told them of the existence of an honorary called Mortar Board at the University of Wisconsin. They wrote to the Wisconsin group requesting a copy of its constitution and bylaws, which they adopted along with the name Mortar Board. At this time both Jack O'Lantern and Mortar Board were competitively interested in the outstanding girls of the junior class. The Iowa State faculty, however, believed that one women's honorary in the school was enough and suggested that they merge. The Mortar Board group would not agree to this and had to convince the faculty of its right to be recognized as a second group. The purpose of this new honorary was the promotion of democracy and good fellowship among women students at Iowa State College and the accomplishment of permanent good for the college.

When the local chapter learned that different groups were uniting throughout the country to establish a national honor society called Mortar Board, they decided to petition for membership. The first year they petitioned, they were not accepted because membership was made up entirely of women enrolled in home economics. The following year two women in industrial science were members, and national membership as a chapter was granted. The chapter was installed on February 7 at the home of charter member Mary Kelly Shearer.

One tradition of the early chapters was during Freshman Days, when all new women students filed out to the open lawn east of the dormitories in the early evening, forming rows in a huge semicircle and facing the black-robed Mortar Board members, who held lighted candles. The Mortar Board president spoke to them of dormitory life and the significance of citizenship. As the women returned to their dormitories, they lit their own small candles from those held by the Mortar Board members.

A yellowed report of the February 7 installation is a letter to "Eleanor" (probably National President Eleanor Stabler Clarke) from Alline Smith (Missouri, 1922) stating that "one active member and two alums missed their train in Des Moines and arrived late so installation ceremony was repeated because they did not have a copy of the initiation ritual. During the ceremony one girl fainted and the Tri-Delt house caught on fire."[63]

Petitions: 1924, 1925.

Installing officer: Section Director Alline Smith.

University of Iowa, 1926

In the spring of 1911 Dean of Women Anna M. Klingenhagen invited all the girls of junior classification to a May morning breakfast. She explained that the purpose of the gathering was the selection of the outstanding members of the class of 1912. Each girl was asked to vote for the twelve classmates whom she considered representative in scholarship, personality, and accomplishments. From the result of the popular vote, the twenty names that stood highest numerically on the list formed the roll of candidates from which the final vote by the junior women determined the twelve who were to form an honorary society for senior women.

The initiation of this original group took place during the first week of the school year on Thursday, September 22, 1911. Beulah Lasher, who had the highest number of votes, was declared president, and Ethyl Martin was elected to serve as secretary. After careful consideration, the name Staff and Circle suggested by Dean Klingenhagen was adopted. "Staff" signified the relationship to the dean of women as members of the staff of her office, and "Circle" signified the friendship among the girls themselves. The purpose of the organization was "to act as advisory council with the Dean of Women and to further the best development—moral, social, and intellectual of the University girls." In 1922 an investment of hundreds of dollars was made in a university songbook that became somewhat of a burden when it did not pan out. In 1924 the program for the year was a survey of occupations for women and the formation into groups of those interested in any special field for study and information. This climaxed in a conference with Alice Betts of Cornell, who was secured as speaker, which "indicates the consciousness of a need still felt and now being met in the program of University Women's Association."[64]

As early as the fall of 1918, the secretary of Staff and Circle wrote a letter of inquiry to Mortar Board. The administration and some alumnae at that time were "seriously concerned lest something of the essential sprit of service for Iowa which characterized Staff and Circle might be lost; there were other concerns against joining." A new method for election was adopted by the 1926 group that was in agreement with the requirement of national Mortar Board. A petition was sent in and granted. The Staff and Circle chapter was installed on October 31 at the Memorial Union. Early projects were a May Frolic, a Sunday tea at the president's house for mothers and fathers and their students, the establishment of a student loan fund for senior women, and a Smarty Party honoring all women who earned a 3.0 grade point average or better the preceding semester.

Petition: 1926.

Installing officer: National Vice President Gertrude Wilharm (Minnesota, 1922).

James Madison University, 1977

The Percy H. Warren Society, named for the dean of the college, was organized in 1965 at Madison College as a local honorary to recognize outstanding senior women. The goal of the honorary was to provide a unifying experience of fellowship for its members and to make contributions to the college campus as the faculty and students deemed advisable. In the 1970s chapter members served as student academic advisors and assisted with the Visiting Artists and Lecture Series, and the chapter gave a scholarship to a Madison student entering graduate school and held a tea for new faculty.

The chapter was installed on March 19 at 1:00 p.m. in the Warren Campus Center Ballroom, followed by a reception and dinner in Chandler Hall.

Petition: 1973.

Installing officers: National Director of Finance Dorothy Moser and Section Coordinator Sharon Sutton Miller.

Kansas State University, 1928

XIX was founded in the spring of 1915 at Kansas State Agricultural College by four women led by Annette Perry. It was to be an organization for women to parallel Scarab, the men's political group, and was to be secret, so even though the women were elected at the end of their junior year, their names were not announced until the spring of their senior year.

For several years XIX could not be considered for a Mortar Board chapter because the college was not recognized by the AAUW. After agreeing to shed its political purpose when it could finally petition Mortar Board, XIX became the forty-first chapter on Saturday, May 26. Those to be initiated met in the upstairs room of the cafeteria, donned caps and gowns, and then walked to a literary society hall in Nichols Gymnasium for the installation ceremony. One commentator wrote that "the yellow tapers, the darkened room, the deep significance of the cap and gown and the very beautiful, yet solemn initiation service made a lasting impression upon all who were there."[65] The installing officer was National President Kathleen Lucy Hammond. A two-course luncheon was served after the ceremony in the cafeteria.

One of chapter's first programs was sponsoring an all-college women's Halloween dinner where the name of the freshman girl having the highest grade point average was announced. In the 1930s and 1940s the chapter sponsored the Spinster's Skip on Valentine's Day, a dance where the King of Hearts was crowned. In the 1950s the chapter's projects involved beautifying the campus. In the early 1970s the members had Sunday Suppers once a month at the homes of alumnae. The chapter historian wrote that "it helped to solve the 'Where do I go for Sunday dinner?' problem."[66]

The flower of XIX was the daisy, and the color was yellow. In 1945, newly tapped members wore gold tassels to show their membership. In the 1960s, they wore mortarboards to class the day after tapping. In 1967, the chapter changed its uniform from black skirts and white blazers to navy shirts and yellow shells. In the 1970s gray shirts became the standard, and black suits became the norm in the early 1990s. In 1968, Mortar Board sold a booklet listing all campus events. Like a programmer, the booklet sold for $1.

After Mortar Board voted to allow men, XIX tapped three in 1976: David Cink, Stephen Hoffman, and Guy Seiler.

Petition: 1927.

Installing officer: National President Kathleen Lucy Hammond.

University of Kansas, 1924

In the spring of 1912 the society of the Torch was established. Inspired by the enthusiasm of Professor of the German Language and Literature Clara Price Newport and Professor of German Alberta Corbin (Kansas suffragette leader for whom Corbin Hall is named), Professor of Latin Hannah Oliver (a survivor of Quantrill's Raid) and Mrs. Charles Easterly (secretary to Dean Olin Templin and Watkins Hall housemother), the new society began to take form.

The members of the first Torch were nominated by the faculty on a scholarship and campus activity basis. It was compulsory that nine members be selected from the campus each year for membership and that their election be kept secret from the spring of their junior year when they were chosen until the spring of their senior year. Later the members were chosen by a committee of faculty and active members. The thought was that by working through others and through other organizations they could better and more unselfishly serve their ideals, relinquishing any acclaim or recognition to others through whom they worked.

Champions: Dr. Price Newport (Swarthmore, 1909), Dr. Corbin (also acting dean of women), Professor Oliver, and Mrs. Charles Easterly.

Kent State University, 1972

A senior women's honor society called Duerna was founded in March 1955, with the name taken from the first two letters of Latin words *ductus, erudite,* and *natura* to remind the members to be "first to give, first to share, first to aid."[67]

The society's name was changed to Laurels in 1956 to symbolize the laurel wreath, which to the ancient Romans meant victory and merit. The colors were yellow and rose, the colors of the sun as it rises and sets for each day of learning. The peace rose was Laurels' flower, a symbol of constant responsibility to work for world peace.

Laurels' purposes were to promote loyalty to Kent State, advance the spirit of service and fellowship among university women, maintain a high standard of scholarship, recognize and encourage leadership, and stimulate and develop character. The goals of Laurels were symbolized in the pin: the laurel wreath for distinction, the open book for knowledge, and the torch symbolizing the influence of women in the world society and the responsibility of all to further understanding and peace.

There was no motto. In place of words, there were thoughts and actions.

In the spring of 1964, the historian announced at initiation that "we hope in the near future to become affiliated with the national Mortar Board whose purposes are scholarship, leadership, and service."[68] On May 7, 1969, showing the influence of Laurels, the *Daily Kent Stater* ran a description of the twenty-five women tapped.

Three years later on March 4 at 2:00 p.m., the installation was held in the student union. University president Glenn Olds and his spouse Eva Olds hosted a reception in the Portage Room.

Petition: 1967.

Installing officers: National Secretary Virginia Gordon and Section Coordinator Lotus Ferin (Washington State, 1945).

Knox College, 1920

In 1919 the Woman's Self Government Association (WSGA) of Knox College felt that there was a definite need on campus for a society that gave special recognition to outstanding girls with high scholarship. Working with Dean of Women Grace Stayt, the WSGA officers laid the groundwork for the organization early in 1920. The first eight members were selected by a faculty group from a list of names recommended by the WSGA executive board. They organized immediately and voted to petition national Mortar Board for a charter.

In April after correspondence with national Mortar Board officers, the name Knox Mortar Board was chosen as the name of the local society, and leadership, scholarship, and service to the college were adopted as membership requirements, with emphasis on character and loyalty. The new members were announced on May 21 at the May fete, and from the crowd of students one senior and six juniors were summoned to the green. Florence Merdian (1920), president (an outstanding tennis player, president of K Club, editor of the newspaper and yearbook, and the secretary of Panhellenic), explained the purpose of the society, and as the new members advanced, they were each given a mortarboard.

Shortly after graduation word came that the petition had been accepted, but no formal installation was to be held. Instead, when the required fees were paid, typewritten copies of the ritual and constitution were mailed to Florence and sent to each member so that "each of the Knox Mortar Board will initiate herself." Several members who were in Chicago for the summer met on July 24 and "closed the installation"[69] by jointly reading the ritual, so they were entitled to wear the pin. Badges were mailed to the eight members from the national officers.

In the 1930s the chapter sponsored the annual Campus Sing; inaugurated an all-college amateur show, the proceeds of which helped restore Old Main; and sponsored the senior caroling before Christmas. The group also conducted the publicity for a lecture series by Alma Archer, newspaper columnist and founder of the well-known charm school the Fifth Avenue School for Smartness, and established a tradition of selling cakes after chapel to raise money.

The charter is dated June 28, 1920, and was hung in the college Business Office for some time; now it is in the Mortar Board Archives.
Petition: 1920.
Champion: Dean Stayt (Knox, 1920).

Lake Erie College, 1975

President Vivian Blanche Small was instrumental in the founding in 1926 of the predecessor society to Mortar Board. At first unnamed, the organization had several faculty, fifty-five alumnae, and twelve student members. Membership was available to those who "received Honor in the academic system of awards"[70] and was retroactive to 1913, as that was the first class that had completed 120 semester hours for a degree.

The next year the organization gained its name, Kappa Alpha Sigma. "Kappa" stood for strength in leadership, "Alpha" for virtue of loyalty to the college, and "Sigma" for knowledge through scholarship. The triangle was chosen to symbolize the bright light of intellect. Gold symbolized the purity of quality.

The long history of the society describes the importance of personal responsibility and challenge. The 1948 *Tiber* (the yearbook) glowed that "the entire population of Lake Erie looks to these girls as future leaders in the outer world, leaders who achieved their first success in college by winning membership in the society which stands for high ideals in both scholarship and leadership."[71]

By 1955, the eligibility requirements were for student members to be chosen by 75 percent of the faculty and confirmed by the current Kappa Alpha Sigma membership. In 1957 Kappa Alpha Sigma was striving for membership in Phi Beta Kappa, but that was not to be. In 1958, the Alpha Lambda Delta society for freshman women came on campus.

By 1968 Kappa Alpha Sigma either disappeared or was replaced in 1969 by the Laurel Society, which had four members that year, and in 1974 nineteen members petitioned Mortar Board for a charter. Some accounts put the Laurel Society with a founding date of 1964, with nine members who approached the president of the Mortar Board Alumnae Club for help in founding a chapter.

The group was inspired by Mortar Board's Ideals and purpose, including support of college ideals and advancement of scholarship and leadership. The students formed a committee and drafted a constitution and bylaws. Laurel's petition was accepted in 1974. Installation took place at 11:00 a.m. on May 11 in the Helen Rockwell Morley Memorial Music Building, and a banquet was held at noon at the Commons Dining Area. Eleven new members, the nineteen petitioners, and ten alumnae were initiated.

Significant events in the history of the Laurel Society during the 1960s and 1970s include the initiation of the Shoestring Concert Series; the establishment of an education library; the organization of an Experimental College and a speakers' series, Cum Multis Alis; the beginning of a Meals on Wheels program; and the establishment of a resource file.

The first man invited to join the Laurel Society chapter was Joseph A. Bash in 1986.

Petition: 1970.

Installing officers: First Vice President Connie Wallace and Section Coordinator Nancy Campbell.

Lakeland College, 1998

Gold Key was established with the specific purpose of petitioning Mortar Board. The chapter was installed at 2:00 p.m. on April 18 in the Bradley Building, with a processional, a piano prelude by Kelly Benedict (Lakeland, 1998), and singing of the "Mortar Board Ode" and "Thy Ideals." Reverend David Lauer assisted with the installation. Fourteen of the petitioning group (which was the Gold Key Society), sixteen new members, and two alumnae were initiated.

Petition: 1997.

Champions: Director of Residence Halls Michelle (Mickey) Grossmann (MacMurray College, 1993), Dean of Campus Life Sandra Gibbons-Vollbrecht, Dean of Graduate Studies Mehraban Khodavandi, and Ginger Peters (Lakeland, 1997), petitioning chapter president.

Installing officer: National Vice President and Section Coordinator Denise Rode.

Lawrence University, 1922

The original honorary society of Lawrence College was Theta Alpha, established in 1914 to unite the women of the college "in closer fellowship and to promote an interest in service to their fellow men."[72] The motto was "Live not unto thy self." The watchword was "Service." The pin consisted of a combination of Greek letters, theta and alpha, the first and last letters of the Greek word "service." This word was engraved on one side of the pin, and on the other side was a star symbolizing the ideal of service. Eligibility for membership consisted of activity along spiritual, intellectual, social, and physical lines. A candidate must have participated in at least two phases of these extracurricular activities.

The duties of active members were to encourage younger women in development along the same four lines and "to give something of herself to aid in the betterment of her fellow students, and to continue in such activity in whatever community she may afterward be placed."[73] Any faculty members who had shown particular interest in student activities could be honorary members upon election by the chapter. Their duties were to advise, criticize, and help the active chapter.

Theta Alpha became a chapter of Mortar Board on October 8. Installing officer Gertrude Wilharm wrote that she arrived in Appleton at 5:15 a.m. that day, "where six girls and several alumni met her train, had a hurried breakfast, and went to the Russell Sage dorm about 7:00 a.m. where the installation service was held in the parlors." A dinner was arranged at noon with the college president and his wife, several faculty members, and the dean of women as guests. A tea was given later where Gertrude met the alumnae. She wrote that the members were "a wholesome group of girls with very high ideals," and she was pleased that they were admitted to Mortar Board.[74]

Installing officer: Vice President Gertrude Wilharm.

Lenoir-Rhyne University, 2008

Arktos has as its motto: "To Learn . . . To Serve . . . To Lead." It was begun with the hope of a chapter of Mortar Board, whose members would be announced annually to the college community at the Honors Convocation. Installation was at 7:00 p.m. Sunday, April 27.

Petition: 2008.

Champions: Professor Jeff Wright and Dean of Students Anita Johnson Gwin (both Lenoir-Rhyne, 2009) and Arktos president Kelly Teague.

Installing Officer: Executive Director Jon Cook.

Longwood University, 1993

In the spring of 1966, the members of Alpha Kappa Gamma decided to disaffiliate with its national organization and petition Mortar Board for membership. The reasons for this decision were many. Although recognizing those qualities of leadership and service on the campus, the organization had become stagnant; its membership consisted of only six other colleges located primarily in the South. The national scholarship requirement for membership was set at not less than a C average, but this was lowered on some member college campuses.

Longwood was striving to reach high levels in both academic and administrative areas, and "we wished to better our college and ourselves. This is why we made the decision to petition Mortar Board." The first petition was rebuffed in 1967 with a request by Director of Expansion Betty Jo Palmer that Longwood's Geist organization "not reapply for a three-year period."[75]

The chapter was installed on April 19 in Wygal Auditorium, with President William F. Dorrill addressing the audience. Fifteen outgoing members and eighteen new members were initiated.

Long-standing programs of Geist were the overall organizational leadership of Oktoberfest and the Geist-Elizabeth Burger Jackson Scholarship.

Petitions: 1966, 1992.

Champions: Director of Alumni Relations Nancy B. Shelton (Longwood, 1994) and instructor of English Camille C. Tinnell (longtime advisors of Geist), Vice President for Student Affairs Phyllis Mable (Longwood, 1999), and President William F. Dorrill.

Installing officers: Expansion Director Jane Merrill and Section Coordinator Anne Foltz (Ohio State, 1954).

Louisiana State University, 1934

Blazers was founded in the school year of 1921–1922 to promote higher ideals of leadership and scholarship. Admission required school spirit, aptitude in many phases of work, and high scholarship. New members were chosen in April from the junior class. Various projects were sponsored to build a loan fund for worthy college students. These projects included Sorority Sing Night, Sorority Stunt Night, and intersorority athletic contests.

When Blazers was installed on Friday afternoon, November 23, as the fifty-seventh chapter of Mortar Board, "we became a part of a much larger group with the same aims—we were sisters of this group which is scattered all over the nation, members of which wear a pin symbolizing all that Mortar Board has been, is and will be." Thirty-one alumnae returned. An all-university convocation in honor of Mortar Board was held on Saturday morning, with President James M. Smith welcoming the new group and Professor of Law Harriet S. Daggett, an alumna, speaking to the history.

In the spring of 1937 a new project was undertaken, one that was felt to be more in keeping with the real purpose of Mortar Board: Leadership Day. The chief desire in sponsoring the program was to train undergraduates for positions of leadership in campus organizations. A point system was accepted in 1938 whereby the number of offices a girl could hold was limited. Another project was to place markers at the foot of trees in the newly laid-out grove to signify Mortar Board's living, growing presence on campus. Ceremonies took place after tapping, with the outgoing and incoming chapters participating together with representatives of alumnae groups.

Petition: 1933.

Champion: Professor Daggett (Louisiana State, 1922).

Installing officer: Editor Hazel Moren Richards, assisted by Elizabeth Winn (Agnes Scott, 1933); Abbie Lyle, Hazel Goza, Georgia Ruth Work, and Marion Brantley (actives of the Florida State College for Women); and Dorothy Mueller Nelson (Iowa, 1930).

Louisiana Polytechnic University, 1974

The Alpha Tau Delta Honor Organization for Senior Women was established in 1955 and patterned after Mortar Board. Communications with Mortar Board and a national visit from Treasurer Joy Moulton occurred in the late 1960s after the campus was recognized by the AAUW. The petition was accepted, and installation was at 3:00 p.m. on April 7 at the Student Center, with more than three dozen alumnae and two dozen new members present.

Petitions: 1962, 1970, 1972.

Champions: Dean of Women June Dyson (Louisiana Tech, 1974).

Installing officers: National President Catherine Evans and Section Coordinator Dottie Moser.

University of Louisville, 1949

On May 3, 1932, the Pallas Club was formed to recognize women of the senior class who had made outstanding contributions through leadership and scholarship. The name came from Pallas Athena, the goddess of peace, wisdom, and service whose head adorns the university's seal.

The most coveted honor on campus was the Pallas Outstanding Freshman Award. The chapter was very active across campus, and members were noted for accomplishments as well.

Mortar Board installation was on March 26 in Robbins Hall, with fifty-seven alumnae initiated and three honorary members, including Dr. Hilda Threlkeld. A banquet was held at the Puritan Hotel.

Petition: 1947.

Champions: Dean of Women Hilda Threlkeld (Louisville, 1949), Physical Education Department head Sue Hall (Nebraska, 1929), and English instructor Elizabeth South Jones (possibly Pittsburgh, 1921).

Installing officer: Expansion Director Rosemary Ginn.

University of Louisiana at Monroe, 1977

The Senior Board began in January 1958 at Northeast Louisiana State College, and charter members were tapped in May by the college's president and dean, who conducted the first tapping ceremony at the Spring Honors Assembly. Late in 1976 the Senior Board was approved for membership. At the time of installation on April 17, the Senior Board had participated in many university and community programs, including campus beautification projects, acting as special hosts for university administrators and alumni, working with Mainline, and ushering for the Northeast Louisiana University Concerts Association.

Petitions: 1964, 1971, 1974, 1975.

Champion: Dean of Women Martha Madden.

Installing officers: National Vice President Val Ogden and Section Coordinator Cathy Randall.

Lyon College, 2001

Much at Lyon honors the Scottish roots of the Presbyterians who founded the college in 1872 in Batesville, Arkansas. The Order of the Tartan fit that theme when it was founded in 1996 as the senior honor society.

The order was installed as a Mortar Board chapter on October 27 with twelve members, three honoraries, and five returning alumni. It was Parents' Weekend.

Champion: Vice President of Student Life and Dean of Students F. Bruce Johnston (Lyon, 2001).

Installing officers: National Alumni Representative Jason Vogel (Nebraska–Lincoln, 1993) and Section Coordinator Cathy Bird (Oklahoma State, 1971).

MacMurray College, 1968

Announcement that the new honorary society Cap & Gown had been founded on April 15, 1924, was made at chapel services on Saturday, May 24. The society was organized under the auspices of the student body president, president of the Students Association, editor of the *Greetings*, president of the Athletic Association, and the president of the YWCA. According to the organizing members, "only representative girls with high scholastic standing who personify the Woman's College ideals will be chosen from the Junior Class." Three juniors were elected to membership the first year. In 1925 the members stated that the primary purposes of the society were "recognition and encouragement of excellence, both in scholarship and general ability. Thus it is an association to further the spirit of our College Motto, 'Knowledge, Faith, Service,' and to act as a medium for the stimulation and maintenance of high standards."[76]

In 1928 the members decided that election of new members should not necessarily follow the precedent of selecting presidents of the four major organizations. There is a void in the records of Cap & Gown from 1929 to 1957. In 1957 the group sponsored a career day, calling it a

Vocation Conference, and helped plan Parents' Day in the fall. In 1963 the members decided they were devoting too much time to paperwork and concentrated on lifting their standards and redefining their objectives with the goal of membership in Mortar Board. Cap & Gown members carried out projects that were of distinct service to the college and the student body. The members of the 1964–1965 chapter prepared a comprehensive report about the group and MacMurray in petitioning Mortar Board.

Installation was held on Sunday, April 21, in the Annie Merner Chapel.

Petitions: 1930, 1958, 1963.

Installing officers: National President Helen Snyder and Section Coordinator Mary DeBaca (Purdue, 1956).

University of Mary Washington, 1959

The founding of Cap & Gown at Mary Washington College took place in 1944. The idea and plan for the organization was formulated by Director of Student Personnel Margaret Russell and would recognize those students who had exhibited outstanding qualities of leadership, scholarship, and service during their three years in college. Not only would the organization be a fitting acknowledgment of the contributions of these women, but it would "foster such continued service on their part as would be beneficial to the life and morale of the college."[77] Sixty seniors met the academic requirement for admission, and the class as a whole voted to select the twelve women who best fulfilled the other requirements of leadership, personality, and service to the college. To adhere more strictly to the standards of Mortar Board, an amendment was made to the constitution in the early 1950s to delete personality as a requirement, and more emphasis was placed on the primary qualifications of leadership, scholarship, and service. Cap & Gown has continually risen in the

estimation of the college community, and election is now considered the highest honor that can come to a student at Mary Washington College.

Installation was on Sunday, May 24, in the Hall of Mirrors in George Washington Hall with seventeen collegiate members and nine alumnae, who were summoned hurriedly to campus (the notice of approval from the expansion director had come just the day before!). The chancellor of the college presided, and almost every member of the administration and many faculty members were present.

Petitions: 1956, 1959.

Champion: Margaret Russell (Mary Washington, 1959).

Installing officers: National Second Vice President Helen Lang and Assistant Dean of Students Mary Ellen Stephenson (Westhampton College, 1935).

University of Maryland, 1934

The Women's Senior Honor Society was founded in the spring of 1925 by Dean of Women Adele Hagner Stamp to bring "together women students of the senior class who have maintained a high standard of scholarship and leadership and who have all times shown their willingness to serve the best interests of the University through its various organizations as well as by an actively loyal spirit toward college authorities."[78] Dean Stamp selected the first three charter members because of their scholarship, womanhood, and service. Public initiation was held early on the morning of Baccalaureate Sunday.

In 1925 the society started the traditional ivy planting on Class Day. Other projects over the years included offering a cup annually to the woman student having the highest scholastic average her entire four years of college, serving as pages and ushers at the conventions of the National Association of Deans of Women (often held in conjunction with the meetings of the AAUW), sponsoring a freshman honor society that in 1931 became Alpha Lambda Delta, and hosting a farewell dinner for all senior women.

The initiation was held on December 8 in the women's student activity room, which was adorned with yellow and white chrysanthemums. Many alumnae returned to be initiated and to attend a formal tea in College Park the next day.

Petition: 1934.

Champion: Adele H. Stamp (Maryland, 1934). The student union is named in her honor.

Installing officer: National Secretary Margaret Charters.

University of Memphis, 1973

Tassel (previously Crown and Sceptre) had as its colors purple and white and an emblem of a sterling silver key with a tassel on it.

The installation was on January 27 in the University Center Ballroom. A reception was held in the William Faulkner Lounge followed by a banquet at the University Center.

Petitions: 1957 and subsequent.

Champions: Dean of Women Flora Hayes Rawls.

Installing officers: National Second Vice President Barbara Cook and Section Coordinator Susan Bowling.

Miami University, 1922

In 1916 six senior girls, selected for their leadership, scholarship, and service to Miami, formed a women's honorary. This group took the name Pleiade in recognition of the six stars in that constellation. But as time went on these women felt it unwise to limit membership to so small a number, so they decided to add the seventh sister, who can be seen with the aid of a telescope. As Miami grew, the society widened still further to include other stars in the sky beyond the vision of the human eye. In 1922 when Pleiade petitioned for Mortar Board membership and was accepted, the National Council expressed its interest and appreciation of the lovely traditions and spirit behind the group and asked that the name be retained as the name of the chapter and also that a part of the pledging service remain the story of the organization and maturing of the society that grew into Mortar Board. With this background have developed certain Mortar Board customs:

Tapping is always done on the University May Day in the presence of the Queen. After pledging, which takes place by candlelight outdoors on lower campus, the actives entertain the pledges with supper and then serenade them in their respective dormitories at midnight. On the following morning the initiates are formally introduced to the student body at a University Assembly. As a farewell to the outgoing group, the new members give a picnic, more famous for its lack of dignity than anything else. Mortar Board members were instrumental in the establishment of [the Beta chapter of Cwens] freshman honorary and encouraged scholarship by awarding prizes and giving scholarship dinners.[79]

Petition: 1922.

University of Miami, 1965

On May 7, 1937, Nu Kappa Tau was founded by Dean of Women Mary B. Merritt, four deans of academic schools, and the chairperson of the faculty committee on organizations "for the purpose of honoring the most outstanding girls on the campus, for the fostering of school pride in intellectual pursuits, for the forwarding of University of Miami ideals, and for the promotion of fellowship among its members."[80] The name stood for the Greek words meaning "victory to us and honor." Nine girls were selected as the charter group. The initiation ceremony centered around the nine muses of Greek mythology. Each initiate drew the name of a muse and thenceforth held that name. A constitution was adopted, and tapping ceremonies became a tradition. Tapping occurred during the Honors Assembly each year; the members, dressed in cap and gown, placed bright orange scarves around the shoulders of those chosen for recognition. At first the organization was purely for the recognition of outstanding upper-class women.

In 1938 the members addressed their first letter to Mortar Board requesting information as to requirements for petitioning for a chapter. The members moved from being a recognition society to being actively engaged in service. One project that was of great value was an annual careers conference to which any interested woman student was invited.

Mortar Board rarely accepted applications from a university not fully accredited by the AAUW. This obstacle was overcome in 1953 through the efforts of professor of German Melanie Rosborough (Miami, 1965), an AAUW national officer. In 1955 the second dean of women, May A. Brunson, made Mortar Board a prime goal, and when President Henry King Stanford came to campus he was a proponent. The chapter was installed on May 14, with 120 members and alumni initiated in the auditorium of the newly built student union. There was a tea in the president's home. The Greater Miami alumni held a luncheon in honor of the National President and Ruth Stanford (Miami, 1967), the president's spouse, the next day.

Through the years, alumnae of Nu Kappa Tau have given solid support to the society. On the twenty-fifth anniversary they returned for a celebration, and five of the original nine muses participated in the gala affair.

William Butler (Miami, 1990), vice president and professor emeritus, did much to help ensure that longtime dean May Brunson was honored for her service to students of the University of Miami. Brunson Drive is named in her honor, largely thanks to Butler's efforts and collaboration with alumnae.

Petitions: 1958, 1962.

Champions: Dean May Brunson (Miami, 1965), President Henry King Stanford, Professor Lynn Rountree Bartlett (California, Berkeley, 1927), Harriet French (West Virginia, 1928), professor of history Ione Stuessy Wright (possibly California, Berkeley).

Michigan State University, 1934

For some time prior to 1916, a need for some organization for women students was apparent. There were several literary societies, an honorary scholarship society, and the YWCA, but there was no organization representative of all women students made up of members from the existing organizations. In 1916 a group of women, including representatives of all the literary societies and the independent women, organized what was called the Sphinx Society. Its purpose was to cut through society lines, to stand for democratic campus spirit, and "to do the thing necessary for a broader and bigger Michigan Agricultural College."[81]

By 1923, the basis for membership had changed. Sphinx members were elected from senior women who had been outstanding in campus leadership, scholarship, and character. A few of the more important projects of Sphinx at the time were conducting the first Freshman Week for women, establishing the traditional Lantern Night, organizing and promoting an activity point system for women, collecting college songs

Hazel Povey Richardson was the owner of this original Sphinx pin, having been one of the first members of the local group at Michigan State, which became a Mortar Board chapter in 1934. On June 4, 1941, Hazel gave the pin to the archives, the same date that she was formally initiated into our Society.

and publishing a songbook in conjunction with the Alumni Association, teaching these songs at freshman lectures and in women's dormitories, contributing more than $50 to the Union Memorial building fund, establishing an $85 loan fund for a needy student, and establishing a social training course for men and women.

In 1924 and again in 1929, Sphinx petitioned unsuccessfully for membership in Mortar Board. The 1929 petition was not considered because the college was not on the accredited list of the AAUW. After that accreditation, Sphinx became a chapter of Mortar Board on November 24, 1934, with thirty alumnae returning on short notice for the ceremony.

Acting Dean L. C. Emmons expressed the college's satisfaction with the approval of its petition for a Mortar Board chapter:

The coming of Mortar Board to the College marks one more step toward the ranking of Michigan State among the leading colleges in the country. Only the establishment of Phi Beta Kappa remain lacking for the complete fulfillment of a long term program.[82]

Since 1935 it was the custom to tap new members at the May Morning Sing, which was staged by the college at the foot of Beaumont Tower, the heart of the campus both geographically and spiritually. The major Mortar Board project for 1937 was the Personalities and Careers Conference, the first move in an attempt to bring a placement bureau to Michigan State. In 1938 the chapter instituted a marriage course for senior women, a coffee for off-campus women as the start of a project to provide them with social opportunities, and the compilation of alumnae files of all former Mortar Board and Sphinx members.

Petitions: 1924, 1929, 1933.

Installing officer: National Expansion Director Katherine Kuhlman, assisted by Dean of Women Elizabeth Conrad (Ohio State, 1920) and faculty members Irene Shaben (Iowa State, 1926), Elizabeth White Daniels[83] (Ohio Wesleyan, 1929), and Nora Null Bunney (Illinois, 1925).

University of Michigan, 1918

The Mortarboard Society was founded at Michigan in the spring of 1905, but the idea was conceived earlier by a few who recognized the need for such an organization in the university. "Four women students, Jane Cochrane, Anna Waugh, Effie Armstrong, and Sue Diack, founded a society which represented the girls of the university and exerted an influence for the betterment on the customs, traditions and general spirit among the women." (The national records of the founders' names also show that Clara Moffat, Alice Reynick, and Anna Workman were among the founding group but do not show the name Jane Cochrane.) The early history of the chapter describes the environment, attitude, and activity:

> The university president and other authorities were never willing to make hard and fast rules but preferred to have the students control themselves by traditions, customs, college spirit and the unwritten laws of the student body. While social and intellectual aims were a part, they were not the fundamental ideals, but social and scholarship qualifications were to be sought for side by side with college spirit, executive ability, and a sincere interest in the welfare of the women of the university. University President Angell and Dean of Women, Mrs. Myra Jordan expressed great satisfaction that such a long felt want should be fulfilled.[84]

In the winter of 1905–1906 the four girls chose the other members. The two sorority girls named six independents, and the two independents named six sorority girls from the senior class. They drew up the constitution and in the spring of 1906 elected fifteen girls from the junior class who were initiated on June 5 in the Barbour gymnasium, with the ceremony followed by a banquet at the Cutting. This account of the founding is in the book where accounts are written by a member of every year telling of the main accomplishments of the society during that year.

In 1905 the society played an active part in securing a Phi Beta Kappa chapter at Michigan. Several chapters (the word chapter meant the class of new members, selected annually) instigated a petition to secure residence halls for women and established a student loan fund.

One of the groups undertook to start agitation against cheating in examinations, one petitioned for a quieter library, and another caused a petition to be sent to the Board of Regents for some new drinking fountains (there was only one on campus at the time) at Tappan Hall and in the Economics Building. One of the largest sources for their income was the sale of French gloves.

Middle Tennessee State University, 2001

In the fall of 1930, a faculty committee was appointed by President P. A. Lyon of the State Teachers' College of Murfreesboro to consider the possibility of organizing an honorary society for young women, a need having been felt for such an organization. After investigating other schools, a decision was made to select a small group of the most outstanding women as charter members of Tau Omicron. The standards were those of the highest educational ideals and the fellowship of the highest type of woman for mutual help to each other and to the university. The purpose of the society was to foster fellowship, scholarship, achievement in educational work, and leadership.

Petitions: 1967, 1970.

Installation date: April 26. (It is not clear how Tau Omicron became Hampton Society, the current chapter name.)

Middlebury College, 1928

For many years Middlebury College had several honorary societies for the men but none for women. In 1912 a group of junior girls met for the purpose of founding a secret society. The original foundation of the society was congeniality, and the name Banshee was chosen because the meetings were held in the middle of the night, long after lights were out. The original group proved to be quite representative of the college women, for in 1912 it contained the president and vice president of student government, four Phi Beta Kappans, and members of the Glee Club, the orchestra, the yearbook staff, weekly paper boards, athletic teams, and the junior play cast. At the suggestion of Dean of Women Eleanor Sybil Ross, it was decided to make Banshee stand for the most representative women in the college, and the threefold basis of membership of scholarship, personality, and college activities was adopted.

The Banshees' chief interest was to maintain goodwill and congeniality among all the women on campus, and this was accomplished by informal social gatherings in the dormitories, the awarding of riding scholarships to members of the Athletic Association, and a Student Friendship Drive in 1925. The same year the Banshees had charge of the Red Cross blood drive and also supervised a special drive for flood-relief work in the college and business section of the town. In 1926 the organization began a fund to be called the Banshee Loan Fund, which would be open to any student of the Women's College who needed it. Money has been raised for this every year by sandwich sales and "benefit moving-pictures."[85]

Petition: 1926.

Champion: Dean Ross (Middlebury, 1928).

Midwestern State University, 1981

The installation was held on March 28 at 2:30 p.m. in the Bolin Science Hall. Immediately following was a reception at the home of President Louis J. Rodriguez and then a banquet at the Wichita Falls Country Club.

Champion: Dean of Students Viola Grady (Midwestern State, 1981).

Installing officers: Expansion Director M. Kathryne MacKenzie and Section Coordinator Katy Gill.

University of Minnesota–Duluth, 2009

Chancellor Kathryn A. Martin wrote offering the institution's full support for a chapter in 2008 after a local group, Tau Delta, was formed for the purpose of petitioning Mortar Board. The group's motto was "honor, service and leadership." Dr. Martin and head of the Economics Department A. Maureen O'Brien were made honorary members at the installation on April 23.

Installing officer: President-elect Dan Turner.

University of Minnesota–Twin Cities, 1919

In 1899 the first of the senior girls' societies at Minnesota was called the "Senior Twenty" and had a pin with "XX" made of gold twisted wire. They were organized solely for social purposes, and the basis of membership was simply that a girl be a "good sport." The class of 1900 adopted a Greek name and added ten members, calling themselves Sigma Theta, and wore a pin of those two Greek letters.

The class of 1901 continued the Greek name but reverted to the 1899 plan of twenty members and adopted the name Sigma Tau. "The Society of the Green Pickle" was the formal name of the senior girls' group in 1902. There were fourteen members, and they wore the Heinz pickle pin as their symbol. The next class called themselves Sigma Beta, and in 1904 the name was changed to Sigma Rho. In 1905 the group reverted to Sigma Tau, and this name continued until 1919, when the active members became the chapter of Mortar Board with the power to select and initiate.

One of the most beloved of Minnesota Mortar Board traditions was the tapping ceremony. On the night before Cap and Gown Day, the Mortar Board girls in caps and gowns began at midnight and serenaded each elected girl at her home with Mortar Board and Minnesota songs. "When the girls came to their doors, they are extended a formal invitation to Mortar Board and to the annual alumni banquet the following evening. They are pledged to secrecy until the luncheon next day when two by two the senior Mortar Boards circle the room and cap the pledges one by one. Initiation takes place when the old and new chapters gather on the campus knoll at sunrise for the ceremony with a breakfast following."[86]

An anecdote related to Dora V. Smith of the 1916 group is worth including:

One of the things I remember about our *Sigma Tau* group of class of 1916 is that certain socialites on campus who were disgruntled at not being selected set up a rival organization. The "new" women's gym was just being finished and there was no water in the swimming pool. We got permission to have a picnic in the pool to which we invited their organization in order to introduce them into the social swim![87]

Mississippi College, 1978

Cap & Gown dates to 1960 and was patterned after Mortar Board. There were thirty-two members initiated from the outgoing and incoming classes. Twenty-seven alumnae also attended the initiation on April 16.

Petitions: 1962, 1970, 1976.

Champions: Dean of Women Louise H. Griffith and Joy Nobles (Mississippi College, 1990), spouse of President Lewis Nobles.

Installing officers: Expansion Director Marylu McEwen and Section Coordinator Cathy Randall.

Mississippi State University, 1986

The Centennial Honor Society was founded on April 14, 1977, when the assistant dean of student life and two graduate students chose the first candidates. Four of the five women initiated graduated, so fifteen more women were tapped in October. There were thirty-one incoming and twelve outgoing actives initiated at the April 6 installation.

Petition: 1984.

Champions: Professor of economics Kathie S. Gilbert (Alabama, 1963) and Assistant Dean of Student Life Frances Lucas (Mississippi State, 1978).

Installing officers: Expansion Director Cathy Randall and Section Coordinator Emma Norris.

Mississippi University for Women, 1942

Star and Scepter was organized to petition for a chapter of Mortar Board in 1926 at Mississippi State College for Women. Its purpose was to encourage a high quality of scholarship, promote participation in all constructive college activities, and inspire high ideals of conduct.

A course in parliamentary procedure was an annual project offered to the entire student body and the community. Tutoring services were offered the last few weeks of each semester, a tea was given in honor of the students recognized on Honors Day, and members acted as guides for Senior Day and planned a teacher evaluation program that was held yearly. Fund-raising included a "Mr. W" pageant, Coke sales at "W" day dances, and typing term papers.

Star and Scepter was installed on December 7, with two dozen alumnae, fourteen members, and three honoraries. A banquet was held at the Golden Goose Tea Room, and President B. L. Parkinson spoke.

Petition: 1941.

Champions: Mrs. B. L. Parkinson, Dean Nellie Keirn, and Professor Gladys Martin (Indiana, 1928).

Installing officer: National Treasurer Jean McIntosh Knickerbocker (Southern Methodist University, 1929), who had just two days before installed the Ole Miss chapter, assisted by assistant professor of speech Laura Crowell (South Dakota, 1928).

University of Mississippi, 1942

For several years before 1936, student leaders had discussed the benefit of having an organization that would not only give recognition to leadership but would also put emphasis on intelligent and democratically minded leadership among women students. To this end a small group organized Tassels, and the members discussed Mortar Board and formulated a program that would parallel the work of a Mortar Board chapter. Though women were admitted to the University in 1882,

> each year only a few had come till about ten years ago when the enrollment of women students began to steadily increase. Despite the fact that this is a man's campus, through the influence of the Women's Student Government, and the women on the faculty, opportunities for women have increased until

at present all the usual campus activities open to university women are open to women here, and the women students play a real part in campus activities.[88]

Tassels assisted Alpha Lambda Delta, helped the Oxford Welfare Club, assisted in directing Freshman Stunt Night, stimulated interest in art exhibits and open forums, and recognized women leaders.

Petition: 1936.

Champions: Dean of Women Estella G. Hefley (Mississippi, 1942) and faculty members Evelyn May and Ruth White (possibly Idaho, 1926).

Installing officer: National Treasurer Jean McIntosh Knickerbocker, who two days later would install the Mississippi University for Women chapter.

University of Missouri–Columbia, 1918

In the fall of 1915 twelve senior women, feeling that the women of the university needed a stimulus for campus activities, met together and established an honorary organization under the name Friars. The constitution stated that "the purpose of this organization shall be summed up in the acrostic 'For Right Ideals Among Right Students.'" All women of junior standing who by their interest in student activities and sterling character had shown themselves in sympathy with Friar ideals were eligible for membership. However, no more than fifteen juniors were taken each spring, and these had to be unanimously elected to active membership. Those were the days when organizations were financially within the reach of everyone, for the Friars set an initiation fee of twenty-five cents for general expenses. One of the driving forces behind the Friars was Anna Workman Fairchild, who was one of the six founders of the local Mortarboard at the University of Michigan. She had come to Missouri with her spouse A. H. R. Fairchild, who was an assistant professor of English. For several years the Friars worked quietly. An epidemic of influenza during the winter of 1918 and 1919 made meetings impossible, so the Friars "slept for a year."[89]

"When they awoke it was with a glorious dawning, for they had thrown off the local cowl of the Friars while they slept to don on waking the national cap of Mortar Board,"[90] trilled the local historian. In the winter of 1919 advisor of women Eva Johnston received a letter from the Wisconsin chapter of Mortar Board suggesting that a chapter of the national organization be established at Missouri. Presumably in consultation with Anna Fairchild, Eva referred the letter to the president of the WSGA and the president of the senior women, both of whom were Friars.

Things moved fast, because by April 1919 Friars was a Mortar Board chapter and was represented at the second national conference in Ann Arbor, Michigan, by Mary Mildred Logan, who was elected as the second National President.

A tapping tradition started at midnight before the new members were announced, when the new members were called and told of their election to Mortar Board. The next morning Mortar Board and two senior men's organizations, Mystical Seven and QEBH, led their hooded pledges to the Columns. As each name was announced, the pledge was unhooded and capped with the mortarboard, which she wore all day. At the end of the day Mortar Board and the men's organizations hosted the senior class and the faculty at a reception in the president's home (this senior day became Tap Day in 1925, and several other societies were permitted to join the festivities as the years went by).

A member in 1923 wrote that "we, who wore the Mortar Board and marched solemnly around our stately columns one day last spring, feel we must give our best. Besides scholarship, leadership and service, it spells comradeship with women of like interests and the pleasure of cooperation in working toward a goal that will broaden the lives of every member."[91]

Petition: 1918.

Champions: Eva Johnston (Missouri, 1918) and Anna Workman Fairchild (Michigan, 1905), who advised the chapter until 1932.

University of Missouri–Kansas City, 1973

Delta Alpha began in 1956 and petitioned Mortar Board in 1970, becoming a chapter on January 27 with two dozen actives and more than forty alumnae present for the ceremony.

Installing officers: Director of Finance Jayne Wade Anderson and Section Coordinator Kathy Kuester Campbell.

Monmouth College, 1972

Tau Pi was founded in 1931 by Dean of Women Mary Ross Potter for senior women and based on scholarship, leadership, and service. Symbolic of its purpose, the name stood for "The Prism" and the lofty goal for members to "take the white light of existence and refract it through their lives into the seven colors of the spectrum, and in so doing make their campus a more lovely place in which to live, and make their own lives reflect the characteristics of true womanhood symbolized in the rainbow colors."[92]

The chapter was active, hosting prospective students in their rooms, giving teas for freshman women, sponsoring special dances, leading book discussions, collecting for UNICEF, helping to move books from the old library to the new one, and baking and selling birthday cakes. Tau Pi awarded an annual trophy to the outstanding freshman woman. The active members met semiannually with alumnae at a tea at homecoming and a breakfast at commencement.

Petitions: 1954, 1966.

Champion: Dean Potter. She had been dean of women at Northwestern for twenty years (except for a two-year hiatus) before moving to Monmouth in 1929. It is likely that she was the champion of petition for Cap and Tassel at Northwestern to become a Mortar Board chapter in 1922 and brought her belief in the senior women's honor society to Monmouth.

Installing officer: Second Vice President Barbara Cook.

Installation date: February 13.

Montana State University, 1927

Cap and Gown's historian wrote that

in November 1919, the members of the Bozeman Pan-Hellenic in order to stimulate high standards of scholarship, to increase participation in college activities, to encourage leadership, and to recognize the highest qualities of womanhood among the women at Montana State College, submitted to the faculty plans for the organization of a senior honorary society to be known as the Cap and Gown. The faculty acted favorably upon the suggestion and a committee was appointed by President [Alfred B.] Atkinson to select the first members of Cap and Gown. The membership was to consist of twenty percent of the senior women so long as the total did not exceed six. The selection of members was made by the committee appointed

on the basis of scholarship—sixty percent, college activities—twenty percent, and character—twenty percent.[93]

At the suggestion of Coach D. V. Graves, who pointed out the lack of any athletic activities for women at Montana State College, the athletic program for women was outlined, and in the spring contests were held and awards were given under the direction of Cap and Gown. The major activities suggested by Cap and Gown for the athletic program were tennis, swimming, and hiking. This was carried on until the fall of 1922, when an athletic director for women was secured. In May 1921 a petition was sent to national Mortar Board, which was refused because Cap and Gown had not been organized long enough. The class of 1922 organized Spurs, the sophomore organization for service on campus, and in 1924 a song contest was sponsored to stimulate the writing of new college songs.

In 1925 a second petition was sent to Mortar Board, but the five nearest chapters withheld approval because of lack of knowledge on their part of standards at Montana State College. In 1927 the petition to Mortar Board was granted.[94]

Installation took place on the afternoon of April 8 followed by a banquet in the dining room of Herrick Hall and then a reception in the Fireplace Room of the Women's Building. Attending the reception were members of the faculty, townspeople, members of the student senate, and the Septemviri Senior Men's Honorary. Spurs acted as ushers and presided over the punch bowl. The historian in 1935 wrote that "it was a most thrilling and inspiring occasion."[95]

The chapter name is now Pi Sigma Alpha, and it is not clear when that change occurred.

Petitions: 1921, 1925.

Champions: Dean of Women Una B. Herrick (Montana State, 1927), in whose honor Herrick Hall was named, and Jessie Louise Donaldson (Montana State, 1927).

Installing officer: Expansion Director E. Luella Galliver (Michigan, 1923).

University of Montana, 1927

On April 1, 1904, a group of women under the leadership of Eloise Knowles,[96] who had begun working for the university while still in school, met informally for the purpose of organizing a secret society for promoting and fostering the spirit of unselfish devotion and loyalty to the University of Montana. Eloise was a member of the first graduating class (one of two graduates) and also the first head of the Fine Arts Department. A committee was appointed to draw up the constitution and bylaws. The name Penetralia was selected as symbolizing the aims of the group. A member wrote that "the strength and uprightedness of the pine, its steadfast, unchanging character, the sweet pervading scent, the healing quality, the protecting kindness—all these find meaning in Penetralia."[97]

Any junior woman, faculty woman, or benefactress who demonstrated unselfish devotion to the best interests of the university could be a member. Membership was restricted to twelve seniors, nine of whom were tapped in their junior year, and not more than four faculty women. Penetralia's activities, particularly tapping and initiation, were conducted with the greatest secrecy. The tradition of tapping and initiation began the night before, when there was a rapping at the door of the neophyte. She found a box with a pine bough in it and a card bidding her to report to the Eloise Knowles Room at five-thirty the next morning and to wear white. (On November 22, 1936, a meeting room in the new student union had been dedicated to the memory of Eloise Knowles, beloved founder of the chapter.)

Initiation was held in the beautiful Aber Memorial Grove in front of the student union at sunrise. The rites were concluded with the initiates donning caps and gowns, which they were privileged to wear all day to classes. They were entertained at breakfast by the seniors.

In late spring Penetralia held its annual and beautiful tree-planting ceremony, setting out a new evergreen each year. They gathered at 5:00 a.m. to hold this rite, placing the names of the girls at the base of tree, with each member shoveling dirt over the root ball. One of Penetralia's first service activities was to furnish a women's restroom, which was financed by assessments made on members. The chapter also bought linen for the infirmary and fostered a loan fund.

Installation was held in the old university radio station in the Little Theatre on April 11. The setting was particularly effective, with its massive grand piano and its walls hung in heavy black velvet curtains.

Petition: 1927.

Installing officers: Expansion Director E. Luella Galliver and Professor Leona Baumgartner[98] (Kansas, 1922).

University of Nebraska at Kearney, 1988

On Sunday, April 24, Xi Phi, which had been founded at the Nebraska State Normal School on December 13, 1924, became a chapter of Mortar Board. More than fifty alumni returned for the Honors Day Program and installation in the Fine Arts Recital Hall at what was by then Kearney State College. The Carillon Bells played "Thy Ideals" as the candidates, nine chartering and sixteen incoming, were presented.

President William R. Nester presided over the banquet in the Ponderosa Room at which the charter was presented.

Petitions: 1964, 1985.

Champions: Journalism instructor Roberta Moomey McKenzie, Director of Career Placement Jacqueline Rosenlof (Nebraska–Lincoln, 1951), and professor of history Philip Holmgren.

Installing officers: Director of Membership Marilyn L. Wirtz (Iowa, 1977), Section Coordinator Marilyn Moomey Nielsen (Nebraska, 1951), and past National President Jayne Wade Anderson.

University of Nebraska–Lincoln, 1921

Thirteen energetic and original senior girls established a permanent organization known as the "Order of the Black Masque." This quotation is from *The Senior Book* in 1905. There had been a long-felt need for this group. The senior boys had their organization of thirteen members known as the Innocents. When the girls organized, they selected the same number for membership.

The first mention of the group was on April 4, 1905, when the university publication carried a story of its establishment. The original members wanted a women's organization that would bring campus leaders into closer friendship and would enable the group to lead certain women's projects on campus. It was a secret order, and the girls wore caps, gowns, and black masks when meeting together in public and at their ceremonies. In 1908 the initiation ritual was written in the seclusion of Miss Louise Pound's library.[99]

For some years the members marched in a pageant before the annual Girls' Basketball Tournament. In 1910 the chapter assisted with the Friday afternoon teas. By 1911 the university was becoming more football conscious. The Black Masques took a special interest in the girls' section at the games. They decorated it, sat there in a body, and wore red and white caps. In 1913 they held a football rally for girls and carried red and white pennants. Later the chapter assisted in the formation of a girls' club that in 1918 became the Women's Self-Governing Association. The chapter sponsored a marriage course series that led to the formation of a marriage and family course with university credit. The chapter also founded the first local freshman women's honorary, which later affiliated with Alpha Lambda Delta. In 1920 the girls voted to apply for a charter of Mortar Board, and the petition was granted. No national officer could come for the installation, so a charter and a "ritual" were sent. The girls initiated themselves on January 4 in the presence of any alumnae who were able to attend. The chapter's concerns continued to focus on women's awareness as well as student awareness.

The chapter has contributed three National Presidents—Katherine Coleman, Helen Snyder, and Jayne Wade Anderson—and hosted national Mortar Board conventions in 1964 and 1970.[100]

Petition: 1920.

Champion: Professor Louise Pound and Olivia Pound (both Nebraska, 1921).

University of New Hampshire, 1938

Cap & Gown was founded in 1927 with four purposes and ideals in mind: "stimulate initiative among the underclass women students on a campus where men are in an overwhelming majority, foster the spirit of friendship between sororities and on the campus as a whole, develop and encourage leadership and fine scholarship, and aid in upholding the honor and traditions of the university." One service program was to form a plan for welcoming freshmen to the school. A Big Sister Committee was formed, and "Cap & Gown members acted as chairmen of smaller committees made up of junior girls." Prospective freshmen were sent letters in the summer acquainting them with school life. They were greeted during freshman week and were helped in adjusting their schedules. Later in the fall, a "big and little sister hot-dog roast was held at a nearby Outing Club cabin."[101]

Several teas were given throughout the year for freshman and transfer women. One of the most interesting and unusual customs of Cap & Gown was editing and publishing a semiannual booklet on courtesy, "which is of especial use to unsophisticated freshmen."[102] On February 19 nine active members and four alumnae were initiated.

Petition: 1937.

Installing officer: National President Katherine Wills Coleman.

New Mexico State University, 1967

In the fall of 1953 the Women's Self-Governing Board, recognizing the need for an honorary fraternity for women, began to investigate the possibility of eventually establishing a chapter of Mortar Board at the New Mexico College of Agriculture and Mechanic Arts. The following spring, fifteen girls were selected for the first roster of Mu Beta. The most important activity of Mu Beta was a scholarship program started in 1956 with an award of $100 to a deserving woman student. The next year awards were presented to the highest-ranking scholar in each class. The awards were presented at the annual Women of Achievement Banquet sponsored by the Associated Women Students.

Service activities included sponsoring panel discussions by students, faculty, and members from the community and the state on contemporary issues of national and university significance. Another program was to interest and acquaint students with graduate school programs.

In 1967 the National Council unanimously granted Mu Beta permission to petition Mortar Board for a chapter, and installation was held at 1:00 p.m. on April 2 in the Milton Student Center, with twenty new initiates and more than fifty alumnae present.

Petitions: 1964, 1967.

Installing officers: First Vice President Helen Snyder and Section Coordinator Shauna Adix.

University of New Mexico, 1936

On May 30, 1921, seven outstanding senior women founded Maia. They portrayed the best in academia as well as leadership and service. They were Eleanor M. Cameron, Blanche Guley, Irene Wicklund, Wilma Snyder, and Estelle Weisenbach. They worked hard over the next two years to establish themselves as a model organization (for Mortar Board).

The group was known as Mortar Board Junior and was always the leader among women's organizations, sponsoring student mixers, dances, luncheons for the different classes, and similar social events for the women and also fostering the Associated Women Students. Maia took a particular interest in the freshman women and attempted to take upon itself the responsibility of orienting them to university life.

In 1930 the members decided to take over a Christmas tradition of lighting luminarias on the campus. This tradition is still held the first week of December and is now called the Hanging of the Greens. Members would travel to the Sandia Mountains to cut greenery they would use to make wreaths and decorations for the ballroom in the student union; they also organized other student groups to participate.

In 1931 the members added the sales of mums at homecoming and managed other traditions such as Stunt Night and the Senior Breakfast.

The first year of Mortar Board Junior was spent completing the details of the organization. Because the university did not have an AAUW rating, the petition to Mortar Board was denied.

Mortar Board Junior was installed on November 7 and changed its name to Maia. More than two dozen alumnae paid the initiation fee, alongside five new members.

Champions: Dean of Women Lena C. Clauve and Director of Libraries Wilma Loy Shelton (both New Mexico, 1936).

Installing officer: National President Coral Vanstrum Stevens.

North Dakota State University, 1964

Senior Staff was organized by Dean of Women Alice Pearl Dinan (who was also a professor of English) in 1922 at North Dakota Agricultural College to work directly with her office "in the furtherance of all plans developed for the improvement of college students, especially . . . women students." Membership was highly selective, and the number elected to membership each year varied from six to ten. Eligibility requirements were high scholarship, demonstrated leadership, sincere interest in and dedicated loyalty to the university, and above all "exemplary womanhood."[103] Senior Staff cosponsored with Blue Key the annual University Honor's Day, the Doctor of Service Banquet, and a special occasion recognizing students on the dean's list of the six colleges.

Nine petitioners and two honoraries, along with twenty-one alumnae, were present at the installation on April 4 in the Union Ballroom, followed by a tea for seventy-five in Meinecke Lounge. A plaque with the first nine members was hung in the student union to commemorate the event.

Petition: 1955.

Champion: Dean Alice Pearl Dinan (Dinan Hall was renamed for her in 1957).

Installing officers: Section Director Helen Snyder and Fellowship Committee member Charlotte Wollaeger (Wisconsin-Madison, 1927).

University of North Dakota, 1932

Quo Vadis was founded on April 22, 1923, by a group of senior women who organized first as the Question Club. The name was changed later to Quo Vadis, whose motto was "Whither goest?" Its question-mark badge, jeweled in pearls and an emerald, typified its never-ending search for truth and betterment for its members and alma mater. Seven policies were agreed upon by the original members:

To promote the honor system by actions and word of mouth; to work for cleaner and better living in our residences; to encourage and patronize all university contests; to assist in raising the standards of our parties and dances; to establish ourselves definitely against intoxicating liquors and cigarettes for both men and women; to build always constructively and never destructively for our Alma Mater, both in school and out of it; and our work will be carried on by our actions rather than by publicity.

Rather than seeking publicity for our organization, it shall be a silent force.[104]

Quo Vadis, with the help of Blue Key, established the Ben Eielson Memorial. The members of Quo Vadis were the life force behind the endowed interclass Carney song contests for many years, and they also helped sponsor Women's League teas, led the drive for a women's building, and sponsored the orientation of freshman women. A moneymaking activity was the Spinster Skip, a dance when the girls pay all the expenses of the evening and even take the gentlemen to and from the ball. Quo Vadis presented a Mortar Board plaque to the freshman woman with the highest average and awarded a cup to the high school that sent the greatest number of students the greatest distance.

Petition: 1931.

Installing officer: National President Katherine Wills Coleman.

Installation date: October 29.

University of North Texas, 1968

On April 19, 1950, fifteen outstanding senior women at North Texas State College were selected by a faculty committee to form an honor organization for senior women. They became the charter members of Meritum on May 11. The dean of women and her successor had designs on a Mortar Board charter from the beginning. Since 1950 Meritum helped with the freshman orientation program. Late in the afternoon of Honors Convocation, the Meritum Calling-Out Ceremony brought the next year's members into the society.

In 1976 Meritum planted a cypress tree by the Marquis bench as a part of Mortar Board's celebration of the bicentennial. In addition to the tangible services performed, there is an intangible service to the campus that can be termed the Meritum ideal, evident in the characteristics of members: loyalty, fellowship, leadership, scholarship, and character.

Petitions: 1962, 1967.

Champions: Dean of Women Imogene Bentley Dickey Mohat (North Texas, 1968), President J. C. Matthews, Vice President James L. Rogers, Dean of Students William C. Lindley, Dean of Arts and Sciences Frank H. Gafford, professor of English Mary E. Whitten, professor of French Marian F. DeShazo, Ruth Hammerle Webb (Ohio University, 1944), and distinguished professor of English Arthur M. Sampley.

Northern Arizona University, 1971

The idea of a senior women's honorary was first conceived at Arizona State College in 1954 when a group of former Spurs (sophomore women's honor group) decided that the campus needed an organization to honor outstanding senior women. Even at this very early stage contact was made with Mortar Board, and Honor Board set its sights on affiliation. The first group of outstanding senior women was chosen in 1957 by faculty members. In addition to honoring senior women for scholarship, service, and leadership, the Honor Board members have endeavored to serve the community and Northern Arizona University through annual projects such as ushering at the yearly Honors Convocation and at graduation, hosting monthly art shows at the University Art Gallery, and serving at the annual Dedicatee Banquet.

The aspiration became a reality on December 11, when Honor Board became the Blue and Gold chapter and was installed with fourteen actives and fifteen alumnae.

Petition: 1963.

Champion: Professor of history Katharine Ferris Nutt (Northern Arizona, 1971).

Installing officers: Expansion Director Mary McAlister and Section Coordinator Kathy Kuester Campbell.

University of Northern Colorado, 1972

In March 1956, a faculty-student committee met to discuss the possibility of forming a senior women's honorary. After many meetings, the first constitution was drawn up setting grade point requirements, activities, and leadership characteristics as qualities of the first and future members. A late evening tapping was held for the newly established Gold Key chapter, and the five members held their first meeting on April 18, 1956. Many projects were discussed, and the tone was set for the activities for years to come. As the membership grew, interest pointed to cultural, societal, and educational experiences. Gold Key helped establish Phi Beta Kappa.

Petitions: 1964, 1971.

Installing officers: National First Vice President Virginia Gordon and Section Coordinator Val Ogden.

Installation date: December 3.

Northern Illinois University, 1971

The senior women's honor society was founded on June 2, 1938. Pleiades, the constellation of seven stars, was the name chosen by the seven original members. According to Greek mythology, the stars were sisters who were transformed by the gods and placed in the sky. They represent character, service, endurance, scholarship, sympathy, understanding, and leadership. The emblem of Pleiades is a bracelet of sterling silver with an arc of seven stars over a castle on a hill. The stars symbolize the everlasting light of truth; the castle on the hill represents the realization of those ideals. The colors are blue and silver; the pledge emblem is a white rose. The purpose of Pleiades is to advance a spirit of service and fellowship, further high scholastic achievement, encourage college loyalty, and promote leadership among all women students.

Two past National Presidents are Pleiades: Denise Rode and Dan Turner.

Installation was on November 21, with twenty-eight actives and seventy-two alumnae.

Petitions: 1960, 1968, 1970.

Installing officer: First Vice President Barbara Cook.

Northern Michigan University, 1979

Telion was founded by the Associated Women Students in the spring of 1970 as an honor society for senior women. Eight charter members chose Telion, from the Greek word meaning "ideal," as the organization's name. A local Mortar Board alumni advisory committee was an encouragement to Telion and was helpful in sharing ideas for projects and procedures. Some of the service activities were investigating the ways student academic advisement could be improved, helping the director of admissions recruit new students across the state, cosponsoring a weeklong series titled "Men and Women in Transition" to increase student awareness of the changing sex roles in our society, and sponsoring a Rape Prevention Workshop with the National Organization for Women and the Northern Michigan's Women's Center.

Petition: 1977.

Installing officers: National Director of Programming Janet Ayres and Section Coordinator Shirley Simanski Spelt (Grinnell College, 1947).

Installation date: April 7.

Northwestern University, 1922

A yellowed petition is on file giving the basis of membership as scholarship, service, and personality. Accomplishments and activities of the chapter, which was called Cap & Tassel, were listed as employment bureau management, a breakfast to welcome the university president, and a card party to raise money.

Petition: 1922.

Champion: Dean of Women/Counselor for Women Mary Ross Potter.

Occidental College, 1947

Dranzen was organized in 1927. According to a Mortar Board officer's chapter visit report in the 1940s, membership was based on "scholarship, well-balanced service upon the campus, force of leadership (initiative, dependability, and integrity of character), attitude of democracy toward all students regardless of race or social standing, and community service." In keeping with its motto, "Doing Is Being," Dranzen was active in its early years in planning freshman orientation, assisting as hosts at college functions, and serving as a liaison between student opinion and administrative action. According to the petition (written during World War II), "With the coming of the war, the departure of Occidental men, and the rapid changes in personnel of the student body brought about by the new three-semester academic year, Dranzen assumed special responsibility for preserving the traditions of the prewar college—especially the cherished Honor Spirit. Through columns in the campus paper, assembly presentations, and tea discussion groups the members of this period kept enthusiasm high for many campus ideals which might otherwise have been lost."[105]

The reason for affiliating with national Mortar Board was that "the war crisis emphasized to Dranzen the need for high standards which Mortar Board is able to keep at consistent high levels." Tapping at that time was held on the Quadrangle in front of Thorne Hall on Senior Class Day, two weeks before graduation. Tapping was described by the dean of women as "exciting and impressive."[106] Service activities included a program of orientation of freshman women and junior transfers and advising sophomore women's honorary Tiger Taps, and whenever there was friction between student and administrative groups, Dranzen worked to alleviate the cause of the misunderstanding.

Petition: 1947.

Installing officer: National President Coral Vanstrum Stevens.

Date of installation: June 13.

Ohio Northern University, 1975

In February 1954 the Student Council founded a senior honorary society to recognize men and women students who had given outstanding service and leadership in extracurricular activities. The Adelphian Literary Society was a force on the campus for four decades before it was reborn in 1954 as a leadership honorary. In 1965 women reorganized under the name Aurora, while the men retained the name Adelphian. Aurora recognized women of the senior class who had given outstanding service and leadership while maintaining high academic standards. The name was adopted from the Greek goddess of the morning or dawn. Writes the chapter historian, "Anticipating their eventual request to petition for membership as a chapter of Mortar Board, the charter members patterned Aurora after the high standards of that society."[107]

Petition: 1973.

Installing officers: Expansion Director Marylu McEwen and Section Coordinator Nancy Campbell (Ohio State, 1972).

Date of installation: April 20.

The Ohio State University, 1914

Alice Ward DeLong returned from a student government meeting at Indiana University with the idea of a senior women's honor society, which was formed in the spring of 1914 after she contacted seven other senior women. The group, which called itself Mortar Board, contacted the university president, William Oxley Thompson, and he gave them permission to select a group of junior women until the appropriate faculty committee could be secured. On June 16, the new members were initiated near Mirror Lake on campus. At the same time the idea was also being worked out on other campuses.

In February 1918 an Ohio State Mortar Board representative met at Syracuse, New York, with four like organizations to discuss forming a national senior honorary. The Ohio State pin was chosen as the new national group's emblem, and Ohio State's initiation service was also used as a basis for the ritual.

Once the roots of the local chapter were firmly established, it began to undertake projects and participate in campus affairs. In the early years the chapter was very socially oriented, with teas, parties, and entertainment. Once the national organization was firmly established,

This gold president's pin may very well be the first badge of the Ohio State chapter. On the back is etched the name of the jeweler, Auld. There was a jeweler by that name in Columbus as early as 1870.

however, the social life declined, and service to the campus increased. As times changed, Mortar Board sought to be relevant to the issues, not merely responding to them but as a leader. In the 1920s the group was concerned with the problems of the Negro student and worked toward proportional representation in student government. The 1940s members were involved with the postwar reconversion issues. The lack of student participation in campus activities and the new "Speakers Rule" were key concerns of the 1950s. The members of the chapters in every decade were involved in the issues of their time. The chapter commemorated its one hundredth anniversary in April 2014 with a three-day celebration. A complete centennial history was written for the occasion by Dr. Virginia Gordon, and copies are in The Ohio State University Archives and the National Office.

Champion: Dean of Women Caroline Breyfogle.

Date of founding: June 16.

Ohio University, 1938

The Cresset chapter, founded in 1913, has its own individual flare, as its history shows. In the spring of 1956 the chapter tapped a foreign student for the first time. Her name was Migonette Yin, a fine arts major from Singapore. Her membership got the chapter to think about helping the International Club. The president of the International Club was contacted to see if Mortar Board could act as tutors for some of its members. Mortar Board set up a few hours each week to meet with an assigned international student, helping with pronunciation of words in the English language, university policies, and American customs.

Since then the Cresset chapter's history has been quiet but enduring. The various activities in which members were involved were talking to a resident at the Athens Mental Health Center, tutoring, and working for all facets of student government and relations.

Petition: June 1932.

Champions: Dean of Women Irma E. Voigt and professor of English Edith Wray.

Installing officer: Expansion Director Katherine Kuhlman.

Installation date: October 15.

Ohio Wesleyan University, 1929

In 1914 when President Herbert Welch was trying to build closer ties between the faculty and students, he chose from among the four classes twelve representative men and women whom he used to assist him in gaining student opinion and leadership. For three years this organization held an honorable place on campus, with members elected by the student body.

During World War I this group became practically useless. In 1919 the women who were then in the organization decided to break away and organize separately to carry on the work of leadership among women. They called themselves the Women's Boosters Club and strived to create the proper attitudes among the student body toward the WSGA, the YWCA, and the Honor Court. The Boosters carried on a vibrant service program that included many parts of homecoming and a big outdoor supper on Campus Night. Members organized a women's cheering section and successfully outcheered the men. At their October 30, 1928, meeting, a committee was appointed to draw up a formal petition to be sent to Mortar Board in the hope that soon the Boosters might become a chapter. By March 25, 1929, the petition was accepted, and installation was held on May 17.

Traditions of election and capping of future Mortar Boards were established. New members were initiated each Monnett Day, having been capped the preceding day during the student chapel service. The new girls wore their caps until sundown, and the retiring members wore their robes until noon.

The National Council approved the chapter's petition to take the name Monnett in 2014, in honor of student and early benefactor of the college Mary Monnett.

Petition: 1928.

Oklahoma Baptist University, 1968

Zeta Chi was founded on April 28, 1955, as a leadership fraternity for senior women by thirteen women whose hope was to affiliate with Mortar Board. The organization was approved by the faculty on May 11. Through its members, plans were made for joint meetings with the three other honor societies, Phi Eta Sigma, Alpha Lambda Delta (Zeta Chi was responsible for bringing this society to campus), and the local men's leadership fraternity. These monthly meetings were designed to broaden the cultural and intellectual outlook of the members. Elected in the spring, newly chosen juniors were pledged in one of the biweekly chapel programs attended by the entire student body. The group was given a series of lectures on study habits and campus life, a panel discussion on combining career and marriage, and "organized lectures for Charm School for one year."[108]

Petitions: 1960, 1968.

Installing officers: First Vice President Shauna Adix and Section Director Mrs. Keith Thomas (Oklahoma State).

Installation date: April 21.

Oklahoma State University, 1940

Six women founded an honor society for senior women on the campus of Oklahoma Agricultural and Mechanical College and chose Achafoa, a Choctaw word meaning "a few rare and precious ones," as their name. Mortar Board was in its sights.

Conducting a well-rounded service program, Achafoa sponsored Orange Quill and Black Quill, honor societies for freshman and sophomore women; supervised a study hall; arranged the AWS Spring Tea; and honored alumnae at homecoming.

Installing officer: National Secretary Rosalie Leslie with assistance of many visitors from other chapters, including Amy Comstock, a founder of Wisconsin.

Oregon State University, 1933

Cap and Gown was organized in the spring of 1926 after nine outstanding junior women were chosen as charter members at the women's honor convocation. Installation was at 4:00 p.m. on November 18 in the lounge of the student union after a luncheon served at the Benton Hotel. Six active and three honorary members (Dean of Women Kate Jameson, Assistant Dean of Women Lorna Jessup, and Leonora Hamilton Kerr, spouse of the president) were initiated by National President Katherine Wills Coleman.

University of Oregon, 1923

The Scroll and Script chapter of Mortar Board was formally chartered at the fourth national conference at Swarthmore College in 1923. National Mortar Board was growing rapidly during this period, and the addition of the University of Oregon and Washington State University that year meant that the honor society had expanded from coast to coast.

The first edition of the *Mortar Board Quarterly* in 1925 included a submission about the chapter's activities:

The biggest plans of our University this year are those concerned with the building program. The Gift Campaign office is expanding all efforts to raise the necessary quota for the plans. The goal is one new building annually and this year's addition is a three-story science building. In line with the program of growth, our Mortar Board chapter has pledged to the Student Union fund and we make $15 payments annually toward this campus edifice, the work on which is to begin soon.[109]

The 1925 chapter reported that it met once a month on Sunday evening, with both active and alumnae members attending. The meetings were held in the apartments of various members, who "took turns at getting tea." A supper followed the business meeting, and discussions were held on various subjects, such as politics, literature, art, and music. The chapter helped the dean of women disseminate a pamphlet on vocational guidance that was distributed by the university to high school students. The members felt fortunate to have Section Director Lillian Stupp, a faculty member who "helped them over all the hard places."[110]

The 1929 chapter worked with freshman orientation by placing an informational bureau at the entrance of the administration building where students could obtain information regarding the campus and registration. The chapter was also involved in a Get-Wise Party for freshman women during orientation week "to acquaint them with the various phases of campus life." A few women students on probation were the special charges of Mortar Board members for "guidance and help with their problems"; members "helped girls who are earning the greater part of their way through school who have little time for actual campus life and contacts."[111] The 1929 chapter reported that

> contacts between Oregon's alumnae and active Mortar Board members are entirely personal. The Mortar Board pledging custom at the University has become a beautiful tradition of Junior Weekend, and with this and the incentive of the Weekend's elaborate entertainment it is a time when alumnae members try hard to be on the campus. At this time alumnae join the actives in pledging and welcoming the new members while renewing contacts with the chapter. Oregon seems especially lucky in having a number of alumnae members living in Eugene. The one event that brings many old and new alumnae together is the annual initiation breakfast following the early morning initiation service.[112]

The moneymaking schemes included sponsoring a formal Mortar Board Ball and a benefit movie. The ball was held during the winter term, with "decorations of immense black, plaster board mortar boards with gold cord tassels and programs in the shape of a mortar board which gave a pleasing dignity, contrasting with the gaily colored gowns and lights." Mortar Board members also helped with campus advertising for the theater near campus and provided reels of a movie about the campus. The 1930 chapter wrote in the *Quarterly* about paying off a $90 debt that was left by the alumnae (no accounting for the origin of the debt). The chapter also initiated a general survey about the relative effects of activities on scholastic achievement and participated in advertising a "personnel and vocation campaign" sponsored by the university.

Reports in the *Quarterly* in the late 1930s describe many chapter activities, including honoring three freshman women with the highest scholarship, giving a subscription for *Fortune* magazine to the "new half-million dollar library," giving a Smarty Party for all women students who received a B average or higher, and sponsoring the annual Mortar Board Ball where "Kwama, the sophomore women's honorary[,] marched under the line of military swords of Skull and Dagger, the corresponding men's honorary."[113] Throughout the school year Mortar Board members had lunch at the different houses on campus. This provided the opportunity to introduce Mortar Board and its purpose to the women on campus.

During the years of World War II, the chapter was responsible for the campus blood bank. Members made appointments for all qualified students and faculty to give blood. The chapter continued to sponsor the Smarty Party "for about eighty or ninety smart freshman girls with a grade point of three point or above." After the war, chapters were more interested in international concerns. Scroll and Script sponsored a full page of national and international news in the campus newspaper and helped with a program "designed to bring students a clearer understanding of international problems and affairs." The 1948 chapter laid the groundwork for a campus-wide honor system by giving speeches at the "living organizations" (fraternity, sorority, independent) about the honor system's operational procedures and methods. The next chapter took over the project and developed it further. Inspired by the theme of the Mortar Board national conference the previous summer, the 1950 chapter focused on "leadership on the campus, the community and the home."[114]

The 1970 chapter sponsored an alumni reunion dinner where members of the 1924 and 1927 chapters shared fond remembrances of their Mortar Board student experiences. Other chapters in the 1970s published a pamphlet on college honor societies and established a Mortar Board monetary award that was given to two graduate fellows for distinguished teaching. Many chapters in the 1980s sponsored a "professor of the month" project where they honored faculty members who were known for their dynamic teaching and student centeredness. Other chapters during this decade were involved in campus beautification projects and environmental issues, a Telefund for the University of Oregon Foundation, and tutoring for various academic departments. The 1989 chapter began with a retreat on the Oregon coast; sold the Mortar Board Planner, a daily calendar and date book; and gave a free day of child care for student parents and the community during the busy Christmas season. The chapter sponsored the "Mortar Board State of the University Address" featuring a speech by the university president that was followed by answering student and faculty questions.

The 1991 chapter participated in University Day, a one-day event where students, faculty, and staff members cleaned and beautified the campus. This included scraping cobwebs and peeling paint from lampposts, planting flowers, power-washing sidewalks, and picking up litter.

The 1992 chapter promoted literacy by making the campus community more aware of illiteracy in the state of Oregon. The chapter partnered with the Literacy Line of Oregon by referring volunteers to tutorial groups and organizations. Members celebrated Mortar Board Week by holding a special activity every day. The Professor of the Month program was continued, with a plaque with the name of the winning faculty member posted in the student union. The 1995 chapter won the Chapter of Excellence national award (similar to today's Gold Torch Award) for outstanding programs and service. Other Scroll and Script chapters in the 1990s raised money by selling university planners through the university bookstore and cleaning up after university basketball games. They continued to honor junior scholars with a 3.75 grade point average or higher with a special banquet and a certificate.

The 2007 chapter continued the traditions of honoring the top one hundred juniors and presenting the Professor of the Term award. All the students on campus voted for their favorite professor, whom Mortar Board recognized with a plaque during one of his or her classes. Chapter members held a book drive and went door-to-door in Eugene, where they collected more than five hundred used children's books that were donated to an elementary school and the public library. The chapter also participated in numerous community service events, including food drives and literacy projects.

Otterbein University, 1988

In the 1970s there were two separate honor societies for men and women. Archaghia was the men's group, and Arete was the women's group. These two merged in 1980 to become Teleiotes, meaning "completeness or perfection." The new society looked to Mortar Board for constitution, bylaws, and programming, petitioning for a charter in

1986. The Westerville, Ohio, campus hosted national visitor Executive Secretary Diane Selby in March 1987, and the petition was approved in November after the chapters in the section voted to approve the addition.

The procession of the May 8 installation in the Campus Center was led by President C. Brent DeVore (Otterbein, 1989) and Vice President for Student Affairs JoAnne VanSant. Nineteen in the petitioning group and thirty-four in the new group were initiated along with eleven alumni of Arete or Teleiotes. Nineteen more alumni from the three groups were initiated in absentia. Advisors Robert Fogal (who performed a piano prelude) and Mary Cay Wells were made honorary members.

Teleiotes is dedicated to contributing to the development of the individual and supporting the ideals of Otterbein. It is defined as an honor society that recognizes achievements but also challenges its members to active participation and continued leadership for the betterment of the campus community.

Petitions: 1980, 1986.

Champions: Vice President VanSant and Dean Wells.

Installing officers: National Director of Communications Gail Harrison and Section Coordinator Pam Richards (Ohio State, 1965).

Pacific Lutheran University, 2014

The Black and Gold chapter was formed to serve as the ultimate recognition for senior leaders who had participated well in the steps of the leadership programming provided by the Office of the Dean of Students.

The chapter was installed and thirty-seven members were initiated, including the president and vice president as honorary members, at a luncheon during the Board of Regents meeting on May 3 in the Anderson University Center.

Champions: President Thomas W. Krise and Vice President for Student Life Laura Majovski (both Pacific Lutheran, 2014), Dean for Student Development Eva Frey Johnson, associate and assistant directors of student involvement and leadership Amber Dehne Ballion and Ian Jamieson, and librarian Lizz Zitron.

Petitions: 1968 (from a society named Tassels), 2013.

Installing officers: National President Marty Starling, assisted by University of Washington advisor Margot N. Smith (San Diego State, 1965). Section Coordinator Doug McManaway (Washington, 2009) and Executive Director Jane Hamblin also were present.

University of the Pacific, 1967

Knolens was created in December 1949 in honor of Emily Walline Knoles, an outstanding woman and the spouse of Tully Cleon Knoles, who had been president of the then College of the Pacific since 1919. About the Knolens, the historian wrote that

one of the outstanding characteristics of this women's honor society is the ability to shift emphases with the changing times. As a result Knolens has sponsored various programs and activities throughout its history. Dialogue has been established concerning campus etiquette and parliamentary procedure. Faculty women have been treated to a breakfast opening Women's Day. Service projects include making foreign students feel at home by offering friendship, entertainment and scholastic services and regularly sponsoring a convocation and sing. Knolens also grants an annual scholarship of fifty dollars to an outstanding sophomore woman. Knolens is a self-sufficient organization. Its programs and activities are self-perpetuating. Income is derived from supervising the creation, publication and distribution of the Campus Address Book.[115]

Petitions: 1956, 1960.
Installing officers: Treasurer Joy Moulton and former Director of Expansion Mary McAlister.
Installation: April 15.

Pennsylvania State University, 1935

In 1926 Pennsylvania State College dean of women Charlotte E. Ray and students Jane E. Smith and Helen Crocker called together eleven outstanding women to form an honorary group with aims parallel to those of Mortar Board. Professor of classical languages Robert E. Dengler aided in the selecting the Greek name, Archousai, and in writing the rituals.

On November 23 nine years later, the Nittany Lion Inn was host to Archousai and guests at the installation of Mortar Board's sixtieth chapter. The 5:00 p.m. installation was attended by President Ralph Dorn Hetzel. A reception for four hundred faculty members and student leaders followed the installation and banquet.

It is interesting to note that seven (presumably of the eleven) were initiated at installation. Jane Smith and Helen Crocker were not among them; they were initiated on April 25, 1936, with four other women.

Champions: Honorary members Dean of Women Ray and First Lady Estelle Heineman Hetzel and alumnae initiates Assistant Dean of Women Ellen Burkholder, assistant professor of physical education Marie Haidt, Fannie E. Haller, and Mary E. Dengler.

Installing officer: Expansion Director Kay Kuhlman, assisted by eight members from the University of Pittsburgh, five from Ohio Wesleyan, four from Penn, and one from the Carnegie Institute.

University of Pennsylvania, 1921

The historian of the Quaker chapter in 1975 wrote that

> while our Mortar Board chapter here at Penn is by no means a new one (installed in 1921), we have only just recently begun keeping a history. . . . A few of the projects of the 1975 group: To help ease the confusion and commotion of move-in, Mortar Board women served iced tea in the dorm lobbies and acted as unofficial greeters, helping make everyone feel welcome; we co-sponsored a reception for women with the Penn Women's Center where we discussed the nature of women's resources here at Penn; on Activities Day we had a booth and sold lemons with peppermint sticks—a popular Penn treat; we presented a program featuring the new head of the combined faculty of Arts and Sciences who spoke on his views of the future of liberal arts education. We will change our selection procedure this year due to the large number of potentially eligible women.[116]

University of Pittsburgh, 1923

The Alpha Lambda Nu chapter of Mortar Board at the University of Pittsburgh began in 1916 as a local society to honor senior women for their scholarship and leadership. Under the guidance and support of Dean of Women Thyrsa Wealtheow Amos, who served as dean from

1919 to 1941, Alpha Lambda Nu began to seek membership in the national college senior honor society Mortar Board, which had been founded in 1918.[117]

In February 1923, Helen Davies of Alpha Lambda Nu presented a case to Mortar Board at its national convention, held that year in Swarthmore, Pennsylvania, requesting that a charter be granted. Her petition was granted immediately, the same time as the petition offered by the Carnegie Institute of Technology. Pitt and Carnegie became the nineteenth and twentieth chapters of Mortar Board later that year.

Mortar Board members were renowned for their leadership in the Women's Self-Government Association, the Debating Association, women's sports clubs, sororities, and residence life. With Dean Amos, Mortar Boards helped to create the women's space, which was so important to women on campus, on the twelfth floor of the Cathedral of Learning.

Champion: Dean Amos (Pittsburgh, 1928).

Pomona College, 1930

Eight senior women, all leaders in undergraduate activities appointed the preceding spring by the outgoing class, met in October 1923 for the purpose of organizing the Senior Women's Honorary. The constitution and the other forms of plans for the society were all made with the hope that some day Mortar Board would install a chapter. The group first inquired about Mortar Board membership in 1925 and inquired again in 1927. The campus was inspected in October 1928, and Expansion Director Lillian Stupp told them they could petition. The vote recorded in handwriting on her notes was a sound "yes."

The installing officers, National Vice President Marion Blanchard Hickey (Washington State University, 1923) and Section Coordinator

Mrs. Albro Lundy, arrived in Claremont on Friday morning, March 28, and held a series of conferences with officers and alumnae. At 4:00 p.m. the cap and gown ceremony was held in a "candlelighted room. Nine members . . . accepted the pledge of Mortar Board." In a ceremony immediately following, "Seventeen alumnae and three honorary members received the trust of the Mortar Board Group."[118]

University of Puget Sound, 1959

Otlah was founded on the College of Puget Sound campus in 1922 and has had a continuous existence since that time. It was felt by the faculty at that time that there was a need for a group of outstanding college women who could aid in the fulfillment of the aims of the college. After careful consideration it was decided to establish a senior honorary for women. The selection of members was made by the faculty members, and each person on the faculty was asked to consider those students who met the eligibility requirements and select one student as their candidate for membership in Otlah. An organization that held high scholarship, campus service, and unquestionable womanly character as its ideals became a reality. The petition of 1959 declared that

> throughout the years the activities of Otlah have been numerous and varied depending upon the needs of the students, the faculty, and the campus. As the campus has grown in size, new areas of service and responsibility have been opened to the Otlah members. Otlah has taken initiative in the formation and continuance of various campus activities and governing bodies such as AWS; the annual leadership conference; the art and lecture series; the annual AWS spring banquet, at which the new Spurs and Otlah members were tapped; and

the freshman and upper class weekly convocations. Since the beginning, . . . Otlah worked toward the type of program that would make it eligible to petition for membership in Mortar Board. The members of Otlah contribute a great deal to the maintenance of the college's values as they give leadership to the student body in the areas of student government, religious emphasis, faculty-student relationships, and in their support and encouragement of high scholarship and ideals.[119]

Petition: 1959.
Installing officer: Section Director Gen DeVleming.
Installation: May 2.

Purdue University, 1926

A local honorary for senior women, S.L.S (for scholarship, leadership, service) was established in 1923 under the guidance of Dean of Women Carolyn Shoemaker. The S.L.S. petition was accepted on November 11, 1926, by the national conference, held at Washington University in St. Louis, and the installation was held just eighteen days later on Monday, November 29, on campus with five collegiate members. At a banquet following in the Fowler Hotel, installing officer National President Kathleen Lucy Hammond welcomed the chapter. New president Mary Zimmer responded with a speech titled "The Responsibilities of a New Chapter," and Dean Shoemaker, who had been made an honorary member, offered a speech titled "What Mortar Board Means to Purdue."

In the 1930s, Mortar Board members assisted with registration, started a big sister program, helped the dean of women revise data for a coed employment bureau, and held a series of teas for outstanding underclasswomen. The chapter also put on the Gingham Gallop, an all-campus dance. Each year the chapter respectfully laid a wreath at the grave of John Purdue, who was buried on campus.

In 1937, the chapter petitioned President Edward C. Elliott for a Women's Placement Bureau. The petition was successful, and Ruth Houghton was hired to run it. Dr. Dorothy C. Stratton (Purdue, 1936) was dean of women. In 1939, the chapter secured modern lighting in the library and tackled upgrading the women's restroom in the library.

To raise money the chapter sold chrysanthemums on Dads' Day, a practice that went on through the beginning of the 1940s. In 1941 Dr. Lillian Gilbreth was made an honorary member. In the war years, suppers for distinguished sophomore women and Smarty Parties for junior women were held. Mortar Boards assumed roles on campus formerly held by men who had left to serve in the military. Dean Stratton also left campus to become the first head of the women's auxiliary of the Coast Guard, SPARS, whose name she coined.

On December 1, 1945, the chapter put reminder calendars, "bound in blue or green," on sale in the student union. The project was so successful, reported Jean Huston, that "we decided to make it an annual one."[120] The proceeds were handsome. For instance, by 1962 the chapter gave $5,000 in scholarships to other students. In 2012 thanks to the continuous sale of the Mortar Board Calendar, the chapter celebrated the award of its millionth dollar for scholarships for Purdue students, awards to clerical and service staff, and prizes to other student organizations to promote their projects.

Also in 1962, Purdue worked to bring Omicron Delta Kappa (ODK), a men's honor society, to campus, and the Century Circle was installed.

Throughout the 1960s, Mortar Boards helped advise Alpha Lambda Delta and also assisted the Office of the Dean of Women in interviewing one thousand freshman women to discuss problems, ideals, and goals after a month of college life.

In 1967 the Fiftieth Anniversary Conference of Mortar Board was held at Purdue, with Dean of Women Helen B. Schleman (Northwestern, 1923) as the conference chair. In 1968 upon Dean Schleman's retirement, the chapter, along with the Women's Residence Council, Panhellenic, the Women's Co-op Association, and Off-Campus Women, started the Helen B. Schleman Gold Medallion to honor a woman (or man) who matched the goals of Dean Schleman. Dean Schleman created an endowment to fund a gift to each recipient.

In 1975 men were introduced to Mortar Board, and advisor Barbara Cook, as national Mortar Board vice president, was in the thick of the process and the special national conference that would bring out that result. In 1976 five of the twenty-nine new members were men.

In 1977 the Tip of the Cap Awards were created, and the chapter also gave $6,000 for an aquatic pond in Horticulture Park to celebrate its fiftieth anniversary.

In 1983 the first Mortar Board Leadership Conference was held in the configuration that has been continued annually to the present. Another 1980s success was the establishment of the Rose Awards (1986) for outstanding clerical and service staff members and also the Senior Women-Athlete Dinner, which was eventually repurposed to the Freshman Scholar-Athlete Dinner. The chapter also began the Mortar Board Volleyball Purdue Premier and has been the only chapter and possibly the only student organization in the country to host an intercollegiate athletic tournament. In 1987 the calendar was netting $30,000, and the chapter presented seven scholarships of $2,500 in a rigorous selection process.

In the fall of 1987 the chapter constructed a marker at a major thoroughfare on campus in honor of Barbara Cook, who was retiring as dean of students; the chapter sought and received permission to be called the Barbara Cook Chapter. In the early 1990s the chapter also dedicated a lovely seating area on the south side of Schleman Hall to honor Dean Emerita Schleman.

In 1991, the calendar included safe sex and safety tips along with events, addresses, and phone numbers. Though criticized for this, calendar chair Kevin Fink said that "Mortar Boards are not stick-your-head-in-the-sand types of people."[121] In 1995 the chapter decided that it was not done honoring Dean Cook, so it started a national fellowship in her honor and is the only collegiate chapter in Mortar Board to make this level of annual contribution ($5,000 at the time of this writing) to the MBNF, of which Cook had been president for two terms in the 1990s.

In 2005, the chapter led other campus groups in raising $16,000 for victims of Hurricane Katrina. In 2007 the Women of Purdue event hosted by the chapter made national news, and the chapter arranged for portraits of all of the deans of women and deans of students, all members of Mortar Board, to be painted and hung in the West Faculty Lounge of the student union.

Gifts to the Women in Crisis Program and the Span Plan for older students and impressive events each year to promote the national program of Mortar Board, Reading Is Leading, are all part of the Barbara Cook chapter legacy.

The chapter in the 2010s is reenvisioning itself with new strategic planning that takes into account declining sales of the paper calendar and expectations for involvement by members while at the same time excelling in the organizations, research, and classwork that caused them to be selected in the first place.

It is no wonder that the chapter won in 2002 the first national award as the top chapter, the Ruth Weimer Mount Chapter Excellence Award. It shared the top honor again in 2014 with the University of Nebraska at Kearney.

THE MORTAR BOARD FORUM

MORTAR BOARD INC., NATIONAL COLLEGE SENIOR HONOR SOCIETY

SPRING ISSUE 2001   VOLUME 31, NUMBER 2

**National Project
"Reading is Leading"
Makes a Difference
Across the Nation**

Purdue hosts an extravagant Reading Is Leading event annually on campus. Starting quarterback Drew Brees was an active participant as a member of the 2000 class; the photo of his reading made the front cover of the *Forum*.

Queens University of Charlotte, 1987

The secret organization Order of the Olympus of Queens College, founded in 1924, became a chapter of the regional group Alpha Kappa Gamma in 1928. There is no record of when this group disbanded, but Alpha Kappa Gamma had grown faint in the 1960s. In 1961 Orb & Sceptre was begun for the seniors of the College of Arts and Sciences.

Twenty-five members were initiated at installation, along with four alumnae who were present. Dr. Clyda Stokes Rent was made an honorary member at the ceremony, held in Belk Chapel.

Petition: 1986.

Installing officers: Vice President M. Kathryne MacKenzie and Section Coordinator Esther Williams (Iowa State, 1950).

University of Redlands, 1955

On May 14, 1943, ten women selected on the basis of leadership, citizenship, and scholarship by the dean of women and three interested faculty women assembled to found a senior women's honorary group. The name W.E.B.S. was chosen to represent the ideals of wisdom, excellence, belief, and service. Ever mindful of the problems of a college campus, W.E.B.S. sought to establish a distinct service program to promote scholarship, student citizenship, and leadership.

In the early years, W.E.B.S. originated the Senior Breakfast and a vocational guidance program and supervised wartime drives such as blood bank. As an organization, these senior women have led in every phase of campus life. As years passed W.E.B.S. began other projects that included the Marriage Series, faculty-student coffees, square dances, the Orientation Dance for new students, and the Smarty Party

to honor women with high scholarship achievement. Yet these "women in blue" were never too busy to offer their services for homecoming or University Day or to participate in all-college affairs. Individually, the integrity, influence, and capabilities of each W.E.B.S. member commanded the respect, friendship, and cooperation of students and faculty alike.

Installation date: April 23.

University of Rhode Island, 1967

Laurels was founded in the spring of 1960. Its standards and purposes were the fostering of the highest standards for scholarship, the encouragement of service and friendship within the university, the recognition of capable leadership, and the promotion of loyalty to the university. A few of the activities of Laurels during the first few years included the Annual Honors Tea, the compilation and distribution of a freshman booklet, the annual Last Lecture Series, the Head Start Follow-up Program, promotion of faculty-student relations, and an undergraduate evaluation of teacher effectiveness.

Petition: 1965.

Installing officer: Editor Pam Chinnis.

Installation: May 14.

Rhodes College, 1964

Just before commencement in May 1937, the Torch Society was formed at Southwestern at Memphis and recognized by faculty and administrators. There were six charter members. The chapter supported many important projects and assisted in obtaining

Southwestern's recognition by the AAUW. Seven women were initiated on April 18.

Petitions: 1955, 1962.

Installing officers: National First Vice President Marianne Wolfe assisted by Section Director Betty Carol Pace Clark.

University of Richmond, 1930

On Saturday, October 25, Pi Alpha became a chapter of Mortar Board at Westhampton College, the women's division of the University of Richmond. There were seven active members, and the privilege of membership was extended to alumnae; no fewer than thirty of them returned and joined the society. Three honorary members were elected: Dean May L. Keller, head of the Latin Department Gertrude M. Beggs, and professor of history Maude Woodfin.

The Blue Room was the site of the 6:00 p.m. installation conducted by Expansion Director Katherine Kuhlman, who was assisted by Shirley Wright, president of the Virginia Gamma chapter at William & Mary. A banquet followed at the Commonwealth Club.

Rowan University, 2001

Gamma Tau Sigma was founded in 1966 as a "prestigious organization comprised of senior students who have taken full advantage of the opportunities the university has to offer by excelling in academics and participating in extracurricular activities."[122] Its emblems were the torch and scroll.

Petition: 2000.

Champions: Gamma Tau Sigma vice president Chris Yates and advisor Esther Mummert.

Salem College, 1984

Arete was established in September 1977 when a group of seniors who had distinguished records of scholarship, leadership, and service met to discuss the possibility of forming a senior honor society. Eleven seniors enthusiastically endorsed the idea and began plans to establish a society modeled after Mortar Board. After selecting the name Arete (a Greek word meaning "excellence"), the group submitted a constitution and took it through the appropriate channels to become a recognized campus organization. As a result of their assessment of campus needs, they conducted informal discussions on the Equal Rights Amendment and compiled a directory of faculty members who would assist them in promoting women's issues.

The first members were tapped during the 1978 Honors Convocation. Since Salem students had more free time in January and needed to be aware of cultural, social, and recreational opportunities in the city and surrounding areas, Arete compiled, prepared, and distributed a January calendar with daily listings of activities. Other service projects included sponsoring a lecture series; meeting with underclassmen to discuss topic such as time management, graduate study, and campus and community enrichment opportunities; sponsoring a GRE Math Review; and teaching word processing.

Petition: 1983.

Champion: Dean of Students Virginia Johnson.

Installing officers: National President Dottie Moser and Section Coordinator Mary Sue Bissell.

Installation: May 5.

San Diego State University, 1965

Cap and Gown Honor Society was founded in 1932 at San Diego State Teachers College and was reported in the *San Diego Union*. Its first meeting was at the home of Francis Boyd. Membership was limited to twelve senior women and one honorary member, who was Mary McMullen. Helen Squires was elected high chancellor. In 1965 Cap and Gown became a chapter of Mortar Board.

The chapter spearheaded the establishment of an Honors Council and began publishing a planner in 1992, which continues to be popular. Reading Is Leading is a perennial project, and in a collaboration with the Alcalá chapter and San Diego alumnae, Cap and Gown stuffs backpacks for a local elementary school. The chapter's annual faculty recognition and tree-planting ceremony are widely attended and very popular, as is its more than two decades-old Faculty and Staff Appreciation Dinner. The chapter won the Ruth Weimer Mount Chapter Excellence Award in 2003 and 2012.

In 2008 the chapter, with approval of the National Council, became the Jane K. Smith Cap and Gown chapter.

Champion: Dean of Activities Margery Ann Warmer (San Diego State, 1965).

University of San Diego, 2000

The Alcalá Senior Honor Society began in the 1999–2000 academic year, with thirty juniors selected for scholarship, leadership, and service.

The chapter's petition was accepted, and on October 22 National President Mabel Freeman conducted the installation with the assistance of former section director Jean Carfagno (Ohio State, 1960). University president Alice B. Hayes became an honorary member.

Alcalá is extremely active and supports the community by helping students at Kearny Mesa High School and raising funds for scholarships, called STRIVE (for "Seeking to Recognize Individual Visions of Excellence"). In 2008, just eight years after becoming a chapter, Alcalá received the Ruth Weimer Mount Chapter Excellence Award.

Champions: President Alice B. Hayes and Director of Financial Aid Judy Lewis Logue (San Diego State, 1965).

Seattle Pacific University, 1994

In the winter of 1992, professor of chemistry and director of the University Scholar Program Wesley Lingren and director of the Center for Special Populations Gwen Spencer discussed creating a senior honor society whose values would correspond with those of the university. There had been a women's honorary, the Falconettes, and a men's, the Centurions, which were local. The time seemed opportune to pursue a national honorary.

Several societies were explored, and Mortar Board was determined to suit best because of its emphasis on scholarship, leadership, and service. University president Curtis Martin enthusiastically endorsed Mortar Board, and the faculty and staff were informed of this goal.

Director Spencer continued to gather information and develop governing documents modeled after Mortar Board. The group was named Ivy Honorary after the significant campus tradition, a pregraduation event where seniors stand in their caps and gowns holding an interconnected circle of ivy. After a community service, the president and administrators cut a section of the ivy for each senior to keep and nurture.

The first students were selected in January 1993. Selected students are tapped by surprise (e.g., in a class, an internship, or an orchestral rehearsal) by a member of the Seattle Pacific University faculty or staff, wearing a cap and gown, who is a Mortar Board member and a member of the Ivy Honorary. The new members are given a certificate, and a sprig of ivy is pinned to their jackets or shirts. They are recognized during homecoming weekend in January and introduced to the student body at homecoming chapel.

Ivy honorees are actively involved as ushers and members of the color guard during the senior class ivy cutting.

Petition: 1993. The president's letter notes that six members of the faculty or staff, including Gwen Spencer, are Mortar Boards.

University of South Alabama, 1979

Mortar Board began at the University of South Alabama in the late 1960s when President Frederick P. Whiddon asked Associate Dean of Students Blanche Cox (South Alabama, 1979) to establish honor societies at the university. In 1969, eight women were selected as charter members of Gold Key. In 1976 following Title IX guidelines, men were included as members for the first time. In 1979, the Gold Key chapter was granted national Mortar Board membership. In 2007, the chapter name was changed, with the approval of the National Council, to the Azalea chapter.

The Azalea chapter has repeatedly received national recognition, with the Golden Torch Award for chapter excellence and the Project Excellence Award for exceptional chapter activities. In 2005 the chapter was named the Most Improved Chapter. Three advisors, Dr. Dennis Fell, Mrs. Sally Cobb (who served as advisor for more than twenty years), and Dr. Sally Steadman, have been honored with the national Excellence in Advising Award.

Chapter projects have included book drives and flower sales to support the national project, Reading Is Leading, "Top Prof" and "Tip of the Cap" recognitions for faculty and staff, scholarships for freshmen and juniors, holiday parties for the children of St. Mary's Home, Philippine relief collections, canned food drives, tutoring, and study breaks for University of South Alabama students.

In 2017 the chapter, with the approval of the National Council, became the Sally Steadman Azalea chapter.

University of South Carolina, 1967

There had been a women's honor group since 1928, when Gamma Omega Pi was founded as a leadership society and patterned after and sponsored by Chi Circle of ODK. Fourteen outstanding women were selected on the basis of scholarship and participation in student activities. Later the group joined Alpha Kappa Gamma, a regional organization. For more than thirty years Alpha Kappa Gamma was known on campus for its outstanding service to the university, its recognition of women who had made significant achievements in scholarship, and its strong contributions to the campus community in leadership and service.

Finally in the 1960s, although there were strong ties of sentiment and tradition with Alpha Kappa Gamma, the Carolina chapter felt that the university and its women leaders were worthy of an honor society truly national in scope. Since Alpha Kappa Gamma had six other chapters in South Carolina and Virginia, the University of South Carolina group gave official notification of its withdrawal from this organization, feeling that it could not be a part of one national, however small, and aspire to belong to another.

Carolina decided to continue as a local honor society and petition Mortar Board. The local name was Alpha Order—"order" signifying a strong society and "alpha," the very first letter of the alphabet, signifying the optimum in all things. Organizing the Associated Women Students on campus was a project of the Alpha Order. Another major project traditionally was a loan fund through which money is made available to students needing financial aid. Each member of the Alpha Order strives to fulfill its stated goal that "the University shall become a better place because we have been there."[123]

Petition: 1964.

Installing officers: Expansion Director Betty Jo Palmer, assisted by Section Director Lynn Rountree Bartlett.

Installation: April 16.

University of South Dakota, 1928

Keystone was founded in 1921 under the guidance of College of Arts and Sciences Dean Frank T. Stockton and Marion Conover (Wisconsin-Madison). They selected a group of six women on the basis of womanliness, scholarship, and activities. From the beginning Keystone set its sights on Mortar Board.

The group developed an enviable reputation, helping the faculty with many projects. Together with the Dakotans, the society for men, Keystone developed a point system to regulate student activities in 1925. The system was adopted by the student government. Senior Swingout was a well-known project, and an outdoor pageant was given in the spring. The chapter was discouraged by Expansion Director Gertrude Wilharm from petitioning in 1925 but did not lose its momentum.

Installation was on November 24 in the home of "one of the active members" by National Treasurer Kay Coleman. Six active and nine alumnae were initiated.[124]

University of South Florida, 1972

In 1957, Grace Allen, spouse of President John Allen, the university's first president, and Professor Margaret Fischer, applied to Mortar Board for a charter. In 1959, the chapter was officially installed as the Athenaeum Chapter of the Mortar Board National Senior Honor Society.

The Oracle described Mrs. Allen as a woman whose passion and vision for University of South Florida inspired many as she helped develop the University from its inception, when it was just a plot of grass overlooking a dirt road called Fowler Avenue, to its status as the nation's ninth-largest university.

The Athenaeum chapter of Mortar Board was one of the first student organizations on the South Florida campus. It was considered a very prestigious honor society in which young women could participate. The women selected for membership became the first University of South Florida ambassadors and assisted Mrs. Allen with university events held on campus.

In 2001, the Athenaeum chapter hosted the Mortar Board national conference. Chapters from all over the country participated in that conference, and the chapter was recognized for its hard work and dedication for coordinating that annual conference.

In the fall of 2003 the Athenaeum chapter initiated its first honorary member, President Judy Genshaft, in a special ceremony. As part of that ceremony, Grace Allen and Margaret Fischer were presented Outstanding Alumni Awards. In the spring 2004 Initiation and Awards Ceremony, the chapter initiated its second honorary member, Provost Renu Khator.

During Chapter President Susan Rodman's term, the chapter initiated Tampa mayor Pam Iorio; her late father and professor emeritus John Iorio; Jenna Welch Bush, daughter of former president George W. and Mrs. Laura Bush (Texas at El Paso, 1995); and professor of psychology Judith Becker Bryant. The honorary members and their families, along with Mortar Board alumna Patricia Bynum Riggs (University of Oklahoma, 1946), wife of former University of South Florida president Carl Riggs, and former county commissioner Jan Kaminis Platt (Florida State, 1957), were present at the 2008 induction ceremony.

The chapter started its annual project called Storybook Forest in the fall of 2003. The first Storybook Forest was held at the University of South Florida Botanical Gardens. The project involved providing underprivileged children from the local area with new books that were collected through the year. The event included a bookmark contest, reading with the children, and snacks. After the inaugural Storybook Forest, the event has been held each year at the University Area Community Center. In 2007, the Athenaeum distributed over $3,500 worth of school supplies, including 350 books, and entertained 350 kids at the annual Storybook Forest event. Athenaeum also won the National Mortar Board Week photo Contest. The tradition continues.

Athenaeum has received numerous national awards for project excellence for the Storybook Forest and the Pet Extravaganza project. In 2003, 2004, 2006, and 2007 the chapter also won the Gold Torch Award.

University of Southern California, 1929

In the fall of 1913 a group of senior women felt the need for a women's honorary organization. Three of them met in a small room of Old College, along with two juniors they had invited. They drew up a constitution and chose the name Torch and Tassel. The torch signified wisdom and knowledge, the tassel signified dignity and achievement, and the combination of the two signified power. The constitution stated that the purpose of the organization "shall be (1) To develop a complete college woman capable, self-reliant, and efficient, (2) to encourage the participation of women in university affairs, and (3) to honor in the eyes of the college world those women who have achieved."[125]

Membership was limited to not more than ten active members; graduate members who returned were active and additional to the limited number. The motive and plans for Torch and Tassel were presented to the administration. On January 22, 1914, formal initiation rites were held around the fireplace in the entrance of Old College as each of the six founders held a lighted torch, signifying the ideals of the group. The dean formally accepted Torch and Tassel as an organization on the campus. Skull and Dagger, the national men's honorary, sent white carnations to the Torch and Tassel members, and all initiates wore violets as part of their recognition.

Fifteen years later Torch and Tassel became a chapter of Mortar Board on January 4. In 1932 a new tradition was inaugurated. The new members of Mortar Board were announced by the display of a silver plaque with their names on it. A case containing a Mortar Board with a gold tassel and the plaque was placed on the Trojan Shrine in front of the university. Early service projects included sponsoring women transferring in their junior year, holding a leadership training class under faculty guidance, establishing a tradition of holding afternoon teas when all women were invited, awarding a freshman scholarship cup to the woman who maintained the highest average that year, and creating a Mortar Board Service Fund to aid coeds who were worthy and not eligible for other loans.

Southern Methodist University, 1932

The secret group called Square was organized in 1916, no later than one year after the founding of Southern Methodist University. This group consisted of three or four women each year, with university librarian Dorothy Amann as advisor and mentor. Around 1926, the group decided to expand to include ten women each year. The name of the group became Decima. Its colors were mustang red and blue, and "Varsity" was its song, written by Dorothy Amann.

Decima learned about Mortar Board from a University of Texas alumna, who told the group details of the organization. In 1930, National President Kay Coleman visited the Southern Methodist campus to investigate Decima. Gene Caldwell, chair of Decima alumnae at the time of Kay's visit, is credited with securing the charter.

Decima became the fiftieth chapter of Mortar Board on February 20. The ceremony took place at Stoneleigh Court and was followed by a formal dinner. In its early years, the chapter typically consisted of ten to thirteen women. Major events for the chapter, which included advisors and alumnae, were the Founders Day banquet, a breakfast following spring initiation, and a breakfast the first Sunday after Thanksgiving.

In early years, tapping was typically held on the steps of Dallas Hall at twilight. Another interesting tradition was the transfer of ribbons. Active members wore red and blue ribbons on their right shoulders for ten days before public tapping. The day after tapping, active members transferred their ribbons to the right shoulders of new pledges.

Petition: 1932.

Southern Nazarene University, 1980

The AWS organized a senior women's honor society in May 1964 with nine charter members at the then Bethany Nazarene University. The name chosen was Athenas (from the Greek goddess of wisdom), and the motto was "Wisdom—Culture—Service." Because of the traditional significance of ivy in the commencement ceremonies, the group's emblem was designed with a wreath of ivy around a mortarboard; within this circle were the letters "BNC" above and the name Athenas below. Although no official ongoing uniform was adopted, the tradition of using blue as an essential color in the official outfit each year was established by this first group.

Early projects ranged from gathering books for a library in India to printing the first calendar of events for students. In 1977 the name was changed to Chi Sigma, signifying "Chosen to Serve."

Petition: 1979.

Champion: Dean of Women Wanda Rhodes, who also spearheaded the start of the AWS.

Installing officer: Expansion Director M. Kathryne MacKenzie.

Installation: March 25.

Spelman University, 1987

Senior Honor Society of Spelman College was begun around 1982 with Mortar Board in mind. Installation of thirty-four petitioning, thirty incoming, and sixteen alumnae members was held on March 22 at 2:00 p.m. in Sisters Chapel. A reception followed in the Sojourner Truth Concourse of the Manley College Center, with Alpha Lambda Delta members assisting.

Honorary members initiated were Drs. Hayward Farrar, Grace B. Smith, and Donald M. Stewart.

Petition: 1985.

Champions: Acting president Barbara L. Carter (Fisk University, 1975) and professor of chemistry Gladys S. Bayse (University of Memphis, 1984).

Installing officers: Director of Finance and Records Bette Swilley and Section Coordinator Esther Williams.

Stephens College, 1986

In April 1979 a new honor society for outstanding senior students was proposed by the Academic Affairs Commission of the Student Government Association and approved by the Faculty Senate. It was modeled after national Mortar Board in hopes of petitioning for membership. The name selected was the Society of Athena, after the Greek goddess of wisdom, defensive war, and justice. Each Athena group has engaged in many activities and service projects, including a forum on graduate school, a lecture series, assisting in the Admissions Office, and helping with the Phonathon. During Stephens' sesquicentennial in 1983, Athena members helped with the inauguration of the first woman president of the college, Mortar Board member Dr. Patsy Hallock Sampson (University of Oklahoma, 1958).

Petition: April 23, 1984.

Stetson University, 1958

As a climax to more than twenty years of hard work and hopeful expectation of almost three hundred members, The Honor was installed as the ninty-ninth chapter on February 23. The Honor was organized in 1935 by its first president, Etter McTeer Turner, who was a freshman in 1931 and remained on campus until retiring as dean of students in 1977.

The Honor held the Women's Leadership Banquet and recognized the outstanding freshman woman each year, sometimes partnering with ODK at homecoming for another banquet. Just two days before the installation, the famed Columbia professor and Mortar Board member Dr. Esther Lloyd-Jones, where Dean Turner had done graduate work, was the speaker at this event. Installation was held in the new student union.

Installing officers: Expansion Director Daisy Parker and historian Hazel Moren Richards.

Swarthmore College, 1918

It was in March 1907 that nine women were chosen by deans, faculty, and alumni to form a society recognizing loyalty, scholarship, and character. The Greek words signifying these characteristics provided the initials for the group, and the chapter developed into the Pi Sigma Alpha chapter after "nationalization."

"The charter members prided themselves on the originality with which they designed their insignia, a mortar board in a dull gold. It was however their very unoriginality with this emblem which brought about the nationalization of a senior honor society. The pin at Ohio State University was almost identical!"[126]

University of Tennessee–Chattanooga, 1953

Quadrangle was organized on Class Night, May 30, 1936, as an honor society for senior women based on character, leadership, scholarship, and service to the University of Chattanooga. Selection was by unanimous vote.

The members worked during Freshman Orientation Week, advised freshmen, administered a point system, and built a card file of activities for every person in school so as to work closely with the Elections Committee for eligibility for offices. The All-Campus Sing was an annual Quadrangle project.

The installation was held on the afternoon of Saturday, December 5, in the new Danforth Chapel for ten active members and thirty honorary and alumnae members. A banquet was held in the gold Room of the Read House.

Champions: First lady of the university and advisor Virginia Golladay Lockmiller, Dean of Students Dorothy Woodworth, professor of history and advisor Theresa Waller, secretary to the dean of liberal arts May Saunders, and former first lady Charlotte Holmes Guerry (all Tennessee-Chattanooga, 1953).

Installing officer: Editor Daisy Parker.

University of Tennessee–Knoxville, 1937

The chapter's historian wrote in 1939 that

contrary to all probable conjectures, the first move toward a senior women's honor society at the University came not from the girls, but from the boys. About the year 1922, several boys representing the Scarabbean Secret Society came to Dean of Women Harriet Grove [*sic*] to discuss the possibility of a senior women's honor society. Dean Grove, though perfectly willing to help start such an organization, thought that perhaps it would be better if the idea for such a group came from the girls themselves. In the spring of 1929 the Women's Student Activities Council met in a retreat and late one night a group of four girls gathered on a small rustic bridge near the Gatlinburg Hotel discussing campus life. The idea of Cap and Gown was born.

The next day on May 21, 1929, two girls came to the Activity Council to ask recognition of this local senior organization for women. This petition was granted with the suggestion that the word "character" be included in the purpose of the organization. The process of election was based on faculty recommendations, open investigation and the unanimous vote of the group. Two women faculty members helped the girls write the initiation ritual and the installation service was held at the Knoxville home of a campus leader.[127]

There were eight charter members.

The historian in 1974 wrote that

on October 18, 1937, Katherine Kuhlman, Mortar Board Expansion Director wrote Dean of Women Harriet Greve to inform her that the Tennessee petition had been approved. In order to attain recognition from Mortar Board, the Cap and Gown chapter tutored freshmen women; held open forums featuring outstanding speakers; and gave an annual award of a five dollar gold piece to the collegian in each of the three lower classes who had been of the most service to her fellow students during the preceding year. A silver loving cup (Aloha Oe) was also presented to the senior most nearly approaching the Ideals of Mortar Board throughout her four years at the University.[128]

During World War II the chapter raised funds, worked at blood banks, sold war bonds and stamps, volunteered at hospitals, and held discussion groups on war marriages and special adjustments to men returning from combat. During the early 1950s the chapter experienced a casualness and indifference toward the ideas of Mortar Board, but this changed within a few years. During the later years, the chapter sponsored many worthwhile service projects that included a graduate school orientation program, a survey on how college women make career choices, and a tutoring program. The chapter also awarded Senior Citations to forty-eight women who exhibited leadership and scholastic qualities and gave an award to the "Most Outstanding Contribution Made by a Woman" on campus.

The installation was held on November 27 in Tyson Center, and members of the HOASC chapter assisted. Thirteen active members assisted, including ten of the previous year's group, and many alumnae of previous classes.

Champion: Dean Greve and instructor of English Mamie Johnston (Tennessee, 1937).

Installing officer: Expansion Director Kay Kuhlman.

Tennessee Technological University, 1975

Gold Circle petitioned to join Mortar Board in 1972, five years after its founding. Its goal was to affiliate with Mortar Board one day; its colors were gold and ivory, and the insignia was a gold circle pin. Women were selected for membership on the basis of scholarship, leadership, and service. Some of the projects of Gold Circle included conducting tours for prospective students on campus, ushering at spring convocation, serving as guides at the President's Reception, hosting a Smarty Party for freshman women on the honor roll, and assisting with blood drives.

Installation took place in the student union on Saturday, April 12. Fourteen petitioners, twenty-three new members, nineteen alumnae, and two honoraries were initiated. Following the ceremony was a reception with punch and cookies, then cocktails followed by a buffet-style banquet dinner.

Installing officers: Second Vice President Kathy Kuester Campbell and Section Coordinator Janis Pierce.

Texas A&M University, 1979

Installation: April 8.

University of Texas at Austin, 1923

Visor was established in 1912 to disseminate knowledge of the traditions of the University of Texas and to foster growth of other traditions, develop a spirit of democracy, and unify the women students of the university. Visor was a secret organization, and whatever projects it undertook were developed by members through their activities in other organizations and with the help of the Office of the Dean of Women.

Initiation of new members was held at 6:00 a.m., after which the new initiates, outgoing members, and alumnae joined for breakfast. A picnic was held so that the new girls learned the names of all the old girls who told of the reaction they experienced when elected to Mortar Board and related the happiest experience of their college career. One traditional activity was for Mortar Board members to announce Visor's newly elected members at Swing-Out each May, an event at which senior women passed campus responsibilities and traditions on to the junior women.

As early as 1927 the chapter raised $14,000 for outdoor lighting along a sidewalk connecting a residence hall (dormitory) and campus, "three or four blocks"[129] away. Other regular achievements were the presentation of the Sophomore Scholarship Cup, Freshman Discussion Evenings, a Vocational Guidance Program, and a Personal Grooming Program. The chapter wrote in 1926 of being concerned to address the honor system and the drinking problems. Visor secured cooperation from the Cowboys (men's organization) to address the drinking issues on campus. Visor also managed the campus calendar of activities for women to help coordinate and avoid conflicts.

Installation: May 11.

Installing officer: Field representative Pauline Wherry.

University of Texas at El Paso, 1972

In 1951 a faculty committee organized an honor society for senior women called Octotillo with the intention of petitioning Mortar Board when eligible. The first five members were chosen for their service, scholarship, and leadership at what was then Texas Western College. After the expansion of the campus with more buildings in the Asian style, the name of the group was changed to Chenrizig in honor of the fabled Tibetan princess who promoted education for her people, including women.

During the initiation of new members, the meaning of the name was read, symbolizing each letter: C for cooperation, H for honor, E for enthusiasm, N for nobility of purpose, R for responsibility, I for intellect, Z for zeal, I for initiative, and G for graciousness. The closed motto was "perennial wisdom." A Maypole was chosen as a background device for the initiation ceremony. Various colored ribbons extended from the top of the Maypole, and each of the new chapter officers was asked to hold a certain colored ribbon. The remaining ribbons represented the new members, and all joined hands to form a circle around the Maypole. This was to signify the "the bond of Service, Scholarship and Leadership."[130]

Chenrizig was installed by Mortar Board on February 13 in the Union Ballroom, with a reception in the Conquistador Lounge. The chapter was apparently installed as "Charter," but in March 2001 Chapter President Karina Franco and advisor Cheryl Howard wrote that the Chenrezig name should be restored because of the special relationship between the University of Texas–El Paso and the country of Bhutan, which is the inspiration for the campus's architecture.

Petitions: 1958, 1964, 1969.

Installing officer: Director of Elections Catherine Evans.

Texas Christian University, 1970

Ampersand began in 1932 to recognize women of high scholastic achievement who had given unselfish service to other students and the university. The name was taken from the Greek symbol meaning "and other things" and representing the object of the society to honor those who had achieved academically and participated significantly in "other things."

Ampersand was discontinued in 1944 when the university adjusted its program to meet the needs of the Navy V-2 program.

In the spring of 1963, Ampersand alumnae in Forth Worth, together with several Texas Christian University faculty women, reestablished the society. The goals were the same.

The group sponsored an annual calendar, cosponsored a Women's Recognition Night, helped with orientation clinics for new students, honored new initiates of Alpha Lambda Delta, and recognized sophomore women of high achievement. Many other activities were added from year to year.

The installation of Ampersand as the 135th chapter was on Saturday, April 18, at 5:00 p.m. in the Robert Carr Chapel, with a banquet following in the Brown-Lupton Student Center Ballroom.

Petition: February 15, 1970.

Champions: Dean of Women Jo Ann James and advisors Drs. Clotilda Winter, Virginia Jarratt, and Judith D. Suther.

Installing officer: National President Helen Snyder, assisted by Carolyn Jenkins Barta (Texas Tech, 1960).

Texas Tech University, 1957

Forum was founded at Texas Technological College in 1927 by Dean of Women Mary W. Doak for fifteen junior and senior women to promote on campus all worthy undertakings, organizations, and movements of the student body; create an unselfish interest in the welfare of the college and its students; furnish a means to a better understanding of human nature by holding as many general social meetings as practicable, thereby helping every student to broaden her scope of friendships; and try to give every woman student a part in some extracurricular activity in which her interests may be broadened and her service fruitful.

Forum's pin was pyramid shaped, and black skirts and white blouses were worn on the regular meeting day. Tapping was in early May, and on the "decided morning, the school song is played from the tower of the Administration Building, and Forum members form a chain, going from class to class and placing a black collar about the shoulders of the chosen members."[131]

The group was well known on campus and conducted the All-College Recognition Day Service, the Big-Little Sister Program, Fireside Forums, Schools of Parliamentary Law, and the first all-college directory. Forum sponsored the Homecoming Queen Contest, began a Town Girls' Club, and held Be Kind to Faculty Week celebrations.

It was Dean Doak's dream that Forum would one day become a Mortar Board chapter. After Texas Tech University was recognized by the AAUW in 1949, correspondence with Mortar Board began in earnest. The installation was on February 9, and thirteen members and seventy alumnae received the Mortar Board pin.

Installing officer: Expansion Director Daisy Parker.

Texas Wesleyan University, 1990

The Quadrangle Senior Women's Honor Society was founded in 1967 by an interested group of faculty women following the example of Mortar Board. Some activities of the organization included nursing home visits, giving trees to campus, the Annual Honors Banquet, and a tea honoring city alumni and Mortar Board officers.

Quadrangle petitioned to join Mortar Board many times, but it was not until 1989 that the first national visitor, Expansion Director Bette Swilley, conducted an inspection. Based on her visit, she determined that it would be a mistake not to install Mortar Board at Texas Wesleyan.

Petitions: 1972, 1975, 1981, 1983, 1988.

Champion: Associate Professor Sue Passmore (Texas Wesleyan, 1994) and Quadrangle president Ralph Adkins.

Installing officers: National Vice President Kathryne MacKenzie, Section Coordinator Nolan Dees (Texas Tech, 1985), and advisor Loralee Pohl.

Installation: Saturday, April 28, at 10:00 a.m.

Texas Woman's University, 1972

Installation: December 2.

Installing officers: National President Shauna Adix and Section Coordinator Connie Wallace.

University of Toledo, 1983

The Peppers Women's Honorary was founded on November 27, 1924, to increase support and attendance for university athletics and other campus events. Since membership was limited to those involved in at least two campus activities, the pep organization was considered an honorary. The installation was at 1:00 p.m. in the Student Union Auditorium with a reception following.

Membership in the Peppers Honor Society consisted of a select group of men and women who maintained high scholarship and participated in campus and community activities.

Installation: May 15.

Installing officers: Director of Finance and Records Bette Swilley and Section Coordinator Patricia Douthitt (Illinois, 1943).

Trinity University, 1973

Installation: March 31

Installing officers: Director of Elections Catherine Evans and Section Coordinator Connie Wallace.

Troy University, 1979

Champion: Dean of Students Gary Branch, who was on ODK's National Council but wished Mortar Board to provide honor *and* service to the campus community.

Tulane University, 1958

Alpha Sigma Sigma was founded at Sophie Newcomb College on March 22, 1915, by five charter members in the class of 1916, Kathleen Black, Regina Janvier, Mina Koch, Julia Schwabacher, and Hermine Ujffey. They saw a need for a women's honorary organization to promote leadership, high scholarship, and loyal service to the college, selecting the name Alpha Sigma Sigma, for "Always Show Spirit." The badge was of a gold senior cap with Greek letters on it. Newly elected members, numbering ten to thirteen, were tapped at an assembly late in the spring. The initiates went through a traditional processional and were then entertained at a tea given by the outgoing members.

The primary contribution to the school then was the organization and direction of the Freshman Orientation Program. Throughout its history at Newcomb, Alpha Sigma Sigma worked with all other organizations on campus for the betterment of the school.

Three of the founders and many alumnae attended the installation on March 1 at 3:30 p.m. in the Alumni House. In 1959 more than fifty alumnae were initiated in a special program.

The Excellence in Teaching Award is held in high esteem by the faculty. Newcomb Awareness Week was started by the 1989 class, and Toast to Newcomb was also started that year. The Newcomb Leadership Conference for Girls was undertaken by the 1996 chapter. The 2008 chapter was the first to admit men.

In 2009, the chapter petitioned for a name change in reaction to the elimination of Newcomb College by Tulane in the aftermath of Hurricane Katrina. Demonstrating its respect for Newcomb College, the chapter is now the Sophie Newcomb Alpha Sigma Sigma chapter.

Petition: 1954.

Champion: Dean of Women Dorothy Riccuitti (Newcomb-Tulane, 1958).

Installing officers: National President Jane Klein Moehle, Expansion Director Daisy Parker, and historian Hazel Moren Richards.

University of Tulsa, 1950

Senior Staff was established on April 19, 1933, by Dean of Women Myrtle Gleason Cole. The purpose of the organization as stated in the initiation service was threefold: to give recognition to and bestow honor upon women students who have attained distinction in scholarship and leadership on campus and who have displayed qualities of fine character in loyalty, honesty, generosity, cooperation, and service; to inspire interest and enthusiasm in all women students in developing themselves into the highest type of womanhood of which they are capable; and to build better and more worthwhile college ideals than now exist.

The beautiful initiation service followed tapping, with candles representing scholarship, service, leadership, and character. A few projects of Senior Staff at that time were the establishment of Lantern, the sophomore honor society; sponsoring the Leadership Conference for women on campus; and holding a tea for new out-of-town women students before there were dormitories.

Senior Staff made application to Mortar Board before World War II, and no national visits were made during that period. Wrote the historian, "After the peace we again filled out the national questionnaire. We presented an informal annual report to Mortar Board for a good many years. Senior Staff was installed as a chapter of Mortar Board in 1950."[132]

The installation was on May 19 in the Tyrrell Hall auditorium for sixty-one alumnae, six honorary members, and sixteen active members. President C. I. Pontius spoke at the banquet, held in the After Five Room of the Hotel Tulsa, that was attended by all the academic deans as well.

Honorary members in addition to Dean Emerita Cole were Drs. Harriet Barclay and Carol Y. Mason, counselor to women Mary Clay Williams, Mrs. E. A Morrow, and Mrs. C. I. Pontius.

Petitions: 1941, 1946.

Champion: Dean Cole (Tulsa, 1950).

Installing officers: National President Rosemary Ginn and Betty Baranoff (Oklahoma State, 1948).

Utah State University, 1970

Sigma Phi Eta was founded in the spring of 1958 and was structured on Mortar Board guidelines with the hope that one day it would be accepted as a chapter. The purpose of Sigma Phi Eta was to stimulate a high type of senior woman in scholastic and leadership activities. Among its traditions and service projects included a dinner for foreign student women; gathering paperbacks to send to servicemen in Vietnam; a tea for junior women who have excelled in scholarship, leadership, and service; and aiding in the Ph.T. (Putting Hubby Through) program that honored the wives of graduates during the commencement activities.

Sigma Phi Eta also completed a graduate brochure containing a list of all fellowships, grants, and scholarships available to women graduate students in all departments on campus along with information on testing deadlines. The chapter brought campus issues to its meetings and, when appropriate, formulated and published group opinions.

The installation was on April 18 in the auditorium, with a reception and banquet following. Thirty-two alumnae returned for the proceedings.

Petitions: 1963, 1969.

Champions: Charter member Margene Isom Thorpe, advisors Sylvia Anita Srnka Carter (George Washington University, 1949) and Mary Ann Bailey Lammers (Montana State, 1967), Dean of Women Helen Lundstrom, and former dean of women Leah Dunford Parkinson, who were made honorary members.

Installing officer: Expansion Director Mary McAlister.

University of Utah, 1933

In the spring of 1921, Bessie Jones and Kenna Cragun attended a convention of the Intermountain and Western Division of Associated

Women Students at which representatives of Mortar Board urged them to organize local groups and work toward petitioning for Mortar Board chapters. Jones and Cragun were so inspired by the aims and ambitions of the national group that they installed on the Utah campus a similar local organization. Under their leadership, on November 17, 1921, a group of outstanding senior girls established the Order of Acorn. Their purpose was to encourage scholarship and extracurricular activities and to provide some definite goal for which underclass students might strive.

Their ideals and ceremonies were based on a triangle of womanhood, activity, and scholarship. Their motto was "Great oaks from little acorns grow." Twelve years after the founding during which time it grew amazingly in prestige and recognition on campus, the Order of Acorn was admitted into Mortar Board. Among the accomplishments of the chapter have been the promotion of the Big Sister Program to aid freshman women, the encouragement and recognition of high scholarship in each class, the leadership classes presented annually to train students in leadership and methods of conducting meetings, and cooperation with Orchesis to aid in the success of their yearly cultural program.

In the *Quarterly* Selma Schonfeld (Utah, 1934) wrote that

> November 13, 1933, was the reddest of red letter days in the calendar of important events at the University of Utah, for on that day the Order of Acorn reached the goal toward which it had been striving since the day of its founding, twelve years previous.[133]

The members greeted National President Kay Coleman as she arrived on the train. It was a crisp, cool, Indian summer morning. Schonfeld continues:

> At one o'clock we reassembled, and over the teacups absorbed the Mortar Board enthusiasm which emanates so vibrantly from Mrs. Coleman's personality. . . . [W]e hurried homeward for freshening purposes and arrived, slightly breathless, at the Alta Club where eight active and twenty-seven alumnae members of the Order of Acorn were initiated.[134]

Dean of Women Jean Slavens, Librarian Esther Nelson, and Mrs. Mary T. Richardson were made honorary members.

Installing officer: National President Kay Coleman, who arrived from Wyoming, where she had just installed Cap & Gown.

Valparaiso University, 1969

Gown and Gavel was founded in 1943 to honor outstanding senior women and to promote leadership in the intellectual, cultural, social, and spiritual programs of Valparaiso. Through the years it has remained a flexible organization, emphasizing projects of service to the entire academic community that have promoted the development of a changing university. In its role of fostering higher intellectual standards, Gown and Gavel attempted to emphasize those academic and cultural areas neglected by other student organizations. Its constitution recognized that one purpose of the membership should be to serve as a liaison between students and faculty as well as students and the administration. To this end, the members participated in varied activities throughout the years—assisting with freshman orientation, sponsoring art exhibits and speakers, raising money to furnish the student union, and planning student chapel services. The chapter also sponsors the annual Awards Day Convocation. An honorary organization for junior women called Aurora was sponsored by Gown and Gavel, and each year a member of Gown and Gavel serves as an advisor to Aurora.

Petitions: 1955, 1963, 1966.

Installation: April 20.

Installing officers: Editor Marthella Holcomb Gitlin (Nebraska–Lincoln, 1946) and Section Director Barbara Cook.

Vanderbilt University, 1940

Bachelor Maids was organized in 1918. At that time three girls from each sorority and three independents were selected for membership. The purpose of Bachelor Maids was to unite in one local group of senior women those recognized for their high standard of scholarship and leadership in collegiate activities, encourage those women to continue their high attainments and to inspire others to strive for such attainments, and mold and maintain this sentiment in matters of local and collegiate interest for mutual understanding and helpfulness. All selections were made with the approval of three faculty advisors. In December 1936, the constitution was revised, and election of members was placed on a point system. In 1939 definite steps were made toward seeking a charter from Mortar Board.

Petition: 1939.

Installation: January 13.

Installing officer: Expansion Director Kay Kuhlman.

University of Vermont, 1924

Akraia was founded on October 13, 1913, to promote college spirit, develop college loyalty, and further the best interests of the women's department at the university. Seventeen senior women were invited to a meeting at which the name, emblem, and constitution were adopted.

The design for the Akraia pin, a plain block "V" mounted on a thin gold circle, was selected later in the year. The society was secret; therefore, the activities were not made public.

Activities of Akraia during the eleven years of its existence as a local honorary included a dance in the fall and spring, teas for underclass women, a revision of the point system in 1916, stunt nights, class get-togethers, a student employment bureau, and general assemblies. In 1921 a Leap Year dance secured proceeds that the group used to improve the Vermonter's Club House. The first Lilac Day was held in 1922 when Dean of Women Pearl Wasson planned that a "magnificent hedge of lilacs be planted every year in a fitting ceremony."[135] The Vermont creed, composed by Dean Wasson, was used by Mortar Board every year at this ceremony. Activities at that time included assisting with Orientation Camp for freshman women, establishing a free tutorial bureau, and sponsoring the Big Sisters Program.

In 1930 Mortar Board gave a prize of $25 to the dormitory ranking highest according to weekly inspection. The chapter presented a cup to the junior girl, working her way through college, who had maintained the highest scholastic rating.

Petition: 1924.

Installing officer: National President Eleanor Stabler Clarke.

Installation: October 18 at Redstone.

Virginia Polytechnic Institute and State University, 1977

Sigma Lambda Sigma was founded in May 1971 by the senior members of Garnet and Gold, an honor society for junior and senior women that had been formed four years previously with the hope of affiliation with Mortar Board. However, at the end of the fourth year, the dean for student programs contacted Mortar Board and found that Garnet and Gold was ineligible due to its inclusion of junior as well as senior women. Thus, Sigma Lambda Sigma was founded in 1971 as an honor society for senior women only, while Garnet and Gold continued as an active organization for the university's junior women.

The late spring of 1971 saw the first selection and initiation of Sigma Lambda Sigma members. Fourteen women were chosen with utmost care and initiated for the 1971–1972 class. During the following year the fourteen members initiated many university and community projects that were to continue for the next several years. The members implemented their desire to be of service to the administration by serving on various curriculum advisory committees, helping with House Council elections, aiding the Alumni Association, and ushering at the Centennial Founders Day Ceremonies. At year's end, twenty-two women were selected to carry on the ideals of Sigma Lambda Sigma.

Installation was on April 30 at 3:30 p.m. in the East Commonwealth Ballroom of Squires. A brief history of Sigma Lambda Sigma was read by Professor Rebecca Powell Lovingood (Ohio State, 1955). A banquet followed the ceremony in the Rehearsal Room.

Installing officers: National Vice President Val Ogden and Section Coordinator Sharon Sutton Miller.

Wake Forest University, 1969

On April 22, 1947, a group of seven girls were asked to meet in the office of Dean of Women Lois Johnson and learned that they had measured up to certain standards of scholarship, leadership, and character, which were determined by an arbitrary point system set up by the dean

and the president of ODK. Dean Johnson thought that Wake Forest College needed a leadership society for girls to correspond to ODK for boys. On April 29, the honorary leadership society for women was officially named Tassels.

The tassel was chosen as a symbol for the organization because in olden times, "it was the yarn used to clean the bow and arrow so that the arrow would follow a straight, true flight. Today it adorns the mortarboard signifying the accomplishment of a student."[136] The constitution was drawn up in 1947 and stated that membership should never exceed 4 percent of the total number of women students at Wake Forest. Each woman considered must have been in the upper 35 percent of the women students in her class in scholarship, must be either a junior or senior, must hold special distinction in at least one field of activity on campus, and must have been of the highest character. An arbitrary point system was observed, fifty points being required for membership. A new constitution was adopted in April 1965, when active membership was confined to 3 percent.

The official emblem consisted of a tassel fashioned of black yarn, the seal of a gold key embossed with a tassel, the school seal, the initials of the college, and the name of the society. Also recorded in the new constitution was the tradition that tapping into the society was to be held before the student body during the chapel period.

Tassels members applied for recognition by the Mortar Board National Council in 1965, when it was suggested that the group become more of a service organization. Tassels cosponsored with ODK a high school leadership conference in 1965 and 1966. This conference was held not only to help high school students from all areas of North Carolina develop their leadership potential but also to introduce them to a college community. Later the chapter organized a system of junior advisors to guide freshman coeds and sponsored a get-together for graduate students. The chapter also conducted panel discussions to acquaint senior women with the prospects of graduate school and the life of women graduate students.

Petitions: 1965, 1969.

Champion: Dean of Women Lu Leake.

Installation: April 26.

Installing officer: Second Vice President Lynn Rountree Bartlett.

Washburn University, 2006

Nonoso Society was founded in 1917 with the purpose of honoring and recognizing college women who are representative of the best Washburn ideals on the basis of service to the college, leadership, and scholarship. New members were called from the junior class by preferential balloting. Nonoso was the women's honorary, and Sagamore was the men's honorary. Nonoso petitioned Mortar Board in 1967.

The Ichabod Club was created with the intention of petitioning for Mortar Board, since Nonoso and Sagamore were still single-gender. As the Washburn campus reinvigoration continued in 2006, Ichabod was perfectly positioned to become Mortar Board. Vice President for Student Life Denise C. Ottinger (Bowling Green, 1974) was the champion for Ichabod. She was also the founding advisor of the Turret Society when it became a Mortar Board chapter at Northwest Missouri State University.

Petition: 1967.

Champions: President Jerry Farley and Dean of the Honors Program Donna LaLonde (both Washburn, 2006) and Vice President for Academic Affairs Ron Wasserstein.

Installing officers: National President Bill Niederer and Vice President Denise C. Ottinger.

Washington State University, 1923

At the senior picnic on May 22, 1913, a committee was selected to work out a constitution for Gamma Tau and a list of eligible "girls." The group was to be an honorary society for upper-class women, eligibility being based on scholarship and participation in college activities. The senior women elected were to form an advisory board to the junior women.

Ten charter members were selected on May 27. At the first initiation ceremony, the members of Gamma Tau wore caps and gowns for the service, while the initiates were dressed in white. The newly elected members wore red and white ribbons on the day that the names of the new members were announced in the chapel. White stood for womanhood; red stood for honor. The song was

Joyous we greet thee, lovely ones,
Chosen of Gamma Tau.
Come sisters dear, and join with us
In honoring all her law.
Her strength, her truth, her vital worth
We'll meet with love and awe.
Then shall we grow in Womanhood
That is blessed in Gamma Tau.

The pin of the emblem of the organization was a hexagon with concave edges of polished gold with the raised letters Gamma Tau. The six points were symbolic of leadership, scholarship, character, personality, loyalty, and stability. The first plane was the road of service; it had no end. The second plane represented the height toward which all were striving, the plane upon which stood the woman to whom honor was due.

Gamma Tau became a chapter of Mortar Board at the State College of Washington on April 15 in an installation conducted by Miss

Hazel Wright. The installation ceremony took place on Round Top, a wooded hill near the campus, at 6:00 a.m. There were eight charter members. Some of the chapter activities given in the very old history include the following:

- Each year the name of the woman with the highest grades in the junior class was engraved on a Mortar Board Scholarship Plaque.
- A point system was introduced that limited a woman's activities to prevent a certain few from participating in the majority of the activities.
- The chapter sponsored the annual Mothers' Luncheon.
- For "fun's sake and as a money-making scheme, they gave two women's choice dances each year."[137]

Washington University in St. Louis, 1922

Keod was a secret society (although it and the other secret societies were listed in the yearbook, *The Hatchet*). It was begun in 1914 with nine charter members. The complementary men's group was Pralma. There was a junior women's honorary, Ternion, and a freshman women's honorary, Clais.

The purpose of Keod was to work for a greater Washington, promote a spirit of cooperation among the student organizations, promote a spirit of appreciation rather than criticism toward both faculty and students, work toward the elimination of politics in elections, and maintain a high standard of ideals for women at Washington University.

Keod petitioned for active membership in Mortar Board in 1919. The first petition was judged by the convention of 1921 as "too insufficient to judge the merit of the organization," according to the minutes.[138]

Some correction evidently took place, as the charter was granted, and Keod was installed as a chapter on May 22. A banquet was held a week later at the Claridge Hotel, where all former members of Keod were initiated into Mortar Board.

In the late 1920s the chapter wanted "to start a vocational library in the Women's Building but the information secured was not very helpful."[139] They gave a Kid Party for all freshman women and sponsored a pep luncheon for all women on campus preceding a football game.

In the fall of 1925 the chapter historian, Helen Bechtell, wrote in the *Quarterly* about Keod's duties to explain traditions to incoming women and have Big and Little Sisters events. *Co-ed Vodvil* was a performance made up of acts from all women's organizations on campus. It was a handsome moneymaker for the chapter.

The Alumnae Tea, wrote Bechtell, was "one of the very pleasant things that finds a place on our program . . . , where all the old grads gather and talk over old times or tell the actives how it was done in their day."[140]

In 1936–1937 the chapter "abolished sorority participation in campus politics and induced Student Council to draw up a new constitution revising the method of all elections." Other activities included sponsoring "an all-school backwards dance, known as the Gold Digger's Ball"; publishing a school calendar; and sponsoring a tea dance every Thursday afternoon in the women's gym, with an admission charge of ten cents a person.[141]

The early 1940s chapters were involved in war activities by functioning as an "Information Committee for the entire campus concerning the latest developments in the civilian defense program."[142] They started a campus chapter of the Red Cross.

The members of the 1969 Keod chapter decided to disaffiliate from Mortar Board and did not select a new group of seniors. The administration did not support this decision, and a method to choose a new group was approved in 1970 by the Mortar Board National Council. The 1975 chapter participated in a citywide televised auction, with profits going to the St. Louis Arts and Education Fund, and sponsored a campus symposium titled "Women in Careers."

University of Washington, 1925

Nine women, with Carrie Cowgill Thompson the spirited catalyst, met in December 1909 and agreed that they and their feminine peers should have both a greater voice in campus affairs and more recognition for work well done. Two prestigious honor societies for men, the Oval Club and Fir Tree, were a tradition at the time. Why not such an honor for senior women? In a *Celebration of Excellence*, Tolo's seventy-fifth anniversary publication, the story continues:

> With belief in their effort, the fledgling honor society sought a name for their new club and met with the popular Professor [of botany and history] Edmond S. Meany, a firm advocate of higher education for women. Meany, a noted historian of the Northwest, suggested the name "Tolo," an Indian word meaning success and achievement. He further reasoned the club's insignia could be a full-feathered Indian headdress with "Tolo" inscribed upon it.
>
> Meany's ideas and his continuing support were received warmly. In fact, during the early years of Tolo, he is said to have "fathered" the organization, so supportive was he of its efforts and directions. Within a decade, his daughter Margaret would

be tapped and would extend the Meany touch by writing Tolo's initiation ritual.[143]

The Tolos were aware that an honor society was not an end in itself. The members knew that "all too many coeds were forced to forgo further university education due to lack of funds." To help meet the need, Tolo Club decided to create a loan fund to help deserving junior and senior women. To raise the funds, the Tolo Club hit upon the solution of having women invite men to a college dance instead of the other way around. The community was enthusiastic, even if some thought that social dancing was improper. With meticulous skill the dance was presented, and the proceeds were placed into the new student loan fund. The dances continued for many years, and the Tolo Club became a Washington tradition. In 1944, *The Daily's* front page reported that one thousand couples were expected to attend the "Mortar Board Tolo."

The Tolo Club was particularly concerned with the trials of "town girls," who commuted but had no place to gather or hot meals to eat, "despite their near heroics in getting to campus each day."[144] Under Carrie Thompson's leadership, the first dining commons was established for women.

World War I's end was a time when Mortar Board national was getting started. The Tolo Club was among many women's honor clubs from major universities to receive an invitation to join, but the club declined, preferring to remain a distinctly local club with its own history. Seven years later, the attraction of being part of the national group was stronger. After Tolo's petition to affiliate was accepted, two classes of actives and nineteen alumnae were initiated on June 17. Four columns from the original territorial building formed the backdrop of the outdoor Sylvan Theater where the Tolo Club became the Tolo chapter of Mortar Board, the thirty-second to be installed.

Section Director Lillian Stupp writes in the *Quarterly* of her experience in coming to Seattle:

Four of us . . . left Portland early Tuesday the sixteenth (June) for the two hundred and eight miles' journey. It was great fun, but rather fatiguing, for I had to drive all the way. By 10:30 we arrived at the address stated, only to find a vacant lot. However, a bit of questioning soon put us to rights—the name of the street had been changed. Weary, we were soon "toted" off to bed, the girls to the Kappa House, and I to the home of Miss Mary Dunn Ward (Assistant Dean of Women, at the University).

Wednesday we drove over the very magnificent boulevard system of Seattle, had luncheon with a group of girls, shopped, then prepared for the installation. It took place in a perfectly beautiful out-door theatre surrounded by hedges and bushes, away from the curious public eye. We stood in front of four tall white Doric columns, while the girls formed in semicircle on the grassy "stage." The day was heavenly, chimes played during the ceremony, and even an aeroplane hummed over our heads. There were so many (forty-nine) that we took all charter members and actives first, then alumnae next. Everyone wore cap and gown over white, and we added a solemn march before and after to add to the impressiveness. A very nice dinner in the common dining room followed. Professor Meany, father of Tolo and Washington traditions, was among us and gave a very inspiring talk.[145]

After the war's end many military men came to campus, putting on-campus housing for women at a premium. Freshman women had no housing at all. "Again Tolo responded. Working with the collegiate group, Tolo alumnae (who had budded with good humor in 1916 as the 'Tolo Twig,' a branch of Tolo) incorporated and bought a house adjacent to campus."[146]

The Tolo House provided housing for twenty-five students a year for several decades. In 1943 the house was sold, and proceeds were placed into the Tolo Loan Fund.

Tolo continued to serve the campus. After forty years, the dances were still a social highlight. "Tips for Tolo" instructed coeds on the finer aspects of the "reverse etiquette" for the evening. The last Tolo dance was held in the early 1950s. Mortar Board's fund-raiser became "[candy] cane raising," which proved profitable and enabled scholarships to be awarded for many years.

Installing officer: Section Director Lillian Stupp.

Wayne State University, 1952

The Starlight Room of the Student Center at Wayne State University was the scene of the installation of the eighty-eighth chapter on December 14. Nine collegiate members and twenty-nine members of the local, Gold Key, were initiated. Head of Testing and Guidance Doris Cline was made an honorary member. Dean Clarence Hillberry, acting president, welcomed the installation team.

Gold Key was begun shortly after the 1933 start of the university by five women students who wished to keep alive the names of those women who had contributed and would contribute so much to the future of the university. They chose a gold key as their emblem, inscribed with the letters Pi, Lambda, Sigma for personality, leadership, and scholarship.

Freshman orientation, lecture series, conferences, and clinics were started by the women of Gold Key.

It appears that the name Laureate is now attached to the chapter. The records for this are not traceable.

Champion: Counselor of women's activities Elizabeth Sargent.

Installing officers: Expansion Director Mildred Rankin (Ohio State, 1945) and Section Director Marie E. Hartwig (Michigan, 1928).

Wesleyan College, 1972

Crown and Sceptre was founded in September 1963 with the purpose of promoting scholarship, encouraging leadership, and bringing tangible benefits to the entire campus through a service program. In the early years the group organized the President's Seminar, an informal campus discussion of modern philosophies, arts, and current affairs; sponsored tutorials before examinations for those students needing extra help; and organized a debate team.

The installation was on March 4. The president and academic dean spoke at the banquet following.

Installing officers: National Secretary Betty Carol Clark and Section Coordinator Cheryl Wilkes.

West Texas A&M University, 1985

Scribes Honorary Society was established in 1974 at West Texas State.

Installation: March 30.

West Virginia University, 1924

Beginning in the early 1930s, the Laurel chapter maintained Laurel Cottage, a cooperative house on campus for women students. The 1934 chapter reported that it sold senior collars and Eskimo Pies to buy "much needed articles for the cottage."[147] The chapters in the 1940s gathered data for a school bus for student teachers and started a system for membership selection in which each girl was graded on a basis of one hundred, with twenty points for character, forty for leadership, thirty for service, and ten for scholarship.

The 1943 chapter sold $648 worth of War Stamp corsages and sponsored a series of guidance meetings for senior women. In the early 1950s the chapter surveyed 2,500 students, 450 faculty members, and 500 alumni to prove the need for a new student union. The survey produced specific recommendations for the interior and location of the new union. The 1954 chapter studied four major campus problems: apathy to convocations, the university's advisor system, the over-and-under participation in activities, and sorority rushing. The chapter's recommendations were adopted by the Convocations Committee.

The 1965 chapter sponsored a meeting of all the women's honor societies on campus to "discuss the role of honoraries in light of every-expanding campus enrollment and the rediscovery of their purpose relative to the contemporary campus."[148] This concern extended into the 1970s.

The traditional activities of the Laurel chapter until the late 1960s included sponsoring the annual Freshman Mix that was held in the fall, the annual homecoming mum sale, and the Laurel Link Day, when new members of all the class honoraries were formally inducted. The 1971 chapter published a booklet titled *Signing Your First Lease* that was "prompted by the fact that the summer of 1972 was the first time that all university women above the rank of freshmen will be allowed to live in off-campus housing."[149] An alumna researched and edited the booklet, and four thousand copies were printed and distributed to the university community.

Installing officer: National President Eleanor Stabler Clarke.

West Virginia Wesleyan College, 1976

Membership in the original Haught Literary Society, begun in 1925 (and named after dean of the college Thomas W. Haught), signified literary attainment by exceptional Wesleyan women through "attempts to formulate and direct the literary judgment of its members."[150] Later it was an honorary organization for senior women who achieved an academic average of 3.0 or higher and served in positions of leadership. The purposes of the organization were to underscore the necessity and value of active, creative citizenship to women who are currently members and encourage high scholarship and worthwhile service on the campus at large. The original literary orientation of the group continued into the 1960s.

The response by the National Council to the society's first petition in 1964 was "no action," but correspondence and updates were sent to Mortar Board throughout the 1960s and 1970s. According to the 1971 petition, "For the past forty-six years, Haught Literary Society has held a worthy position on the Wesleyan campus, recognizing scholastic excellence and outstanding leadership among Wesleyan women."[151] A few of the activities and programs mentioned in reports included serving as ushers for the Founders Day Convocation on homecoming weekend; sponsoring a town hall for the president to discuss the college's long-range plans; giving a Smarty Party for freshman girls; founding a sophomore women's honorary, Soquinta; and establishing the Haught Book Exchange in the library. The chapter is now the Haught Honor chapter.

Petitions: 1964, 1971, 1976.

Champion: Dean of Students Richard A. Cunningham.

Western Carolina University, 1983

Cap and Gown was established in March 1976 with Mortar Board in mind. Installation was on April 10 at 2:00 p.m. in the Music Recital Hall.

Installing officers: Director of Communications Cathy Randall and Section Director Esther Williams.

Western Illinois University, 1976

Vice President for Student Affairs G. R. Schwartz set a goal to charter a senior women's honorary. His exploratory meetings with faculty, staff, and outstanding student leaders identified a great need for a women's honorary that would recognize outstanding scholarship, service, and leadership skills. In the fall of 1968 a group of women were selected by a group of faculty and staff to start working on the formation of this organization. Governing documents were written, and the Council on Student Welfare chartered the group, named Arista. Immediate projects and constitutions were written to equate the high standards of Mortar Board, as it was hoped that sometime in the future the group could become a chapter.

Arista strove to use the potential of its membership for university service and demonstrated this through Arista's many campus and community projects. The chapter organized the Emphasis on Women's Week to show concern with the status of women in the university and the community, held leadership clinics for underclass students, counseled National Merit finalists who were thinking of attending the university, helped establish a freshman women's honorary that later became Alpha Lambda Delta, and brought noted speakers such as Margaret Mead to campus. The chapter was installed on Sunday,

April 4, at 10:00 a.m. in the Heritage Room by Expansion Director Marylu McEwen.

Petition: 1974.

Western Michigan University, 1963

The first meeting to establish an organization to honor outstanding junior women at Western Michigan College was held on April 29, 1941, in the Dean of Women's Office, and seven senior women

In the spring of 1995, Western Michigan created a T-shirt display to emphasize the prevalence and effects of sexual and relationship violence.

determined the yardsticks by which new members were to be measured: high scholastic achievement, excellent leadership qualities, and fine character. It was decided to tap the first group of junior women at the traditional June Breakfast.

Arista, the name given the organization, was translated from the Greek as meaning "the best." The colors chosen were black and gold, and the flower was the talisman rose. Seven juniors were tapped on June 17, 1941. During 1941 and 1942, Aristans met frequently to discuss projects and planned two affairs, the June Breakfast and Tea and "a chocolate for sophomore women having a 3.0 average." During World War II, Arista served as a "clearinghouse for administering such jobs as rolling bandages, knitting for the Red Cross, baking cookies for the U.S.O., sewing for French War Relief, [and working as nurse's aides.]"[152] In later years Arista members continued to sponsor the January Sophomore Honor Chocolate, organized campus lectures and movies, and held a Leadership Training Workshop for sophomore women.

Petitions: 1954, 1961.

Installation date: April 27.

Westminster College, 1955

Target was organized in 1933 to bring a chapter of Mortar Board to the campus, and on December 18 Dean of Women Mary Turner and representatives from all of the women's organizations met to select the outstanding senior women. Each candidate was considered on the basis of Mortar Board requirements: scholastic standing, campus contribution through activity, and character through personality.

The motto of Target was "We who lead must keep our armour bright." The aims for the new group were tutoring, eliminating small clubs, enlightening and placing freshmen in activities, and developing and encouraging a women's employment bureau, plaques, keys for honors class day, a library fund, and professions for women.

The first call day was held on May 1, 1934, when the notes of a trumpet announced the commencement of the public pledge service. All the senior members sat in a semicircle with a large target made of pasteboard and covered in circles of first blue and then white paper. Large blue and white arrows with each member's name on one were drawn from this target, and the name was read by a senior member. Each new junior responded by coming forward, and the senior member escorted her to the senior member's chair, with the senior member standing behind her. This tradition continued for many years.

In 1945, the group revised its constitution so that it could more nearly approximate the national Mortar Board standards. Service projects of Target's early chapters included buying furniture for the browsing room of the library, purchasing furniture for the ladies' room in Old Main and the Science Hall and bonds for the student union building, and donating a radio to the college infirmary. The group also held book drives, gave a tea for sophomore women, and presented an engraved bracelet to a junior woman who had achieved a 2.0 average or better and was outstanding in scholarship, leadership, character, and service. Later chapters in the 1960s and 1970s held seminars with the Placement Office; sponsored speakers on the topic "Women in Today's World"; wrote a booklet titled *Senior Survival Kit* about apartment leasing, insurance, and jobs; gave a scholarship to an outstanding sophomore woman; and "tried to promote quiet in the library."[153]

Louise Fitch reported that the "Internal Life" group of the faculty had approved the establishment of Cap and Gown, an honorary senior women's society. Five women were chosen. They withdrew from the Order of Waiilatpu and elected nine alumnae members into Cap and Gown on November 24, 1924.

Securing a chapter of Mortar Board was the goal of the group from the start, and the group petitioned for a chapter after one year. The petition was approved, and Expansion Director Luella Galliver installed the chapter on October 16.

In 1932 the chapter sponsored an afternoon Thanksgiving tea dance for students "to make their holiday away from home a pleasant memory."[154] In 1934 the chapter began maintaining a Kotex shop in the dormitory where boxes were sold at any time, day or night. In 1936 the chapter succeeded in securing the pledge of every sorority on campus to refuse to participate in coalitions, vote trading, and other practices. A parchment scroll was presented to the freshman girls who had a 3.0 average or above, and it hung in the library in Prentiss Hall.

In 1941 the chapter held a reunion breakfast for Mortar Board alumnae during commencement week. Other activities until the 1970s included organizing a vocational career conference for women, revising "Songs of Whitman College, 1923" with a running history of the college, sponsoring a car caravan for freshmen to point out the highlights of Walla Walla, initiating the John F. Kennedy Book Fund Drive, raising funds for a gift to the library, and holding a campus discussion on the relevancy of a liberal arts education in small groups with five professors.

Whitman College, 1926

The first honorary society was the Order of Waiilatpu, founded in 1920, that included both men and women. In 1924 Dean of Women

Wichita State University, 1954

Honor Five was organized at Fairmount College (which had until 1887 been called Wichita Ladies College or Congregational Female

College) in 1917 and became affiliated with Mortar Board in 1954. Later the chapter was called Fairmount, perhaps when more than five women were selected for membership and in recognition of the institution's history.

Willamette University, 1958

Cap and Gown was founded in March 1933 after corresponding with Mortar Board Expansion Director Kay Kuhlman in 1932. The name was borrowed from Oregon State College, and the constitution was modeled after that of the college. The purpose was "to foster the highest development of character among women students, to maintain a high standard of scholarship, to recognize genuine leadership and sincere service, and to further the best interests of the University in every way." In carrying out the purpose, the members were "concerned with the stimulation of better student-faculty relationships and understanding." It was not long before Cap and Gown was recognized as "dean's assistant counsel."[155]

In 1950 Cap and Gown took the lead in founding the program of women's self-government and also the AWS. The members were also counselors for freshmen and for women in the residence halls.

In 1954 Cap and Gown established the Olive Dahl Memorial Loan Fund to provide small emergency student loans. Chapter members assisted with university functions such as weekend visits of prospective students, Parents' Weekend, and the president's receptions for new students. Later chapters sponsored a leadership training program, held a Smarty Party for women scholarship holders, presented an annual award to a sophomore woman who "exhibited the most improvement during the year in the ideals of Mortar Board,"[156] and held a campus graduate school program. The 1964 chapter sponsored for the first time a highly controversial project that asked students to evaluate their courses, including their critique of teachers, materials, and what they had learned in the course.

The installation was on April 27, and eight actives and thirty-two alumnae were initiated before a host of parents and faculty and student organizations. A banquet was served at Lausanne Hall, and President G. Herbert Smith welcomed the "distinguished new addition" to Willamette.

Petitions: 1951, 1958.

Champion: Dean of Women Olive Dahl.

Installing officer: Section Director Gen DeVleming, with assistance from Mrs. Richard Hill and Marjorie Chester (both Oregon) and Margaret Dowell Gravatt, MD (Minnesota, around 1943).

College of William and Mary, 1928

Alpha Club, the only honorary society for senior women, recognized the value of women whose intelligence in scholastic work has "been carried over into the campus activities and services which they have rendered to their fellow students."[157]

The installation of the forty-second chapter was on Saturday, December 8, for six active members and three honorary members, Dean of Women Grace W. Landrum, Emily M. Hall, and Martha Barksdale. "Following a delightful supper at the quaint old White Heron tea-room, thirteen alumnae were initiated by the new chapter."[158]

It is not clear why the chapter is now called Virginia Gamma.

Installing officer: Former First Vice President Irene Rems.

William Jewell College, 1978

Panaegis was founded on October 23, 1928, as a secret women's honorary by P. Casper Harvey. It was limited to seven senior women who were to serve the best interests of the college. Panaegis was the most prestigious honor society on campus for fifty years. The name is derived from "pan," meaning "universal," and "aegis" alluding to the shield that Zeus gave Athena, the goddess of wisdom. In 1947 there was some interest in Mortar Board, but the first petition was in 1964.

Brown Theater was the site of the installation.

University of Wisconsin–Eau Claire, 1976

The original 1969 members of Gold Caps were concerned at first with visibility. They were the ones who selected the name of Gold Caps, with "C.A.P." standing for "challenge always present." They wrote the constitution so that they might apply for recognition by the Student Senate as a chartered organization. The next group spent many hours working on a committee to reevaluate the closing hours for women on this campus. As a result of their survey, they were able to convince the administration that closing hours were no longer necessary in the residence halls for female students. The 1971 group sponsored a week of events especially for women called "Female Focus" that included bringing Gloria Steinem and Florence Kennedy to campus to speak on women's liberation and holding discussions on women's issues, a Faculty Symposium on contraception and abortion, a Teach-in called a "Sex-In," and a women's concert and art exhibit. They also revitalized the Chancellor's Roundtable, where students could have a dialogue with the chancellor and administrators.

Installation was held on April 24 in Schofield Auditorium at 1:00 p.m., with a reception in the Skylite Lounge and a banquet in the Southwoods Room.

Installing officers: Second Vice President Kathy Kuester Campbell and Section Coordinator Shirley Spelt.

University of Wisconsin–Madison, 1920

Mortar Board was founded on January 31, 1909. It was felt that an honorary group of women who could do something worthwhile for their campus would add to the value of college contacts. Two seniors called together eight more seniors and formulated plans for such a society. The name Mortar Board was given from the beginning, and the pin—very much like the national pin only smaller and with no lettering—was designed by a future member. The colors were black and gold, and the flower was a yellow tulip. "To be of service to our campus . . . was our first thought."[159] As a service project, a $100 scholarship was established to be given each year to a junior woman to enable her to continue her studies. This fund was raised by a personal subscription of $10 from each member—the first dues. Although the chapter at Wisconsin was not present at the first Mortar Board organization meeting at Syracuse on February 15, 1918, it was asked to join soon after and was installed on June 15 by National President Mary Mildred Logan.

The group established the first cooperative house for university women at Wisconsin, called the Mortar Board Cottage. Because of its success, several other such houses were established. In 1919 the chapter started the tradition of the May Day supper held in connection with the preliminary eliminations of the All University Sing. Initiation was early the Sunday morning of Parents' Weekend, with the president of the new chapter elected by the outgoing chapter before the new members were notified. The chapter members appeared at the house of the new members the evening before the Senior Swing Out, when their names would be announced.

University of Wisconsin–Milwaukee, 1975

Two outstanding senior women were invited to serve on the first selection committee for the first Women's Honor Society in May 1966. These two women were not eligible to be members of the charter group because they were seniors, but they possessed all other necessary qualifications. Honoratae was established similar in structure and goals to Mortar Board. Early projects included Coffee Hours for new faculty women, tutorial help for Milwaukee Inner Core students, assistance in the Voter's Registration office, a reading service for blind students, and the Family Friday tradition that featured a dinner and children's entertainment.

Petition: 1973.

Installing officers: Secretary Val Ogden and National Secretary and Section Coordinator Alice Krebs

Installation: April 26.

Wittenberg University, 1967

The purpose of the 1922 founding of the first senior women's honorary, Arrow and Mask, was to petition for membership in Mortar Board. The philosophy of the group was expressed in its motto "Dwelle in Sothfastnesse," which means "Live in Truth." Although Arrow and Mask petitioned Mortar Board for membership in 1930, 1938, and 1950, it was not accepted until 1967. Until the late 1940s, Arrow and Mask was strictly an honorary with the primary concerns of self-perpetuation, social gatherings of campus women to encourage scholarship, conferring honor on others, and rehonoring alumnae. This changed with its later emphasis on becoming a service-oriented group.

In the 1940s the group held a Fireside Tea at Christmas for freshman women, "put out a booklet on campus fashions and acquainting women students from town with the women living on campus," and compiled information regarding homes for children and the aged in Springfield for use by campus organizations considering volunteer work. The 1950s marked a dramatic change in the attitudes of the group, since this was a "time of communication and role consciousness." In the 1960s the chapter sponsored a discussion series on careers after college, took over freshman orientation with informal discussion on campus life, spoke out against discrimination in Greek groups, set up a taxi service for rides to Dayton Airport, revised the college catalog, set up a "reaction bulletin board for opinions on *anything*," and discussed college problems informally with administrators. The 1970s opened with an emphasis on communication, but Mortar Board's efforts were directed not only to disseminating information but also toward bringing people together—tackling the polarization of groups on campus. The president of the 1970 chapter, Maureen March, wrote in her annual report that "Mortar Board helped us at Wittenberg to realize that honor does not come on university stationery, but from the hearts and minds of others. Honor is not empty nor an end in itself. It is instead only a beginning and it was *only* the beginning of our chapter."[160]

Installing officers: National President Ruth Weimer and Section Director Virginia Gordon.

Installation: April 17 at 4:00 p.m. in the Alumni Room with a dinner following.

In the spring of 1924 six senior women, recognizing the need for a senior women's society, formed the organization known as Cap and Gown. These women were selected on the basis of scholarship, leadership, and service and were sponsored by the dean of women and a faculty member. In 1925 many of the traditional projects of Mortar Board were begun, including sponsoring the traditional senior women's breakfast and furnishing and maintaining a social room for university women. In 1926 Cap and Gown began publishing a recognition list acknowledging the qualities of scholarship, leadership, and service among women of the sophomore and freshman classes. An annual tea for junior women was given near the close of the year. Installation by National President Kay Coleman was on November 10 in the Nellie Tayloe Ross (the first woman governor in the United States) Room, the furnishing of which had been a project of Cap and Gown. A formal banquet was held at the Summit Tavern.

Other worthwhile projects were sponsoring the Torchlight Sing and Project Trip, where the dean of women and a senior girl toured various sections of the state in an effort to interest high school students in the university.

In June 2012 the 1958–1959 class of the chapter presented a series of charcoal drawings by member Ruth Eileen Bragg portraying all of the deans of women. The Luella Galliver Fund helped fund the project.

Champion: Dean of Women Luella Galliver, who had been a section director and a member of National Council.

The D'Artagnan Senior Service Society was formed in 1991 for admission to Mortar Board. It was championed by President James E. Hoff, advisor James T. Snodgrass, and Director of Student Activities David Coleman. The chapter was installed on April 25 by Director of Expansion and Alumni Emma Coburn Norris and Section Coordinator Mabel Freeman. A brunch followed in the Terrace Room with remarks from President Hoff.

Notes

1. Chapter History, 1993.

2. Ibid.

3. Jane Hamblin, then an advisor at Purdue, recalls the moment after the announcement of the chapter's renaming at the Mortar Board Homecoming Breakfast before three hundred collegiate and alumni members and dignitaries: "Dean Cook had a look of utter surprise, mixed with uncertainty, on her face; and then her deanly demeanor kicked in, and she said, 'I don't think you all can *do* that!'" Later that day a university marker at a prime entrance to campus was dedicated to Dean Cook by the Barbara Cook chapter of Mortar Board, assisted by many friends of the chapter and presided over by Chapter President Rod Frazier.

4. *Mortar Board Quarterly* 28, no. 2 (March 1942): 89–93.

5. The Ohio State University Archives, Mortar Board: National (RG 50/a-1/4/45), "National Council: Expansion Director: Annual Report: 1926–1949" (hereafter Expansion Reports, 1926–1949).

6. Expansion Reports, 1926–1949.

7. Ibid.

8. Ibid.

9. Ibid.

10. Ibid.

11. Ibid.

12. The Ohio State University Archives, Mortar Board: National (RG 50/a-1/5/44), "National Council: Expansion Director: Annual Reports: 1950–1977" (hereafter Expansion Reports, 1950–1977).

13. Expansion Reports, 1950–1977.

14. Ibid.

15. Ibid.

16. Letter to National Council, May 17, 1968.

17. Ibid.

18. Ibid.

19. Expansion Reports, 1950–1977.

20. Ibid.

21. Ibid.

22. Ibid.

23. The Ohio State University Archives, Mortar Board: National (RG 50/a-1/13/28), "Appendix B: Final Report of the Committee on Expansion."

24. Ibid.

25. Ibid.

26. Minutes, National Council, October 22–23, 1999.

27. National Council Minutes, July 20, 2005.

28. Petition of Pacific Lutheran University, October 15, 2013.

29. Expansion Reports, 1926–1949.

30. Chapter History, 1993.

31. Petition of Arizona State University, 1963.

32. Chapter History, 1993.

33. Petition of Birmingham Southern, 1935.

34. Ibid.

35. Ibid.

36. Ibid.

37. Chapter History, 1993.

38. Ibid.

39. Ibid.

40. Ibid.

41. Ibid.

42. Ibid.

43. Ibid.

44. Petition of Chapman University, 2007.

45. Ibid.

46. Chapter History, 1993.

47. Ibid.

48. Ibid.

49. Jessica R. Cattelino, *A History of Der Hexenkreis, 1892–1996* (Ithaca, NY: Cornell University Press, 1996), 1.

50. Ibid., 7.

51. Chapter History, 1993.

52. Ibid.

53. Expansion Reports, 1926–1949.

54. Chapter History, 1993.

55. *Mortar Board Quarterly* 7, no. 4 (May 1931): 72. This Mrs. Richards is Hazel Moren Richards of the Minnesota chapter, not Wisconsin. She relocated to Tallahassee.

56. Chapter History, 1993.

57. Ibid.

58. Ibid.

59. Chapter History, 1938.

60. Chapter History, 1993.

61. Chapter History, 1938.

62. Expansion Reports, 1926–1949.

63. Chapter History, 1993.

64. Chapter History, 1968.

65. Ibid.

66. Chapter history, 1993.

67. Ibid.

68. Chapter History, 1938.

69. Chapter History, 1993.

70. Ibid.

71. Chapter History, 1938.

72. Ibid.

73. Ibid.

74. Ibid.

75. Expansion Reports, 1975.

76. Chapter History, 1938.

77. Petition of the Mary Washington College, 1956.

78. Chapter History, 1938.

79. Ibid.

80. Chapter History, 1993.

81. Ibid.

82. *Michigan Record,* November 1934, 9.

83. Of members initiated at Ohio Wesleyan University in this era, there is only Elizabeth White. Further research is needed.

84. Chapter History, 1993.

85. Chapter History, 1938.

86. Ibid.

87. Ibid.

88. Chapter History, 1940.

89. Chapter History, 1938.

90. Ibid.

91. Ibid.

92. Chapter History, 1968.

93. Chapter History, 1938.

94. Chapter History, 1935.

95. Ibid.

96. Eloise Knowles also is credited with starting Theta Pi, which became a chapter of Kappa Alpha Theta at Montana. She remained at the university until illness forced her to move to California in 1915. She died the next year at the age of forty-four.

97. Chapter History, 1968.

98. With a Kansas PhD and a Yale MD, Professor Baumgartner became the first woman commissioner of public health in New York City in 1954, and in 1962 she became the assistant director of the U.S. Agency for International Development. She retired from Harvard Medical School in 1972.

99. Dr. Louise Pound was a noted professor and famous folklorist. Willa Cather was a close friend. Professor Pound was the sister of legal scholar and Harvard Law School dean Roscoe Pound.

100. From a 1938 history of the chapter. Another history lists the installation date as October 1920.

101. Chapter History, 1968.

102. Ibid.

103. Chapter History, 1993.

104. Chapter History, 1968.

105. Ibid.

106. Ibid.

107. Chapter History, 1993.

108. Ibid.

109. *Mortar Board Quarterly* 1, no. 1 (January 1925): 10.

110. Chapter History, 1938.

111. Ibid.

112. Ibid.

113. Chapter History, 1968.

114. Ibid.

115. Ibid.

116. Chapter history, 1975.

117. About the same time Dean Amos, for whom Amos Hall is named, was beginning a national honor society of her own for sophomore women called Cwens, which eventually became the national sophomore society Lambda Sigma.

118. *Mortar Board Quarterly* 6, no. 3 (May 1930): 183.

119. Chapter History, 1968.

120. *Mortar Board Quarterly* 22, no. 2 (March 1946): 132.

121. Chapter History, 1990–1997.

122. Membership flyer included with petition.

123. Petition of Alpha Order, 1964.

124. Chapter History, 1993.

125. Chapter History, 1938.

126. Hazel Moren Richards, "Mortar Board's Forty Years," *Mortar Board Quarterly* 24 (January 1958): 45.

127. Chapter History, 1974.

128. Ibid.

129. Chapter History, 1938.

130. Chapter History, 1993.

131. Joanne Holmes, "Installation of Forum—97th Mortar Board Chapter," *Mortar Board Quarterly* 33 (1957): 83.

132. Chapter History, 1968.

133. Schonfeld, Selma. "Installation Notes: The Fifty-Fourth Chapter," *Mortar Board Quarterly* 10, no. 2 (March 1934): 82.

134. Ibid.

135. Chapter History, 1938.

136. Chapter History, 1993.

137. Chapter History, 1930.

138. Expansion Reports, 1926–1949.

139. Chapter History, 1938.

140. *Mortar Board Quarterly* 1, no. 3 (November 1925): 74.

141. Ibid.

142. Chapter History, 1993.

143. "Celebration of Excellence," chapter history for the 75th anniversary of Tolo.

144. Ibid.

145. *Mortar Board Quarterly* 1, no. 3 (November 1925): 61.

146. "Celebration of Excellence."

147. Chapter History, 1938.

148. Chapter History, 1993.

149. Ibid.

150. Ibid.

151. Ibid.

152. Ibid.

153. Chapter History, 1968.

154. Ibid.

155. Ibid.

156. Ibid.

157. Ibid.

158. Chapter History, 1993.

159. Chapter History, 1929.

160. Chapter History, 1993.

4

The Bonds of Mortar Board

Alumni

One of the enduring strengths of Mortar Board over one hundred years has been the commitment, loyalty, and involvement of its alumni.[1] Some of the original delegates who founded the Society in 1918 became the alumnae who convened the second meeting in Ann Arbor in 1919 to continue the founding plan. It was at this convention that the role of alumnae was clarified: "The general sentiment of the Convention was in favor of National Officers being elected as Alumnae." The new alumni officers elected were president, vice president, secretary, treasurer, and historian. The 1920 constitution stated, however, that while the national officers were responsible for the ongoing business of the Society, "the conventions shall be the supreme governing body of this fraternity."[2] Thus, Mortar Board became the rare national honor Society to be governed by student members. (The

1973 delegates officially clarified the National Council's governing role when they added to the constitution "In the interim between National Conferences, the governing of the Society shall be vested in the National Council.") The national organization continues to flourish under this shared pattern of governing by students and alumni. Active student members offer a contemporary perspective, while alumni provide the organization's continuity and support at the national, regional, and local levels. The enormous contributions of Mortar Board alumni to the Society over the past one hundred years cannot be overstated. Since student members' focus is on chapter involvement during their senior year, alumni volunteers have provided the time, leadership, and stability that have sustained the Society and ensured its vitality and continuity.

The Milwaukee alums did much to support the collegiate chapter at the University of Milwaukee; most were from other chapters. Scholarships, food, and advice were always on hand. In the early 2010s the chapter grayed out. Rather than waste away, the members voted to close and to return a healthy treasury to the National Office, whose training room is now named in honor of the Milwaukee alumnae. This apron, with each patch embroidered by a different member, is a reminder of times past and the camaraderie that came through Mortar Board after graduation.

Mortar Board Alumni Clubs/Chapters

Alumni support at the local level appeared immediately after Mortar Board's founding in 1918. The first alumnae club was formed in 1919 in Ann Arbor, Michigan, to help plan the second national meeting of the new Society. The second alumnae club emerged in Columbus, Ohio, in 1921 to help plan the third meeting. This was a time when many alumni groups connected to colleges and college-related societies were forming across the country. Although the first recorded college alumni group met at Yale in 1792, Williams College in Massachusetts claims that its "Society of Alumni," founded in 1821, is the oldest alumni association still in existence in the United States. Mortar Board alumni were following a time-tested practice of supporting and staying involved with their college affiliations.

During Mortar Board's lifetime, over ninety alumni chapters have been formed. Alumnae interest and involvement were recognized by the 1920 constitution, which stated that "five or more alumnae may associate themselves as an Alumnae Club."[3] As new alumnae groups formed, others went inactive or restarted after a period of time.

Two general types of clubs or chapters emerged from the beginning. Alumnae from newly installed chapters often organized to support a particular collegiate chapter. Many of them continued to serve the Society nationally. Another type of chapter was established in large metropolitan areas, with members representing many different collegiate chapters. Northwestern and the University of Illinois alumnae offer a good example of how this type of club started in the early years. When Section Director Mary Liz Ramier, a University of Illinois member who lived in Chicago at the time, discovered at the 1925 convention that alumnae who lived in the Chicago area were interested in meeting, she contacted thirty-one members "with the expressed purpose of continuing the fellowship of college days and to unify the scattered strength of Mortar Board after graduation."[4] Fourteen braved a raging February blizzard to attend the meeting. As the president of the new club indicated,

> The general opinion was that we must not insist on too much activity in the lives already involved with business, families and other organizations. But if we can, in our stated meetings and gatherings, perpetuate our loyalty to Mortar Board and our sense of Mortar Board ideals, honor and spirit, we shall be accomplishing our purpose.[5]

This sentiment summarizes the inherent purpose of many alumni chapters then and since. Since Mortar Board members individually were so involved in work, community, and volunteer activities, they should spend time together at Mortar Board events that were more educational and social. (The fractious slogan of the Iowa City alumni chapter, founded in 1928 was, "We meet to eat and rest our feet.") Many alumni chapters, however, continue to sponsor local scholarship funds, leadership programs, and service projects.

The number of members in a given club has seen a wide range over the years. For example, in 1962 the smallest group was 17 in San Diego County, while the largest was in Seattle, with 800 listed on the roster (all did not actively participate). The 1962 Washington, D.C., club is an example of an extremely active group, with 258 dues-paying members representing sixty-seven different colleges and universities and members who graduated from 1911 through 1960.

Frequency of meetings varied from once a year to six times or more. The diverse profile of each Mortar Board alumni chapter defines why and where it was organized and the type of activities and programs it offers. Each group is unique because of these differences. Although the wide range of activities and programs reflects a club's individuality and

In 1940 the
Chicago Alumnae Club
set out to help
underprivileged teens
through the
Service Council Club.

interests, many support local active chapters in a variety of ways (programming, offering general financial assistance or gift memberships, helping with tapping and initiation, establishing scholarship funds, serving as chapter advisors).

The early *Quarterly* devoted a great deal of space to alumni news, including club activities and portraits of outstanding alumnae. (The first section about alumnae in the *Quarterly* in 1927 listed engagements, marriages, births, and personals. The third issue contained a full-page reproduction of the announcement of Mary Liz Hanger's marriage to Arthur Charles Ramier, a rather impractical practice that was seldom repeated).

Alumnae club programs in the 1920s mainly consisted of supporting the local chapter with tapping and initiation. Some clubs sponsored local scholarship programs for student members who were pursuing undergraduate or graduate study. In 1930 the alumnae section of the *Quarterly* was called "Around the Tea Tables," which was apropos since drinking tea was part of many social functions. During the Great Depression, the *Quarterly* featured job interview techniques and published interviews with alumnae who represented many career fields (or vocations as they were called then). Sixteen clubs existed in 1930, and it was decided that year to call the alumnae groups by the city where they were located rather than a college's name. At first the national organization assessed each alumna member fifty cents annually, but in 1932 it was decided to assess the alumnae clubs $3 a year instead to cover printing, postage, and other incidentals. 2018 alumni chapters are assessed $25 annually.

There was regular correspondence between the alumnae clubs and the national secretary in the early years, since she was their liaison with the National Council. In a 1932 report to the ninth biennial Mortar Board convention, National Secretary Dorothy W. Grieser (Illinois, 1921), wrote that

> the alumnae clubs have shown an increase in membership as well as numbers. The fact the alumnae clubs, most of which are rather young, have done so well with the slight support of the national organization is particularly gratifying to those interested in the alumnae club plan of Mortar Board. The fine spirit and friendship developed in the meetings and the active interest taken in the affairs of the active chapters is indicative of future strength and support to Mortar Board.[6]

During World War II, many of the alumnae clubs stopped meeting as formal groups. There were forty-two alumni clubs listed in 1942, but not all were active. The chairperson of the Committee on Alumnae Affairs at the time reported that "we have suffered some heavy casualties and even a few mortalities in our alumnae clubs."[7] Alumnae serving in the armed forces were profiled in the *Quarterly,* and one article highlighted Eleanor Roosevelt's interview on her famous radio program of two Mortar Board alumni who held prominent government positions, mentioned in chapter 2.

A special alumnae session was held for the first time as part of the 1955 national conference. Historian Hazel Moren Richards led a discussion about the role of alumnae clubs in the community. They were urged to "devote one or more meetings each year to discuss community problems and how Mortar Board members can take part." Although Mortar Board alumnae had donated to local scholarship funds for many years, some asked how they could contribute to the national organization (and deduct their donation as a charitable contribution). The Mortar Board Foundation Fund was first approved at the 1955 convention. Alumni donations made it possible to award the first two graduate fellowships during that convention. Thirty-nine Mortar Board alumnae clubs were still on the roster in 1962, and forty-eight clubs were listed in the *Mortar Board Forum* (the publication that had replaced the *Quarterly*) in 1972. The 1970 delegates passed a resolution emphasizing the importance of "increasing the attention to the functioning and growth" of alumnae clubs.[8]

The Title IX legislation that was the impetus for accepting men into Mortar Board in 1975 led to mixed reactions among its alumnae and had a strong effect on alumni clubs. One club wrote to the national alumni affairs chair in 1976, stating that "many of our members are concerned about the initiation of men into Mortar Board. We would like to be kept informed as to how this may necessitate changes in alumnae clubs."[9] (It wasn't until the 1995 national conference that the delegates officially changed the spelling of "alumnae" to "alumni" to reflect the Latin gender-neutral plural.) At that time "alumni club" was changed to "alumni chapter," since "clubs sounded too much like women's groups." Delegates to the 1976 triennial conference recognized the contributions of alumni as "a valuable source of information and inspiration for collegiate chapters" and encouraged chapters to use them as a resource for orientation for new members. There was a strong push for active chapters to compile a record of their alumni with current addresses for their own use and to send to the National Office.

As women continued to enter the workforce in greater numbers in the 1960s, their participation and time spent in club activity and volunteerism began to decline. The U.S. Bureau of Labor Statistics reported that 60 percent of women were participating in the labor force during this period. In a 1966 *Quarterly* article titled "The Role of Women Today," the president of the Fargo, North Dakota, alumnae Alpha Ottis (University of North Dakota, 1935), offered the opinion that "while the typical college woman desires to establish a home, she is finding many doors open to her in a multitude of jobs and professions which were not possible twenty-five years ago."[10]

This increase in the number of working women, especially professional women, began to have a negative influence on women's participation in "clubs" and the time it required. The role of women in society along with other cultural and societal changes has influenced the number and active participation in Mortar Board alumni clubs. The effect of an increasingly mobile society was felt as early as 1932, when it was noted in an alumni report that "the (Detroit) Club has suffered because all of their officers have moved out of town!"[11] This increase in mobility over the years has made it especially difficult to sustain contact with new graduates—and even alumni.

Although the total number of Mortar Board alumni clubs has declined for these and other reasons, others are thriving. New and old friendships, interesting programs, traditions, and association with a collegiate chapter all contribute to the enjoyment, importance, value, and continuity of an alumni chapter.

Alumni Involvement as a Priority

In the 1980s Mortar Board began looking for ways to increase alumni involvement with the national organization, and those efforts continued over the next three decades. An "alumni part" was added to the initiation ceremony so that outgoing collegians could be welcomed as alumni (and since 2012 to the Mortar Board Alumni Association [MBAA]) and reminded to stay connected:

> Although active collegiate membership in Mortar Board lasts only one year, the commitment to excellence in scholarship, leadership, and service is one of lifelong duration. Do you pledge to continue your commitment to the pursuit of excellence in scholarship[,] leadership and service? (here, the seniors, standing, say "I do.")[12]

An "alumni liaison" position was added as a collegiate chapter officer at the 1987 conference to strengthen the ties between the chapter's collegiate members and their alumni. The Alumni Career Network was formed in 1993 in response to collegiate members' desire for career information. Collegiate members could contact the National Office for names of alumni volunteers who shared information about their area of expertise. Alumni contacts were also available in geographical areas where new members were searching for a job.

The impetus to further develop alumni involvement continued into the 1990s. The 1991 delegates passed a conference resolution for the Society to (1) provide a single, clear source of information for alumni; (2) consider a lifetime membership fee; and (3) make available a permanent subscription to the *Mortar Board Forum*. At the 1995 conference the delegates repeated this resolution, and a committee was appointed to study how to form a national alumni association with a lifetime membership fee.

One of the important goals of the 1997 Mortar Board strategic plan was to "develop programs to maintain ongoing contact with alumni members,"[13] and the National Alumni Standing Committee was formed in 1998.

All alumni were contacted for the first time in Mortar Board history in 1998 when the Alumni Sustaining Members program was created. In addition to supporting the national organization, alumni were "given the opportunity to support their collegiate chapter, a local chapter or an alumni chapter" through a membership fee that was paid on an annual basis or as a lifetime lump sum. The 2007 delegates urged the National Council to address the need to "consistently involve alumni at all levels of leadership and service and to develop an executable plan to support such an initiative."[14]

A task force formed in 2009 to develop an alumni program recommended that a new position be established in the National Office for an alumni engagement officer, who was added part-time to the staff in 2010. Creating this position ensured that more direct contact with alumni was expanded and maintained.

National leaders developed a five-year strategic plan in 2011 to strengthen Mortar Board's position and mission. One of the goals was "to create a unified Mortar Board culture of lifetime membership."[15] The National Office staff were already on the case with the threefold strategy of "finding" alumni so the culture could be created, keeping track of and being meaningfully in touch with alumni, and creating connections with new alumni.

Finding Alumni

The upgrades in technology resources since 1990 and the improvement in software and applications that allow for the management of data have been used by the National Office to improve the quality of member records. E-mail addresses of members began to be collected rather late in the game, but presently the e-newsletter *MBits* that goes out every two months to all alumni is sent to forty thousand valid e-mail addresses. An e-mail address is an important part of the log-in process on the Mortar Board website.

So, the National Office has adequate tools to keep track of alumni. Staff members have implemented concentrated tactics to *find* alumni whose addresses have languished for many years and, consequently, are very stale. This operation is made more formidable because for all of its talk about lifelong membership, Mortar Board wasn't very good at keeping track of collegiate members upon their graduation. It was a practice off and on over several decades that a member received the *Mortar Board Forum* for one year after graduation (sent to a home address), but this practice was stopped in 2010, as the return on investment was poor and the resources of mailing the magazine were better diverted to alumni of "a certain age" who preferred to read printed communications. (The magazine is digitized to be readable by members—anyone—on the Internet, and notifications of new issues are sent by e-mail with a link to the URL where the issue can be found.)

That level of communication was insufficient to engender great connectedness, so Mortar Board has faced a challenge that fraternal organizations—or those with annual dues—encounter to a lesser degree: reestablishing connections with its alumni, a great many of whom had not heard from Mortar Board in forty, fifty, or even sixty years.

The staff members in the National Office have spent a great deal of time assessing address quality, and the directory project, begun in 2010, was the first step in finding alumni. The project took longer than expected, because for thousands of alumni it was the first time in decades they had heard from Mortar Board. They were often wary of the yellow card in the mail followed by the phone call. The call-center agents experienced a great deal of push-back, but the company managing the operation persisted. The *Mortar Board Register of Scholar-Leaders* was published in 2012 after a sufficient number of contacts had been made to make the project worthwhile.

The Society's 250,000 alumni were listed alphabetically in print (and on CD-ROM) and organized by institutions and chapters, with a section of international members. (The very first Mortar Board alumnae directory published in 1930 listed almost 6,900 members.) The 2012 directory also included a career networking section that listed members by fifty-two occupations based on the *Dictionary of Occupational Titles*.

When the *Register of Scholar-Leaders* was published in 2012, the result was an upgrade in records of more than ten thousand members, which was a real boost to address quality and for the staff members in the National Office.

Services that, for a charge, help organizations find their alumni also have been contracted by the National Office to upgrade information, and since 2012 thousands more records have been refined and confirmed in tactically segmented batches that will assist in developing connections with alumni.

Association best practices are implemented by the staff, who standardize information that is collected, and alumni are regularly reminded to update addresses through e-mail communications and through the *Forum*.

For many years, Mortar Board volunteers had laboriously typed each chapter's new members' names on 4″ × 6″ index cards stored in gray army surplus–type metal file drawers. The National Office is the home now for these "Legacy Cards," and staff members joke that in case of fire, the eight file drawers are the first thing to be rescued (there is a redundant set of photocopies, actually, stored off-site). The cards, which tell an amazing part of the Society's history, are often used to confirm older memberships, correct misspellings and to add, slowly chapter by chapter, the names of members initiated before 1990 that could not be entered into the first relational database when it went live in the National Office in the early 1990s. This is another step, though much less instantaneously satisfying, to the record of members in a digitized format so they can be found.

A grassroots group of members called the Keeper Network was established in 2012 "to help the National Office keep track of alumni—their awards, honors, good news, and sad news." These members notify the staff about life events of members. In addition to the phone call or e-mail from alums, Expansion Specialist Bridget Williams Golden uses "alert tools" that she has set to learn when Mortar Board members are mentioned. Very often, these are in obituaries. Bridget diligently marks the records of these members as deceased so that e-mails and print mailings are not accidentally sent to them. She also alerts Executive Director Jane Hamblin, who posts an online condolence or handwrites a note of sympathy to family members. Although this is both tedious and a little depressing, it is part of the process of building the "unified culture of lifetime membership" described in the 2011 strategic plan and is important for address quality and efficiency.

In 2017 after vast improvement from the days of a database that was maintained on typewritten cards, Mortar Board runs a respectable association management operation that includes managing member records, taking member payments, handling conference registrations, accepting donations, and taking payments for items in the Mortar Board Store.

Keeping Track of and Meaningfully in Touch with Alumni

An important milestone was reached in 2012 when the MBAA was launched. The purpose is to "extend the legacy and tradition of Mortar Board beyond the collegiate experience to encompass Mortar Board's quarter-of-a-million alumni so they can connect distinctly and formally worldwide." The names of the 106 charter members who contributed $500 were placed on the charter, which is displayed in the National Office. While some alumni are actively involved as National Council officers, section coordinators, trustees, or chapter advisors, many outstanding alumni lend their prestige and support for the Society in other important ways.

The MBAA has been an important vehicle for driving connections with members who truly believe in Mortar Board as a lifetime experience and want to keep tabs on the Society. In addition to the charter members, there are some four hundred lifetime members and scores of annual members.

The idea of a Mortar Board alumni association had been bandied about for some time. The Alumni Sustaining Membership program of the late 1990s proved overly complex in its apportionment of dues. Though it was feared (slightly) that the MBAA would detract from members' contributions to the fund-raising efforts of the Mortar Board National Foundation Fund (MBNF), the MBAA has instead served to enhance connectedness and increase awareness and giving. The staff communicates regularly with MBAA members through a quarterly e-newsletter and shows members the links between the Society's

Centennial Campaign, fellowship programs, and alumni networking possibilities. The growth of a "unified culture of lifetime membership" is sequoia-like, but the seedlings are planted and tended to very ably. Under expert care of staff members, the growth will also be massive and sequoia-like.

The "Volunteer Interest Form" on the Mortar Board website helps members stay in touch and indicate that they would like to be involved, and staff and national leaders draw from respondents to these forms and from MBAA members to fill out award-review committees, read fellowship applications, and serve on work groups. The National Council, especially under the coaching of past National President Marty Starling, has been committed to creating a pool of volunteers to serve at all levels.

Part of creating a "culture of lifetime membership" is Mortar Board's affinity program. The Society's partnership with Nationwide™ since 2011 provides members with discounts on all types of insurance (cars, homes, RVs, motorcycles, boats, and even pets) that more than make up for the cost of membership. Other offerings of reductions on hotels, car rentals, and office supplies are fairly standard for a membership organization. Mortar Board has a partnership with a test preparation company that offers discounts to its members using a simple code, along with other incentives for collegiate chapters to make money.

Since 1973, membership in Mortar Board (because it is a member of the Association of College Honor Societies) meets one of the requirements for entrance at the GS-7 level in numerous professional and technical occupations in the federal service.

In 2016 Mortar Board started a partnership with Portfolium, which allows all collegiate members, new alumni, and members of the MBAA to have access to the online network that showcases members' portfolios to hundreds of employers through LinkedIn. Collegiate members can showcase their college activities and projects in a way that levels the playing field with more seasoned job seekers who are already in the workforce. This type of career-building platform enhances younger members' chances for satisfaction in the world of work.

Creating Connections with New Alumni

New alumni are congratulated with digital greetings at their scheduled graduation dates and receive Mortar Board's *MBits* e-newsletter. These highlight Portfolium, fellowships, and member discounts such as Nationwide. The use of webinars to work with recent alumni and help them network for jobs or review their résumés is contemplated by the National Council and staff.

The MBNF has established its Tapping Society to create a cohort of newer donors.

Many newer members like the opportunity of having quick exchanges and chances to help. This is hard for a national organization to pull off, but e-mail and cloud-based sharing of files can allow for work to get done.

Mortar Board Alumni Awards

Recognition of outstanding Mortar Board alumni began in 1989 with the creation of the Alumni Achievement Award, which "honors an alumni member who is more than ten years past initiation and has demonstrated outstanding long-lasting achievement in her/his profession or notable, signal service to a broad community." The Distinguished Lifetime Membership was established in 1995 and honors an alumni member "who has retained significant and meaningful connections and service to Mortar Board through collegiate or alumni chapters, programs, or events and epitomizes the meaning of lifetime of service to Mortar Board."[16]

The Emerging Leader Award was established in 2013 to honor an alumni member who was initiated as a collegiate member and is between one and twenty years past initiation. The award recipient must demonstrate remarkable accomplishment in her/his profession far ahead of others of the same cohort or be noted for outstanding community service. Nominations for the alumni awards are made annually, and the recipients have been honored at national conferences.

The first Outstanding Alumni Chapter Award was given in 2001. The purpose of the award is to recognize an alumni chapter that has exhibited sustained excellence, outstanding accomplishments, and lifelong dedication to the Mortar Board Ideals of scholarship, leadership, and service.

Teams of Mortar Board members are coordinated to review award nominations, which are evaluated year-round under the direction of staff member Bridget Williams Golden.

Mortar Board Alumni Chapter History Summaries

To illustrate the role that alumni clubs and chapters have played in the lives of Mortar Board alumni for one hundred years, current alumni chapters were contacted and asked to contribute a summary of their histories for this centennial volume. The chapters that responded provide excellent examples of how Mortar Board alumni have organized, maintained programs and activities, and enjoyed contact with other members after graduation. These histories demonstrate how alumni chapters have supported the collegiate chapters in their geographical area, established scholarship funds, and offered educational and service opportunities for the enrichment of their members and their communities. They also provide examples of how current alumni chapters continue to offer opportunities for Mortar Board alumni to enjoy interesting programs, projects, and each other.

Burlington, Vermont

The first alumni chapter in Burlington, Vermont, was established in 1946, and by the 1960s membership had increased to eighty members. An early tradition was for the alumni to hold a breakfast for the collegiate chapter at the University of Vermont during commencement activities. Programs during that time also included a tea in honor of Marion Patterson, dean of women from 1922 to 1937, when she returned to Burlington for the dedication of a residence hall named in her honor; a talk about the Peace Corps by a volunteer; and a slide presentation of the Ivory Coast.

In the late 1960s alumnae established a memorial fund for Margaret Wing, former assistant dean of women, and assisted the University of Vermont collegiate chapter in its efforts to name a dormitory in her honor. Currently the alumni sponsor an annual Mortar Board Breakfast for all alumni in the area but especially for those who are returning for their class reunions. The alumni group provides financial assistance to the collegiate chapter at the University of Vermont by helping to fund the cost of sending the delegate to the national conference as well as supporting other Akraia chapter projects.

Columbus, Ohio

The Greater Columbus Mortar Board Alumni Chapter was founded in 1921 to support the second national convention. The alumni in the area have enjoyed a strong bond with members from many chapters across the country for over ninety-seven years. In 1924, the Columbus Mortar Board Alumnae Club, as it was then called, gave twenty volumes of the *Life and Work of Theodore Roosevelt* to The Ohio State University library. During the early years the alumnae held supper meetings every other month during the school year, usually at the home of a member, where they shared stories about their work and experiences.

Programs in the 1960s and 1970s highlighted societal topics including "Young College Marriages: How Happy are They?," "Television: Is It Intellectual?," and "Today's Environmental Problems." Other topics through the years included voting rights, child behavior, and community leadership and service. The 1980s topics focused on the arts and community events with presentations such as "A Bicentennial Look at Columbus" and "Making Columbus a Healthier, Safer Place to Live." More recent programs included tours of Ohio State's renovated William Oxley Thompson Library and the new Ohio Union and hosting speakers on a wide variety of educational and cultural topics.

In 1953, The Ohio State University Board of Trustees accepted a gift of $300 from the Columbus alumnae to establish a scholarship fund. Through the years Mortar Board members nationwide have generously contributed to the fund, which now boasts an endowment of $600,000. In 2014 the Mortar Board Scholarship Endowment Fund supported sixty-three scholarships for Ohio State students (not Mortar Boards) amounting to $39,093. The alumni chapter also contributes to the MBNF annually through both its treasury and individual member contributions.

The Greater Columbus Alumni Chapter, as it is now called, annually sponsors a reception for the initiation of Ohio State collegiate members and has been especially dedicated to celebrating collegiate chapter anniversaries. In 1939, the Columbus Alumnae Club of Mortar Board marked the twenty-fifth anniversary of the collegiate chapter's 1914 founding with a tea at the home of Harriet Day Bricker

(Ohio State, 1918), the wife of Ohio senator John W. Bricker. In 1989 alumni celebrated the seventy-fifth anniversary with a luncheon, the receipt of scrolls from the Ohio Legislature, inspirational speakers, the honoring of founders and older members, and the dedication of the Mortar Board Court on campus.

To celebrate the one hundredth anniversary of the Ohio State collegiate chapter in 2014, the alumni raised funds to name a suite of rooms after Mortar Board in the newly renovated Thompson Library. Alumni also took part in the Ohio State chapter's centennial celebration with various programs and a dinner gala at the university. The Greater Columbus Alumni Chapter received the Outstanding Alumni Chapter Award for programming and service in 2003.

Denver, Colorado

The Metro Denver Alumni Chapter was founded in 1950 as a women's organization to further the principles and perpetuate the Ideals of Mortar Board. Programs have included "Communistic Tactics, Fronts and Infiltrations" (1961–1962); "Nitty Gritty of the New Generation on Campus," "Antique Silver," and "Why Negro Colleges Today?" (1967–1968); "Don't Be Caught with a Cranky Carburetor," a practical demonstration (1977); and "Escape from Hungary," member Marta Sipeki's story of her family's flight to Austria—while Soviet soldiers shot at them—during the 1956 Hungarian Uprising (2012).

In 1956 the chapter was asked by the British embassy in Washington, D.C., to organize a celebration in Denver honoring Ghana's (Gold Coast) March 6 independence. Given the chapter's location in a large metropolitan area, over the years members have served to welcome visitors and newcomers. In the 1950s and 1960s, members cooperated with several national organizations to provide travel assistance and home hospitality to foreign graduate students in the area and later joined the University of Denver in its welcoming and orientation program for foreign students. In the ensuing years, the chapter has worked closely with the Mortar Board National Office to locate and invite Mortar Board alumni who are new to the area to take part in the group. Denver alumni awarded fellowships to graduate students in Colorado, Utah, and Wyoming between 2001 and 2012. The chapter has published a directory and a roster every other year since 1963 and started its own newsletter in 1993. In 2001, the Denver chapter received the first Outstanding Alumni Chapter Award.

Iowa City, Iowa

"We meet to eat and rest our feet!" The Iowa City alumnae have followed this slogan since the club's founding in 1928. The members, who over the years have numbered more than one hundred, hold monthly potluck suppers where conviviality, stimulating conversation, and friendship are the hallmarks. In the past, the alumni have provided an advisor for the University of Iowa collegiate chapter, hosted collegiate members at a fall potluck, and participated in chapter Founders Day celebrations. In addition, the alumni president participates in the collegiate chapter initiation ceremony.

Knoxville, Tennessee

The Carson-Newman Mortar Board Alumni Chapter was founded in 2005 with sixty-five members. According to the chapter's 2007–2008 annual report, members held an annual Mortar Board Tea at homecoming in conjunction with the Carson-Newman collegiate chapter and have established the Janie Swann Huggins Endowed Mortar Board Scholarship and the Anne Hunter Hughes Endowed Mortar Board Scholarship. In 2008 to commemorate the Carson-Newman collegiate chapter's fiftieth anniversary, alumni joined collegiate members to hold a special homecoming reception, a reading and storytelling event for area children, a 5K run, and a preservation effort to help safeguard historical Carson-Newman Mortar Board scrapbook collections. The alumni chapter has begun a campaign to raise $50,000 toward scholarships.

Lafayette, Indiana

The Greater Lafayette Area Mortar Board Alumni chapter (known locally as GLAMBAC) was founded in 2000 to perpetuate the Ideals of Mortar Board, assist active chapters in their programs when possible, bring together persons of similar interests, and sustain enduring friendships among all its members. Programs have included "Transitioning Life Changes" by Sam Postlewaith, retired biology professor, and Chuck Boonstra at University Place Continuing Care Retirement Community (2007); many programs on happenings and development at Purdue University (Dean Rhonda Phillips of Purdue's new Honors College in 2015, for example); and a tour of a Frank Lloyd Wright home with members of the collegiate chapter during the 2001–2002 academic year. Alumni have provided financial assistance to the Purdue University collegiate chapter projects to install historical markers on campus. In addition, alumni chapter officers attend the annual fall student retreat to brief collegiate members about their chapter namesake, Barbara Cook, Purdue University dean of students emerita who was an advisor for forty years. Alumni participate as speakers and volunteers for the Mortar Board Leadership Conference and also participate in the spring initiation ceremony.

Of particular note: Five successive Purdue University deans of women or students—all Mortar Board members—pursued shared human rights and equality for all when they served from 1933 through 1995. Their story is delightfully chronicled in the 2014 book *The Deans' Bible: Five Purdue Women and Their Quest for Equality* by Angie Klink. In it, Ms. Klink describes a Bible that was passed down from dean to dean at each transition between them. That Bible in 2013 was transferred to the Purdue University Archives.

In September 2014 the Purdue Center for Student Excellence and Leadership building was dedicated and received its official name, the Krach Leadership Center, in honor of Purdue's immediate past chair of the Purdue Board of Trustees Keith Krach (Purdue, 1978), a 2012 Mortar Board Alumni Achievement Award recipient. The center houses virtually all student activities, including the Barbara Cook chapter and its advisors. At the 2014 homecoming, the Commons and the Conference Room in the center were named for the five deans.

Lawrence, Kansas

Founded in 1911 and chartered in 1924, the Lawrence Mortar Board Alumni chapter makes special efforts to support the collegiate chapter at the University of Kansas. The alumnae completed restoration of the original collegiate chapter's Torch Charter, which was placed on permanent display in the University of Kansas Spencer Library in 1974. Since then the chapter has held a commencement brunch and honored alumnae celebrating their fiftieth year of Mortar Board membership. Records as far back as the 1930s show that the chapter has granted scholarships, and currently alumni present annual scholarships in memory of deceased members.

In 1993 in honor of the seventy-fifth anniversary of Mortar Board, the University of Kansas collegians planned a program for the alumni group. Active members interviewed alumni and then made brief reports on traditions, remembrances, and unusual events. President Mary Alice Demeritt Gordon (Kansas, 1954) wrote in the alumni club's annual report that "alumni members immensely enjoyed reminiscing and the actives were intrigued by some of the past traditions."[17]

Lubbock, Texas

Founded as Forum in 1954, the Lubbock, Texas, Mortar Board Alumni Association was chartered in 1957. In its 1957–1958 annual report, the club reported that being nascent, "we just 'meet, eat, greet and beat it.'" Within three years, however, members became increasingly active and planned programs including "Phi Beta Kappa on Tech Campus," "Challenge to Our American Heritage," "Satire as Criticism," and "Narcotics in Lubbock." In 1979–1980 members chose a theme for the year: leisure. At each meeting they discussed different aspects of what people feel is leisure time. The most successful meeting featured as guest speaker, a psychology professor from Texas Tech whose topic was "Leisure without Guilt." This was also the first year the club awarded a scholarship to a Mortar Board member for graduate study.

In the 1980s programs took on a regional tone, with topics including dress and customs of the early days in West Texas, historical architecture at Texas Tech University, and wildflowers of West Texas. During the 2001–2002 year a collegiate member undertook a project of expanding the Mortar Board archives, taping interviews with many alumni. In September 2001, the alumni met with the actives at the Southwest Collection/Special Collections Library for the dedication of these archives. In this time frame the group's focus also turned

international: programs included "Vietnam: Yesterday, Today and Tomorrow," "Life from an Irishman's Point of View," and "The Life of Women in Africa." Through the years the chapter has hosted a spaghetti supper for Texas Tech collegiate members and more recently met with them for lunch. The alumni chapter has continued to award scholarships to students for graduate school and continuing studies.

Miami, Florida

The Miami alumnae assisted the Nu Kappa Tau collegians, organized in February 1964, at the University of Miami toward their successful installation as a Mortar Board chapter in 1965. Over the years, the alumni have continued significant involvement with the collegiate chapter. The alumni and college students go to the Salvation Army's warehouse in Miami-Dade each December for the Angel Tree program, when they bag thousands of Christmas gifts for needy children in the county. The members also have read and participated in art activities along with the University of Miami students at the local Ronald McDonald House for children battling serious illnesses. As a result of this volunteer work, the members saw the need for children's books in Spanish, French, and Creole and collected books in those languages at several meetings. The alumni participate in the collegiate chapter's initiations and Senior Send-Offs and invite the chapter advisor and president to be guests at the Carita S. Vonk (Miami, 1965) Homecoming Luncheon in conjunction with the Audrey Finkelstein (also Miami, 1965) Experience at homecoming. They also welcome students' presence at luncheon meetings and outings.

For many decades the Miami alumni have awarded the Ruth and Henry King Stanford Award to the president of the University of Miami Mortar Board chapter for outstanding scholarship, leadership, and service. Henry King Stanford was the president of the University of Miami who was instrumental in bringing Mortar Board to the university. The alumni chapter meets at least twice a year. Program topics since the group's inception have included 1970s discussions titled "Parents and Sex Education" with Lynn Rountree Bartlett, a University of Miami professor and past national vice president; "Keys to Success" with a young metaphysician; and "Volunteer Community Action—An American Phenomenon." During the 1995–1996 year Thelma Gibson, the widow of civil rights leader Father Theodore R. Gibson and a member of the Miami Centennial Committee, presented a program on the settling of Coconut Grove in 1896 by Bahamian blacks. In 2001 Aubrey Simms, former administrative assistant of University of Miami presidents Henry King Stanford and Edward Foote II, presented "Remembrances," which focused on her Tuskegee childhood when a frequent dinner guest was George Washington Carver. The Miami Mortar Board chapter was given the Mortar Board Outstanding Alumni Chapter Award in 2004.

Muncie, Indiana

The alumni in Muncie organized in 1971 to support the collegiate members at Ball State University at their tapping and initiation events. The tapping is particularly popular because it is held at the university president's residence. When John Worthen served as university president from 1984 to 2000, his wife Sandra Damewood Worthen (American University, 1984) attended the tapping celebration. In conjunction with the national service project Reading Is Leading, the alumni have conducted book drives and collected approximately three hundred books annually to donate to community organizations. During 2011–2012 members read *The Glass Castle* by Jeannette Walls, the Common Reader assigned to incoming freshmen, and participated in a book discussion. Many had attended the author's talk about her book on campus that fall.

Successful programs have included presentations and slide shows by members who have traveled internationally and a spring 2006 luncheon at which Kay Bales, dean of the Division of Student Affairs, spoke about trends among students on campus in today's world, their interests in service, and the opportunities for becoming involved in student activities. In 2006, the chapter received the Outstanding Alumni Chapter Award.

San Diego, California

Alumni living in the San Diego area have formed one of the largest alumni chapters in Mortar Board. Alumni assisted in the installation of the collegiate chapter at San Diego State in 1965 and helped establish a chapter at the University of San Diego in 2000. The group didn't have a smooth path to its current success; an initial effort to form a chapter in 1961 fizzled for a year in 1972. In 1973 to attract even greater participation by alumnae living in the area, San Diego's alumnae board produced its Conclave, with prominent regional experts giving presentations about lively topics. Meredith Brokaw's (South Dakota, 1961) spouse, NBC Los Angeles news anchor Tom Brokaw, gave a warm and witty opening keynote very supportive of Mortar Board. In late 1978, however, alumni interest waned despite a roster of nearly 450 members. Tenacity prevailed, and in 1989 136 dues-paying members showed resurgence toward Mortar Board's purpose to support the ideals of the university, to advance a spirit of scholarship, to recognize and encourage leadership, to provide service, and to establish the opportunity for a meaningful exchange of ideas as individuals and as a group. Activity has remained strong ever since, and members have established Distinguished Alumna/us and Outstanding Service Awards.

In September 2005, alumni and students celebrated forty years of Mortar Board at San Diego State University with a high tea and a display of scrapbooks dating from 1932.

The chapter now has one hundred dues-paying members and a mailing list of more than eight hundred. Members annually hold a Mortar Board Alumni Honors Reception, which is attended by the San Diego State University and University of San Diego provosts or presidents, and award up to $15,000 in scholarships to students going to graduate school. Actively involved with the collegiate members at both universities, alumni participate in their initiation ceremonies, provide lunch for their annual Backpack Stuffing events, and host End of the Year Luncheons for the students. Members also participate in tapping and stocking stuffing for the military at San Diego State University.

The chapter's life is featured in the autumn 2016 *Forum*.

Seattle, Washington

Mortar Board alumnae in the Seattle area first organized in 1916 as Tolo Twig, which was renamed the Tolo Association. It was chartered into the national Mortar Board organization in the mid-1920s. In 1978 it became the Mortar Board Alumni/Tolo Association but then in 1998 became a private foundation: Mortar Board Alumni/Tolo Foundation. Now one of the nation's largest and most active Mortar Board alumni groups, its membership includes approximately 1,300 alumni representing sixty universities. Nearly 150 members participate in events and governance and contribute financially. The foundation is now "alumni home" to Mortar Board active chapters at the University of Washington, the University of Puget Sound, Seattle Pacific University, and Pacific Lutheran University.

Visionary thinking was an early Tolo characteristic. Tolo alumnae purchased a home near the University of Washington campus to provide much-needed housing for women students. When in 1925 the alumnae assumed many of the responsibilities of Tolo House, it became necessary to incorporate under the laws of the State of Washington, with over two hundred alumnae signing the articles of incorporation. Tolo House offered a natural forum for working more closely with the collegiate Tolo chapter. Proceeds of the eventual Tolo House sale were among funds set aside for student financial aid. The Tolo Foundation's scholarship program for deserving University of Washington students has been a central focus for decades. In the past ten years alone, the foundation has awarded $343,300 in scholarships.

Since the 1940s, the annual meeting has been the key gathering event for alumni. Alumni from a wide spectrum of graduation years attend to honor graduating University of Washington Mortar Board seniors and alumni celebrating their fiftieth, twenty-fifth, and tenth anniversaries. Featured speakers have been respected leaders and prominent faculty, such as NASA astronaut Bonnie Dunbar, philanthropist and civic leader; alumna Mary Maxwell Gates (Washington, 1949); Washington state attorney general Rob McKenna (Washington, 1983); and professor and conservation biologist Dee Boersma (Central Michigan University, 1973). Ever the innovators, alumnae in the early decades presented an educational television series featuring women whose stories sought to inspire others. Banquets, homecoming open houses, and book reviews were among other reasons to gather. Opportunities for learning were opened to the community, as seminars and conclaves became "town and gown" occasions.

In 1993, Seattle's Mortar Board alumni conceived and led a successful statewide campaign to name a major Seattle interstate floating bridge for its inventive designer and engineer, Homer M. Hadley, whose spouse, the revered Margaret Hadley, was a member of Tolo Club's first tapped class.

The Mortar Board Alumni/Tolo Foundation received the Mortar Board Outstanding Alumni Chapter Award in 2002 in recognition of its sustained excellence, outstanding accomplishments, and lifelong dedication to the Ideals of Mortar Board scholarship, leadership, and service.

State College, Pennsylvania

While living in East Lansing, Michigan, Phoebe Forrest Link (Penn State, 1947) became a member of a Mortar Board alumnae group there. After she and her husband returned to State College, Pennsylvania, she ran ads in the local newspaper seeking members for a local Mortar Board alumnae club, establishing it in 1968. The group has been going strong ever since, with the exception of one inactive year in 1978–1979. Members represent more than fifteen different alma maters.

In 2001 the chapter held its first of what would become an annual alumni luncheon, in coordination with Pennsylvania State University's traditional Reunion Weekend, to honor members celebrating fifty-, fifty-five-, and sixty-year reunions. The members also give two scholarships to Penn State collegiate members: $1,500 for graduate study from the Helen Eakin Eisenhower Memorial Scholarship and the Charlotte E. Ray (Penn State, 1935) Scholarship endowments. During the 2003–2004 year, the College of Health and Human Development's Women's Leadership Initiative arranged "Mentor Meetings" with Mortar Board alumni. The enthusiastic student response resulted in renewed and increased awareness of Mortar Board on the Penn State campus, and the program was indicative of the important role that alumni can take in the lives of college students.

One twenty-two-year-old member, Jill Pakulski, conducted an intergenerational interview in 2004 with Mrs. Link as an assignment for the Women's Leadership Initiative. They shared a common bond: Jill's grandmother had died when she was a senior in high school, and Phoebe's husband had died just a few months before the two met. "We are both at a time of transition, just 60 years apart," Jill wrote, noting how Phoebe helped her make a decision to go to Columbia University for graduate school and offered advice for the transition to New York life. "You don't have to prove anything your first year. This is an incubation period for you. Find sanctity in the silence and learn from it."[18] In recent years, the group has faced struggles similar to those of other alumni groups across the nation: recruiting new members who are recent graduates and can keep the organization viable.

Stillwater, Oklahoma

Alumnae in Stillwater contacted the National Office in 1972 to say that their group had been in existence for five years but was not affiliated with the national organization. The required information was sent in 1973, with the constitution listing the organization's purpose as twofold: first, to promote and provide intellectual, cultural, and social interchange among its members, and second, to cooperate with the chapter on the Oklahoma State campus in the promotion of its aims and activities. During that year approximately twenty members attended each of four programs, which featured topics of election, Oklahoma wildlife, Native Americans, and old age. The members served breakfast for the actives and newly tapped students and assisted in the formal initiation and reception.

The Washington, D.C., Alumnae Club celebrated its fortieth anniversary in February 1974 at the Kennedy Center for the Performing Arts. Awards were presented to Julie Nixon Eisenhower, who spoke about the unusual idea that a woman might become president of the United States, and to Captain M. Janet Lewis, U.S. Navy, deputy chief of naval material for management and organization.

The group's 1974–1975 programs covered an interesting theme of expansion with four meetings: "Expanding Your Role: Is Today's Woman Really Any Different from Yesterday's?," "Expanding Your Fellowship: Communication Is the Key," "Expanding Your World: Archaeology in the Middle East," and "Expanding Your Waist: To Expand or Not to Expand . . . That Is the Question." Other interesting programs over the years included "Women in the Courtroom" (1979–1980), "The Proliferation of Religious Cults in America" (1979), and "Women's Role in International Development" (1985–1986). The 1985–1986 report indicated that the alumnae initiated a new tradition: together with the collegiate chapter they created a new award, the "Mortar Board Medallion for the Distinguished Professional," to honor a professional each year for superior academic achievements, significant professional contributions, and outstanding service to her or his community. In the late 1980s, the group held spring luncheons to honor the collegiate members with the special touch of inviting their mothers to attend. In 1990–1991, the alumni helped the collegiate chapter celebrate the golden anniversary of Mortar Board on the Oklahoma State campus.

Notes

1. The spelling of "alumnae/alumni" used in this chapter reflects the timing of the archival documents. Since women composed the original membership, "alumna/alumnae" were used until men became members in 1975, when the term was changed to "alumni."

2. The Ohio State University Archives, Mortar Board: National (50-a-1/3), "Constitution and By-Laws: 1920–1975."

3. Ibid.

4. Ibid.

5. *Mortar Board Quarterly* 1, no. 1 (1925): 9.

6. The Ohio State University Archives, Mortar Board: National (50-a-2/18), "Conference and Convention: Minutes, 1932."

7. Committee Reports to National Council, 1941–1942, Committee on Alumnae Affairs.

8. Minutes of the Mortar Board National Conference,1970, Lincoln, Nebraska, 1.

9. The Ohio State University Archives, Mortar Board: National (50/a-8/11), "Alumni Club: Correspondence: 1976–1986."

10. *Mortar Board Quarterly* 42, no. 4 (April 1966): 45.

11. Committee Reports to National Council, 1931–1932, Committee on Alumnae Affairs.

12. "Initiation Handbook," Mortar Board, http://www.mortarboard.org/Collegiate/Resources/.

13. Strategic Plan, Mortar Board, Inc. 1997, internal document of the National Office.

14. Minutes of the Mortar Board National Conference, 2007, Columbus, OH, 4.

15. Strategic Plan, Mortar Board, Inc. 2012–2017, internal document of the National Office.

16. "Alumni Awards," Mortar Board, http://www.mortarboard.org/Alumni/AlumniAwards/.

17. Chapter History, 1993.

18. Personal correspondence, July 5, 2004.

5

The Mortar Board National Foundation

Founding of the Mortar Board National Foundation

At the sixteenth national convention of Mortar Board in 1955 on the campus of Michigan State University, a resolution was adopted unanimously to create the

> Mortar Board Foundation Fund, or such other identifying name as shall appear proper to the Committee, the appointment of which is hereinafter provided for, to receive gifts, bequests or devises, either outright or in trust; a Committee shall be appointed by the national President, with the consent of the National Council, to establish such fund; the attorney for the Corporation shall be empowered to make application

> for a ruling of the Internal Revenue Department, requesting that such funds and/or other property, or income therefrom, be exempt from federal income, estate or social security taxes; that no general campaign be inaugurated to publicize the creation of the Fund, but that dissemination of information as to its aims and purposes be left to the discretion of the Committee or Trustees appointed to administer the fund.[1]

Simply put, the Mortar Board National Foundation Fund (MBNF) was established "for charitable, scientific, literary and educational purposes, to advance the spirit of service and fellowship among university women, to promote and maintain a high standard of scholarship, to recognize and encourage leadership, and to stimulate and develop a higher type of college woman."[2]

The connection between Mortar Board, Inc., and the MBNF was very strong. In the beginning the MBNF's officers were appointed by Mortar Board, Inc., especially the chairperson. Through the 1950s, the Foundation (or Foundation Committee, as it was called at first) prepared reports to be delivered to the National Council. By 1961, the Internal Revenue Service "approved the tax exempt status of the Mortar Board Foundation Fund."[3] In July 1961, the trustees of the MBNF for the first time on their own appointed all of the officers: Chairperson Thelma Lockwood (Texas at Austin, 1923), Secretary Rosemary Lucas Ginn, and Treasurer Coral Vanstrum Stevens.[4]

The trust agreement that established the MBNF has been revised many times over the decades since its first adoption. Mortar Board became coeducational in 1975, so by the time of the 1996 revision of the trust agreement, the MBNF's purpose had lost its reference to a "higher type of college woman" and instead incorporated the purpose of Mortar Board, Inc.:

> for charitable, scientific, literary and educational purposes, to promote equal opportunities among all peoples, to emphasize the advancement of the status of women, to support the ideals of the university, to advance a spirit of scholarship, to recognize and encourage leadership, and to provide service, in such manner as the Trustees shall from time to time in their absolute and uncontrolled discretion determine.[5]

In 2003, the purpose added "Said Foundation shall support Mortar Board, Inc. in furthering the ideals of scholarship, leadership, and service" to the "for charitable, scientific, literary" language of the 1996 version of the trust agreement.

This language was reaffirmed by the trustees in 2014.

Fellowship Program

At the time of the establishment of the MBNF, Mortar Board, Inc., presented fellowships named in honor of Katherine Wills Coleman, a program that had been passed by the twelfth national convention of Mortar Board in June 1941. The first two fellowships of $500 were given in 1942 and paid from the Mortar Board, Inc., treasury. The program continued through the 1950s with one or two $500 awards given, depending on the resources of Mortar Board, Inc.[6]

The MBNF began controlling the Katherine Wills Coleman Fellowship Program fully for the first time in 1961, although the National Council still appointed the chairperson of the Selection Committee. Mortar Board, Inc., contributed to fellowships in the MBNF through 2008.[7] (Readers will remember that the National Office wasn't established until 1970.)

In 1982 five fellowships were presented, and by 1989 the MBNF was presenting twelve fellowships for a total of $12,000 annually and making decisions on developing endowment growth by enlisting a financial planner's assistance.[8] Fellowships often honored retiring national Mortar Board leaders with a named fellowship in the year that they stepped down from their volunteer duties, and much time was spent deciding how these honors would be accorded.

By 1994, the MBNF was presenting a total of $18,000 in fellowships. From 2000 through 2009, fellowship program totals ranged from a low of $24,000 to a high of $60,000. The adoption of a spending policy would later prevent this roller-coaster approach to the annual amount of fellowships. From 2011 through 2014, the average fellowship total each year was $36,625.

In 2011, wrestling with the reality that college costs were escalating well beyond the earnings of the endowments, the MBNF Board of Trustees, with Sally Steadman as president, declared that the threshold to create a named, endowed fellowship would be $50,000 and for a named, program endowment would be $10,000. At the same time, the board expressed its wish that no single fellowship be smaller than $5,000 annually.

To improve its endowment earnings growth, the MBNF in 2011 approved the spending policy to indicate how investments were to be allocated among asset classes and specified that supported accounts would be provided 4 percent (at the time of this writing the percentage is 3.5) of a rolling twelve-quarter average of endowment balances. The trustees and staff realized that to fully fund a $5,000 fellowship, an endowment of $125,000 would be needed. In 2013 there were only two fellowship endowment funds at that level. If the MBNF wanted to add to the number of endowed fellowships and increase the number of fellowships given, significant donations would need to be acquired. The prospects of soliciting that size gift from a single donor (or even several donors) were slight.

The number of fellowships stabilized and then declined when the earnings from several endowments were pooled to reach the $5,000 fellowship target that the Board of Trustees had established. In 2011 the number of fellowships was eight, and prospects for increasing that number did not appear bright.

It was evident to the fellowship selection committee that fellows would be pursuing their degree objectives with or without Mortar Board's help. What had started as a true enabling program in the 1940s had evolved into an assistance program. That is, the MBNF's fellowships of $3,500 or $5,000 were helpful but not instrumental to the cost of attendance in a graduate or professional program.[9]

Chapter Project Grants

Also during the 1990s and 2000s a number of chapter project grants were provided,[10] but by 2015 no grants were given. No endowed funds supported this initiative, so the Board of Trustees had been trying to budget funds from its operating account every year. By 2015 after individual unrestricted contributions leveled, the board decided to suspend the program.

Fund-Raising

The MBNF has been described over the years as "the fundraising arm of Mortar Board," with its mission being "to enhance [the] society by supporting Mortar Board members in their scholarly endeavors and in service to their communities."[11] The early leaders of the MBNF, nearly every one of whom has served as a leader Mortar Board, Inc., were so vividly aware of how critical funds were for women seeking graduate degrees that fund-raising for long-term growth did not seem to sink in until the mid-2000s. Also, it is vital to note that endowment funding concepts that fund-raisers apply today were incipient or nonexistent.

As the MBNF established itself, the trustees raised funds from several sources. One ready source was Mortar Board, Inc., which had been funding fellowships for years. In 1982 Mortar Board, Inc., began the practice of giving 5 percent of collegiate membership fees annually to the MBNF for fellowships. In 1985, the annual percentage was raised to 6 percent. This practice continued through 2009.[12]

The MBNF also received 40 percent of alumni sustaining dues from Mortar Board, Inc., toward other programs of the MBNF.[13] Sales of Mortar Board merchandise (about 35 percent of operating income)[14] and individual donations added to the MBNF's coffers along with royalty programs[15] such as an affinity credit card and insurance and sometimes very healthy contributions from alumni clubs.[16] Unrestricted and restricted donations from individuals to the MBNF from 1994 through 2013 averaged $32,609, with a high of $78,000 in 2001 and a low of $13,000 in 2009.

In July 1990 the MBNF undertook the Seventy-Fifth Anniversary Campaign for Fellowship Funding, a catalyst for which was a $20,000 gift from Mary Liz Ramier, who had assisted in establishing the MBNF. Her gift was the largest ever received by the MBNF up to that time, and the trustees decided to offer additional fellowships each year. Spurred by the large gift, the board, during the presidency of Barbara Cook, set a goal to raise $200,000[17] in new endowment money so that by 1993, twenty fellowships of $2,000 could be given to Mortar Board members.[18] In its spring 1992 newsletter the MBNF reported

Mary Liz Ramier drove from Indianapolis to Columbus in 1990 (at around the age of ninety) to hand-deliver a check for $20,000 to jump-start the seventy-fifth anniversary campaign in the MBNF.

$30,000 received or pledged thus far and saw its purpose at that time as being "to further the educational objectives of Mortar Board, Inc. Chief among its services to Mortar Board members is the raising of money to finance national Mortar Board fellowships."[19]

Throughout the 1980s and 1990s, the trustees were always working toward merchandise or affinity prospects as well as annual-giving issues. In 1982 the board discussed merchandising quantities of cocktail napkins, scarves, and small tote bags. Charms were sold for $12 from the National Office. Discussions around annual giving analyzed how to manage the mailings themselves. Most address changes that were found during these years were often as a result of the MBNF's efforts to contact members for donations. In 1993 the trustees urgently struggled with the idea of adding the additional affinity opportunity of a long-distance telephone card beyond the bank card already offered.

Toward the end of the 1990s under the presidency of Gail Harrison Corvette, the MBNF launched the campaign "A Million in the Millennium" to increase its endowed funds. The trustees' focus was on fellowships still, but the idea of increasing giving and getting the endowment to seven figures—as well as reaching that goal—must have represented a great encouragement for the board members who had labored so long.

At the end of her term as MBNF president, Ms. Harrison Corvette established the first endowment in the MBNF that was not connected to a fellowship. Her Gail Harrison Corvette Leadership Endowment would provide funding for national conference leadership initiatives.

Focus on the Future: The Centennial Campaign

In January 2011, Mortar Board began discussing the possibility of a comprehensive campaign and invited a professional fund-raiser to talk with the national leadership. Some feasibility work was done by trustees shortly thereafter. A Board of Trustees decision in February 2011 *not* to conduct a comprehensive campaign spurred the MBNF to prepare itself for the time when that decision would be favorable.

The MBNF developed a spending policy; began a regular review of its investment policy; wrote the gift-acceptance policy; revised lengthy policy manuals, combining them into the *Handbook for National Leaders;* and wrote the "National Leader Gift Understanding."

The Mortar Board Alumni Association was created in 2012 to help build alumni affinity, and the trust agreement was modified in January 2014 to allow for nine trustees instead of seven. A special giving incentive for more recent members, the Tapping Society, was formed to encourage a pattern of giving to the MBNF.

Significantly, Mortar Board created the expectation that all national leaders would be donors at whatever level their means would allow, and quarterly requests for contributions were developed and implemented each year either digitally or via print or both. The *Mortar Board Forum* was increased from two issues per year to four. Approximately forty thousand new postal and e-mail addresses have been imported into Association Management Software that Mortar Board now uses, which taken alone is a significant tool to use in fund-raising and donor connections.

The MBNF trustees, under the leadership of President Denise Rode, decided that enough groundwork had been done so as to reconsider the earlier decision, so on June 22, 2015, the board voted to conduct a comprehensive fund-raising campaign in connection with Mortar Board's one hundredth anniversary in 2018. The name of the campaign would simply be the Centennial Campaign, CenCam for short. The goal would be $500,000 by the end of the centennial year of 2018.

Section Coordinator Chris Wilkins is welcomed into the Tapping Society by staff member Tracey Fox at the 2016 Mortar Board national conference in Indianapolis. Only the newest members may join this special group by giving to the MBNF for three years within a four-year span after initiation. It's not the amount, it's the habit!

Since the discussions leading up to this decision had begun in January 2011, the board agreed to "start" CenCam retroactively in a silent phase to January 1, 2011. Denise appointed Marty Starling as the chair and Sally Watlington as the vice chair of CenCam.

The silent phase was buoyed by gifts to the MBNF that were significant. Dr. Starling and Drs. Sally and John Steadman created program endowments that would directly benefit the operations of Mortar Board, Inc., as a whole. These were the second and third endowments, following Gail Harrison Corvette's, that were not related to fellowship funding.

Bob Sorensen and Linda Sorensen (Purdue, 1962) created the first MBNF endowment whose earnings could be used for whatever purpose the board designated, what MBNF calls a Type A fund. The death of Barbara Cook resulted in an estate gift whose purpose was to create an endowment that, like that of the Sorensens, would allow its earnings to be used for a purpose designated by the board. Sally Watlington followed with another Type A endowment gift for program funding. The phrase "off to the races" comes to mind.

The board created a Centennial Endowment fund where contributions that were intended for CenCam could be placed. This too was a Type A fund.

All of the trustees contributed to CenCam and all National Council members did too, representing a shift in the attitude toward support of the Society with one's pocketbook. The goal of $500,000 was quickly reached; another goal of $750,000 was set and surpassed.

The public launch of CenCam was held at the 2016 national conference in Indianapolis. The new goal of $1 million was announced, and at the time of this writing it too has been surpassed, and the MBNF is deliberating the next goals.

The first endowment in the MBNF whose earnings were unrestricted was created in 2012 by Linda and Bob Sorensen (Purdue, 1962 and 2000, respectively). Both have served as advisors to the Barbara Cook chapter and are charter members of the MBAA. Bob has chaired the MBNF and the Investment Advisory Committee. Linda and Bob's children, Scott Sorensen and Anne Sorensen Inman (Purdue, 1987 and 1989, respectively), flank them in this photo.

On July 23, 2016, Centennial Campaign chair Marty Starling and vice chair Sally Watlington launched the Mortar Board Centennial Campaign with a goal to raise $1 million in funding to help support Mortar Board for the next one hundred years.

From a small committee under the wing of Mortar Board, Inc., to a full-fledged Board of Trustees, the MBNF has accepted squarely the obligation in its trust agreement to support Mortar Board, Inc. Fellowships will still be given, but the broader purpose of the MBNF is much more apparent now.

Chapter Endowments

The Chapter Endowment Program has been part of the MBNF since 2009, when the policies were written by the MBNF under the leadership of Dr. Sorensen and Dr. Steadman. Late in 2012 the first

chapter to take advantage of this program in the MBNF was the Tolo Alumni Council. There was a calm period after that until CenCam started focusing on the value of the program in earnest.

The MBNF encourages collegiate chapters to establish Centennial Chapter Endowments to commemorate the one hundredth anniversary of Mortar Board's founding. This qualifies the chapter to be recognized forever as a donor to CenCam.

Beyond this recognition, the chapter endowment will provide unending financial support for the chapter's future activity. This endowment is an expression of the chapter's commitment to the relevance of Mortar Board's purpose, to Mortar Board's reputation as the premier college senior honor society, and to the longevity of both the chapter and the national organization. The MBNF has set an ambitious goal of having at least twenty chapters establish endowments before the end of the centennial year 2018. The threshold is $10,000 over a five-year period.

Alumni of the chapter may be the ones to start the fund for their chapter. Twenty alumni, each donating $500, would have the fund up and running instantly, with a distribution to the chapter to follow. The endowment is the perfect place for loyal members to give to the MBNF each year while at the same time designating their gift for their chapter's endowment.

The chapter endowment is a vibrant way for the MBNF to stimulate giving from members whose loyalty is more solidly placed

The Tolo chapter at Washington began the first chapter operations endowment. The more in the endowment, the larger the earnings each year for the chapter to use. It's a win-win: national gets your money, and your chapter gets your money.

with their alma mater. If ever there were a definition of a win-win, this is it.

Contact Jane Hamblin or any member of the National Office staff to learn more about CenCam and chapter endowments:

Mortar Board
National Office
1200 Chambers Road, 201
Columbus, OH 43212
(614) 488-4094
www.mortarboard.org
jhamblin@mortarboard.rog

Notes

1. Minutes of the Sixteenth National Convention of Mortar Board, July 1–4, 1955, Kellogg Continuation Center, East Lansing, Michigan, 10.

2. MBNF Trust Agreement, 1955.

3. Minutes of the Meeting of the National Council and Section Directors of Mortar Board, Inc., June 29–July 5, 1961, Union Club, Oklahoma State University, Stillwater, Oklahoma.

4. Post-Convention Minutes of the Meeting of the National Council of Mortar Board, Inc., July 6, 1961, Union Club Oklahoma State University.

5. The Bylaws of Mortar Board, Inc.

6. There were seventy-eight chapters of Mortar Board at the time. Eligible members were required to be unmarried, under the age of twenty-five, and accepted to a master's or doctoral program. Members of the selection committee often included deans of women as well as members of the Mortar Board, Inc., National Council. They were appointed by the National Council. The fellowship amount was raised to $1,000 in 1956, and the decision on a second fellowship was deferred until the "Mortar Board Foundation Fund Committee is in operation" (Minutes of the National Council, August 6, 1956). Financial need was not a consideration as of 1958.

7. From 1970 through 2008, Mortar Board, Inc., gave $400,000 toward fellowships.

8. Mortar Board National Foundation Fund Trustees Meeting, July 22–23, 1988, West Lafayette, Indiana.

9. Thanks to Bob Sorensen for this sentence.

10. Over sixteen years, the average of chapter project grants annually was $3,500. There were two outlier years, 2008 and 2009, when the grants were tripled, skewing the average. Without these, the average was closer to $2,500 annually.

11. MBNF 2003–2004 report to the national conference.

12. With a few years unaccounted for, audit reports show that at least $415,724 was paid by Mortar Board, Inc., to the MBNF between 1982 and 2009; the last payment from Mortar Board, Inc., to the MBNF was $50,000 in 2009, which was designated to offset the loss of income from merchandise which Mortar Board, Inc., would take over in 2010.

13. This program began in 2002, and over eight reporting periods $22,357 was given to the MBNF by Mortar Board, Inc.

14. The MBNF netted $481,450 from merchandise sales from 1994 through 2008, the last year the MBNF ran the program.

15. The royalties averaged about $11,000 annually from 1992 through 2012.

16. In the February 1987 MBNF newsletter, Catherine Evans reported that seventeen alumni clubs, one "active chapter," and eighty-three individuals gave $6,356. The St. Louis alumni club gave $500, and the Washington, D.C., club gave $2,000.

17. By July 14, 1993, the MBNF had raised $86,006.

18. Letter from MBNF president Barbara I. Cook in February 1991 to individual donors requesting a tax-deductible contribution of $1,000.

19. MBNF quarterly newsletter, Spring 1992.

6

The Challenge of the Future

Study the Past if you would divine the future.
—Confucius

Mortar Board's remarkable history provides a steadfast foundation upon which to build our future. Although trying to predict the future direction of Mortar Board in our constantly changing and fast-paced world might seem presumptuous, there are feasible short-term and long-term goals for Mortar Board.

Influences That Lie Ahead

Many factors will directly or indirectly influence how Mortar Board navigates the future, some within and others outside of our control: an evolving higher education system, the characteristics and attitudes of future generations of students, the value that students place in honor societies, and the relevance of this organization as it meets the needs of its collegiate and alumni members.

Higher Education Influences

In chapter 1 we learned that to appreciate Mortar Board's amazing history, we must examine it within the context of higher education, Mortar Board's home. There is a symbiotic relationship between higher education and Mortar Board. Many higher education leaders agree that present challenges of implementing new ways for teaching digital learners, graduating more students, and lowering the cost of a college education will continue to be important in the future.[1] Perhaps one of the most important challenges is how technology is transforming the way colleges offer teaching and learning.

Books, articles, and online sources projecting the future of higher education are voluminous. Mortar Board leaders must continue to be in tune with the research and trends that could affect how this changing milieu might influence our policies, programs, and services. Our history gives us markers that we should keep in our sights, such as the effect of federal legislation (Title IX, the Buckley Amendment, etc.), institutional retrenchment when enrollments decline or investments are lower, and the priorities that college administrations or governing boards set (staff reductions or changes, for example, that affect student organizations). Of course, world affairs and tragedies here at home (Kent State, 9/11, Hurricane Katrina) are only predictable in their unpredictability. Can Mortar Board be ready to make a difference or make a stand in these eventualities? Mortar Board must watch all of these markers, and since Mortar Board students are involved in out-of-class activities and cocurricular learning experiences, monitoring research in the field of student affairs especially can yield important insights.

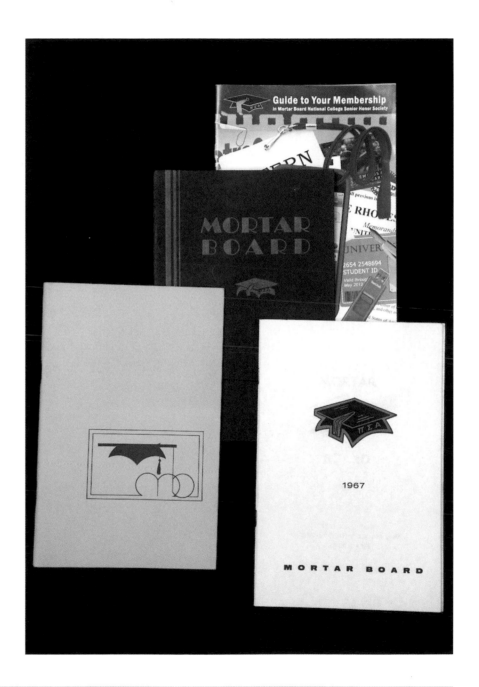

From the first guide to membership printed in the mid-1930s (black) to the present day when the guide is online only, Mortar Board has delivered clear information about the Society, even if the look of the logo has changed over time (note the stylized logo used in the 1970s and 1980s on the yellow cover).

Future Student Characteristics

Mortar Board's future is intimately tied to the characteristics and attitudes of the students it serves. Over many generations, the Society has been guided first by the interests and needs of its collegiate members and collegiate chapters. The last of the millennials (born in the late 1990s) will be in the minority in the next decade. The next generation (those born around 2000) might be called the postmillennials or Generation Z—or, better yet, Generation C for *connectivity*. This is the first generation to know the Internet and the World Wide Web from infancy. Interacting on social media has long been part of their lives.

Those who write about this generation suggest that they will be open-minded, tolerant, and respectful of others. Through the power of social media and the Internet, they already are more aware of what is transpiring around them than past generations. Since they also are described as community-oriented, they will fit comfortably into Mortar Board's Ideals of service and leadership. Conjecture? Surely. And still this has implications for Mortar Board planners. Can Mortar Board turn on the plugged-in denizens of Gen C?

Can Mortar Board's idealism and enthusiasm for its purpose help create what Robert Putnam calls "an era of civic inventiveness" that reinvigorates interest in social capital?[2] Gen C could be connected through both technology and *belonging* to our Society as well as being, as Dr. Komives explained in chapter 1, the Responsibles.

The Future of College Honor Societies

Although there was a hodge-podge of "honor societies" in existence before 1925, it wasn't until the Association of College Honor Societies (ACHS) was founded in that year that a coordinating body was formed for establishing standards and recognizing different classifications of honor societies. Mortar Board was invited to become a member of the ACHS in 1937 and since that time has made valuable contributions to its viability and leadership. The ACHS makes an important distinction between an "honorary" and an "honor society." As described in chapter 1, Mortar Board has always taken pride in being a "leadership honor society" as opposed to a "scholarship honor society." Mortar Board members are not only honored for recognized scholarship, service, and leadership but are also expected to contribute additional service to their campuses as a group.

Annual reports to the ACHS by its member societies reflect many common challenges. Some suggest that there is a continuing lack of interest in honor societies in general. Some societies report their membership numbers remain steady, while others are experiencing a decline. Financial security, lack of institutional support, how to remain relevant to alumni, how to educate first-generation students who may have no knowledge of honor societies and their value, keeping good advisors, and funding student travel to conferences are all on the list of challenges for our sister societies. Mortar Board has experienced all of these to some degree and has met these challenges in a variety of ways:

- Mortar Board is confronting its financial challenges through careful budgeting and by exploring viable resources to pay for creative programs and services, especially the cost of national conferences. A recent Mortar Board task force report on this problem offered insights into possible solutions that may involve change for the better.
- Maintaining or increasing membership levels is basic to the financial health of the organization. This is a complicated challenge, because declining membership means a reduction in revenues. Mortar Board leaders are actively engaged in

encouraging chapters to select the number of new members allowed by the bylaws, working actively with individual chapters that are experiencing problems, and contacting those defunct chapters that might be interested in reactivation.

- The value of faculty and staff advisors to our chapters is incalculable. One of the most frequent challenges mentioned in the ACHS reports is the difficulty in attracting and maintaining chapter advisors to student organizations. Mortar Board has incorporated the Leadership Excellence and Advisor Development program that certifies advisors of student organizations after educating them about the importance of the work they do.
- To encourage alumni support and involvement, Mortar Board established the Mortar Board Alumni Association (MBAA) that not only solicits financial support but also acts as a resource for recruiting new leaders.
- The Mortar Board National Foundation Fund (MBNF) is vigorously conducting a comprehensive campaign, the Centennial Campaign (CenCam), to provide the type of

Donors who give $500 or more during the course of the campaign are eligible for membership in the distinctive giving group, The 1918 Society.

funding for Mortar Board, Inc., that will support leadership development and officer onboarding for new members each year. The goal of $1 million has been surpassed. All members should react with a gift when the MBNF says that "every member has a chance to contribute to Mortar Board's tomorrow by giving to CenCam today."

Relevance to Future Students

Throughout our history it is obvious that Mortar Board has been relevant to members, or the Society would not continue to exist. How do we determine our approaches to this important issue as we enter our second century? What have we learned from the past that can help us maintain the relevance of Mortar Board for our future members?

Students seek to become Mortar Board members for many reasons: honor and recognition, emerging awareness that they are becoming a leader, validation that they belong, the opportunity to work and learn from a special group of outstanding leaders, the anticipation of receiving valuable experiences and skills from Mortar Board's programs and services, fulfilling a long-held aspiration to be a part of the prestigious Mortar Board, building connections with others, padding a résumé, etc. Will these reasons still be relevant for future candidates? Since these and others have stood the test of time, one can reasonably surmise that they will continue to be viable.

Mortar Board's Future Challenges

The new and continuing challenges that Mortar Board faces in the future will require constant monitoring and informed decision making.

Courses of action will evolve from creative thinking and study. The guiding force for determining these actions is the Mortar Board purpose, whose eight tenets are

* contributing to the self-awareness of its members,
* promoting equal opportunities among all peoples,
* emphasizing the advancement of the status of women,
* supporting the ideals of the college or university,
* advancing a spirit of scholarship,
* recognizing and encouraging leadership,
* providing service, and
* establishing the opportunity for a meaningful exchange of ideas as individuals and as a group.

National President Dave Whitman and President-elect Gail Harrison Corvette will lead Mortar Board to and then past its one hundredth year. What will constitute the hallmark of their success?

The challenge to both collegiate and alumni chapters is how to incorporate into their programs the ideas stated in the Mortar Board purpose so that they continue to provide high-impact practices that contribute to the quality of student life on campus (or, in the case of alumni, meaningful programs that showcase Mortar Board in the community). Chapters must conduct a program related to one of these that is high-level, meaningful, and cost effective; do it well; reflect; and repeat next year but better.

Other challenges are complex and must be identified, updated, and confronted continually, for example:

* *Establish financial stability nationally.* As Mortar Board begins its next century, it must find ways to stabilize its financial position. It can no longer rely on membership fees and other traditional funding for conferences, programs, and operations. More diverse revenue streams must be identified to maintain an operating budget that ensures its future financial health.
* *Establish financial stability at the chapter level.* There should be no poor chapter. Find one fund-raiser that also provides a value to the campus, and put the money in the bank. Follow the adage of leaving your chapter better than you found it. Every chapter (collegiate and alumni) should also build an endowment in the MBNF so that it has a perpetual annual source of funding.
* *Realize that Mortar Board is not a service organization.* Yes, members are selected for their service, but a Mortar Board chapter must not compete with other organizations to do the types of projects that anyone and everyone can do. With their rich and broad experiences and leadership, Mortar Board members have the keen knowledge and observations to identify

what needs to be done to create high-impact programs. They must leverage the capacity of their diverse involvements and consolidate their force to benefit their campus.[3]

- *Continue strengthening collegiate chapters.* As evidenced in chapter 3, strong, involved chapters are the bedrock of the Society. A positive capstone experience for Mortar Board members is the key to a chapter's success. Chapters that focus on their members and embrace the idea of building connections among members first and then representing Mortar Board on campus through high-impact programs will present themselves well in the eyes of future members and faculty and administrators alike, year after year.

- *Select from the entire group of those eligible.* Do the work to select candidates who meet *all three* of Mortar Board's criteria (see our *Membership Selection Handbook* for more about this). Mortar Board is the university's (or college's) honor society. Include the entire campus community in nominating true scholars, real leaders, and committed servants as candidates for membership. If everyone on campus has a chance to nominate, the chapter will ensure that it is as egalitarian as possible. Numbers will rise, and opportunities for greater synergy among a diverse class, year after year, will grow.

- *Sustain alumni leadership.* A recent task force emphasized the importance of alumni leadership. Throughout its history Mortar Board has been fortunate to have strong, committed leaders. It is especially important to actively recruit outstanding Mortar Board alumni to fill leadership positions at all levels. Training programs must continue the learning and mentoring process. Although volunteers provide the leadership and guidance for the Society, the National Office provides the continuity and direction that is essential to the ongoing success of the organization. The position of executive director must carefully be filled with an experienced and loyal professional who can select and direct capable staff members.

- *Continue to rely on strong alumni connections and support.* Alumni have been the glue that has held the Society together. The MBAA is a pivotal resource. Alumni at all levels, from local alumni chapters to those in national leadership, must continue this proud tradition of connection and support. Max DePree wrote that "to give one's time doesn't always mean giving one's involvement."[4] Be involved in Mortar Board.

- *Establish strong communication connections.* Communicating with digital-savvy collegiate and alumni members in the future requires an understanding of changing technology and how it can be used. All types of communication with and among students, alumni, National Council members, section coordinators, trustees, and other leaders must be employed for a cohesive and efficient organization. Many of these functions are ultimately the responsibility of the National Office staff, and input from various stakeholders, especially collegiate members, should be sought on a regular basis.

- *Make CenCam a success.* The MBNF is setting Mortar Board up well for the second century with financial backing from endowment funds, the use of whose earnings can be designated by the board. The success of this campaign is paramount to Mortar Board's success.

Mortar Board's greatest assets will continue to be its outstanding collegiate members, the commitment and guidance of its national leaders, and the dedication and work of the executive director and staff. The MBNF trustees will continue to make indelible contributions to the organization. Another important asset is the pool of loyal alumni who will supply future leadership and resources. The collective vision of all of these stakeholders will direct responses to future challenges.

As Mortar Board's first century ends, we believe that this Society will continue to make a difference in members' lives. They in turn will provide high-impact programs for their campuses. Mortar Board will continue to be a force on campuses through our relevance and purpose. As in the past, we will continue to put our collegiate members' interests and needs first; attract committed, capable volunteers and professional staff; create and provide relevant programs and services for future students and alumni; and employ the most effective communication methods and technology with all shareholders. Building on the foundation that past collegiate and alumni members have bequeathed to us, we enthusiastically anticipate the challenges of our beloved Mortar Board's second century.

Notes

1. "A Meeting of Minds," *The New York Times*, June 23, 2016, F4.
2. Robert D. Putnam, *Bowling Alone: The Collapse and Revival of American Community* (New York: Simon & Schuster, 2000).
3. Credit here to Susan Komives from her good thoughts in chapter 1.
4. Max DePree, *Leadership Is an Art* (New York: Doubleday, 1989), 132.

Index